Mushakôji Saneatsu

Long Corridor

1996

LONG CORRIDOR

『長い廊下』英訳武者小路実篤詩集

The Selected Poetry of

Mushakôji Saneatsu

1996

For

Shôji Toshiko

東海林淑子に捧げる

gifted teacher
able colleague
loyal friend
dear little sister

Copyright © 1996 by **Yakusha**, Stanwood, WA
Photograph, Introduction, Prefaces, Translations, and Notes
Copyright © 1996 by Robert Epp

first edition 1996

Manufactured in the United States of America
Printed on acid-free paper by
Thomson–Shore, Inc., Dexter, MI 48130-0305

Mushakôji [surname] Saneatsu [given] (1885–1976)
    [Poems. English. 1996]
    Long Corridor : Poetry / Mushakôji Saneatsu;
    translated from the Japanese
    by Robert Epp

    396 pp.   15 x 23 cm.
    Notes, Chronology, Appendixes, English and Japanese Indexes
    ISBN 1-880276-70-4

Library of Congress Catalog Card Number: **95-60539**

Available from **Yakusha**
Post Office Box #666, Stanwood, WA 98292–0666
$30.00 (postpaid—U.S. currency only) Hardcover

CONTENTS

INTRODUCTORY

Photograph • 9
Acknowledgments • 11
Conventions • 13
Introduction • 15

THE POETRY

I. Myself & Others • 47

II. Work & Love • 109

III. Art & Poetry • 175

IV. God & Country • 233

SUPPLEMENTARY

Chronology • 287
Notes • 309

Appendix I: Chronological Listing of the Poems • 349
Appendix II: Views of Mushakôji's Work • 359
Appendix III: Mushakôji on His Poetry • 363
Appendix IV: Poetry Collections • 371

English Index • 375
Japanese Index • 385

Yakusha Offerings • 397

THE ME OF WORDS

In this book you'll find
the me of words
and the me of silence.

The me of words is me,
but the me of silence is more me.

— Mushakôji Saneatsu —
1970?

九十歳の武者小路実篤（昭和五十年夏）
調布市のお宅の庭にて（撮影・悦富）
Mushakôji Saneatsu at age 90 (late summer 1975)
in front of his home in Chôfu, Tokyo

ACKNOWLEDGMENTS

Those who, in one way or other, have assisted me in making this and other collections in the **Yakusha** series are far too numerous to list. I must, however, offer special words of gratitude to at least the following individuals:

Mushakôji Saneatsu —— Before he died, the poet granted interviews and responded generously, sometimes in writing, to many irksome inquiries.

Mushakôji Tatsuko, the poet's youngest daughter —— She kindly provided indispensable materials difficult to come by and also cheerfully and promptly responded to a number of questions concerning family and bibliographic matters.

Professor Iida Gakuji —— Warm friend and lucid instructor who provided immeasurable, generous, and insightful help on questions of grammar, meaning, and nuance. I also add sincere appreciation for the gracious hospitality he and his *odoriko* Masae provided over several decades.

Professor Nagata Masao —— Old reliable! His laborious checking of my translations brought to light the usual battalion of sophomoric miscues, correction of which has spared me unmentionable and countless embarrassments.

Professor Erhard Essig —— Over many years he read and reacted to countless pages of manuscript. I treasure his positive and helpful suggestions, not to mention his steady encouragement along the way.

Paul Pallmeyer —— For stimulating and thoughtful input, including a host of stylistic suggestions, improvements in clarity or grammar, and correction of factual errors.

Haraguchi Saburô —— His thorough research filled in a number of blanks; I have countless reasons to feel much indebted to his scholarly expertise and friendship.

Yamamoto Yoshifumi (a.k.a. Nishide Kimikazu) —— For support, inspiration, and insightful comments on some Mushakôji poems, recorded for me in the early 1970s. He comprehensively expanded appreciation of the verse of Mushakôji and several other modern Japanese poets.

Mitsuko —— She again offered substantive help, both by help with
the supplementary materials and by her extremely patient
and meticulous checks on every conceivable aspect of this
collection. Along the way, she uncovered the usual un-
countable and unaccountable oversights and miscues—
always far more than I have the courage to admit. Fur-
thermore, she offered innumerable creative and valuable
suggestions throughout the preparation of *Long Corridor*.

Dating back to when I began making these translations, I furthermore incurred
non-repayable debts of thoughtfulness and hospitality to Tamesada Nobuyuki and
his late wife Yukiko in Machida, to the late Iida Kakuyoshi and his widow Aya in
Kodaira, and to Shôji Toshio and Toshiko in Urawa.

✦   ✦   ✦

It is obvious yet necessary to note that the final versions of these poems—as well as
all data and its presentation in the Introduction, prefaces to the poetry sections,
Chronology, Notes, Publications, Appendixes, Indexes, and elsewhere—remain, of
course, the translator's sole responsibility.

CONVENTIONS

Names of Japanese nationals appear in the natural East Asian order, surname first. Saneatsu (sah-nay-ah-tsoo) is consequently the poet's given name. In the past, most Japanese have read the graphs of his surname Mushakôji (moo-shah-koh-jee) as Musha-no-kôji. Contemporary biographical dictionaries uniformly continue to use the *no*. This *no* is not the euphonic particle found in, say, the surname Kinoshita, but the genitive connector that corresponds to von in German. This aristocratic name thus means Musha of Kôji. The poet told me, however, that his name is far "more democratic" if he omits the *no*; he positively stated that he preferred that I read it that way. When he signed the books he gave me, he made a point of writing phonetic *katakana* alongside his graphs; these omitted the *no*.

A superscript or raised asterisk ***** following the title of a poem indicates an entry in the Notes, page 309 ff. These I arrange in ABC order omitting initial articles. A bullet or raised period • after the last line of poetry on a page notifies the reader that the first line on the following page begins a new stanza. Elsewhere the bullet separates variant readings or meanings of a term, etc.

Special symbols in the Notes include a pointing finger ☞, a down–slanting arrow ↘, and a five–pointed star ☆. The ☞ calls attention to another entry (in small caps) or to a poem (in quotation marks) followed by its page number in *Long Corridor*. The ↘ marks a break that signifies added, related, or—most often—gratuitous comments. The ☆ indicates a major break in provided information.

In the Introduction or prefatory remarks to each poetry section, the first appearance of annotated terms are in small caps. These direct the reader to an entry in the Notes. Shirakaba refers most often to the group of humanists that issued a journal bearing their name. References to the magazine I italicize.

✦   ✦   ✦

Most translations in *Long Corridor* are equilinear. If the original has ten lines, the English has ten lines (counting those flush to the left margin). This convention honors Mushakôji's concept of what constitutes a line of verse, which often differs from mine. Because preserving the poem intact on a single page frequently takes priority over an equilinear rendering, at times I combine lines rather than allow the last line or two of the poem to spill onto the following page. This is particularly the case when the spill occurs on an overleaf. With the exception of longer poems that clearly have too few breaks, in principle I aim to preserve the poet's stanzas.

Japanese customarily write poetry from the top to the bottom of the page; lines at times can therefore become quite long. In translation, they have a tendency to become even longer. The fact that English must be written from left to right further intensifies line length. This often forces me to break a line to fit available space. Because I prefer to decide where to break each line I indent, I never allow the lines to wrap automatically. In the relatively few instances where the poet indents his lines, I make this clear by adding several spaces beyond my usual indentations.

With very few exceptions, Mushakôji wrote his poems using everyday conversational Japanese. In an era when accepted poetic style required a certain amount of artificial "poetic" diction, the language of his earliest verse was so "natural" and unaffected that it drew sneers. I know of no way to indicate this in English. For biographical data, please refer to the Chronology, page 287 ff.

Appendix I offers a chronological listing that allows an interested reader to place the poems in historical context. Mushakôji strongly objected to a chronological arrangement of his verse, for he feared it might imply an inauthentic interest in artistic growth; cf. page 44.

Appendix II gathers seven views of Mushakôji and his work. The purpose is to give a selective but brief overview of the way certain near contemporaries regarded him. This appendix contains statements by writers born between and 1892 and 1904. They are thus from seven to nineteen years younger than he. Their assessments are mostly positive; more important, they are fair.

Appendix III presents summary selections from fourteen Mushakôji essays. These offer a potpourri of his views on poetry. Most are predictably spontaneous. As usual, he does not make systematic comments or try to act as an apologist for his ideas. He simply states his subjective views in a forthright manner.

Appendix IV lists all known poetry collections published between 1924 and 1989. I add several books that contain a substantial number of new free-verse works. This list indicates the minuscule part that poetry occupies among the more than 700 books Mushakôji published in his lifetime.

❖   ❖   ❖

There are no doubt countless approaches to an appreciation of Mushakôji's verse. Each suggestion in what follows has contributed in some small way to my personal understanding of his work or helped me penetrate his thinking. That is, of course, no guarantee that others may necessarily benefit from my experience. I expect, however, that an undergraduate unfamiliar with or unsure of how to read Mushakôji's poems could find some data in *Long Corridor* helpful. These details may prime one's pump, so to speak, and thus spur a more meaningful reading of the text.

It is my hope, too, that these materials may at least make Mushakôji Saneatsu's unique poetry, person, and aesthetic readily available to the non-specialist.

INTRODUCTION

Mushakôji Saneatsu (1885–1976) was a painter, dramatist, novelist, essayist, moralist, and social engineer. He was a mentor to humanity and a poet as well. *Long Corridor* presents his verse, most of which celebrates life and joy, for Mushakôji rejected art that was as negative and as depressing as the news. His poems deal not with being overcome but with overcoming. A mere glance at their content reveals also how frequently they present views on such diverse topics as morality and the problems of communal life, painting and the artist, authentic existence and inauthentic critics, or God and faith. No introduction to Mushakôji's verse can justifiably sidestep these concerns. Not only do such matters inspire most works in this collection, they are vital ingredients of his eclectic aesthetic.

The term "eclectic" points to an aspect of this poet that many regard a failing. He subscribes to no specific literary theory. Rather, he has adapted bits from this thinker or that, East or West, past or present. Appropriating what appeals to the heart or what promises to be serviceable has never been a sanctioned way to fashion a poetic. Scholars refrain from conferring status on the subjectively selective or the unsystematic. Only an integrated system meets requirements for coherence and unity. Since authorities aver that one can create a legitimate literary theory only on the basis of strict logical analysis, they reject ad-hoc eclectic views like Mushakôji's. The complexity of poetry and literature, after all, disallows unfocused, amateurish procedures. An eclectic aesthetic, moreover, often characterizes chameleon types who dissipate their artistic gifts by adapting to every new trend. How might the piecemeal be viable or convincing? Eclecticism may thus degenerate into temporizing or mere expediency. In a word, because Mushakôji's hodgepodge aesthetic can by no means measure up, scholars evidently assign his poetic a failing grade.

Most of these negative characterizations of an eclectic aesthetic are beyond debate. It is debatable, however, whether all aptly apply to Mushakôji's work. However selective or patchwork his principles, they served him well for more than seventy years. Nor over those decades of poetry writing did he make a single chameleon-like switch. Analysts may call the eclectic elements of his aesthetic either hash or a mishmash. They cannot claim that Mushakôji ever changed the "hash" to fit expectations, be up-to-date, or impress others—especially critics. His views of art and poetry display notable stability and consistency. Some readers might instead wish that the poet had made conscious attempts to vary his manner of writing. Stability in this case allows the reproachful tag "no professional growth."

Apparent changes turn out to be shifts in approach or slightly altered emphases. By design, Mushakôji's verse does not develop. This poet, in truth, considered conscious transformations of art the height of insincerity. Most offensive were variations manufactured to be different or to convey impressions of growth and profundity. Mushakôji rejected all such self-conscious artifice. True, he supports a kaleidoscopic aesthetic. Even if his artistic principles resemble a miscellany, however, he deserves credit for steadfastly resisting temptations to pander to critical tastes. He always felt compelled to produce poetry his way—spontaneously and intuitively. His art derived from his heart not his head. Despite the apparently illogical and emotional cradle of this approach, Mushakôji's aesthetic has, to repeat, been steadfast. Doing it his way produced a poetic more stable than any of the arcane and erudite theories scholars derive through rational gymnastics or analysis.

The title of this collection relates to Mushakôji's wish to write as he wishes without being intimidated by critics or social conventions. The poem "Long Corridor" appeared in 1909 when he was twenty-four; cf. page 55. The issues this piece deals with thus date from early adulthood. Using this work to title an introduction to Mushakôji the poet and the man by no means implies that I regard "Long Corridor" a masterpiece. The intrinsic worth of the poem is irrelevant. It is important rather that this work serves several key functions. "Long Corridor" is a metaphor of Mushakôji's lengthy life and the path of his commitment to SINCERITY, truth, and love; cf. page 114 ff. It's straight as a hallway. Less obviously, the title suggests a crucial theme of his verse and thought: the strains and inconsistencies that create anxiety in a sensitive individual. These include tensions between emotion and reason, particularly as they affect the integrity of the poet's aesthetic.

Predictable strains exist also between assertive desires for selfhood and an authoritarian ethos. One important aspect of these strains is the ancient relationship between liberty and duty. From beginning to end, Mushakôji believed that people must earn moments of autonomy by first discharging their responsibilities. He couldn't possibly consent to the way that some now pervert this relationship by according "inalienable rights" to practically everything alive. Another aspect hints at the equally old and troublesome stress between social expectations and the individual's expression of free will. The poem "Long Corridor" depicts the persona as a self-indulgent child who wants to clomp down the hallway, shouting all the way. The child also wants metaphorically to cater to adult (or critics') prescriptions of how to behave (or write). Third-party expectations habitually triumph in Japan, a land where blind conformity rules. Racing loudly down a hallway is behavior most appropriate to children innocent of social constraints. Because most enjoy the comforts of conformism, they cannot approve such comportment in a man of twenty-four. By complying, the persona rejects the right to uninhibited self-expression.

Racing raucously down a resonant, wood-floored corridor also symbolizes Mushakôji's aesthetic values. The innocent and harmless act of dashing noisily through the hallway may, at most, offend adult propriety. But the persona surrenders something precious by deciding not to run and shout. He allows concern for other people's (i.e., critics') opinions to constrain his spontaneity; cf. page 177 ff. Mushakôji's verse consistently touches on this artistic dilemma. His aesthetic may be eclectic. It is neither irresolute nor opportunistic. The poem "Long Corridor" presents the poet's basic attitudes toward art. These include notably the authentic artist's—and person's—need to remain committed to a private agenda regardless of what others say. Clomping down the hallway is equally a polemical symbol. It attacks critics and academics, many of whom Mushakôji regarded as pitiful "control freaks" who aggressively and sometimes spitefully try to make their standards normative. Using every imaginable ploy in their attempt to intimidate artists, critics shamelessly berate the work of any who refuse to perform according to their aesthetic criteria; cf. pages 215 ff. "Long Corridor" depicts the malaise many an artist feels in the face of critics whose acrid pen can influence decisions to refrain from spontaneous, uninhibited behavior. How wholesome if the persona simply gave in to the urge and clomped shouting down the hallway!

Aside from making us wonder how a person can be free and remain related, the title poem implies other ubiquitous problems facing the artist. Must the poet be socially responsible? If so, how balance art and activism? How might an individual committed to being himself survive in a rigidly conformist society? Very many Mushakôji poems—successes or failures, long or short—touch on, if they do not deal directly with, these significant issues. Although we cannot expect him to impersonate a systematic philosopher or thinker, we can expect honesty. That much he unfailingly delivers. The manner in which he deals with these problems is always uncomplicated, disarmingly earnest, and straightforward. Throughout, Mushakôji's verse implies the need to address similar universal issues. He does so unpretentiously, never trying to impress us with world-quaking profundities. Nor does his work puzzle readers with esoteric terminology and serpentine reasoning. More important, the poems doggedly confront these problems in a society that rarely accorded one iota of value to the individual and his welfare.

Mushakôji's verse overflowed from his heart. The unadorned expression of how he felt about these questions makes his views accessible to all. His elemental concerns furthermore focus his viewpoints by constant reiteration. Along the way, he reveals both the breadth of his eclecticism and the sources of his polemic, many of which can be identified. Everywhere his work repudiates the cliché that modern poetry has little to say about human happiness or joy. To appreciate the scope of his convictions and offer background for a better understanding of his verse, I survey several areas I believe molded his aesthetic and his views of life. His commitments and values neither came to him in a dream nor were they presented to him ready-made in a lecture, essay, or volume dealing with poetics. Rather, he absorbed scattered ideas from whatever he read: Taoism or Mencius, the Bible or Tolstoy, European or Japanese writings, philosophy or literature. Familiarity with these influences on his ideas may increase some readers' appreciation of his verse.

However, the following remarks in no way mean to imply that Mushakôji's poetry requires an understanding of quietism, moralism, HUMANISM, or any other ideology. Nor should the reader infer that he manipulates these ideas so he might obliquely achieve certain aesthetic or moral ends. Of course, principles derived from these ideologies fertilized his thinking on a wide range of issues. But however much fertilizer a plant absorbs, it never turns into fertilizer. Similarly, these ideas stimulated Mushakôji even as they allowed his thought to remain distinctively his own. This poet, a tireless moralist and polemicist, is interested mainly in arousing others to discover and nourish their inner selves. He hopes each reader will determine his or her rate of growth and method of maturation.

I. QUIETIST ASPECTS

Quietist refers to the state of spiritual serenity that the ancient Taoist or the more modern Zen practitioner might wish to attain. My use of the term in *Long Corridor* has no relation to mysticism, passive contemplation, or the "beatific annihilation of the will" often associated with quietism. The quietist's serenity is important primarily because Mushakôji's verse consistently portrays Taoist–Zen viewpoints. Quietism also configured his philosophy of life and art—his favorite Asian painters were Zen priests—and thus influenced his aesthetic or poetic.

All references to Taoism imply the ancient search for happiness and "ultimate reality." This connects with both the Asian fetish for long life and the yearning for a harmonious unity that might embrace every single being and object on Earth. Taoists sought a chemical elixir to lengthen life's span. Like later alchemists in the West, some even hoped to gain immortality. Exploiting the occult aspects of longevity transformed Taoism into a cult of magicians and necromancers, which did not in the least appeal to Mushakôji. For him, long life, happiness, and harmony rather promised productivity and the opportunity to achieve artistic excellence. In his case, interest in longevity thus also had an aesthetic dimension. Indeed, his adaptations of Taoism contain interest solely because of this commitment to artistic endeavors. The alchemist's efforts to transform lead into gold through chemistry or magic, for example, intrigued him as a metaphor of his attempts to excel through hard work and persistence. He believed that sheer effort could transmute inferior talent into the gold of art. One way to manage this feat echoes the Taoist search for equanimity. Mushakôji believed that the "wordless doctrine" of intuition creates spiritual quiescence, which in turn leads to a covenant of peace with the basic laws of the universe. This produces a composure that not only opens individuals to their potentials but allows them to accept the laws of nature, including death. The serenity of acceptance, in turn, enables one to be authentic and to make the most of the self. Taoist equanimity lies at the heart of Mushakôji's poetic.

Composure, acceptance, peace of mind, equanimity—these states absorb the quietist. They also bring to mind the intuitive artist who hopes to outstrip, even defy, the ability of language to capture or define his activity. Taoist artists correctly claim that they can't discover appropriate words to express completely the meaning of what they feel. Who can? Who can explain adequately what it means or feels like to be loved? Taoists knew three millennia ago the impossibility of pouring mother love into a test tube and analyzing it. Mushakôji, aware of this reality, shows in his verse a healthy disregard for the serial, sequential language that characterizes debate and logic. That is why he rarely appears concerned to weed out repetitions or more effectively focus his points. The very terms "weed out" and "focus" suggest exactly the conscious, intentional activities that he believes betray the genuineness and purity of the poetry. After all, the intellect prescribes the criteria for either activity.

The inability to put our most intense and shared experiences or feelings into words by no means makes them unreal or renders them valueless. Nor does linguistic ineptness in these areas signify, as critics urge, stupidity or lack of worth. Words or language may not be worthless, either, but they are by no means almighty. There are many tasks they cannot accomplish. To recognize that is the beginning of wisdom. As poets manipulate symbols to convey what words alone cannot, Taoists sought to achieve a non-verbal serenity that no human can give them and that no one can satisfactorily represent using only words. Mushakôji expresses this philosophical ideal in an appropriately terse manner: "The me of words is me, / but the me of silence is more me"; cf. page 8. Silence indeed can be far more arresting than spoken words. Adopting that attitude constitutes a sure step toward equanimity and spiritual serenity.

It is similarly daunting to describe the Tao. That is why it remains "the Tao," literally "the path." Some render it "reason" in the spiritual sense. Others equate it with the equally untranslatable Christian idea of the *Logos* and offer "the Word." "The law" or "the Way" are other versions. It is far less of a challenge to describe important Taoist-Zen behaviors that Mushakôji either adored or adopted. Chief of these is spontaneity, a state that requires a lack of self-consciousness; cf. page 177. Paradoxically, one escapes the ego-centered self through self-reflection. More accurately, one overcomes it by searching out and reflecting on one's true inner being. Individuals can conform to the Tao only if they are no longer full of the self and its desires and only if they have cultivated sympathy for all things. That allows the Taoist to leap with "passionate intuition to the very heart of things." Authentic verse, Mushakôji believed, must emerge from just such fervently focused intuition.

Taoism and Zen call the ideal state of being or creativity *wu-wei*, which means "no action." Lao Tzu, the presumed founder of Taoism, conceived *wu-wei* as a means to deal with the turbulent times in which he lived. *Wu-wei* accordingly began as a specific method for coping with an era of barbarous internecine warfare characterized by pillage, slaughter, tyranny, treason, and cannibalism. The more conditions deteriorated, the more cruel aggressions increased the people's sufferings. Hoping to brake the vicious spiral, Lao Tzu taught pacifism. He said, don't respond to but ignore aggressive challenges, for not contending diminishes aggression. By yielding, one might survive. Being rather than doing, attitude rather than action, attracting rather than compelling people to your views will, he urged, succeed where overt action fails. To persevere, humans must imitate the lessons of WATER. By passively seeking its level, water overcomes every barrier. This tells us that yielding is to surmount but grasping is to forfeit. The nature of water is crucial to an understanding of basic Taoist doctrine because it teaches that striving for perfection readily invites competition. That results in a vicious circle of more aggression, for competitiveness merely opens the door to those who exult in belligerence. Wisdom instructed Lao Tzu that the tallest tree gets axed. To avoid downfall, it's best neither to have high aspirations nor to be visible.

The *wu-wei* aspect of quietist thought also describes the state of mind necessary to become an authentic person, the only kind capable of producing genuine art. Whether in poetry or painting, Mushakôji agreed that the work must be generated when the mind is in its ideal creative state, one which assumes an openness to intuition and spontaneity. The artist does not, however, sit around waiting for inspiration to call him to his pen or brushes. He keeps perpetually busy at his desk or easel, hoping always to be "ready" the moment the heart opens and spontaneously gushes with insight. *Wu-wei* obviously does not mean doing nothing, but rather describes a state of fruitful readiness for aesthetic response. That's why *wu-wei* is "actionless action." Though typically paradoxical, this simply means that intellect does not self-consciously guide the artist's actions. The late Alan Watts offered the colloquial "no sweat" as a convincing translation of *wu-wei*. Watts' astute insight gets to the heart of the matter. Mushakôji sought authenticity by paring away the layers of intellectuality, intentionality, and artifice that he imagined cloud the beauties locked within the human heart. He aspired above all to produce poetry that might naturally percolate from the innermost recesses of the self. In his judgment, sincere verse alone has *virtue* in that now unfamiliar ancient sense of affective force—the unique power to communicate with and move others.

Another Taoist entrée to ideal existence, perhaps as primal as *wu-wei*, enables the spontaneity that so enthralled Mushakôji. This is the need to appropriate the attitude of the natural man. To become authentic and spontaneous requires cultivating naturalness in the self. Taoism, which taught that individuals with such characteristics alone are capable of redeeming civilization, never urged an image of revolutionaries assaulting the barricades. Assertive leadership cannot earn redemption. Actually, to be known is to lose the power to influence and thus to forfeit one's *virtue*. Redemption happens the quietist's way—like yeast working on dough. The human being who operates in this way is precisely the sort Mushakôji praises throughout his oeuvre. That is the person he hoped to become. He aimed also to be free of distorted values and to have a heart that society and its ethos have not smudged. Poem after poem echoes these Taoist-Zenist teachings. The natural human being finds merit in "primitive" sincerity and purity of heart. Social rules created to enforce conformity have not encumbered his spirit.

The quietist's emancipation from ego lifts him above greed and pettiness. He strives, after all, not with others but with himself as he tries to make the most of the gifts he has been given. He wants to unleash the life force throbbing within his gentle, loving heart. His innermost self embodies the power to counteract society's expected conformity—not to mention the deleterious influences of the politician, the academic, the critic, and the pressures of public opinion. The soul of the natural man exists at a pre-conscious, primitive state that is pure in the sense a child is pure. Mushakôji believed that good poetry flowed only from the heart of such a natural human being. Truth stems from the unconscious, from that part of the heart not redesigned or deformed by intellect, by discursive logic, or by conscious attempts to please or conform to standards not generated in the deepest recesses of the self. Whatever falls short of that cannot be authentic; cf. page 49 ff.

These characteristics echo the Taoist concept of the uncarved block, *p'u*. For centuries *p'u*, the primal and sacred "stuff" of the universe, has served as a significant artistic ideal for Zen artists. It is easy to understand why. One scholar defines *p'u* as the capacity of the unconscious that enables the mind to achieve its objectives. "Non-action" or *wu-wei* thus applies to any spontaneous activity, with or without aesthetic dimensions and regardless of how long it took to foster the spontaneity. Connections between *p'u* and *wu-wei* hint at the aptness of Alan Watts' "no sweat" rendering. Terms like extrasensory perception or even automatic writing suggest modern twists to this ancient idea. Trying too self-consciously to create or shape something may make one bungle the job. The pole vaulter who hopes to excel, for example, must master the various complex phases of the event. Vaulters must be so practiced and expert at these phases that they need expend no conscious energy thinking about them. Each phase must be executed with "no sweat." By the time one thinks about what to do, it's too late. Certain tasks, which for Mushakôji include writing poetry and painting pictures, similarly have the best chance to succeed when the artist exerts less rather than more conscious control over applying preparation to performance. This assumes a foundation of disciplined training the enables and empowers spontaneity. The trick is to tap into the natural self, the innermost person, the heart, and then let "it" do the work.

For this method to prevail, the mind requires more than dedicated preparation. It must be unconditionally serene and, above all, involved. The artist may seed the clouds or water his plants. He need not wait for inspiration or sincerity to strike. That requires preparation of mood and attitudes. The serenity that allows one to tap into his *p'u* demands, for example, that his heart be free of hostility, guilt, and aggressiveness. Only then will it be possible to release the inner self and become genuinely creative. The issue is never whether critics or others judge the product of spontaneous creative release as "high art." Judgmental concerns entice artists to a pathological regard for third-party opinions. In the realm of the natural self and the heart (that is, the domain of *p'u*), critical and scholarly opinions contain minimal meaning or importance. The question is far more elemental: has the artistic effort originated from the proper attitude or source? Only if it has might the result contain the power—the sincerity, the purity, the resonance, or the *virtue*—needed to move those exposed to the work. These views reflect the laws of nature. They are not philosophical constructs subject to debate.

Considering *p'u* as sacred primal stuff is by no means limited to Taoism. An echo of this idea appears in *Exodus* 20:25, where Jehovah commands Moses: "And if you make an altar of stone for me, do not build it of cut stone, for by putting a tool to it you desecrate it." Hewing or shaping a rock violates its natural "purity" and robs it of primal power. Once having lost its virtue, the stone can no longer honor the Lord. A human being who projects his ideas or notions of beauty on the natural stone renders it unnatural. He rapes it. No longer in its original uncarved state (*p'u*), such a stone has lost not only its incipient capacities but every ounce of potentiality as well. Small wonder Jehovah determined that an artificially-shaped rock had been desecrated. Taoists made an identical judgment. Their rebuke applied not only to natural materials like stone and wood but to humans as well. The society that imposes its views or prescribes behavior despoils its members. Mushakôji's consistent view was that when critics impose their standards on his *p'u* they defile him and his work. Stones, wood, or humans in their original state have an inner "stuff" that loses its sincerity and latency the moment someone imposes his will on it. Even the well-intentioned can menace artistic integrity!

As silence, serenity, spontaneity, *wu-wei*, and *p'u* indicate, Taoism lays primary stress on the inner person. Mushakôji's poetry displays identical interests in an interior province where each person can be an individual and make the most of every aptitude. This blessed state constitutes what Mushakôji likes to call the kingdom of God. This kingdom materializes whenever love reigns and individuals willingly cooperate—so long as they do so in a way that does not compromise integrity. Neither in Taoism nor in Mushakôji's verse does this kingdom have anything to do with commonplace notions of heaven as a reward beyond the grave. A person enters this paradise in the here and now by returning to the state of the uncarved block, thus becoming his true self. It takes very nearly an act of "grace," exerted by a power beyond the conscious will, to arrive at this quietist state. Those who have received that grace will be disposed to renounce contrivance and artifice, scheming for gain, and egocentricity. Both Mushakôji and the Taoist also believed that the perfect man is most assuredly a spiritual being and that true rightness derives from an epiphany that enables one to act spontaneously in every phase of existence.

Many admonitions of the Taoist philosopher Chuang Tzu (?369–286 B.C.) overlap Mushakôji's polemic. Chuang urged people to cultivate their inner powers. He adamantly insisted that they pay more attention to what they have within themselves than what they can get from others. Chuang cautioned: Don't wear yourself out trying to change the unchangeable. Man's soul, his innermost self, is impervious to external influences and disturbances. One achieves serenity and happiness by communicating with that self. Because humankind's primary goal is to be such a quietist, he thought the wise will instruct themselves. They neither pose as teachers nor lord it over others. Chuang also thought that to be known and honored in life is to lose the Way, for how can a person be openly admired and preserve his or her integrity? And how can one lose one's integrity and remain at peace with one's self? No one who calls attention to oneself, who seeks adulation, fame, and crowds can remain in a state of blessedness. Once one does so, Chuang averred, that person too soon becomes tempted to purchase adulation and acceptance—in short, one becomes corrupted. Rather, one should discover a means of living in the world without being influenced by it. It is best to do nothing aimed at gaining the favors of others, best to be buried like Chuang among hoi poloi.

Although Mushakôji well knew that reality presents inducements difficult to resist, and that some turmoil doubtless exists under even the most placid surface, he would surely cry Hallelujah! to each of Chuang's admonitions. In his art Mushakôji wanted little more than to provide people a place to stretch out on the mats and feel contented. Even an inattentive overview of the poetry will show that these ideals appear everywhere. He never abandoned his hopes to be just such a quietist.

II. MORALIST ASPECTS

How could a quietist be a moralist? Isn't that an obvious incongruity? Moralist suggests a teacher of ethics intensely interested in—and perhaps dedicated to influencing—the behavior of others. It is impossible to find people more adamantly opposed to moralists, ethics teachers, and their activities than quietists. Taoists abhorred the Confucian stress on the ethical helmsman or the morally superior sage. They regarded as pernicious any who invented duties, laws, and standards of goodness, and they always spoke vigorously against the pretensions of those who claimed to know what it meant to be "righteous" or to act "properly." Because Taoists believed that no human beings—but particularly the powerful—have the right to prescribe our behavior, those who appropriate that right ultimately offend and undermine both the individual's confidence and group harmony [wa].

Mushakôji shed incompatibilities between quietism and moralism the way a frog sheds water. Like most Taoists, he was thoroughly convinced of the artificiality of all externally-imposed morality, which permits tyrants and pedants to warp and embitter man's spirit. Unlike the Taoists, he was not bashful about urging people to act in specific ways. He hoped, however, that self-examination and self-discovery might teach them how to support and not sap the individual's autonomy or spirit. For, almost paradoxically, he sided with the Taoists in wanting to achieve spiritual serenity and so to exist without conscious striving. From the viewpoint of logical consistency, his philosophy of life and aesthetic principles may have been in conflict. But both derived from subjective perceptions that worked well for him. That's what counted. After all, even Mencius infused his moralist position with certain quietist principles. His ability to integrate elements of Taoist thought into Confucianism provides a precedent for this strange coupling.

Mencius followed Confucius in asserting that humans should act benevolently to all. That aspect of human behavior became, some maintain, the keynote of Confucian teaching. Mencius, however, went beyond his master. He allowed people the need for intuition and spontaneity. These, after all, contribute to fashioning the whole person, which was Mushakôji's concern whether he wrote poetry, drama, or fiction. That's why he fully grasped the devotion Mencius shows to "rectifying" the heart—in short, to set it right. A rectified heart nurtures an individual who is whole, that is, "human-hearted" and benevolent. Mencius might concede that those who nourish their intuitive powers and spontaneity will be even more whole. That makes people whose hearts have been set right peerless, for the rectified heart grants the individual immeasurable moral power. This, in turn, infuses a telling charisma of affective force—*virtue* in the ancient sense. Such a person becomes a paragon capable of inspiring others to become better people.

Taoists found Confucian prescriptions for rectifying the inner self excessively authoritarian. The true Taoist abhorred the thought of becoming a standard of perfection. That, in any case, merely proved to all that he was not authentic. In the arena of human behavior, Mushakôji's views almost duplicate what Mencius urges. In his art, however, he lays greater stress on Taoist concepts, in particular on

23

intuition and spontaneity. His reasons are obvious. Confucianists were most interested in human interaction and group harmony. These ideas might apply to life in the NEW VILLAGE, but Confucian prescriptions for behavior bore little or no relation to the aesthetic issues that so persistently confront a painter and poet.

Mencius also believed fully in humanity's basic goodness. He thought that most people desired to become better human beings. This view was not foreign to the Taoist affirmation that innate dispositions will not betray a person. There was, however, a catch. These dispositions must be kept "pure," which means free from pollution by external values. Unfortunately, society and moralist teachers like the Confucianists bent natural human inclinations out of kilter. Mushakôji, who similarly regarded most humans capable of and disposed toward goodness, agreed with the claim of Mencius that humankind's tendency toward goodness shows in the way people commiserate with those in distress. What human would not rush to aid a child about to fall into a well? Those with a rectified heart will endeavor to develop their innate sense of compassion, feelings of shame or modesty, and sense of right and wrong. These "large" noble qualities of the heart make people more human. To nurture them means to escape animality and become a genuine person.

A doctrine that enjoins people to develop their inner selves assumes that they are free to make and then actualize their choices. This may not require believing in free will as a philosopher might define it, but it comes close. Nurturing inner tendencies requires personal decision and efforts, if not a considerable amount of willpower. This urged Mencius to place confidence in individual liberty. He was realist enough to know the frustrations lurking in the quest for a rectified heart. He thus cautioned against unrealistic expectations. Although one constantly tries to do right, it is rarely possible to exert control over other people or the external world. As Taoists maintained, while you can bend yourself you cannot make others straight. After doing everything possible, one leaves the rest to fate or heaven, precisely Mushakôji's view of the matter; cf. page 273. Riches and honors cannot corrupt the ideal person who practices these Taoist principles, nor can poverty or misery force a compromise of principles. Neither power nor force can compel capitulation. Taoists could easily share with Mencius many of these descriptions of the "great" person. That, too, is very much the sort of being Mushakôji hoped to be.

Embedded in this agenda are other ideals that Mencius shares with the Taoists. It is of prime importance to Confucianist and Taoist alike to be in or regain harmony with the universe and its laws. To live harmoniously and become an ideal person often requires recovering what has been lost: one's childlike nature, for instance. The infant is closest to the truth and the Tao. Even Mencius believed it necessary that people preserve their childlike, intuitive hearts. He accordingly adopted an outlook that mirrors Taoist views on this issue. Mencius divided mental activity into two rough categories. The active type requires discursive reasoning. The passive type involves intuition, which encompasses "good" knowledge. Intuitive knowledge is superior because it issues from the inner self and thus possesses far greater potential to affect the person and others from within. Such knowledge is superior also because tyrants or moralist teachers have not warped it.

Through the ages, however, Chinese moralists have preferred discursive reasoning and logic over intuition. This was especially the case in their attempts to discover how to help human beings live with each other in harmony. Taoists, by contrast, taught that one achieves harmony by avoiding reliance on words and dogmas. Heart communicates with heart. Their idea was to keep the world of language distinct from the world of reality, which is far, far more nuanced and complex than writing and speech. They regarded confusion of these two spheres a significant cause of the moral confusion in the world. Despite being forced to make a living through words, Mushakôji interestingly accords silence the superior status, at least in poetry. As mentioned earlier, he thinks the "me of silence" a more genuine reflection of his true self than the "me of words"; cf. page 8.

Confucianists dealt with moral issues in black and white terms. Truth for them was rarely relative. Taoists, on the other hand, believed truth was always relative. Certitude in these matters they found loathsome because they regarded it unlikely that outsiders could make evenhanded judgments or non-dogmatic decisions about others. In the positive sense, a non-judgmental attitude encourages acceptance and understanding, words that characterize the attitude of an indulgent parent, not the behavior of a critic or moralist. In the negative sense, moral relativism not only makes every black-and-white assessment suspect, it encourages one to doubt statements that hint of dogmatism—including those by Taoists. On this issue Mushakôji remains predictably eclectic. An offending individual inevitably urges him to exact appropriate discipline. Acceptance, common sense, and understanding, however, often temper his judgment. The exception is the arrogance that academic critics display. It is not that Mushakôji's views of behavior are relative or subject to argument. Rather, a deep love of people and the fervent hope in their ability to get back on track eases his judgmental nature; cf. pages 117 and 136, middle.

A familiar anecdote illustrates the Taoist's non-judgmental and thus non-aggressive interpretation of an apparent untruth. Ask two forty-year-old women their age and one may say "I am forty," her actual age. The other may respond, "I am thirty-five." Confucianists and sects that similarly presume to have the whole truth will label the second woman's response a falsehood. Taoists point out, however, that the woman clearly means, "I fear getting old." In her own terms, then, she speaks the truth. If people around her recognize that, what harm can there be in accepting her statement? The wise "moralist" will indeed realize, as Taoists believed, that relativity of this sort dominates language at nearly every level. Consider the word "chilly." Can it conceivably mean the same to an Eskimo as to someone living in the Tropics? The Taoist urges the listener not to judge. He must instead try to discern what each expression means and so determine what the speaker really wants to say. This sound linguistic advice applies to any situation. If people behaved in this way, Taoists believed, they could break the circle of aggressiveness. Then they would not find themselves constantly reacting in a hostile manner to hostility. Confucianists, of course, stood diametrically opposed to that view.

Few aspects of moral behavior bore greater import for Mushakôji than self-discipline, a major key to success. Throughout his career, self-discipline remained an extremely important objective. This was true whether in art, the New Village community, or everyday existence in society. For him, as for many another ethics oriented teacher, self-discipline meant more than paying attention to planning and then ascertaining that the plans get carried out. Even a self-starter needs to move beyond just being and staying busy. Busyness, after all, can become inappropriate or even destructive if it heads in the wrong direction or serves only itself. Fruitful discipline meant learning to achieve a productive balance between duty and freedom, aims and abilities. Confucianists attached importance to being active and laboring incessantly in every aspect of life. They were no strangers to the bromide that idleness is the devil's workshop. By contrast, Taoists placed consistent reliance on spontaneity in aesthetic and other endeavors. This put them at odds with all conscious and intentional activities. Taoists equally opposed stress on aims and agendas, programs and productivity, which they thought made a human being inauthentic, tense, and unhappy. Obviously, nobody embracing Taoist principles could conceivably become qualified to administer a state!

Predictably, Mushakôji steers a middle course. On balance, however, his work ethic, if not his inspiration, remains flatly Confucianist. He harmonizes any disparities by asserting that spontaneity does not arise in a vacuum of inactivity. To repeat: the painter must constantly be at his easel handling his brushes. The poet must constantly be at his desk brandishing his pen. Spontaneity might then "happen" to a person. It is more apt to occur during steadfast involvement, however, than during inactivity. The moment spontaneity strikes, the artist mystically bridges the gap between conscious activity and non-action. He finds himself in the zone of the intuitions and achieves *wu-wei*. Because realizing this state is a gift, somewhat akin to grace, few subjects have a clear idea how they attained it. This much Mushakôji knows: he can only make himself open to its occurrence. He cannot actively will or consciously generate spontaneity; cf. page 177 ff.

The teachings of Confucius appeal to everyday people. If you wish a peaceful and harmonious world, Confucianism says, accept authority. You must also be obedient to superiors in the family and the state, act graciously toward inferiors, and discipline yourself. You must become fully associated with society to realize your true self. Moral injunctions like these will be clear to everyone, and people can accept or reject them. Classical Taoist teachings, by contrast, appeal only to elitists—the seer, the dreamer, the mystic. If you wish a peaceful and harmonious polity, Taoism says, reject authority, escape the world, and obey only your inner voice. You must dissociate yourself from society to hear that voice and realize your true self. This way, furthermore, requires one to uncover the emptiness in the self, suppress intentional behavior, and learn to be a child again. Since the common mentality illustrates Erich Fromm's notion that people desire to "escape from freedom," how many can possibly accept these Taoist prescriptions? They will prove altogether too daunting for the average person. Either school offers its dos and don'ts, but Confucianism's directives are clear, Taoism's are cloudy. Similar contradictions occur throughout Mushakôji's eclectic approach. Astonishingly, they produce no recognizable tensions in him. Perhaps his love and respect for humanity made it possible to blend most inconsistencies. It is also true, I reiterate, that his

Taoist aspects manifest themselves most dominantly in the creative process. When he operates as a social man, Confucian elements are more noticeable.

Many poems written between 1918 and 1926, the years Mushakôji lived in the New Village, demonstrate the pedagogical function of his moralist stance. These works, which occupy over forty percent of his poetic corpus, serve as sermonettes, didactic behavioral tracts, catechetical instructions in humanhood, or tutorials in cooperative action. Traditional Japanese methods of empowering the superego, harnessing the ego, and sublimating the id were neo-Confucianist adaptations. Without these moral controls, Japan's hierarchical neighborhood-style communities would have found it difficult to realize a high level of conformity. Mushakôji persistently desired to escape these constraints and the diminishment of personhood they so successfully achieve. Depriving people of happiness affects creativity, cooperation, and the ability to fulfill the self. Becoming self-reliant or independent in the usual Japanese surroundings, Mushakôji felt, would require a fresh social context where people could escape the suffocating demands of a hierarchical body politic. How in that milieu realize the feat of being free to act as an individual and yet remain part of the community? This question provided the germ of his vision. He would establish a close-knit society offering opportunities for human beings to realize their every dream. In this "New Village," people could learn to be free yet related, expressive rather than exploited; cf. pages 146–147 and 150.

Japan's closed, hierarchical polity traditionally accepts the leadership of authority figures. This practice increased the challenge, for Mushakôji's new society rejected conventional leadership. He would instead appeal to the individual's creative potentials and exploit the natural human desire to be liberated from conventions. Mushakôji wanted to believe both that sensitive persons felt driven to discover who they are and that they desired to be more self-reliant. Turning from society's paternalistic embrace would, however, prove extremely difficult for any deficient in Mushakôji's commitments to responsibility, self-discipline, and hard work. Liberation from conformity allowed some to regard themselves freed to self-indulgence, not to a realization of inner potentials or to help and respect others. Systematic indoctrination might overcome this tendency, but indoctrination was as abhorrent to Mushakôji as organizational skills were non-existent. The New Village thus contained neither an authoritarian voice nor a political manipulator. Leadership consisted primarily of the great teacher who—like the Confucian sage—optimistically led by example and encouraging words. That is, the village was so consciously un-managed that it surely resembled a congregation of Taoists.

Mushakôji's New Village movement reflects far more than a reaction to his vertical society. It constitutes also an indictment of monopoly capitalism, the dehumanizing factory system, and the modern city. He is no Luddite calling for the destruction of machines. He wishes only to call people back to a wholesome natural environment where they might begin from scratch to build morally acceptable and humane social and factory systems; cf. pages 145 and 151. His judgments of certain features in modern society intended less to cause its destruction than its redemption. Strategy in this process begins with the moralist urge to return to man's "natural state." Among other characteristics, this state features absolute openness to nature and the power of the Creator • God. Because humanist concerns propel the spirit of this strategy, we find no presumption to discover knowledge about God, nature, or even *Ten* (Heaven, a Confucian tag for the absolute). Like the Taoist, Mushakôji believed that knowledge *about* is artificial and thus useless.

Ten differs from our idea of heaven. It neither implies looking ahead nor suggests a point of arrival. The Confucianist rather saw heaven as the abode of the ancestors. To be "good" implied following the ancestors' way. Those who did so lived in accord with the "will of heaven." Only acquiescence to this will can bring happiness. Awakening to the inner self implied turning from that way, which promised disaster. Confucianists hence curbed every teaching or tendency that encouraged self-sufficiency and freedom from the rule of the past. Those who looked to individual happiness in the future offended heaven and invited misery. Always concerned to move ahead and improve himself, Mushakôji could neither look to the past nor defer to precedents set by ancestors or authorities. He tried instead to get people to refashion how they live, interact, and work together. Renewal required shedding the old skin so one might not be imprisoned by the past. The New Village hence encouraged members to develop private inner values rather than conform to rules established by others, particularly by figures from another age. Human beings acquire power by acting in consonance with values that live in the heart, not by conforming to the presumed will of deceased ancestors.

Living values loomed paramount in Mushakôji's moral stance. People with such values endeavor to improve their total inheritance. That way they not only enjoy a responsible existence but enrich the people of the future as well; cf. pages 117–118. Mushakôji felt most involved and fulfilled whenever he was immediately engaged in self-improvement that promised moral and personal betterment. No doubt about it, he fully accepted the reproof: "Let the dead bury their dead" (*Luke* 9:60). His orientation was not to the past but to a present-tense involvement in life and living, in work and self-fulfillment. Involvement must be the watchword for all committed to improving themselves so as to build a better future. That's why Mushakôji taught that people had better do now what they can for themselves and for others because they have no second chance.

He believed that not even the most benign institution can ordain genuine moral change. That can come only from within. For him, indeed, inner change was the source of everything good and positive. His ethical viewpoints and his beliefs consequently contribute trenchantly to the "emotional reality" his poems create. His moral stance, which serves as a metaphor of his emotions, symbolizes his state of mind and its dedication to humankind. These are the sources of human renewal.

III. HUMANIST ASPECTS

Throughout *Long Corridor* I use HUMANISM in its essential and uncomplicated sense: concern for the interests and welfare of human beings. In certain particulars Mushakôji may resemble the Renaissance humanist. In many others, he does not. He studied the ancient greats to learn what they teach about living. He thought little of abstractions but honored ideas that provide a springboard for action in daily life. From start to finish, however, humanism for him was simply a deep concern for humankind's fulfillment and happiness. He dealt consistently with life's mundane concerns because in them he found the heart [*kokoro*], humanity's source of beauty, love, and truth. Mushakôji hoped always to manage a balance between an intuitive drive for right action and a grateful acceptance of givens. His humanism merges then with quietism and moralism to create a unique philosophy of life.

Elements of the SHIRAKABA spirit most tellingly characterize the humanist essence of Mushakôji's poetry. Between its 1910 founding and 1923 demise—that is, through almost the entire 1912–1926 Taishô era—the *Shirakaba* magazine exerted great influence on Japan's literary arena. Its pages provided broad intellectual excitement by introducing aesthetic ideals, social critiques, and cultural values from the West. The journal also stimulated literary circles with a steady diet of European values like ideas of social equality, personal liberty, and individualism. The menu offered every genre, from plays to paintings, poetry to prose, polemics to panegyrics. It included translations and original articles, as well as photographs of art work and sculpture. The steady humanist commitment of Shirakaba writers provided a seawall that helped prevent many from being swamped by the tsunami of anarchism, Marxism, and other philosophies lashing Japan's shores in those days. Ideas like liberty and free expression particularly fascinated the intellectual community. After all, those years witnessed increased tensions between the state and the individual. During much of the Taishô period, moreover, the *Shirakaba* arguably served as the touchstone if not the arbiter of humanist taste in literature.

Shirakaba associates reacted against NATURALISM and naturalist writers whose techniques then dominated the literary scene. Concerned to break with tradition and interested in being up-to-date, many Japanese writers tried to imitate European experiments with naturalism. Successful imitation, however, required embracing Emile Zola's literary theories. To adopt his stress on factual, realistic representation called for precise descriptions of life's actual circumstances. That involved no threat to those rooted in a tradition of diary writing. It was more problematic to master Zola's ideal of objective novelistic technique or rationally-conceived plot structure. Aside from the "scientific" organization of fiction, his approach required a politically active attitude, for a prime naturalist objective was to change the world and the social conditions that affect human beings. Naturalists believed the state could bring about changes in society if only statesmen had access to systematic analyses of people's needs and the social realities that conditioned them. This increased the novelist's motivation to organize his work to a level where it might function as an instrument of communal reconstruction. European writers hoped these techniques might shield them from fatalism, which meant, among other things, surrender to the status quo. Intellectuals give in to reality when they feel unable to stimulate social change, affect political events, or renew traditional values.

Zola's theories assumed a socio-political system dedicated to human welfare. That presented no problem in a region with a history of charity and rudimentary respect for social well-being. Europe was, after all, the center of Christianity as well as the cradle of humanism. Nor did theorists nurtured in that tradition risk appearing ridiculous if they chose to imply the writer's responsibility to help improve social conditions. In Japan, by contrast, neither government nor public support of charity or humanism existed. Because the family basically looked after human welfare, the state had more than enough leisure to devote its resources to the maintenance of polity order, which it pursued relentlessly. Naturalist objectives accordingly required considerable alteration before they could don a kimono. Japanese writers knew they had little chance of influencing society. Nor did they enjoy a cultural background where science and reason commanded respect—especially when applied to literature, which Japanese entrust to the emotions, the real seat of imaginative power. How, then, could the average Japanese writer become oriented to social concerns? These differences required essential overhaul and reconstruction of naturalist principles. Japanese began by flatly rejecting the scientific, logical, political, organizational, and social reform aspects of naturalism. For them, European techniques merely offered opportunities to free the self from the pervasive family system. Japanese egotists had discovered "scientific" backing for their unabashed self-indulgence. That resulted in a narrow agenda focused on the solipsistic self. What could possibly compel them to develop a sense of responsibility toward themselves, their art, or their society?

It was very easy to demand but extremely hard to gain freedom from the coercive relationships of their familial society. Since they were unable to influence social values, naturalist writers moved inward and flouted the norms they could not reform. They concentrated on the id, the human being's well of instinctive impulses and demands for immediate satisfaction. Their focus on self-indulgence and exploiting libido effectively short-circuited any possibility of developing sensitivity to social conditions. Egocentricity and self-indulgence, after all, choke out commiseration for those who suffer from social injustices. The confessional called for subjectivity and candor. That, too, involved writers in the self, thus further discouraging objective interest in bettering society. The emphasis lay solely on the "natural" presentation of raw reality, which defined success as ability to present life exactly as the writer felt it. Being true to experience quickened, as well, a rejection of novelistic structure, analysis, and logic. When Japanese deserted commitment to social reform, they also rejected the plot organization and authorial detachment that European naturalists believed necessary to seed that reform.

The predilection in Japanese culture for submissiveness systematically undermines humanist concerns. In that environment, submitting to authority is normal behavior. Defiance becomes an act as unnatural as it is unwise. Naturalist writers had the strength to reject traditional society and its demands. They fell short, however, of resisting self-indulgence. Distancing themselves from convention rather than from instinct had consequences. It made them hostages to diary-style unstructured writing. How much intentional plot construction and objective analysis does a confessional require? Actually, readers preferred it that way: little plot, no analysis. The shock value of these revelations increased marketability, to be sure, but popularity did not rest exclusively on the sordid interests of the voyeur. Far more titillating was the popular perception of these works as blows against tradition or assertions of autonomy. By parading the writer's culturally eccentric behavior, confessionals allowed readers to imagine themselves similarly free to act out their fantasies, whether against conventions or flesh-and-blood authority. One commentator consequently describes the single-minded dedication to the confessional mode as "self-burlesque." Exposing deviant behavior fascinated readers who neither missed nor wanted overt scrutiny of life. These confessionals created a realm of illusion where lack of fictive plot structure became an asset. Why should readers concern themselves with the whys or wherefores? The writer's burlesque allowed readers total subjectivity and freedom to appropriate the diarist's experiences. That, in turn, emancipated the psyche, if but momentarily, from overwhelming social pressures to conform. Readers found it far easier to see themselves in the story's primary character than to fret over subtle plot shifts and conflict resolution.

Shirakaba humanists rejected these features. The slightest hint of blindness to human welfare and dignity alienated them. They could not, however, exclude all naturalist emphasis on private experience. After all, man was the measure, and to become authentic assumed release from the constrictions of the polity and its ethos. Total disagreement on that issue never materialized. Nor did Mushakôji and his colleagues willingly accept intentional organization, especially for poetry. To emulate Zola's structural precepts required, however, a degree of objectivity and discursive analytical skills that few Japanese then felt compelled to master. Mushakôji abandoned them not because they were unnecessary to self-indulgent confession but because he felt they undermined sincerity. Some shared agreement aside, Shirakaba associates questioned the negative way egocentric disclosures affected writing quality. Optimistic and idealistic hope for self-improvement, they thought, gave their writing a superior configuration and quality.

Major tensions with naturalism derived, of course, from the Shirakaba humanists' idealist stance. They held that moral, spiritual, or supernatural values count, for ideas have significance. Naturalists rather contended that the confessed self could not help being exactly as they portrayed it. They supposed that natural causes and laws explained all phenomena and that environment and heredity, not ideas, conditioned how people think and behave. Ever the bona fide humanist, Mushakôji averred that ideas, ideals, and even faith allow humans to transcend their social situation. Trust in God and free will contradicted the naturalist's convictions that heredity and environment broadly condition, if they do not determine, human behavior. Naturalist writers saw people as pawns of their animal instincts or social situation and thus powerless to influence their society. Regarding free will an illusion, naturalists ignored problems of willpower, ethical judgment, or good and evil. Unlike Europeans, Japanese naturalists did not imagine they could stimulate political action to reform society. They never regarded themselves social engineers.

Despite being aware from his youth of the diverse ways that his heredity affected him, Mushakôji could not accept the naturalist's environmental determinism. He saw such views as indifference to the nurture of individualism.

Japanese naturalists think negatively. For all their bravado and anti-traditional rhetoric, their zero potential to alter either circumstances or environment made many cynical and gloomy. Even if they tried, they could neither engineer a new society nor transform the values of fellow citizens. They realized, as well, that they confronted immovable and implacable enemies: human instinct, conventional ethos [shikitari], and the government's investments in inertia. Intensely aware that they lacked the ability to budge, much less conquer, these foes, they became—unlike their European counterparts—ever more fatalistic. This produced pessimism. Alas! the cultural rebel's lot was not a happy one. For all its sincerity, unappealing moods of hopelessness, boredom, and suffering shadowed the naturalist confessional.

By contrast, an appealing optimism characterized Shirakaba writers. Trust in the power of ideas and faith in human potential unfailingly made them sanguine about the future. Their positive approach rested firmly on respect for individuals and hopes for—in fact, confidence in—the welfare and progress of the race; cf. page 52. They thus stressed self-fulfillment and the realization of individual happiness. Most pages of Mushakôji's poetry demonstrate how deeply he imbibed these criteria. He replaced naturalism's dreary and depressing aspects with cheerfulness, idealism, joy, and hope. His expectations for the future of humankind had roots in both the present and the past. His poetry implies that now is the time for growth, for decision, for moving ahead. His interest in the past recalls a revolutionary who uses history as a lever to improve the present. Mushakôji desired, for example, to recapture the child's pristine heart. That opens people to heart-to-heart communication and exposes others to the artist's sincerity. Many Japanese readers and critics find such an approach infinitely more affecting than skillful writing techniques. However ingeniously presented, words that fail to move the heart are powerless. Besides, mere technique stems from the conscious brain. It can therefore be more cultivated than felt, which makes it suspect. Faith in the innocence of the heart Mushakôji regarded as the Asian road to human wholeness. That guaranteed that the idealists would be going somewhere. The naturalists were headed nowhere. The founders wanted the Shirakaba to reflect this buoyant, hopeful optimism.

Determined to devote their journal to literature and the fine arts, the associates forged a creative atmosphere attractive to painters and sculptors as well as writers. Shirakaba humanists avoided conflict by agreeing to disagree. Interested both in realizing their human potentials and in achieving collegiality, they regarded themselves artistic equals and cooperated harmoniously. Many were standouts in their fields. The Shirakaba ambience allowed them to celebrate their humanity and genius without feeling pressured to present a homogeneous ideological front. Once the magazine became established, fellows perceived little need to limit its content to their work. Nor did writers use the pages of Shirakaba simply as a springboard to enter the literary mainstream. Hence their wholesome cooperation rather than the customary range of adversary relationships and pernicious jealousies. Stable friendships demonstrated humanism at work. Better, the exceptional congeniality of Shirakaba relations showed that a humanism built on mutual esteem could succeed in Japan's hierarchical society. They moreover promoted each other's welfare and so created associations that extended beyond the dozen years of the magazine's life.

Their apolitical humanism still attracts attention. Some scholars and critics enjoy chiding the Shirakaba's non-political stance as a major failing. It is not possible to understand how any but Marxists (whose agenda is political action) or political scientists (who need fodder for articles or dissertations) might seriously expect idealist artists to act politically. The Taishô political climate dictated the fruitlessness of expecting artists to enter the political arena. Humanist commitments to citizen welfare and individual advancement emerge from the belief that ideals enable action. Naturalist assertions that environment determines private values and that intellectuals are obliged to help alter the environment did not in the least appeal. Shirakaba adherents stood behind free will and individual responsibility, too, and so they never imagined that transforming the person requires political changes. Although privileged or elitist status may have colored their views, their position developed from solid beliefs in idealism and the power of ideas.

Were Shirakaba writers unaware of the fate awaiting the political activist? Given the realities of Japan's closed, hierarchical society, who but a sadist might require artists and writers to pursue a political platform? Even had Shirakaba associates banded together and devoted themselves to the task, it is unclear how they might have made an impact on the political scene. Trying to do so would have identified them as troublemakers and subjected them to government scrutiny. In those days, Japanese imagined that only Socialists or Marxists behaved in that way. Social activities promised only to suffocate their art. Besides, what experienced revolutionary had managed to make the slightest dent in the reactionary armor of Japan's body politic? Those on the Left accomplished little beyond filling jails and squabbling about doctrines. Can Shirakaba faultfinders demonstrate the political success of a single voluntary organization? How, then, expect non-political Taishô artists to dedicate themselves to social action?

In those days, perfectly innocent statements invited censorship; GOVERNMENT OFFICIALS ②. The fear of attracting undue attention effectively inhibited idealist and other writers from involvement in political activity. Nor were they in the least motivated to wrest democratic rights, liberties, or concessions of any kind from the state. They concentrated rather on arresting the attention of their readers and raising awareness on issues like responsible individuality. To Mushakôji's way of thinking, extending that activity to the political arena, becoming activists, or associating with politicians would only corrupt writers. Never in his career did he believe that existence as an authentic individual required him to take political action. Nor did he ever imagine the need to apply to Japan's body politic his own commitment to personal integrity. The small stage he chose made a strong enough statement for him. His New Village experiment demonstrated the wisdom of Aristotle's observation that the "good life" is inconceivable outside the community that supports it. If the community achieved that aim, its size would be irrelevant.

Not all Shirakaba intellectuals were as dedicated to humanism as Mushakôji. Nor was a one as unrestrained in hoping for the future of the individual in Japan. Ideas interested them all, to be sure, but Mushakôji determined to show more hope in people and human values than in abstractions. The way he advocated this hope made him appear at times a reincarnation of Dr. PANGLOSS. Close inspection will surely modify the first impressions that associate Mushakôji with this Pollyanna whom Voltaire describes in *Candide*. Buoyant ingenuousness aside, Mushakôji was realistic. He knew how unlikely it would be for most to adopt his views. He also knew how persistently the values of his society undermined most humanist ideals. Despite that, he retained a childlike optimism and charming naiveté. At his most ingenuous, Mushakôji could never condone the uncritical acceptance of reality that typifies Dr. Pangloss and his slogan: "All is for the best." Nor could his humanism allow him to embrace the vacuous Pangloss bromide, "This is the best of all possible worlds." Not yet! Mushakôji regarded himself a child of a flawed society he felt a responsibility to improve. His poetry attests to the universal values of an indefatigable humanist, not to a preposterous Pollyanna.

Interestingly, *Candide* shares with Mushakôji a profound disquiet over an ancient conundrum: Given a benevolent Maker, how can the evil prosper while the good suffer? The Old Testament morality play *Job* suggests that evil and tragedy are inexplicably obvious aspects of creation. Shadows, after all, make us appreciate sunlight. Mushakôji's view was typically East Asian. People must not be satisfied merely to accept the inevitable and remain passively in harmony with the laws of the universe. They must also actively do their utmost to improve themselves and their world. Accepting everything as "the best of all possible worlds" may reduce conflict. It bears little resemblance to human choices in the real world. Mushakôji accepts the views of Mencius, who taught that the superior—that is, the "human-hearted"—person should always try to act ethically. Because he cannot control others, social forces, or nature, he must leave the outcome to heaven.

Mushakôji more closely resembles certain unfamiliar aspects of DON QUIXOTE, who asserts, "I know who I am and who I may be, if I choose." That awareness informs Mushakôji's interest in differentiating himself from the herd, gaining a sense of personal identity and worth, and becoming aware of his potentials. In pursuit of these ends, much of his verse fearlessly if not flawlessly jousts with the windmills of traditional values—which were, and remain, far from illusions. In no other way could he define his self. His realism reflected a life lived as a human being among other humans with whom he hoped to have an I-and-Thou relationship. Like Quixote, the point of his jousting was to show others how to discover and then realize the self and its possibilities. He ardently hoped that they, too, might seek self-knowledge and find happiness. Transcendental aspects of this humanist faith included a sense of piety, dedication, and conscientiousness, an attitude of reverence toward nature and the Maker of humankind, and an urge to conform to the "will of the universe." His humanism embraces all these ideas, each of which is rooted in the belief that people are always perfectible if never perfect.

IV. SUBJECTIVIST ASPECTS

In Mushakôji's thought, subjectivism links with and empowers quietism, moralism, and humanism. It does so by enabling conscience and the psyche to serve as the sole arbiters of moral or aesthetic judgment. This clearly implies that subjective elements dominate experience. That, of course, restricts knowledge principally to the conscious self and its sensory states. Mushakôji's subjectivist thought contrasts with customary prescriptions in important ways. He locates the aware self in the heart or *kokoro* and interjects a religious dimension that reflects his belief that God implanted certain truths in his *kokoro*; cf. page 235 ff. This infuses these values with a touch of the sacred. The subjectivist believes his private visions are so true that their virtue can harmonize life's inner and outer realities.

Truth stands foremost among Mushakôji's subjective standards. As the correlative of error, we usually define truth objectively, but the *kokoro* is as objective as taste. The lyric poet by definition habitually deals with inner states of mind and subjective matters of taste. For him, truth is what delights or depresses. It is the law of the heart. Mushakôji accordingly finds his ultimate artistic pleasure in sharing the content of his *kokoro*. In the West, critics expect even lyric poets to exert intellectual control over the heart's outpourings and intuitions. Editing clarifies insights. Applying judgment excises the irrelevant, which helps improve coherence of imagery and metaphor. These cerebral operations sharpen the work's focus. Objective considerations of this sort are, however, alien to the subjectivism that dominates Mushakôji's verse. His views stand as exceptions to all common-sense literary criteria, which he does not accept simply because they are objective.

This explains why Mushakôji opposes revising the feelings that ooze up from his heart. He believes that even a hint of amending can erode truth. In passages where he explains, describes, or voices his views of poetry (cf. page 363 ff.), his statements, like his verse, rarely derive from discursive logic, close reasoning, or keen analysis. All editing and rewriting falls into the "by-all-means-avoid" category. He knows what happens once a poet begins to revise a message from the *kokoro*. Revision unleashes the energies of the conscious intellect, which crowds out the heart's truth. Allowing ratiocination to dominate the process furthermore stifles spontaneity. Either way, truth cannot survive. Mushakôji's standards instead reflect the spontaneous, intuitive patterns that characterize his entire aesthetic. This gives them a special flavor, to be sure, but his subjective principles unmistakably make his work vulnerable to endless faultfinding by the professional critic. Few academics are either willing or prepared to judge him by his private norms.

Redaction not only puts truth in jeopardy, it degrades sincerity. Mushakôji insists on delivering to the reader the "holy" and impromptu thoughts and insights of his heart. However ragged and rough, they are both true and sincere. Only sincerity can nourish the heart's truths. The moment a poet begins to edit his outpourings is the moment intellect may betray the heart's purity. Attempts to fashion private feelings into public writing must reflect standards that, however agreeable to others, may be foreign to a passion for sincerity. Allowing alien, cerebral concerns to rule the *kokoro* creates falsehood, not art. The reason is disarmingly simple. Submitting to standards imposed from without, whether by critics or academics, perverts the natural efflorescence of SINCERITY; cf. page 213 ff. From Mushakôji's viewpoint, the slightest insincerity disqualifies the writing as true poetry. He intends to convey as forthrightly as possible the truths buried in his *kokoro*. Readers intent on letting their hearts converse with Mushakôji's heart will be satisfied to bask in the poet's earnestness. Those with expectations foreign to this intention should find a poet who speaks their language.

Concern for sincerity and spontaneity reveals an unrelenting commitment to expressing subjective truths about humanity. Mushakôji nowhere states that he dedicates his verse to these "truth-functions" of poetry. Work collected in *Long Corridor* nevertheless reveals that this is the case. Little of his corpus relates to the "science of pleasure" or to the traditional Japanese appreciation of natural beauty. He is so busy identifying with humankind that he rarely identifies with nature. His is the vision of William Wordsworth, who writes in his Preface to the second edition of *Lyrical Ballads*, "The Poet binds together by passion and knowledge the vast empire of human society, as it is spread over the whole Earth, and over all time." This intimates concern for universal human truth, Mushakôji's arena of artistic activity. Aesthetic aspects of truth may be particular and subjective as opposed to the universal and objective nature of scientific truth. That by no means makes them any less important for the human being who may wish to be fulfilled or happy. How convincing might it be to tell those who thirst for self-knowledge and artistic growth that their hopes are "unscientific"? Or that their desires lack objective validity? Human concerns also turn Mushakôji against the grain of traditional expectations that poetry be "beautiful." For him, beautifully-crafted—that is to say artificial—expressions describing lovely scenery constitute an oxymoron. True beauty is beauty of the inner person. That alone is sufficiently potent to rescue the world from disaster. Consciously crafted verse reveals not the perspicacious truths of the *kokoro* but the esoteric truisms of the conscious intellect. Such poetry is synthetic or counterfeit and thus earns rejection. Mushakôji wants his verse rather to exude the energies of life and the truths that help people live fully.

These concerns touch on critical aspects of *makoto*, a traditional East Asian concept. The celebrated haiku poet Kamijima (a.k.a. Ueshima) Onitsura (1661–1783) describes *makoto*—literally, "true words"—as the principle that gives poetry soul and universality. *Makoto* not only signifies being true or the absence of falsehood but contains a hint of integrity and moral uprightness. Mencius calls it "the way of Heaven." He taught that striving for *makoto* is the proper goal of all human beings. These ideas coincide almost exactly with Mushakôji's. Of course, to develop *makoto* requires incessant training to make it as spontaneous as an athletic skill. Like any such skill, it requires constant polishing. *Makoto*, concerned with character rather than muscles, derives more from the heart, the *kokoro*, than from words. For all that, the *makoto* state may be less an achievement than a gift or a grace. *Makoto* makes a poem timeless. A poet with *makoto* will not use artifice in his work, for that would make him untrue to the self. Nor will he attempt to show off his wit or erudition. If one uses imagery and action alone, the work will lack *makoto*. Onitsura assures us that poetry containing *makoto* will never age. All good poetry is infused with it and is thus timeless. He felt certain that *makoto* would free verse from gratuitous wordplay and ornamentation. Poems with *makoto* characteristics read fluently, are simple, and yet have profound implications for humanity and for life. The work of those blessed with the *makoto* state also exudes joyfulness and buoyancy. Contrived "objective" poetry may have greater immediate interest or impact, but it does not hold up to the test of time and consequently cannot be "good."

Makoto must, however, emerge naturally and spontaneously or it may forfeit its affective power—its virtue. That's part of its mystery. To avoid falsehood and contrivance, one cannot achieve *makoto* by a mere conscious attempt. That would make it only one more poetic device. To repeat, achieving *makoto* requires considerable psychic discipline, which most resembles the activity *wu-wei* describes; cf. page 20. It requires constant "no sweat" attention, for example, to appreciate the simple and the plain over the complex and the ornamented. It's a matter of good taste, something that must be inculcated. Onitsura admired the eulalia [*susuki*, a type of pampas grass] because this autumn plant has no pretensions. It lacks flowers and variegated colors, and yet its simple gold against green leaves projects a unique dignity. That's a learned taste. Onitsura says *susuki* "hides its elegance from fools, but reveals it to the sensitive." Only the initiated can agree. The sensitive alone recognize value in plainness and spontaneity and thus often praise subjective writers whom critics regard as commonplace or childish. The sensitized palate, after all, values naiveté and innocence—pure manifestations of the *kokoro* and its truths.

East Asian philosophers like Mencius or poets like Onitsura do not monopolize these insights into the nature of art. The British philosopher John Stuart Mill made a number of similar observations. He thought that poetry—less the antithesis of prose than of science, he said—has as much claim as science or fiction to represent truth. The narrative and plot, tensions and solutions, character development or comments of fiction make an emotional impact. Poetry by contrast concerns itself solely with emotions. Great poets know the truth by self-observation, Mill claimed, even though a poet may not, like a novelist, have a detailed scientific knowledge of humankind. But the poet does know that his self and the nature of humanity count most. Unlike a biologist, a poet sees through the lion to truths beyond it. He perceives the awe, the terror, and the wonder of the beast. Poetry, Mill believed, is impassioned truth—human thought tinged with feelings. The true poet is so dedicated to exposing his heart that, unlike a dramatist, he may not always be aware of his audience. In any event, Mill thought the bard delivers a soliloquy that does not consciously court sympathy, for poetry is a fruit of solitude and meditation. Stage eloquence rather derives from human interaction. If you need applause, don't go into poetry. Mushakôji's verse contains correlatives of most of Mill's statements.

Another aspect of the *kokoro* that Mushakôji delights in relates to his concern for authenticity; cf. page 49 ff. His definition leans toward the subjective. The scholar's, by contrast, leans toward the objective. These views resist resolution. The scholar finds Mushakôji's work shallow or "sappy" and therefore inauthentic. Mushakôji implies that inauthenticity corrupts the intellectual's discourse. The academician traditionally frets about keeping his theories up to date. He feels compelled to project a sense of superiority or to put others down and call attention to himself, his work, and his areas of competence. Above all, he must be *right*. Academics glorify the objective and the abstract, assuming always that their theories are rooted in reality. Some label this a neurosis or "false consciousness." Mushakôji simply regarded it a pretentious sham. He rejected these ploys, dispensed with scholarly rhetoric, and expressed his heart in plain language. In his view, only the subjective can be pure or "true." He was also aware of the irony that the very powers of insight or organization, imagination or analysis, that raise writing to a higher level threaten at the same time also to rob the writer of authenticity. To call attention to themselves, some strive for higher levels of writing—bogus excellence that encourages inauthentic gestures. Such behavior threatens to distance the writer from his *kokoro*, the fountainhead of poetic excellence and inspiration. From Mushakôji's view, all "bad"—meaning all inauthentic—verse shares the same characteristic. It stems from the conscious, intentional aspects of the psyche, areas of the mind dedicated to concealing what is most natural and true. This is the antithesis of *makoto*. Since smug self-awareness tries to impress or intimidate others, and since it is dedicated to pose and pretense, it is the most non-*makoto* or false.

Attitudes favoring *makoto* values permeate Mushakôji's views of critics; cf. page 213 ff. His subjectivity, in turn, earns the opprobrium of any committed to classic standards. We rarely confront unbecoming displays of emotion in his verse, a customary reproach of the classicist. Nor does Mushakôji typically become excessively imaginative. But classicists, those celebrated despisers of undisciplined, rhapsodic writing, will find much in his poetry to scorn. As steadfast proponents of self-control, they advise restraint over the enthusiasm that characterizes some of Mushakôji's verse. They also stress the importance of form to control subjectivity and accord merit to objective intellectual properties like design, balance, and proportion. These Mushakôji's introspective approach rejected. He nonetheless did reflect the classicist's favoring of ideas and morals over diction and verbal decoration. Classicists, however, support language that is more formal, dignified, and refined than he cared for. Wishing to improve humanity, classicists not only prefer themes with a moral purpose but require an edifying tone. These qualities match Mushakôji's poetic objectives, too, though his definition of "edifying tone" no doubt differs from theirs. In sum, however, he dissociates himself entirely from the objectivity, rationality, and concern for surfaces that most classicists honor.

Above all, Mushakôji saw poetry as the voice of the naked heart. Because the honesty of any writing reflects the condition of the heart, a poem's beauty depends not on rhetorical devices but on the integrity of the *kokoro*. As Thomas Carlyle urged, "Be true, if you would be believed." Consequently, Mushakôji could never regard writing as a matter either of polished surfaces or of artificially-ordered contents. Classicists believe it important to pay attention to poetic surfaces, which imply far more than the words themselves can say or mean. That is equally true of many standard idioms. One cannot, for example, possibly make full sense of an expression like "How do you do?" simply by grammatical analysis of the words. The whole consists of more than its lexical parts. It is also true that a universal peculiarity of poetry is that you cannot grasp the subject matter or master the content of a work simply by reference to its surface. On top of that, consciously manipulating surfaces to move or impress the reader ran against Mushakôji's aesthetic. He aspired only to open his heart and let bubble up whatever would surface. The result is a corpus so free of guile that all its "secrets" are instantly apparent—accordingly, the cliché that Mushakôji's poetry needs no annotation. For that matter, the expression "How do you do?" needs no annotation, either, at least not for those who know how to interpret it. No one can claim, however, that every subjective insight embedded in Mushakôji's verse will be immediately obvious to every reader. It is deceptively easy, for example, to overlook his polemic against indigenous social values. Even the gaze of those well tutored in Japanese culture effortlessly melts into the blandness of Mushakôji's prosaic surface language. Their negative views of his surfaces blind them to the consistent critical stance that pervades his content.

Prosaic surfaces should not desensitize readers to an obvious fact. For all his subjectivity, the content of Mushakôji's work suggests revolt. Work that prescribes how people should live constitutes stern opposition to standard cultural attitudes. He by no means accepts the "spiritual" ethos of his society but urges private models of existence. He also hopes others will look at reality as critically as he does. Mushakôji's minimum regard—particularly in his verse—for the serial, sequential language that characterizes debate and logic corresponds with his revolt against authority. Despite having to make a living with his pen, he resisted or resented editorial comments. He always wanted to write only what he wanted to write and only in the way he wanted to write it; cf. page 218. That is, as a quietist, as a critical moralist and humanist, or as a subjectivist. When writing for the commercial market, it was rarely possible to follow this ideal. When he wrote poetry, however, he seldom felt constrained by any "rules" but his own—the subjective code of the *kokoro* that did not hesitate to revolt against the cultural status quo.

This code transforms Mushakôji's verse to make it uniformly polemical and pedagogical. He is a polemicist in the sense that much of his verse implicitly argues a point of view. He is a pedagogue in that he urges others to consider his views. In the process, he aims to reform attitudes and values and teach people how to be happy. Bland ideas presented haphazardly and clothed in simple and direct language can nonetheless be wolves in sheep's clothing. Mushakôji's perspective rails against prevailing values and urges alternative solutions to human dilemmas. To most readers, the surfaces of his language appear so lacking in artistry, however, that it is altogether too easy to see the innocuous persona as little more (or less?) than the gushing Dr. PANGLOSS; cf. page 34. Despite that, Mushakôji's commonplace language masks a frontal attack on or refutation of a host of cultural targets and conventional platitudes concerning behavior. The list includes the dogmas of the naturalists, indigenous social values that demean the individual, the cruelties of authoritarians who demand conformity, as well as the airs of pompous scholars and critics, of the pretentious, and the snobbishly self-important.

Small wonder that Mushakôji finds the role of the poet charged with subjective importance. His belief that art originates in the heart brings to mind the "naive poet" the German poet-dramatist Johann Schiller describes. Or it makes one recall the advice that Sir Philip Sidney reports from his Muse: "Look in thy heart, and write." Mushakôji is natural, instinctual, and never self-conscious about his craft. Nor does he concern himself with elegance. His primary objective is to convey the unrefined truths of his *kokoro*. Indeed, a thorough distrust of refinement in poetic diction characterizes Mushakôji's work, early to late. Truth, he firmly believed, never ages or matures, nor does it need fancy dress—it definitely delights in wearing the Emperor's clothes! Unlike scientific truths that fresh discoveries repeatedly revise, the heart's truth cannot possibly become obsolescent. The authenticated poet may have admirers and imitators. He doesn't acquire disciples to whom he might convey an art that can only be "caught." Besides, it would be both fraudulent and inauthentic to pretend he is able to "bottle" and distribute his craft. No genuine artist regards poetry a commodity that a machine could stamp out.

The above makes clear, as well, the minimal sense of aesthetic satisfaction we find in Mushakôji's verse. He refuses to manipulate referents. He will not fashion the multiple meanings academicians expect in verse. Nor will he create the pleasurable expressions associated with poetic diction. He also refuses to fabricate language, whatever euphemisms label the outcome: whether ornate, beautiful, condensed, rich, or pleasure-giving. His art remains earnestly rooted in the truths of the heart stated spontaneously and totally without artifice. His poetry features a dialog between his intuitions and what he observes occurring in the real world. This allows him to concentrate on what he regarded as an urgent problem affecting the human condition: lack of perspective. Humankind faces difficulties not primarily because of slums, unemployment, or poor factory conditions but because human beings neglect the sense of fairness, justice, and love innate to the heart. The subjective quality of the human being, not the objective quantity of laws and regulations, creates the fabric of society. Poetry should make people aware, he thought, how they have misused, refused, or abused their spiritual and mental inheritance. At almost every stage, we find Mushakôji practicing this brand of cultural criticism. He deals in human values and always believed that making them clear and presenting them clearly allowed him to discharge his responsibilities as poet, citizen, and human being. He also believed he could be authentic as an artist and a man by being true to his most subjective self: his intuitions and inspirations.

Mushakôji's belief that subjective meant pure and unadorned generated an introspective aesthetic very impatient with fabricated ambiguities and adornment. Scholars have long been aware of the high-frequency appearance in Mushakôji's writings of subjective expressions such as *ki* [mind • spirit • mood • intention • temper, and the like]. The topic of many verbs using this *ki* is, in fact, not even an individuated "I" but the persona's pure, inner nature. The *ki* mindset implies a self who acts most naturally in response to inner drives. Readers can accept, reject, or ignore what this aesthetic stance produced. Are they at liberty to criticize Mushakôji for being himself and responding to the spirit that moved him? His subjective verse focuses on his "being-in-the-world," to borrow a rhetorical flourish from Heidegger. The only way to appreciate his poems is to engage him there.

V . ACTIVIST · NON-ACTIVIST ASPECTS

Whether we choose to see Mushakôji as quietist or moralist, HUMANIST or subjectivist, he regarded himself an activist. He preferred never to wallow in ideology but to exercise his beliefs and realize his ideals. He could yoke his poetry to the four concepts discussed to this point because he tried to practice what he preached. An "active quietist" or an "active subjectivist" sounds at best like an oxymoron and at worst like a contradiction in terms. The dynamic of "no-sweat" actionless action and Mushakôji's record in the arena of life, however, enable this yoking and force us to disregard commonsensical appearances.

Mushakôji's canon depicts a busy arena of pro-human activity. His countrymen nevertheless do not perceive him as an activist. He wrote thousands of lines of humanist verse, but few of his poems are known abroad and many Japanese are unaware he wrote poetry. Younger people, unfamiliar with his role in founding and nurturing the New Village, often think of him passively as "the old man who paints squash [*kabocha*]." Nor will traditional lovers of lyric poetry who assume that verse focuses exclusively on quiescent beauty and personal feelings find what they are looking for in Mushakôji. His perspectives are broadly energetic, person-oriented, and melioristic, for he believed we must aggressively contribute to private and thus to social amelioration or betterment. Beyond his eternal hope for improvement of the self and human life, his verse reveals a glorification of physical labor and a robust love of life and humanity. Above all, he hoped people might change the way they see and treat themselves and each other. No description of the real Mushakôji and his values suggests an inert spectator satisfied to observe life from the balcony.

The three-character compound *bi · ai · shin* [beauty · love · truth] exemplifies his favorite themes. When these concepts appear in the poetry, Mushakôji radically expands their meanings. Truth · *shin* not only relates to authentic existence [*hontô no seikatsu*; cf. page 49 ff.] but results partly from efforts to animate authenticity in daily life. One achieves truth by harmonizing sincerity and behavior. Because love · *ai* relates to altruism, possibly even to *agapé* (cf. page 114 ff.), it, too, suggests more than a realm of spiritual quiescence or harmony. Love is not stasis. It implies taking the initiative and contributing to others. Even beauty · *bi* extends well beyond the customary passive notion of objects merely beheld. It serves as Mushakôji's ideal of the universe, which makes beauty an object humans hope to achieve because it contains the potential to transform the world. The most beautiful and perfect existence is God, who confronts humankind with an unrealizable ideal. Paradise at least can be experienced in time and space. That realm of perfect beauty can exist, Mushakôji believed, wherever people actively create a harmonic balance among *bi-ai-shin* values as they work step-by-step to realize them in the real world. The dynamic aspect is ever present. In sum, Mushakôji did not see beauty, love, and truth as static principles. They rather describe vigorous conditions of activity in daily human life. That describes as well what Mushakôji took to be the call of his verse. Poems that urge people to realize themselves are not mere inert documents.

Verse urging improvement of the self and society must be direct. Unlike the "profound poetry" scholars praise, it should require no deciphering skills. An in-depth grasp of Mushakôji poems may require at most intimacy with several key concepts. Because the surfaces of his work are lucid, they cause little puzzlement and surrender meaning without multiple re-readings or deep pondering. To per-ceive this poet's lessons requires minimal effort. To practice his lessons requires maximum application. His writing, invariably if deceptively accessible, rarely appears to exploit the feature of his language that makes the reader responsible for making sense of a text. Even when Japanese tribal writers do not write primarily for their cliques, few feel accountable for providing crisply-stated topics, referents, and transitions. Those are the reader's responsibilities. Most poets expect readers to engage their work imaginatively and often with considerable intellectual involve-ment. Mushakôji requires only a sensitive or receptive reader, the sort who can appreciate foreign movies and silent films without captions or music. His poems do not call for decipherment or analysis. They call for taking action in life.

Japan's ethos conditions the people to engage texts intuitively, not logically. The cultural stress on filling in is a notable aspect of the Japanese love for the unor-ganized and offhand. "Reader responsibility" in Japan is especially the rule in writ-ings that relate to the emotional life. The cultural demand on readers or listeners to be responsible for bridging the blanks and organizing the facts often baffles writers trained in the West. Alexandra Tolstoy (1884–1979), daughter of the famed novel-ist, would definitely have included herself among the baffled. Around 1930 she was in Japan to give a series of lectures about her father's work; cf. TOLSTOY'S WORDS. Her Japanese advisers insisted that she lump all her details together instead of discussing them serially, discursively, and analytically—as most lecturers in the West would be expected to do. "Put it all into one," they told her, and "all the people will be pleased." For them, context was far more fascinating than content. Those who have tried to teach a native Japanese student to write a cogent analysis of a literary work can appreciate Alexandra's bafflement. Japanese love being seduced by ambiguities, purposeful or otherwise. Writing that involves a high degree of the reader's active input tempts people to imagine themselves interactive partners with the author, even perhaps contributors to the work. Japanese miss that experience when reading Mushakôji's verse. Subliminally, many consequently resent the consistent clarity that denies their participation in the creative process.

Longer poems best show how Mushakôji ignores accepted organizational prin-ciples. Linear, serial, or cumulative development implies the self-conscious applica-tion of technique. For Mushakôji, that spells insincerity, which he wished to avoid. In his more capacious works one rather finds a circularity that conforms to the unpredictable spontaneity of emotion, not to the predictable designs of logic. When Mushakôji writes poetry, his intuitions are active, his intellect non-active. When prolixity results naturally from spontaneous encounter, however, he would not agree that the lines constantly repeat themselves—as boring as it is disconcerting to many a reader. The work simply offers what are at each moment of awareness the poet's truest feelings. The issue is sincerity, not organizational coherence. This distressing feature not only prevents the label "art" from being associated with many Mushakôji's poems, it connects as well with that deep-seated national characteristic:

distressing feature not only prevents the label "art" from being associated with many Mushakôji's poems, it connects as well with that deep-seated national characteristic: the propensity to relish the disorganized, vague, indeterminate, and natural. These are positive qualities because they imply that intellect has not exerted its baneful influence on the impressions of the heart. And that suggests SINCERITY or genuineness. By claiming that Mushakôji wrote almost no verse that requires decipherment, however, I do not mean to imply that certain readers unfamiliar with his work might not benefit from background knowledge. Obviously, the surfeit of notes and introductory remarks in *Long Corridor* suggests otherwise.

His notions of focused activity and his expectations of the reader simply differ from the average. They also diverge from what taste-makers in academe expect. The results of his creative processes at least do not match their standards. Critics unaccountably behave as though this is unthinkable, as though only their standards are valid. Since unpredictability is the essence of creativity, however, academic standards that fail to account for deviations must be inadequate. This is true whether divergence from touted norms involves painters or poets—or, for that matter, teachers, designers, researchers, scientists, or business people. More often than not, creativity is a process of self-discovery. The open mind is always susceptible to surprise. That means that the artist in the least sensitive to the potentials of his media may find the creative process disturbingly dynamic. Mushakôji would surely applaud this rejection of stasis, for he saw creativity as a happening. It is thus not possible to avoid some on-going interaction between the artist and his brush, the poet and his pen. Even the creative cook, according to Julia Child, is an individual able to perceive and make the most of accidentally successful combinations of ingredients. Interaction between the media or matter and the artist or creator brands creativity a dynamic enterprise that can produce unexpected results.

From the outset, Mushakôji averred that his creative writings, especially his verse, were crystallizations of heartfelt feelings. The heart alone is the repository of life's truths. Only the *kokoro* comprehends the nature of the self. Because it can intuit and penetrate directly to essences, the heart confronts reality as it is and not as the self or others might wish to perceive it. That allows the intuitive poet to see through sham or the self-conscious agendas of artists dedicated to creating something new, shockingly different, or challengingly complex. Mushakôji's prescription for "genuine" or authentic poetry is pithy: Stay intimately in touch with the heart and its truth. That's enough. What follows can only be positive. The poet will then understand reality and be satisfied to rely on common sense, insist on simplicity and directness, and avoid the flashy or manufactured pose. More than merely succinct, these principles reflect an unaffected naiveté that easily identifies with the activities of the childlike mind. Ingenuousness nurses the strengths that help one resist pandering to the critics. Forthrightness also appeals to many readers. Only a poet with these strengths might write for Everyman. Only a person with these principles will refuse to acknowledge the rites and solemnities that bind those who represent academe. Mushakôji regarded all such people inauthentic, perhaps even absurd charlatans—precisely what the naive child cannot be.

Two years after Mushakôji's death, *Kindai shijin hyakunin* [100 Modern Japanese Poets] (*Taiyô*, fall 1978) introduced him in a positive way as a poet. Samples of his "characteristic verse" also continue to appear in anthologies. Establishment critics nevertheless generally assign him a marginal position among free-verse poets. Even those who react favorably to his verse, however, hesitate giving it high marks as art; cf. page 357 ff. Some mainline critics either resist labeling his verse poetry or only reluctantly mention his name when they write about valued modern poets.

One reason for negative reactions to Mushakôji is surely, as Professor Donald Keene observes, that "his works seem to belong to another age." His love for repetition calls to mind *norito*, ancient Shintô prayers that embody the mystical power of incantation [*kotodama*]. Though one critic thinks many Mushakôji poems sound like broken records, he confesses that the repetitions have an eerily purifying effect. Redundancies may remind others of the repetitious nature of popular songs. Mushakôji's ideal human values also echo those of earlier writers like Goethe, for example, whose *"reine Menschlichkeit"* [unalloyed • pure humanity] refers to the individual's highest innate qualities. Mushakôji might label them sincerity.

Japanologists, most of whom refuse to evaluate free verse, merely echo native critics on these issues. Or they adopt one famed translator's view that Mushakôji's works do not fit into the categories of literature that interest him. Pre-determined literary classifications make it easy to conclude that Mushakôji's work fails to match preconceptions. Being from "another age," his verse lies beneath academic consideration. This view resists seeing poetry as a vari-splendored art that appeals in different ways to readers on different levels. It is too easy to dismiss a poet's work for these reasons. Why not weigh it on its own terms rather than on artificially determined scales? Why not recognize its significant, timely, or seminal themes?

Through interviews and correspondence, Mushakôji objected to chronological arrangement of his verse. "I wrote every poem from the heart," he told me. The heart, a person's north star, does not change over time. Early to late, he wished only to communicate felt truths, and he thought it unnatural to assume that his art developed or reached stages or plateaus. His view was that "progression" indicates the self-conscious poet who writes more with his head than his heart. Artistic "progress" he found meaningless, and artists who experiment with new techniques he regarded inauthentic. Appendix I on page 349 enables any interested in doing so to study the poems in the order they appeared.

I have grouped the 465 works in *Long Corridor* into four areas, each of which represents an essential concern of this poet: Myself & Others, Work & Love, Art & Poetry, and God & Country. Because many works can conceivably fit into more than one category, an element of arbitrariness exists in my choices. A preface to each section provides additional background that some readers may find helpful.

THE POETRY

Poets were humanity's first teachers.

— Horace —
Ars Poetica

The poet is the rock of defense for human nature.

— William Wordsworth —
Preface to *The Lyrical Ballads*

Prose is limited to the ground. Sometimes it crawls, sometimes it walks, sometimes it runs. It cannot, however, disengage itself from the ground. When a plane taxies down the runway, still incapable of liftoff, you don't yet have poetry. But when it lifts off you get a poem . . . . When words take wing, you end up with poetry.

— Mushakôji Saneatsu —
1947

PART I

MYSELF & OTHERS

EPITAPH

This man wrote novels, but he cannot
be limited by the label "novelist." He
painted pictures, but neither can he be
limited by the label "painter." Calling
him a thinker and philosopher somehow
falls short. This man trekked domains
that no label can limit.

— Nakagawa Kazumasa —
Western-style painter
(1893-1991)

PART I presents many works that imply or present Mushakôji's beliefs in authenticity and progress. Typically, he avoids a theoretical mode. He believed that relying on hypothetical constructs and ratiocination to explain the facts of existence excuses a person from coming directly to terms with them. Indeed, to immerse oneself in theories *about* reality and truth becomes an effective means of sidestepping them. Mushakôji thus disfavored every technique, whether it focuses on human beings or texts, that did not confront reality face to face with simple, everyday words. This antipathy lies at the core of his concerns for SINCERITY and spontaneity; cf. page 177. We must keep this in mind whenever his work deals with what it means to be a true—that is, an authentic—person [*hontô no ningen*].

✤   ✤   ✤

AUTHENTICITY requires confronting and searching for the truth about ourselves. One Greek root of the word means having full control of or power over the self. Platitude or not, the Socratic injunction "Know thyself!" effectively directs attention to the crux of the matter. It is hard to be or become a genuine person until the self has at least a passing acquaintance with the realities and the potentials of its inner being. Understanding the self and seeing what it could become makes one realize the need to reject the false selves that society, the media, critics, academics, and the like try to impose on us. Authenticity may then be possible. If we believe we are fated to be manipulated and used, however, or if we see ourselves as no more than consumers, authenticity will lie beyond our grasp. To know the self requires exerting our will, rejecting the masks we love to hide behind, and returning to primordial human values. That, Mushakôji believed, allows a person to be the self he or she really is.

To be authentic, all agree, requires being true to the self—not a simple task. Those true to the self will not be fakers, act pretentious, or counterfeit themselves. Mushakôji's ideal authentic person furthermore sees each fellow human being as an individual (a "thou") to be loved, not as an object (an "it") to be managed. In any Confucian social setting, however, acting authentically can rarely be easy. Barriers to authenticity include hierarchical social codes that nurture political posturing for power over others, require endless vertical role playing, and relentlessly discourage acceptance of outsiders. What individuals feel or how they see themselves counts far less than how the group expects them to behave. The polity forces individuals to thirst for membership, but belonging is a Faustian bargain that exacts inauthentic behavior. Either adapt to the norms or be a nonentity. One can always talk about wanting to dash loudly down the hallway; cf. pages 16 ff. and 55. An individual, in the end, refrains—inevitably for the wrong reasons—from realizing this desire. Surrender to the expectations of others results in inauthentic decisions.

No sensible person makes a constant issue of being authentic. That would risk displaying an adolescent self-indulgence, which is inauthenticity itself. At some point, however, the individual must decide to take the initiative. The decision to act: that, as Mushakôji's verse incessantly suggests, is the wisest beginning. It is another matter entirely to be perfectly happy with the price that acting authentically compels in a society like Japan's. Or to know the satisfaction that taking such action gives. Those who wish to savor that gratification require release from the control of the active, intentional mind, which associates with quietist and moralist concerns; cf. page 24 ff. Scholars who analyze Martin Heidegger's formulae for escaping emptiness and achieving authenticity typically refer to the Tao-Zen approach to spontaneity. Mushakôji may never have read Heidegger. Because this philosopher's ideas were well reported in Germany during the 1930s, when the poet's brother was the Japanese Ambassador in Berlin, however, the brothers very likely discussed Heidegger's ideas. Actually, Mushakôji had by then been concerned with and writing about authenticity for twenty-five years. All along he was interested, without ever using these highbrow terms, in achieving and maintaining an "authentic stance" in life and in becoming a "realized being."

He felt certain that authenticity is possible only if people escape being objectified. That meant eschewing intellectuality, something the active, intentional human mind loves to do. It also adores making theories about—and thus demeaning and emasculating—everything. Some believe that the development of modern industrial capitalism exaggerated the mind's natural passion to make others into objects. As capitalism fabricates consumer goods, it creates a society that transforms workers and everything else into abstractions. People in that milieu then come to treat themselves and others as goods. Worse, they suppose that is the natural way to behave. Certain theorists nevertheless imply that the pre-capitalist person, especially someone attached to the soil, found it easier to live a more authentic existence. They also point out the unparalleled success that capitalist urban society, and the parasitic mass media that it feeds, now enjoys in transforming people into commodities. For all that, Japan's traditional vertical, age-graded, and basically agricultural polity somehow managed for several centuries without modern capitalism to transform people into role-playing objects. Wherever or however they become objectified, mere commodities cannot act authentically. That's why every society and every age needs a prophetic voice or a poet like Mushakôji. He glowed with the hope that people, despite having become neutered "things," always will be able to discover who they really are. After all, nature has given everyone at least a pinch of sympathy for others, a tad of free will, and the desire to improve the self.

To locate and appropriate that self, however, takes effort. It requires, as well, faith, self-confidence, resolve, and determination. These are, in any event, what Mushakôji constantly prescribes. Even they may be insufficient without the proper catalyst. To discover and recover the self may require a nudge from "the other"— that ineffable power beyond the self that becomes available only to those who open themselves to it. Making oneself vulnerable to spontaneity may require a willingness to surrender to this inexplicable force, which some call "grace" or God. How else avoid third-party values that loom as palpable realities, whether in a hierarchical polity or a consumer society? Surrendering to their invasion of the self looks easy, almost natural. It is less natural and less easy to open one's heart to a sudden intuitive perception of reality—to the touch of that "other"—and then to let the extraordinary happen. That is to experience an epiphany, which demonstrates how the no-sweat, actionless action of *wu-wei* empowers the heart; cf. page 20.

One can then leap across what had been perceived as an impenetrable barrier. Although nothing specifically Christian is involved, this process echoes the catchword, popular in some circles, "Let go and let God." Spontaneous desires to be authentic displace conscious striving and enable the visitation of grace, the activity of the "other." Mushakôji unashamedly labels this extraordinary force "God." Taoists may resist that label because they regarded naming the indescribable and the mysterious as arrogant as the ancient Hebrew found saying aloud the name Elohim. "It" happens. That is description enough. Even an existential philosopher like Heidegger, who describes these events because he has far more trust in language than Taoists, avers that authenticity is not wholly the product of private effort. It cannot be owned because it is inexplicably given to a person.

Mushakôji never tires of telling us that to achieve authenticity and to enable its continual renewal requires constant effort. Without maintenance, muscle tone and enlightenment as well as body and spirit will lose sharpness and conditioning. Similarly, no individual can expect to reach a state of authenticity once and expect it to last forever. Letting up means reversion to the false self that egotistically attempts to manipulate, always showing minimum concern for other people, especially strangers. That self displays no interest in learning the truth about itself. When conscience calls us to become what we are meant to be, we must heed its call and open our minds. Openness is the opposite of inauthenticity. Authentic people must, above all, be sensitive to their selves, to their mortality, to their consciences, and to opportunities for growth. Mushakôji's poetic corpus everywhere urges this sensitivity, for the authentic person realizes the human being's finiteness, limitations, and mortality. Acquiring these liberating views demands release from self-willfulness, from discursive thinking, and from its tendency to objectify everything. These call for the meditative efforts Mushakôji delights in describing.

Meditative thinking is neither linear nor deductive, neither systematic nor representational. It is patently not discursive. That means it cannot be academically respectable, which concerned Mushakôji far less than being inauthentic. His primary goal, after all, was to tap not into the mind but into the heart. Indeed, authenticity called for the rejection of intellectual approaches to reality. Authenticity nests in the heart, where Mushakôji sought less to discover new ideas than to rediscover and recover the simple sincerity and openness that people were once capable of. These existed well before the birth of academe—even before the activities of scholars and critics became metaphors for one of civilization's chief spiritual ailments: the persistent burial of primordial intuition and glorification of self-conscious, self-congratulatory rationality. For Mushakôji, the critic typifies the egoist who serves the self and shamelessly manipulates others. Not only is that self dedicated to making others into objects or things, it encourages the tendency to conceal the truth about the inner self and to be as closed as possible. This is precisely the way Mushakôji saw academics. Closure of the inner self, philosophers think, best defines the inauthentic state. We are, they tell us, often happier being "they" or "them" than being an open "I." Personal and social progress begins only when the individual feels comfortably at home with its self.

PROGRESS and belief in it broadly influenced Mushakôji's work and thought. This is discernible in much of what he writes about humanity, work, the self, love, and the NEW VILLAGE, for example. His hopes for progress also touch every aspect of his values, whether quietist or moralist, humanist or activist. The following clarification of this belief in progress derives from inferences based on his writings.

Early philosophers regarded progress a function of human values, not material comforts. Classical Greek idealists, for example, thought that progress resulted from the accumulation and extension of knowledge. They firmly believed that education might enlighten, ultimately improve humans, and cause the unity of humankind. That was Mushakôji's dream as well. He furthermore thought that people should advance continuously toward these ideals and that each must accept responsibility for social unity. The Industrial Revolution altered these idealist emphases. Once the development of science and technology accelerated the appearance of new inventions and the growth of world-wide commerce, it became feasible to imagine that humans could manage the environment and control society. By focusing attention on an affluent now, however, material progress victimizes humane values even as it emasculates not only the remembered past but the hoped-for future of the spirit. That erodes idealist dreams for spiritual unity and the betterment of morality and human values. Irresponsible material progress creates results that now haunt us: the waste of natural resources, the pollution of water, air, and earth, not to mention urban sprawl. Because these results sap human hope and personal responsibility, they explain Mushakôji's disenchantment with the scientific, technological, and rational aspects of progress. He desired progress and he wanted to use both machines and technology to facilitate it. But he also realized that material progress deficient in ethical values negates or undermines many humanist ideals. Even as progress provides the leisure to guarantee the "good life," it fails to provide conditions for realizing the spirit. A hungry, hopeless, alienated, or anxious individual has little readiness for becoming, and no motivation to be, authentic.

Leisure is the key to spiritual growth and authenticity. Until modern times, average citizens who led a life of physical drudgery and minimal pleasures had little spare time. Once only philosophers concerned themselves with authenticity. It was a luxury that few other than the elite or monks and social dropouts like hermits could enjoy. Thanks to material progress, people in the developed countries have experienced a phenomenal increase in leisure time. This allows them to attend to interests beyond making a living. Ideally, for Mushakôji at any rate, that should mean directing free time and untapped energies to spiritual or non-material areas of self-improvement. This ideal remains, however, a dream, a possibility. The reality is that added leisure encourages in most the pursuit of recreational activities, hobbies, and private pleasures. In an age that the mass media control, these pursuits enable the "couch potato" syndrome, which mesmerizes and empties the mind. Hence the modern increase in leisure time produces effects opposite of the Greek ideal. This results in tensions between material pleasures and spiritual values—tensions that remain far from resolution. In a word, manifestly expanded leisure has yet to result in improved human values and spiritual growth. Augmented leisure consequently begs for an ethical compass—or even a poet—to direct it and keep people from becoming so involved in the physical benefits of material progress that they incapacitate their potentials for true humanhood. Mushakôji knew all too well that ethical concerns sway if they do not always determine the material goals of progress. His dedication to progress accordingly aims to influence man's spiritual space—his attitudes, values, and ideals.

Philosophers East or West share Mushakôji's hopes that progress might stimulate spiritual improvement. Almost two millennia before progress made an affluent life possible for more than a tiny elite, East Asian philosophers devoted close attention to the tensions between the material and the spiritual. Buddhists and Taoists in particular realized that man's desire to be attached—whether to others or self, things or ideas, hopes or desires—invites human misery and unhappiness. Malignant attachments include even the urge to be up-to-date or accepted. A craving for progress or for being "modern" can consequently endanger spiritual growth. That's why distinguished thinkers taught that our insatiable wanting erodes spiritual objectives. To develop new values, however, requires one to be free of the chains of conventions, social norms, and prevailing values that hold humans captive. Those deficient in the will to be liberated must be fated to endure the endless cycle of attachments that acquisition implies. Material progress increases the will to acquire but decreases attention to values and the spirit, for people have always been inordinately interested in what rusts. Matthew Arnold, for one, recognized these tensions when he wrote that culture is not having. It is being and becoming. Like Arnold, Mushakôji hoped that poetry might redeem people by helping them *become.* These observations, as well as the notion that the less you *have* the more you can *be,* perfectly agree with his views, early to late. Mushakôji thought material progress threatened to transform the self into a mere object that could no longer be genuinely human. These ideas imply the alarming obverse side of progress, which can harvest alienation and inauthenticity as readily as it fosters political freedoms and material affluence.

We humans have failed to reduce tensions between the material and the spiritual aspects of progress. The consequences have as lethal an effect on the spirit as they have had on the environment. The failures of progress motivate among intellectuals and writers a heightened disenchantment with technology and science. Those committed to the spirit even question whether material progress is worth the effort. The negative aspects of these tensions rarely appear in his verse, yet Mushakôji was aware of the way greed and industry pollute the environment. He also realized how the machine castrates; cf. page 155. He chose in his verse to stress the positive influences of love and the potentials of human will. His hope lay always in the heart, which he believed was evolving toward a loving acceptance of others. People are the wonder of creation not simply because of their intellect and ability to conquer the physical world or devise ingenious machines to perform tedious or repetitive tasks. He believed people are wonders because the heart empowers them to become more than they now are. The heart alone can sanctify and make congenial the coldly impartial, objective realm of technology. And only the heart can resolve tensions between spirit and matter. Mushakôji hoped that we might eventually baptize progress and bring it under the dominion of the caring heart.

That goal and his dedication to HUMANISM (cf. page 29 ff.) rooted Mushakôji to ethical commitments. Their nature emerges in his call for liberty and rights balanced by responsibility, or in his tireless urging that humanity move ahead. The drive for progress was not movement for the sake of movement. Increased material comforts didn't interest him unless they nourished spiritual values. He couldn't, for instance, imagine that any who chose plumbing over a chamber pot would magically become more ethical, more sincere, or more authentic. Mushakôji's idea of progress meant expanding opportunities to save people from themselves and their attachments. They could then have the leisure to consider being more authentic, more equal, more free, and to show more love and consideration for others. It was, indeed, always a matter—so dear to the idealist—of making physical matter subservient to ideas and the spirit. Progress should aim to nurture values and social conditions that enable citizens to live up to the humanist's highest expectations. Male or female, those with high or low status, should enjoy a happy and productive life—above all, an existence where one gladly discharges every responsibility.

No one can achieve that existence short of consistent attempts to reach specific human goals. These include improving one's spiritual lifestyle, expanding private perspectives, and above all refurbishing inner values and adopting more flexible views. Mushakôji always hoped that future generations might also profit from his and earlier human toil and creative investments of energy. He states these views specifically in poems dedicated to people of the past and people of the future; cf. page 117 f. Throughout the corpus, however, he demonstrates his dogged hope in the power of ideas to beget a new future and to legitimize the ancestors' labors. Desire for these objectives should stimulate a person not only to expect but to work for progress. This implies creating, or at least dreaming of, an ideal community in the present, one that would be an earthly "paradise." Mushakôji couldn't possibly imagine that his dreams might lead nowhere or could never be realized. That's why he never thought of a utopia, which means "no place." Rather, commitment to progress stimulated him to dream of a radically new polity. This idea exerted a steady and persuasive impetus on his thought. It must be clear, however, that he never believed progress in the sense of linear development and stages of growth applied to his work as either poet or painter. What intrigued him was potential for progress in human values, notably in the realm of the spirit. His hopes imply humankind's infinite improvement, always an objective close to his heart.

For Mushakôji, spiritual progress aims for a heaven on Earth that will predictably consist of a fellowship of earthlings. In this life they will love, praise, and freely help one another. Hence, the end of human progress will be intramundane salvation. An unrelenting though unconscious commitment to stated ancient Greek ideals of progress supported his belief. Beyond that, Mushakôji resisted surrendering his unqualified confidence in the human's ability to overcome egotism. Not being self-centered empowers people to realize a satisfying and "perfect" existence.

Long corridor *

Taking huge strides,
I'd like to clomp briskly
down a long corridor.
Here and there along the way I'd like to shout,
Heeeey!

What a waste
to stomp vigorously
where there are no reverberations.
How dismal shouting where there are no echoes.
How forlorn hearing my shouts melt vacantly away.

My thudding feet
echoing everywhere,
my *Heeeey!*
echoing everywhere
—— I want to clomp childlike through those echoes.

A foolish wish,
an idle hope.
Living in town,
I haven't clomped down a corridor for more than a decade,
nor have I shouted, *Heeeey!*

Oh, to carry on and shout like an uninhibited child
—— indifferent to gossip, indifferent to others,
shouting through the echoes of my clomps
in a space that reverberates with my
Heeeey!

Gossip *

I inherited from Mother her incredible dread of gossip.
To overcome this cursed trait,
I scorn it.
Gossip! You only appear dreadful.
I ridicule your emptiness.

Rumors about Him

Trying to drown the pain of a broken heart,
he took a walk to cheer himself.
Along the way he heard people saying:
"There goes an egotist."
"There goes a snob."
"There goes a show-off."
"There goes a fop."
"There goes a dolt."

Overhearing such statements
made him wretched,
so he wildly increased his pace.
It then occurred to him,
"Is the me they see the real me?"
He continued his walk
feeling far more cheerful than ever.

Maligned *

Both those who shrivel up
when they're maligned
and those who get carried away
when they're praised
lack a sense of self.
Such people
are spiritual dwarfs.

Fleet-footed Rumors

"If you try to hide from them,
you'll fail.
You can't flee rumors, for they're too fleet-footed."

When I heard that rumor,
I grinned and responded:
"That's no rumor."

Fate smiles
even on me, doesn't it?
The one who guides me
allows me liberty.
Fate pats me on the back and says,
"You're strong enough now,
you'll be all right.

Press on —— do it your way."

"Fate, didn't you say
it's all right to remain on Earth
to realize your dreams?"

Rumors are fleet-footed.
But since it's no longer necessary
for us to live anonymously,
come on, everyone, show your faces.
Though fleet of foot,
rumors may be slower
than my pen.

AN INFANT'S JOY

Seeing an infant's joy
makes me think that joy is wholesome and natural
and that sadness exists to teach us never to let go of joy.
People who can't rejoice are somehow abnormal.
Joy wells up from within.
The joyful infant
surely symbolizes joy.

The ability to rejoice is human.
I suspect that something's wrong somewhere
with people unable to rejoice
over an infant's joy.

WHEN I WAS A CHILD (i)

– 1 –

When I was a child, Mother often told me I'd end up a lunatic.
These days I frequently recall her words.
I have the sense that I've lost my physical flexibility
and that my perseverance has flagged.
I should be prudent! Prudent!

– 2 –

Unlimited ambition.
Limited physical strength.
All the same, I'll move calmly on
and continue to grow like the cedar
that never gives up reaching for heaven
though aware it can't be reached.

WHEN I WAS A CHILD (ii)

When I was a child, I remember
those summer mornings
when I went at daybreak to the beach
and walked around
barefooted
letting the waves wash my feet.
I feel like strolling the strand at dawn.

FROM CHILDHOOD

From childhood,
I longed for a park.
I wanted to live
in a beautiful park.
Make me
a lovely park.

SINCE CHILDHOOD

Hurrah! —— for those who since childhood schooled me in adversity.
Hurrah! —— for those who never degraded me though they were struggling, too.
Despite being spoiled since childhood,
      Hurrah! —— for whoever gave me deep piety,
constantly chastised my lack of study,
and tirelessly disciplined me.

CHILD

The child reaches out his hand.
Parents want to pile apples on it.
The child's hand is too small to hold them all.
I'm that child. Humanity is the parent.
I can't grumble about humankind.

PARENTS

Parents are dolts.
Forgetting how close I am to the grave,
I hope my child will soon grow up.
I want her to start talking soon.
I want her soon to be able to walk.
I want her to be a child of five or six.
I want her to be seven or eight.

I want her to be twelve or thirteen.
I want her to be fifteen or sixteen.
I want her to be seventeen or eighteen.
I don't yet think much beyond that.
I'm a doting parent of forty
with a five-month-old child.

SON OF MY FATHER, MY MOTHER

I'm their little darling,
the son of my father and my mother.
Father and Mother are the offspring of courtiers and peasants.
I'm the son of dream and reality.

They say Father was morbidly churlish.
Mother is morbidly persevering.
I understand that Father never sidestepped an argument with anyone.
Mother absolutely detests confrontation.
I'm the son of this pair.

I'm filled with contradictions.
Mild mannered and self-indulgent,
a bad loser, hard to please.
I'm the son of my father, my mother.

WHO IS MY FATHER? *

Once I asked Mother,
"What sort of man was Father?"
She said,
"I'll tell you when you're twenty.
He was a wonderful man. If only he'd lived . . . ."
Mother died when I was sixteen.
I knew nothing about my father.
Mother called him "a wonderful man,"
though I don't know what was wonderful about him.
I do know, however, what's most important:
a wonderful father breathes in my blood.

WELL, ALL RIGHT

Well, all right,
I can put my life
to some use
—— even with setbacks.

To TALK OF MYSELF

On spring days I feel ashamed
to talk excessively of me.

I FEEL LIKE LAUGHING

I feel like laughing at myself,
laughing from the pit of my belly.
And then
I'd like to tell myself: "You disgust me."
I'd like to say: "I hoped you'd do better than you have."
I'd like to say: "Doesn't my saying that upset you?"
Yes, I feel like laughing
from the pit of my belly.

To MY MIND

To my mind
I am precious.

A REAL PERSON *

I'd like to be a real person
—— a person
neither used by
nor subservient to others.

I'd like to be a real person
who neither manipulates others
nor corrupts them,
and so is never corrupted.

I'd like to be a real person
who draws
the freshest springs of life
from the deepest springs within his self.

I truly love
an authentic person whom everyone recognizes
as a genuine human being.

I scorn the crafty,
those who lie,
and people who indifferently denounce those
guilty of the very sins that they commit. •

A real person
who can get through life
unafraid of stating his intentions
—— that's the type I like,
a real person.

A real person
—— isn't it enough being a real person?
A real person!

II (i)

I'm delighted with and thankful for those
who happily welcomed
my coming into this world
—— parasite though I be.

I understand Mother's father
regularly said,
"It's an offense against the state
that a man like me should live."
Some found him morbid.
Mother's mother nevertheless
respected this grandfather
like a god,
and his relatives adored him.
Nobody imagined he was
not qualified to exist,
but that's how he thought of himself.
Having inherited his blood,
I understand how he felt.
(In my case, it's an offense not against the state
but against something I don't clearly comprehend.)

Nevertheless, whenever I feel that way
I say with self-awareness:
"I live for them.
I endure being desolate for them
—— for those who are lovable, earnest,
and desolate like me."

I'm delighted and grateful
that there are people who rejoice
over my having been born
—— parasite though I be.

I (ii)

I'm neither sage
nor prophet.
I'm just a person
—— just a person hoping for the happiness of all.

WELL, ME TOO

Well, I think I'll stand up now.
Or shall I remain seated a while?

GROWTH *

I happened to stretch
toward a branch I could never touch
and found I could easily reach it.

NO MATTER WHAT

No matter what anyone says,
I take no path I have no confidence in.

No matter what anyone says,
whatever I find unjust, I find unjust.

No matter what anyone says,
what I cannot approve of I do not approve.

I'M A HUGE ROCK

I'm a huge rock.
However much you hammer
or strike me,
I remain a huge rock.
Whatever you do to me,
I stay at the spot
where I should be.
If you don't mind hurting your hand,
go ahead and strike.
If you want no pain,
you'll have to pat me.

KING OF THE HILL

I'm the king
of a tiny hill.
I close my eyes
to those wiser than I
—— I'm the king
of a tiny hill.

I'M AN EGOTIST

I'm an egotist
and do whatever I please.
I'd like you to tolerate me a while.
Soon the time will come
when I can give you
my best effort.
I'd like you to let me stray
till I'm fifty.
I intend to focus my capacities
after I mature.

LONELINESS (i) *

However often I drive it off,
loneliness slinks back into my mind.
However often I drive it off,
loneliness returns to me like my dog.

LONELINESS (ii) *

Loneliness still besieges me
the way clouds from time to time
shut out the sun.
One day I'll break through those clouds
—— like the sun.

NEITHER A SAGE . . .

I am neither a sage
nor a man of virtue.
I'm just a selfish person
in awe of God.

I BELIEVE

I believe and do not doubt.
However much I try,
I cannot doubt that my dreams are being realized!
Or that a realm in harmony with the will of humankind
is being realized on Earth!
Or that the village will gradually develop!
However much I try,
I cannot doubt.

BELIEVE ME

Believe me, I'm a person who can be trusted.
When it comes to women, however,
I'm not perfectly reliable.
That's because it appears that nature intemperately created me
to find women
extremely charming.
Indeed, perhaps all men have been made that way . . . .
I'm nevertheless a fellow who can't take an altogether false step,
for God always keeps an eye on me.

I RESPECT (i)

I respect and gladly bend my knee
to the person who, beyond what he can do for himself,
leaves everything to God,
who loves all people,
who applies himself.

I RESPECT (ii)

I respect those
who don't give in to fate,
who get up though they've stumbled,
who move on without stumbling,
who can endure
whatever they must.

On any occasion,
there's always room for one to move on.
If you're weary, it's all right to rest.
Resting lets you move ahead.
The person who day by day becomes slightly wiser

—— that individual I respect.

Many in this world are indeed worthy of respect.
This is how the world advances:
step by step.

PEOPLE I RESPECT

People I respect
have discriminating minds.
They are individuals who think precisely.
They gradually approach
their chosen
goals.

PEOPLE I LIKE

The saint doesn't surrender.
The hero may surrender but triumphs spiritually.
The contented scholar triumphs but doesn't gloat.
        He's not appalled if he surrenders.
Tenacious humans struggle till they prevail.
Those who continue to move ahead, however weary they may be
        —— such people I like, as well.
But I also like those who remain calm and praise Providence.

MORAL PRINCIPLE *

Japanese
and Asians
are committed to moral principle.
I respect
Japanese
and Asians
committed to moral principle.

YOU and I ARE BEAUTIFUL

You are beautiful. I am beautiful.
I am beautiful. You are beautiful.
The world is full of beautiful beings.
People want to admire each other
the way mountains admire each other,
the way stars admire each other.

FOR ME

For me,
I am my own best teacher.
At the same time, I am my own best disciple.
That's how everyone should be.

I'M MADE OF STEEL

The more I'm tempered,
the stronger I'll be
and the greater my resilience.
I am steel.
I have nothing to fear.
Satan! God!
Temper me!
Test how strong I can be.

MY SHELL

My shell proves I am.
There's no reason I'd have a shell
if I hadn't been.

I CAN DO IT, I CAN DO IT

I can do it,
I can do it.
If I get serious about it,
I can do it.

If I think I can't do it,
I can't.
If I think I can do it,
I can.

I want to move on
affirmatively,
unconditionally convinced
that I can do
the doable.

I can do it,
I can do it,
I'm sure I can!

New life *

Someone once asked me, "When did you begin your new life?"
I simply stumbled into it.
One day a door I thought was closed happened to open, so I walked in.
I entered effortlessly, nonchalantly.
I entered because the time was ripe.
I entered without exertion.
That's why I live carefree.
Actually, I continue to live without exerting myself.

Lofty aspirations

Oh, new-born race
with lofty aspirations,
sound discretion,
wills of iron,
lively and sunny hearts!
I've been awaiting your birth.
Bless you.

Someone said *

Someone said,
"If this were my land,
I'd really be able to develop it.
What superior harvests
I could reap!"
But what about
that little empty lot
within the person
—— that utterly wasted lot . . . ?
"What happened to your lot?"
"I couldn't do a thing with such a tiny area."
If you can't even exploit your small field,
how do you suppose you might exploit a large one?
Why not make your little plot into something magnificent?
Why not make more of it than anyone possibly could?
Then you can expect someone
to offer you a bigger field.
First, make the best possible use
of whatever you've been given
and leave the rest to fate.
Fate will then become
your docile aide.

E VE *

When Adam awoke and looked around,
he saw a woman
standing proudly,
stark naked.
—— Such beauty!
She had no knowledge either of shyness
or of distinctions between good and evil.
She merely sensed the power of her lifeblood
and stood praising nature.
Astonished,
Adam simply gazed
at the woman's fantastic beauty
—— at her hair, her face, her cheeks, her lips;
at the contour of her shoulders, her breasts, her nipples;
stomach, waist, her hands and legs
—— not a single feature failed to make him happy
. . . her delicate lines, her complexion.
God said to Adam, who was absorbed in observing her:
"What do you think? Anything that doesn't please you?
If so, shall I change it for you?"
"No, no . . . there's nothing to change.
I'd be nonplused if you made her any better."
Having gushed out of the spring of life,
Eve was wholesome and perfect.
Is this but a tale of the past?
No, it's as much a tale of the present
as of the past,
and a tale of the future as well.
In truth, this is the beauty, Eve.

M ARY MAGDALENE *

What beauty in the repentant
Mary Magdalene.
Do you know about her?
What if Mary Magdalene
had committed suicide?
Hadn't she become the epitome of beauty
because she lived
beyond suicide
—— lived for the love of God and humanity?
Lovable, lovable
Mary Magdalene.

TWO WOMEN

Two women dig a well in a lonely place.
Moved to tears, a man observes them.
He can't do a thing to help.
He only blesses the
two from afar.
He prays they might be able to get along.
The two women silently
dig a well in a lonely place.
May light glow richly from their well.

BEAUTIFUL WOMAN *

I get an odd sensation
when I see a beautiful woman.
Why did nature create such a creature?
To make men miserable
and thus beget the spirit of conquest?

TO MY WIFE

My devastated heart
requires your presence.
You must be by my side.
Smiling, you can hurdle, you can negotiate
the maze of neglected tasks
that besiege my heart.
You alone
can steal into my heart.

My devastated heart
requires your being at my side.

MOMMY *

Taking a break from my work,
I went to my wife's room
and got involved in reading the rest of the paper.

My wife was absorbed in
patching my everyday kimono.
I somehow sensed Mother's likeness
in her guileless figure
and inadvertently called her
"Mommy." •

I felt a sense of love and esteem as I said it,
but apparently she didn't feel very good about being called "mommy"
by someone fifteen years her senior.
My unassuming wife said,
"Please don't call me 'mommy.'"
I acceded to her request
and agreed not to say it again.
It would be peculiar trying to explain myself,
so I left it at that.

That evening she was weary and went to bed before me.
When I came to bed
she said,
"It's all right to call me 'mommy.'"
I said nothing in response,
but the thought that my feelings had communicated to my wife
put me in a good mood.

Though I'm eighty-three,
I still long for Mother.
Men generally strut around,
but in their strutting they yearn for their mothers.
Though women depend on men,
they somehow have the mind of the mother.
I sensed that directly.

(This is not—is not, isn't, is definitely not—a poem.)

SONG OF A GIGANTIC TREE

It's appropriate
that I glorify the universe.
My blossoms bloom in their time.
My fruit appears in its time.
Nature regards these favorably
and everywhere scatters my seeds.
People regard this favorably
and help the seeds mature.
Thus do I plant my seeds everywhere
and make the most of my precious life.
I'm satisfied to become an ever more splendid tree.
I'm satisfied to become a more and more universally adored tree.
I'm content.
I love all things.
All things love me.
I am content.

I'M A PINE

I'm a pine.
Whether it rains or there's wind,
I'm a pine, a single pine tree.
As long as I'm a pine
I'll feel proud of being one,
and I'll live as much like a pine as I can.
I am a pine.

A PINE TRYING TO BE A CEDAR

A pine trying to be a cedar will waver.
When the pine is a pine, it is natural, it is free, and will not waver.

WE'RE A GROVE OF CEDARS

We're a grove of cedars
—— united
yet independent.
We're human beings
—— united
yet independent.

SAPLING and SPRING

"You say that
spring is coming,
spring is coming,
it's definitely coming.
But when will it come?
Isn't it rather getting colder and colder?
Do you think I can bear this cold?
You're lying to me.
I'm going to die —— die."
"No. Spring is coming,
spring is coming,
it's definitely coming.
I know it's coming.
However cold it is now,
however unbearably cold,
I know that spring is on its way."
"You're an optimist.
Spring's not on its way.
Spring is not coming.

It's never, ever coming.
It'll just get colder
and soon everything will freeze and die."
"No, spring is coming,
it's definitely on its way."
"I'll no longer be fooled,
whatever you may say.
I can't continue enduring the cold."
"Hold on a while longer,
just a bit more."
"I no longer have the strength."
"Oh, spring, spring —— come quickly.
My young friend is dying.
Please come quickly."
But what choice has spring other than calmly
        to bide its time?

TREES IN THE RAIN

Trees stand silent
in the gentle drizzle.
One cannot confront his fate
more unassumingly
than they.

ENDLESS RAIN

Rain continues falling.
Water roars
through the gorge.
Hills look chalky through the rain.
Huge wind-driven
raindrops
pound the soil,
lash the leaves,
beat on roofs,
and rebound.
I'm at my desk
writing poetry.
Energy brims
within,
and I feel
the herald of joy
dashing at me
full speed.
Rain! Pound with all your might.

Leaves,
don't yield
but rebuff the drops.
Let the streams roar on!
We'll live as vigorously
as we're allowed.
It's a delight
that energy burgeons
within each of us.

GENTLE RAIN

Rain gently falls.
I'm writing down words as they occur to me
in my second-floor room at an inn.

I think I'll pour some hot water into the earthen pot
and have some tea.
That gives me joy.

Many human beings
are suffering now.
Of course, some are happy
and some are not.
I sympathize
with those who are unhappy
and think, if only their fortunes
might soon change!

How wonderful if everyone
could love each other,
help each other,
respect each other,
be grateful to each other,
and live like brothers and sisters!
That day is slow to come,
but I sense its steady approach.

BEAUTIFUL FLOWERS

Beautiful flowers bloom.
Clear water flows.
A pond, an arbor,
an ordinary Japanese garden
holding something extraordinary:
a warm human heart.

FLOWERS

Flowers can't help blooming
on such a fine day.

CLOSING MY EYES *

Closing my eyes
one scene becomes clearly visible:
my favorite landscape.

Fields connected endlessly
on level rural land.
A single ribbon road
extending through crisscrossing paddy ridges.

Along the road a small stream and five or six wintering oaks.
Groves in the distance, faint low hills,
and country houses here and there among dense woods.

Three or four peasant girls walk together
down the road.
Nothing more.
It's nevertheless strangely nostalgic.

NATURE'S EYE

Human beings aren't alone in loving beauty.
Nature loves beauty, too.
If so, does nature have a discerning eye?
She does. The eye of nature is the human eye. Nature wishes to view
    its beauties through human eyes. Unless explained in this way,
    you can't verify the beauty of this bloom.

I ADORE FALL *

I adore fall.
Hankering for something,
autumn-like breezes stir.
A sense of yearning surges up,
and even death seems agreeable.
Somehow
I feel empty.
I admire the beautiful.
I ache also for the past,
for the future,
and for the domain of dreams.

VOLCANO

"Volcano!
Don't you dare blow your top.
If you do, many of the living
will suffer a miserable fate."
"Of course, I'm aware of that.
That's why I harness my energies
as best I can.
That's not to say, however, that I'll always
be able to persist.
It's up to you to take precautions.
Take care."

FLORIST

A florist
raises flowers.
He grows no plant
that does not exist in nature.
He merely harvests,
ever more unadulterated and abundantly,
what already exists.
To succeed he must closely conform to
nature's laws.

SILENCE (i)

Here a realm of silence.
A realm fulfilled.
A realm that accepts nothing but truth.
A realm where all are content
to be what they are.
I live peacefully in that realm,
painting pictures,
silently fulfilled,
    . . . content.

BUDDHA *

The man Buddha
was an extraordinary fellow.
He became the living truth.
He's immortal now.

LORD OF THE CASTLE

Is the lord of the castle balmy or bright?
Is he living or dead?
Whether it rains or snows,
whether its stormy or clear,
he simply looks down at us from his castle window.

Whether we say, "Let's celebrate this year's bumper crop,"
or, "Let's bewail this year's crop failure,"
he always looks down at us with the same expression.

Nor did the lord's mien change
when someone was killed beneath that window,
when a beauty was raped beneath that window,
or when a traveler starved to death beneath that window.

His hair recently turned white and wrinkles crease his brow,
yet he continues looking down on us
with the same expression.
Is he living or dead?
Is he balmy or bright?
No one knows. No one knows.

GOVERNMENT OFFICIALS *

Government officials are great fools, you know.
They figure they have the authority to order people around.
They even say primary schools can't put on such-and-such a play.
Idiots!
Do they imagine that pupils will become better people
if only they don't stage certain plays?
Because we can't leave these decisions to local authorities,
you'd best forego
sending your children to such schools.
Surely it's simple-minded to claim everything will be fine
if only people refrain from putting on certain plays.
In the end, it may be best to let it up to the school.
If performing or watching drama corrupts people,
what is proper for them to watch?
If that corrupts, must we not then
forbid newspapers and magazines, as well?
And enforce a curfew?
And shut up young girls all day in their homes?
The temperament that moves officials to meddle in everything
outrages me.

Dostoyevski's Face *

I have yet to see
a face more grim than Dostoyevski's.
Nor eyes more piercing.
When I look at his face,
my loneliness and anguish seem so trite.
I hang his portrait in my room now
and jeer at loneliness, at grief.

Tolstoy's Words *

Most of the time when I read Tolstoy
I indeed agree with him.
The day is coming when
the seeds that Tolstoy sowed
will surpass the seeds that Marx sowed.
First there's the need to know truly how to love and reverence human life.

Eggshell *

Tolstoy mercilessly denounced the dunce
who tried to return a just-hatched chick
to its eggshell.
With identical vigor
I'd like to denounce the dunce
who would irrationally
break the shell
and remove the unhatched chick.

Lenin's Embalmed Remains *

"These are Lenin's embalmed remains.
Hats off. Hats off."
It's pathetic being obliged to show respect to a mummy.
It's far more pathetic having one's remains mummified.
They say even dogs don't much care having people see their remains.
How pathetic that Lenin
has his corpse on display.
The faces of the soldiers
who respectfully guard the mummy
—— they're pathetic, too.
Well now, the fact that the icon of that materialist state
is a mummy
makes an ironic parallel.

GIANT (i) *

I had a dream.

A giant appeared before me
and said,
"I contend with all
who in the name of humanity
demean human beings:
statesmen,
military men,
educators, religionists,
doctors, scholars,
artists, men of letters
—— all are my foes
because they arrogantly degrade people . . . ."
I timidly asked,
"Do they actually debase us that much?"
The giant's eyes glinted angrily,
and he shouted like thunder,
"Ignoramus!"

I awoke.

GIANT (ii) *

I'm a man
who dreams
that a giant
will stomp into our lives
with weighty
footsteps.
Come ahead,
giant!

GIANT (iii) *

I respect a giant
with one head
and two arms and legs.
I also respect
a giant
with a hundred heads and two hundred limbs.

Or one with a thousand heads and two thousand limbs.
Or one with ten thousand heads and twenty thousand limbs.
Or even one with a million heads and two million limbs. •

I hope
that such giants
might appear here and there
to toil for humankind.

I hope we might become such giants
and work
for the people,
for Japan,
for humanity.
Yes, you giants
come ahead!
Shouldn't you
join hands with each other
and labor for life?

GIANTS ONLY WALK *

Giants only walk
because they want to.
When they no longer wish to walk,
they sit down.
If they want to rest, they rest.
They walk
only because they want to.

THE GIANT ADVANCES *

Although he's no tank,
the giant advances
tank-like.
He advances tactfully.
He detours
where he should.
He greets those he's supposed to greet.
He goes around flowering plants as he passes by.
He walks along singing some song,
glancing up at and acclaiming tall trees.
No one can resist him,
and yet the giant advances
scattering love to everyone.
Only those who repel his just advance
will be subdued,
but even they
laud his fairness and love.
The giant advances,

ever onward.
Many companions
come to serve under him.
Thus does the giant
advance
to an ideal land,
to a realm where everyone
dwells in beauty.

A GIANT'S FOOTPRINT *

I once tried stepping
in a giant's footprint.
How tiny my foot.
Blushing,
I stepped back
and looked again
at the giant's track.
For shame
—— you dwarf!

A GIANT APPEARED *

A giant appeared.
He regarded those in high spirits
charming fellows
but not very bright.
He figured his world
did not include the likes of them.

The giant sang and danced
as he strolled the mountain path,
but his manner
differed entirely
from those who are tipsy.
His rapture came from within.
He truly was absorbed,
life surging from within.

The giant's progress,
the magnitude of his footprints
—— he imagined he took ordinary steps,
yet left mighty tracks.

The giant
hasn't the slightest desire

to have people understand him.
He does, however, hope to live
in accord with his ideals.
His inner life governs him.

The giant, too, is human,
not omnipotent.
He makes mistakes
and doesn't always understand everything.
But when in life he does the best he can,
he successfully does the work of a giant.

Perhaps there are no giants
in our world.
Perhaps it's better not having such creatures.
We'll be impoverished, however, if we have only dwarfs.
We'll be distressed if in our vast world
some few among us
don't have enormous know-how.

Indifferent, slovenly, and callous monsters
will cause us problems.
But those who waver on small issues,
are ignorant of how to live.
They give us problems, too.

I want to live with serenity.
I want to live on the basis of my beliefs.
I want to live taking confident strides,
not losing my footing even in the storm.
I laud the giant.
I laud the giant who lives boldly
on the basis of his beliefs.

WHAT THE GENIUS SAID

The genius said,
"Take whatever you can from my inner self."
The fool took foolish aspects from the inner self of the genius
and then made fun of him.
Actually, however, the fool looked into a mirror
        and mocked himself.

To MY ELDERS *

Listen, fellows,
make me a bunch of hoops
and I'll show you I can smash them to bits.
Though I may be bound by the organic hoops that nature made,
I'll not be bound by the hoops you make.
If you think I'm kidding,
try making me a few hoops.
I'll smash every one.

From MY THREE CHILDREN *

Letters came from my three children.
They asked me to come home soon.
My oldest daughter said, "All three of us pray for your return."
My second daughter said, "Please do hurry home."
The youngest girl said, "Please hurry back.
If you don't, we'll all get sick, you know."
I want to go home,
but I just can't until I complete my assignments.
"The father whose children
think of him like this
is lucky.
I'm going to carry out my tasks as fast as I can and come home.
But if you can't hold out till then,
I'll rush back."
I put this in a letter and sent it off.
As I wrote, I imagined
it was an especially lonely time for them.
Now all three have gotten over my absence,
and I suspect they've put me out of mind.
I hope so.

TIME PASSES FAST

Time passes fast (they tell me).
The faster the better for me.
I'm on the other side of the globe from home.
If it's daytime there, here it's night.
If it's daytime here, it's night in Japan.
I'm crossing the Atlantic
lying in my bunk aboard ship,
no one to keep me company.
The sun has set today.
Time passes fast (they tell me).

The faster the better for me.
The faster these thirty days pass the better.
Joys await me in Japan.
They wait with outstretched arms for my return.
I hope to rush to their embrace.

MANY HARDSHIPS *

I've experienced many hardships
and many pleasures, too,
but seeing America
has become a bit more pleasant now.
Meeting Saitô again has also been a delight.
I'll be fine once I span America
and board a Japanese ship,
for I'll have many acquaintances on board.
They all know I'm a poor sailor
who gets seasick in public.
It's only a matter of time now.

ON A TRAIN TO SAN FRANCISCO *

Train, you've been sitting here forever —— as though you've expired.
When will you move on?
What are you waiting for?
You stagnate in repugnant silence.
And yet once you get going you do run fast, don't you?
I'm confident you'll reach San Francisco
on time.
Don't be late, hear!

MY MIND

How wonderful if my mind were like a water main.
I could then just open a tap
to supply as much water as I like
for the stream of magazine reporters who stop by.

But my mind is quite mulish.
When the water dries up, there's not a drop to be had.
It makes no difference how long I'm at my desk
or how much I rack my brains.

They're waiting impatiently for me.
I don't want to go back on my word.
When my mind dries up, it won't yield a drop of water,

no matter how much I shout.

We've all had enough, I know.
I more than anyone.
I'm just waiting
till my mind shapes up.
When it does, so much water will gush out
that I'll be unable to stanch the flow,
however much I try.

It's somewhat like the way you wait
hoping the weather will clear up tomorrow.
Since weather is absolutely unpredictable,
I'm undeniably at a loss.

It would be especially wonderful
if my mind were like a water main.
If it were, everyone would be content
and so would I.
This obstinate mind of mine!

GRIM REAPER

I don't want to die now.
I don't want to die till I finish this task.
Grim Reaper, don't laugh!
Not wanting to die
until one's work is done
is a human bias.
One dies when he dies.
But it's a fact that one does not wish to die until his time.
Don't laugh at that,
Grim Reaper!
Aren't you making that fearful face
because that's your hope, too?

DEATH'S DREAD

Who furnished us with the depths of death's dread?
Who gave us the robust joys of sexual desire?
Who gave human beings the joys of ecstasy
and afflictions difficult to bear?
Who gave these things to us?
He alone knows the reasons
he gives us life.

DEATH

I was at my desk
when this fellow whispered to me,
"You figure you'll live forever, don't you? . . . Forever."
"No," I answered.
"Nevertheless," he said,
"you figure you'll live to fifty."

"Well . . . ," I said.
By then I felt a bit anxious
and asked softly, "Won't I . . . ?"

"Well . . . ," he said with a smile,
and disappeared.

DEATH'S DESOLATION

Death's desolation
—— I'd like to savor it
when I die.

HOWEVER

If, however, I take only a sip of death,
I suppose I'll be depressed.
Maybe it's best not to savor it.

LIKE A TORTOISE *

Having supplied myself with a refuge for resignation,
I live shameless in this world
—— a tortoise.

I escape into that refuge when I feel anxious.
After the feeling leaves, I move shamelessly about
—— a tortoise.

Not because I have an iron will or a heart of steel,
but because I have a solid refuge
—— a tortoise.

Thus I calmly go my own, my carefree way,
with typical sluggish zeal
—— a tortoise.

OLD HEN

I'm an old hen.
By now, I've created a vast quantity of eggs.
I can't end my day
without producing an egg.
One day an annoying official came by
and told me to record every last egg
I'd ever laid.
I can lay eggs,
but I can't count.
Because I dread officials,
I'd like to tally up all my eggs,
but there's no way I can do it.
That made me want to stop producing eggs,
but I can't stop
laying.
Regardless of what I'm told,
I can't help producing eggs.
I just can't count them.

WOLF and SHEEP

Clad in a robe, the wolf says,
"Peace. Peace."
The sheep joyfully says,
"Peace. Peace."
In this way the wolf peacefully eats
as much of the sheep as he wants,
and the sheep is peacefully eaten
till the wolf feels sated.

TWO LIONS *

It's certainly true
that the person chasing two hares
won't catch either one.
But one of my friends, a famous hunter,
told me,
"Someone chased two lions
and caught both of them.
Who managed that?
The man called William Blake."

ANGRY LION

Whatever does the angry lion do?
He roars and roars.
He runs and runs.
If his prey has eluded him,
he roars
into the hills and savanna.
He roars till he's weary from mane to tail.
He runs and runs,
then roars and roars
till he's absolutely spent.

SLEEPING LION

A sleeping lion
stretched out its legs,
and yawned a vast yawn.
I no sooner thought that this time for sure
he'd open his eyes
and get up,
than he once again went calmly back to sleep.
Soon, I suppose,
he'll waken
—— when people are completely off guard
and have forgotten about him.

THAT LION

"Why is that lion so upset?"
"A fly's caught in his ear."
"Yet fury, however intense, won't free the fly."
"But he's furious because he wants to be."
"He's an idiot."
"When he's that upset, however, he's a bit stronger."
"He's quieted down. Do you think he's done for?"
"The fly got away."

WHAT THE FLY TOLD THE LION

The fly told the lion,
"You have no wings.
You can't view things from a high place.
I'm not in the least afraid of you,
however much you roar.

Only dragonflies
terrorize me.
They're quite
wonderful creatures.
But spiders are knaves."
Laughing, the lion thought of the fly
as a surprisingly charming fellow.
—— I don't know
what this poem means.

FLIES

Flies are a nuisance!
They alight on your head.
They buzz around your ears.
They alight on your shoulders.
They alight on your back.
They alight on your hands.
Whenever they do, they buzz and buzz.
It's a bother to kill them,
but if you let them be
they get brazen,
fly around
buzzing
and again alight on you.
How annoying.

TWO HORSES

There were two horses.
Both were beautiful.
Both fast.

People looked at the two horses
and argued about
which one was better
than the other.
One group praised the one horse,
another group praised the other.

The two horses spoke to each other:
"You're beautiful.
Surely, you're beautiful.
But I'm beautiful, too.
Surely, I am beautiful, too." •

Neither horse knew
which was more attractive.
They simply admired each other.
"No matter what anyone claims,"
the two horses said,
"you and I are beautiful and fast."
They smiled contentedly.

AGE OF ADVERSITY FOR THE RACE HORSE

The race horse made a point of lagging behind a nag.
    He soon became weary and everyone made fun of him.
"Why don't you run faster?"
"If I do they'll all get mad at me."
Once, however, he ran as fast as he could.
Surprisingly, everyone thought he'd gone mad.
For the first time, however, the race horse felt buoyant. For the first time
    he could cheerfully eat his meal.
        "Trotting slowly is quite tiring, you know. Just using your
        head and being careful does you in. That's why I have no
        choice. Even if you're mad at me, even if you hate me, and
        even if you insult me —— sorry, I'm going to gallop."

HORSE DEPRIVED OF LIBERTY

The horse pulled around
hither and yon
eventually became deprived of its self.
Then he was told, "It's all right now.
Go off on your own."
But the horse had already forgotten
what it meant
to be on its own.
The moment the horse was freed,
it stood immobile —— dazed.

TWO-HORSE CART

I want to be under control.
I want to be engrossed.
I want always to be calm.
I always want to burst into flame.

I'm riding a two-horse cart
—— one horse like water,

one like fire.
If I do not skillfully control these two horses,
I'm bound to run off the cliff,
and so I don't want to forget: be under control.

If I run off the cliff,
I'll disappoint many people.
I intend to drive these two horses deftly
till I reach my goal.

Some may find this
an impossible task.
I'd like to say, however, that this shows
why humans fascinate.

Calmness and ardor,
water and fire
—— aware of being under control,
but at the same time flaming up in such a way
that one can always move ahead.
Yet I can't forget: be under control.

WILD GEESE and DRAKES IN THE ZOO

Wild geese and drakes in the zoo
somehow never settle down.
I suppose something irresistibly attracts them.
And yet they don't fly off
toward the attraction.
Not knowing what to do,
they think day in and day out
that they'd simply like to fly north.
I well understand how they feel.
I similarly am unable to fly to places
I'd love to visit.
Nor do I know what to do about it.

WATCHING FISH SWIM

Watching fish swim
is indeed delightful.
Their unrestricted freedom,
their endless activity
—— they are life itself.
Their lively bodies . . .
I love watching
fish swim.

A MAN FISHES *

A man fishes in a large river.
Well, what will he catch?
Carp? Catfish?
No, he'll net equanimity.

APPLE TREES and PEAR TREES

I'm a squirrel
and I love
apple trees and pear trees,
grapes and mandarin oranges.

I love hopping
because I'm a rabbit.
I love climbing trees
because I'm a monkey.

If a lion roars,
I roar, too.
If a horse gallops, I gallop, too.
If an ostrich dances, I also dance.

RHAPSODIZING ON MY BIRTHDAY *

When I was born
twenty-six years ago today,
my family was in an uproar.
That day my grandmother fainted
after an uncle stormed into the house
saying he'd kill my aunt for being unfaithful.

I heard that
the doctor who examined Grandmother
said there was no need to worry.
She'd be all right.
The doctor thought she'd fainted
because of excessive concern
over Mother's travail
in giving me birth.

Mother was most concerned
about Grandmother, they told me,
and so I arrived a bit earlier
than expected,

my face purple.

The events of that day
have left no trace.
More than half of those
who then rejoiced
at my birth
are now dead.

And today
I turned twenty-six.

Thus I've spent half a lifetime
accomplishing nothing,
showing not the slightest
promise.

I'm restless
—— restless.

Father died when I was three.
I've been told that, though I was so young,
he looked at me and said,
"If someone does a splendid job bringing up this boy,
he'll be one of the finest in the world."

Whenever I have doubts about myself,
Mother encourages me
by repeating Father's words.
She says I have a lucky star.

And yet, and yet, and yet . . .
her encouragement only makes me more restless.
To be sure, I have the mental ability
and yet
I don't know how I should put it to use.

I'm already
twenty-six,
anxious to become as great
as Cézanne,
Hodler,
or Van Gogh
—— like the grade school kid wanting to be a general.
I'm an overgrown baby,
my mouth still reeking of the nipple.

How can I constantly be as nonchalant as I am now,

so ready to indulge such fantasies?

Say, do you think you're a genius?
Do you imagine you wear the aura
surrounding genius?
Do you suppose it's only a matter of,
"Ask and it will be given you"?
Do you think that if you constantly eye the shelf
with that sweetcake in mind
it will automatically drop into your mouth?

Though you speak modestly
so people won't regard you a fool,
you dream big and in your heart deride others.
Be quick rather to deride yourself
—— a coward, a milksop, a poor loser.

Was your father a prophet?
Are you a fatalist?

If, however, you live a life of leisure,
that may be an acceptable and an agreeable way
to conceal your weaknesses.
Nothing is as ugly as a genius who promotes himself.
Listen,
you must know your self.
If you're a genius, live like one.
If a mediocrity, live like one.
Unless you make a choice, you'll do nothing with your life.

I've been thinking all along
that if I'm a mediocrity
I might as well do nothing with my life
—— that's why I've taken the most insolent path.
That's why I sneer at those who worry about clothes and such.
I'd like to feel proud of my nakedness.
Gold requires no plating.

On my twenty-sixth birthday,
I look back on the way I've trod.
I always calculated I could be on top on every occasion.
It looks at least as though I'll have the spirit of a three-year old
till I'm a hundred!

So these days I figure
I should leave this world
a megalomaniac.
I'm resolved nevertheless not to be vacuous.

I don't intend to separate skin from muscle.
I intend to have pride in myself as my Maker made me.

I don't intend to walk the streets
concealing my homely face.
Nor do I intend to go out in public and shrink before others.

I'll try to live as long as ordained.
I'll try to solve the riddle that I am.

Today I'm leaving for Otaru, blessing the fact that
the greater the riddle the greater the man.
I'm going to where my first love lives.

A MAN

I've turned fifty-six.
Sometimes I say to myself,
I hope soon to be a marvelous person.
I don't know
if becoming a marvelous person means
to write marvelous novels,
to paint marvelous pictures,
or to save humanity.
I know only that in saying it
I simply feel capable both of having hope
and of being youthfully energetic.
I hope soon to be a marvelous man.

THE MORNING OF MY SEVENTY-FOURTH BIRTHDAY *

Today is my seventy-fourth birthday.
Possibly because I've been hearing about artificial satellites,
it was quite interesting to think that today my tour on the globe
        completed its seventy-fourth revolution around the sun.
I don't find that anything has especially changed.
To think of my birthday makes me more aware
        of being born seventy-four years ago on this Earth.
I don't know whether it was good or bad that I was born,
for the final judgment on my life isn't in yet.
Nor can one determine that the world will be peaceful
        and that life will be tranquil and safe,
so I can never disregard prudence and awe.
I must admit nonetheless that humans move steadily ahead
        with objectives in mind.
Each life has its own ideal. Humanity entertains a more clear-cut ideal.
Aware of these or not, we must advance toward our goals. •

We don't know how far we can go, but I think that life
    wills making as much progress as possible.
I rejoice over the fact that my dogged determination to comply with that will
    has not yet weakened.
Thus each day I intend to move farther and farther ahead.
I haven't the leisure to dwell on the past. I desire to study every day
    —— frankly that's how I feel now.
I look forward, in a word, to going as far as I can.

MY EIGHTY-SEVENTH BIRTHDAY

I'm eighty-seven today,
which means that on Earth I'll be starting on
my eighty-eighth circuit around the sun.
As you know, I photographed the irises that were blooming in our yard
to present to you who've gathered here to celebrate this day.
I'd like each of you to accept a copy as a memento.
I'd also like each of you to remain among us in good health.
It's extraordinary to be born in this world.
May each of you live here in happiness.
That's my intention, too.

AT EIGHTY-EIGHT *

In the old days when you turned eighty-eight
you entered the *"beiju"* year
and observed your *beiju* festival.
In my case I'll be eighty-seven this year,
which means I'm a year shy of *beiju*,
of being called eighty-eight.
Despite that, however, I've decided to follow an ancient custom
and have them celebrate my eighty-eighth birthday this year.
I figure I'll celebrate this event a bit early
and this year try to accompany everyone on the globe
and make my eighty-eighth circuit around the sun.
Even if I make another revolution,
I won't feel especially different.
My eighty-eighth revolution
around the sun will, however,
be a joyful occasion for me,
but it won't mean the world has particularly changed.
Just to think about it, however,
is somehow a joy.

One writes the numbers 8–10–8
to get the *bei* of the compound graph *beiju*.
That is to say, *bei* or the graph for uncooked rice

simply produces the number eighty eight.
As a Japanese that delights me.
The *beiju* age signifies that death is near.
Having put dying out of mind,
living to eighty-eight has, however, been a joy.
Not thinking that I'll soon die,
and being surrounded by people younger than I,
puts me in a sprightly mood.
I therefore put on the mien of an old man.
I rejoice in my foolishness.
I don't give a thought to anything like death
but affirm the attitude that I'll live forever.
I'm fond of myself living like this.
I'm fond of this foolish self.

An OLD MAN'S DREAMS

I don't know how much longer I'll live.
I leave questions of life and death to fate.
I'm concerned only to make the most of my abilities.
Making use of them, I hope to paint.
I don't know how much longer I'll live.
Nor do I know the extent of my skill.

Death is beyond my control.
I want, however, to paint as much as I can.
I find that absorbing.
I'm already eighty-nine,
so I want to try to stretch further,
make the most of my abilities,
and paint good pictures.
That's my happy-go-lucky thought.

This happy-go-lucky eighty-nine year-old man
intends to study constantly
without holding back.
Pushing farther and farther onward
into what encompasses the self —— that's life.
The enticement of being unaware of when I'll die
is my enticement.

Health

I'm an old man now.
Sometimes I take sick.
Each time I do,

I feel grateful for my health.

What joy in being able to get out of bed in good health,
in being able to work in good health!
Those who complain
despite being healthy enough to work
can't reasonably wish for more.

But I'm grateful
once I recover, however,
and regain my health.
Aware of my gratitude,
I want to return to work with care.

AN OLD MAN ON LIFE'S SUPEREXPRESS *

Time passes very quickly.
A week goes by in a wink.
It's as though I'm on a superexpress
dashing toward death.
Aware of that,
I'm unruffled
and will remain
unruffled.
Until the superexpress
reaches its destination,
I'll continue calmly writing what I want to write.
I'll continue making my crude paintings
in praise of the beauty
that nature has made
—— that's how I'm constituted.
I can't do what I cannot do,
but what I can do, I do.

I make no attempt to do what I cannot,
but I want honestly to do what I can.
To be of use to humanity,
somebody will do for me
what I cannot do.
Hurrah
for those who eagerly do
what I find impossible!

However I think of it,
I believe that
all people born in this world
want to fulfill their destiny.

In reality, however, not everyone can.
Impossible or not,
the hope for fulfillment is a fact.
Actually, the majority cannot achieve that dream.
It's truly regrettable
that some interfere with their aims.
However deplorable,
a fact is a fact,
actuality is actuality.
It's also a fact, however,
that we cannot resign ourselves to this reality.
As long as I live,
I am destined
to hope always
that all might realize their potentials.

Each individual thinks selfishly and willfully,
giving no consideration to others
—— "Everything's fine as long as I get mine."
Some think that way,
but they deserve our compassion
if they finally do concentrate selfishly
on making something of themselves.
Reality, however, doesn't permit that to occur.
Reality indeed exists.
These people are heartless and lack humanity.
They regard the death of a human being
with as little import
as they regard a pebble.
True human beings, thankfully, are not like that.
Those with surplus energy are not like that.
Those capable of human feelings are not like that.
In the human realm,
we must value the lives
and the destinies of all.

I ride the superexpress with an air of composure.
On it I sincerely want to do what I'd like to do
and do what I can.
If I'm able to do that,
I can live tranquilly with a joyful heart.
Believing in humanity,
believing in people who can do what I cannot,
and believing that I am a genuine human being,
I'll live as long as I can with peace of mind
and be grateful for being able to do so.
True tears unaffectedly moisten my eyes.

TWO CALLERS *

Yesterday morning a guest appeared.
I went out wondering who it was
and found an old fellow in our entry.
His chauffeur was carrying a large book.
I recognized him immediately.
A hundred-year-old man
had taken the trouble to stop by.

When I asked if he'd come in he said,
"I've other stops to make."
Since he indicated he'd be leaving at once,
I accompanied him to the car
without trying to detain him.
Coming alone by car,
one-hundred-year-old Hirakushi Denchû
showed up at my place to deliver a book.

I moved into this house when I was seventy.
During the sixteen years since,
I've greeted two people
over one hundred years of age.
One of them was the one-hundred-two-year-old person
who years ago showed me around the site of the New Village in Hyûga.

The second was one-hundred-year-old Hirakushi Denchû.
I was delighted to greet two people
over a hundred years old.
I want to work,
living as long as I can.
Because I was born into this world,
it goes without saying that as long as I'm still here
I want to do honest work.

VISION?

Some live with the belief
that there's no contradiction
between authentically realizing the self
and the authentic existence of others,
and that in a genuine sense tensions between the self and others can be reconciled.
Some label these believers "visionaries."
But living like that is to exist as a true human being!
The authentic human living like an authentic person
—— is that a vision?

IDEALIST WHO WALKS TESTING A STONE BRIDGE

Somebody told me
I'm not a man of action
—— someone who doesn't know me.
I'm far more a man of action than he dreams.
I'm an idealist who walks across a stone bridge
testing it.

VISIONARY

I'm the sort of visionary
who crosses a stone bridge only after testing it.

SONG OF THE VISIONARY *

That's right. I'm trying to take money from people poorer than I.
I'm trying to take more and more and more of it.
I'm not compelling them to give it to me. I do think, however, that if I had more power, money would naturally follow.
My work is not accumulating money.
I'm quite satisfied merely to be myself. Then, as an inevitable consequence, the money will follow.
What will I do with the money?
I won't build a Buddhist temple with it.
I'll build a theater. I'll build an art museum. We don't yet have one in Japan. Then I'll build a hospital and a dormitory. We don't yet have them in Japan, either.
Can I do such things?
Ah, if only I had the power! Then the money will naturally follow. I'd of course be able to build whatever I want to build. But that power, that power —— that power alone is the source of my concern.
I'd be satisfied if only that power seethed up in me, if only I had more power, if only I could be my true self. That's enough. Then I wouldn't have to overstrain. I could get by without temporizing. Like the sun.
But . . . there is a *but* —— I must sense my lack of power.
I'm mortified. And yet . . . and yet I do not by any means resign myself. I can't neglect my fundamental self. I woulkd never try so hard to accumulate money that I'd give up being myself. That would be humiliating.
I do not, however, turn down whatever might come in.
I do not refuse money even from the poor. No doubt they'd be happy if only I make the most of their money.
In any event, I have no choice but to go as far as I can with this. I have no choice but to try going on till my strength is spent.
Go ahead and laugh at me, if you will, but my determination is not mistaken. It's just that I then lacked an abundance of capacity.
It's most dreadful for me not having a bounty of capability. Oh, capabilities —— multiply!

THE WONDERS OF THE SUN *

I turned ninety this year.
Day after day
the sun rises,
shows itself, and says,
"The more I shine,
the more I want you to look at me.
I rarely feel like looking at myself."
The sun is an unimaginable
entity.
Simply to observe it
off in the distance
is a wonder to me.
It's truly a phenomenal presence,
a truly wonderful presence
that I can't even imagine
looking at.
For us,
the sun is a fantastic,
a truly enormous entity.
We cannot grasp either its vastness
or its existence
any more than we can imagine
the magnitude of the universe.
Nor can we grasp the actuality of the sun or the universe
—— they are truly vast.
Both seem without guile.
We haven't a clue as to what they are.
We simply can't imagine
their vast power, their complexity.
I hope that they remain immutable,
that they'll be an ever-constant presence.
They are constants . . . and they enchant us.
Indeed, they're excessively enchanting.
They daunt us, for they are awesome, awesome
—— simply too awesome for words.

SUN

The sun
takes what it will
and gives what it will.
It stands above good and bad, right and wrong
—— symbolizing
those who live
the way it lives.

SUN and MOON *

One day when Sun and Moon met
they happened to talk about Earth.
Moon described
fascinatingly, interestingly,
and beautifully
how Earth looks at night.
When Sun heard the description he looked dubious.
"There can't be such places on Earth," he said.
"Ever since it was born, I've constantly gazed at Earth
but never once saw
what you describe."
Moon pondered a while and then—as though making a discovery—said,
"I see, I see.
Whenever you look at Earth, night turns to day.
That's right. Whenever you take a look,
it becomes daytime on Earth."
"I wonder . . . ," Sun said,
but he had no idea what Moon meant.
They then talked of other things and parted.
Ever since, Sun has been eager to see the nighttime Earth.
He has watched it vigilantly for eons,
but he never caught a single glimpse of Earth at night.
Sun then smiled to himself and said,
"That Moon! She's just hallucinating."

WATER *

Trying different approaches,
water crashes again and again
with all its might
into whatever blocks its way.
The barriers remain intact,
so water has no choice
but to batter them
and move on along its path.
I sense within myself
its mighty will.
However frequently held in check,
water invariably makes a path somewhere
and enters the sea.
I sense its will
streaming within my self.
As long as I'm alive,
I'll definitely not hold my energies
in check.

Flowing River

A flowing river doesn't become composed
until it flows into the sea.
But can it be content simply to flow straight to the sea?
Of course not!
Its aim is to enter the sea,
but at each moment during its flow
it views whatever it can,
relishes whatever it can,
and expects to merge with the ocean
as beautifully and as abundantly as possible
—— without having lived an empty life,
without becoming bored.
Still, its aim is to enter the sea,
not to enjoy itself along the way.
Nor could it be satisfied to dry up en route.
River, don't regret
that you're unable to stop
at a single place along the way.
Just enjoy the beauties that repeatedly arise en route
and flow on —— to the sea!

In the Typhoon

I want to become an inflexible crag,
not someone who resigns himself to the storm.
I want furthermore to become a person
able to generate the light and peace
of the typhoon's eye.

Whenever I See a Japanese Movie

It disgusts me
to see a Japanese movie
because some woman is almost always committing suicide.
Why not choose to go on living?
It's a bit absurd to die
because a man abandons
or dishonors you.
Go on living —— go on living,
go on loving life.

PURSE *

The hero placidly urges his horse on,
and without looking back
laughs at the purse the sordid old man reaches out to him.
This is truly a conventional yet an auspicious scene.
I imagine a world where life rules money, not the opposite.
    I think that money will then be little more than a handy aide.

A BIG SHIP

A big ship
is aware of the magnetic power of its compass.
A young man is aware of the magnetic power of the compass in his heart.
It longs to be attracted,
but the magnet isn't sufficiently powerful, so it's useless.
The magnet's strength will amplify till one day it easily attracts
the large objects it longs to draw
—— if only the magnet amplifies its capacity bit by bit.

BOOKSHOP

I miss having a bookshop nearby.
The delights
of going to a bookshop
and sauntering through good books,
my heart leaping up . . . !
I miss not having a bookshop handy.
I miss not being able to meet the people I'd like now to meet
from past or present, East or West.

STUDY

Study,
study,
grinding study.
Concentrated study alone
produces miracles,
changes lead to gold,
ducks to swans.

IF YOU BREAK EVERY OIL LAMP

Electric lights do not appear
just because you break every oil lamp.
Oil lamps disappear
because electric lights appear.
A new house does not appear
when you knock down the old one.
The old house disappears
when a new one appears.

BROAD-MINDED MAN

A broad-minded man has a brain
that doesn't reach its capacity
however much wisdom he absorbs from others
—— the opposite of the narrow mind.

TRAVELER!

"Traveler!
where are you bound?
Where do you travel with no companion?
Haven't you gone too far?"
"I go
where I please.
I go to places that delight me.
I travel alone,
or with two or three others,
or with a hundred, a thousand, or even ten thousand others.
I cannot turn back.
I go where I'm bound."

BE HONEST

Be honest,
be honest.
Even if it's unpleasant, be honest
and don't flatter people to get in their good graces.
Be honest,
be honest
—— honest to truth.

CLAY FIGURINE —— *HANIWA* *

I understand this figurine, evidently a famous artifact,
came from Kaminakajô, Kumagaya, Saitama Prefecture.
At a glance, I find it attractive.
I don't know much about it, but it appeals to me.
This *haniwa* seems a pleasing piece.
I figured it was a curiosity when I saw it
in the current issue of an art magazine.
It apparently won popular recognition.
It's as absorbing as a poem.
I know very little about it,
but I find it interesting to look at.
It's a somewhat amiable piece.
Observing it, a Japanese will feel entranced.
An engaging artifact, it's quite fetching.
I feel it throbs with the amiable temperament of our race.
It pleases me.

STONE, STONE

Stone, stone.
For what purpose
does a stone exist?
Stone —— its existence is non-existence.
Stone —— kicked but not offended.
Stone —— that doesn't object to my sketching it.
Lonely stone.
I like you.
You like me, too, don't you?

NOUVEAU RICHE

He's rich now,
but he couldn't make the most of his gifts,
his individuality,
his life.
Such a man I cannot praise.

SELF and OTHERS

The other in me.
The me in others.
When they joyfully meet one another,
that becomes the shared joy of all.

They

The solemn way they live seems painfully foolish to me.
They lack the heart
capable of sensing how unbearably wretched it is
not to live life solemnly.

Master! Master! *

"Master! Master!
How many times should I get up
if I fall?
. . . Seven?"

"No!
Even should you fall seventy times seven times,
you must still get up."

The Fountain's Lament

Until the day it dries up,
the fountain will lament:
"I can't keep from
spouting water."

Joy

Joy, what is your source?
Some fathomless place, I suppose.
Surely you're the offspring of nature,
or at least of humanity.
You're certainly too profound
for an individual to beget.

Humanity

Humanity is incredibly vast,
a broad stream.
Whatever happens,
this river will flow leisurely toward the sea.
Nothing can resist it.
Humanity is incredibly vast,
a broad stream.

What We Call the City

I can't imagine that what we call the city
stands on a firm foundation.
Vaguely in a flurry,
city folk appear neither considerate nor deliberate.
They live by external stimuli,
apparently indifferent to what burgeons from within.

New World

We must fashion the new world
on the basis of a fresh view of human life.
Issue no commands!
Honor the fact that people have minds!

Transitional Period

I want to be a poet who sings songs of dawn's light.
I'd like to sing of life's burgeoning power.
My heart burns with hope.
My breast bursts with energy.
I no longer think I'll deplore this transitional period.
Blazing with hope, I want to sing songs that delight in transition.

Songs of decaying beauty no longer appeal to me.
Only songs with the power to soar into the skies appeal.
Those born before me live in a different age than I do.
Nature gives fresh strength to all who are renewed.
She gives us longings. She gives us hope.
Transitional period! What a beautiful, youthful term!

PART II

WORK & LOVE

Blessed is he who has found his work;
let him ask no other blessedness.
He has a work, a life-purpose;
he has found it, and
will follow it!

— Thomas Carlyle —
1843

PART II contains poems dealing chiefly with Mushakôji's work ethic and commitment to love [*ai*]. He applied these principles to himself and to the NEW VILLAGE, which he fervently hoped they might both guide and govern. Paragraphs immediately below provide details about the founding of the village not included in either the Introduction or the Notes. A brief discussion of love, primarily from the Christian perspective of *agapé*, then offers background for the shorter second section that gathers works on affection and friendship.

✦   ✦   ✦

LIFE IN THE NEW VILLAGE left a deep imprint on Mushakôji and his verse. The poetry published over the seven years he resided in the village comprises a disproportionate 47% of the 465 works in *Long Corridor*. Actually, since some 43% of his collected verse appeared during those years (1918.11–1925.12), this does not appreciably distort the record. The village occupies such an important place in his thought that events that led to its founding may be of interest.

Physical and intellectual dimensions molded Mushakôji's dream community. His antipathy to the paternalistic ideology of Japan's authoritarian samurai-type family system influenced either dimension. Physical aspects of the dream included creating a community where each member would work cooperatively as an equal. The aim was to provide food, shelter, clothing, and whatever utensils villagers could manufacture. Ideally, physical toil sanctified each member's existence and allowed him or her to live as a true—that is, an authentic—human. All were to share as common property the land, the workshops, and cultural facilities. The interests, tastes, skills, and physical capabilities of each member presumably influenced work assignments. Schools, textbooks, and medical services were to be provided free of charge. No maids, servants, or hired hands—and certainly no "coolies" [*ninpu*]— could be assigned the manual labor and "dirty work." Members themselves must perform even the most menial tasks. Villagers planned to utilize machinery to the full extent so they might earn free time for study or leisure activities. Mushakôji furthermore hoped to establish a common fund to permit trips and the purchase of items the members could not themselves fashion. The dream to escape a capitalist society ironically required a bit of capital.

Intellectual aspects of the dream assumed equal dedication to hard work, individual responsibility, and expansion or enrichment of viewpoint. Mushakôji hoped, for example, to provide each member with sufficient instruction in a foreign language to become fluent. He also planned to construct a playhouse and library. Above all, he believed that the village should enable each to fulfill his or her private dreams to become an independent, responsible, and self-reliant team member. That would enable all to realize every personal potential. Working and living cooperatively also requires one to respect the individuality and tastes of others. The plan presented the rare opportunity to become authentic in a society that has historically insisted on identifying individualism and personal liberty with egocentric selfishness. Accomplishing that goal would be a notable feat in Japan's age-graded, hierarchical, and conformist society. Mushakôji's earnest conviction that such a commune was possible, even in Japan, affected many.

Reactions varied. Some were sympathetic and some wanted to donate money, but a few desired to experience life in the new community. Interested parties agreed to meet once a month for discussions. Although only seven or eight attended the first meeting, the number increased each month. Later the group rented a modest house in Tokyo in which three or four supporters lived. This became the official headquarters for the New Village movement. These members published in July, 1918, the first issue of their monthly journal, *Atarashiki Mura* [New Village]. Before the end of the summer they received many letters of encouragement, some containing donations. The associates then began to consider buying land on which to establish the village. Initially, they wanted a plot close enough to Tokyo so visitors could easily make a round-trip in one day. They could not arrive at a consensus, but one night Mushakôji suddenly awoke with the idea that Hyûga (an area occupying the southeastern sector of Miyazaki Prefecture on the southernmost island of Kyûshû; IN HYÛGA'S HILLS) might be a possibility. The day before somebody had mentioned Hyûga to him, and the name fermented in his mind. For centuries the region was associated with the birth of the nation because of Takachiho-no-Mine (elevation 5,165'), the mountain on which Japan's mythical founding gods and the Emperor's forefathers descended. Planting their community in such a location would surely make a statement about creating a new order in Japan.

Mushakôji immediately felt positive about this possibility. Choosing Hyûga occurred to him naturally. He did not argue that Kyûshû would be better than the Kantô area or Tokyo because land was far cheaper there. No, the idea came to him as in a dream. It was as though God had spoken. Members quickly accepted the "revelation" and decided to give public speeches about and conduct discussions on the village. They held the first of many meetings on 14 September 1918 in the Hongô section of Tokyo. The next day many gathered at Mushakôji's home in Abiko, Chiba Prefecture. There they decided to send a search party to Hyûga to look for land. Mushakôji left Abiko on 20 September and on the 23rd he and three other committee members boarded a train at Tokyo Station. Along the way they stopped at Nagano, Matsumoto, Nagoya, Kyôto, Ôsaka, Kôbe, and Fukuoka on Kyûshû to talk with those who shared their dreams. On 10 October the party landed in Totoro (now Nobeoka) in the northern part of Miyazaki Prefecture. Nobeoka, a former castle town at the mouth of the Gokase River, was since the early 1920s the largest industrial city on Kyûshû's east coast.

On 11 October they began investigating nearby rural areas for an appropriate piece of land. Several problems cropped up. Some conservative country folk feared the group consisted of Communists. Few ideologies were more menacing. Others mistook the committee members for "city slickers" interested in exploiting cheap rural labor. If the village head or the local constabulary opposed their plans, the group had no choice but to move on. Using maps to aid their search, the party divided into two groups and continued the quest. One location appealed, but the asking price was ¥70 (then ca. $35) per *tan* [ca. 0.245 acres], well over their ¥50 per *tan* budget. Letters from supporters encouraged them to begin their search anew.

Mushakôji's wife Fusako, another committee member's wife, and several ardent backers joined them. With almost a dozen involved in the search, the team tried to conserve funds by renting a house in Takajô. This village lies several miles northeast of Miyakonojô, the major city in a mountain-enclosed basin located in the southeast corner of Miyazaki Prefecture. The searchers were running low on funds, so their sense of urgency increased. Worse, only two or three of the party escaped the immediate post-World War I flu epidemic that ravaged the area.

Despite setbacks, they eventually prevailed. Mushakôji and another member went to the small seaport of Obi (renamed Nichinan following a 1950 amalgamation of communities) where they encountered a familiar frustration. While making inquiries at the county courthouse, they met the mayor of Ichiki, who indicated interest in their project. That afternoon he took them to his village, showed them various pieces of property, and encouraged them to live there. He arranged to meet them later but never appeared. Mushakôji afterward discovered that local police had advised him to back off. People in one of the next villages they visited reportedly lost interest the moment they noticed how fast the strangers from the capital walked. Conservative Kyûshû rural clansmen did not welcome being visited by bustling Tokyoites who also might be hustlers. The search party felt discouraged. The very next morning, however, Fusako sent good news from Takajô, where the local people had lowered the land price to the budgeted ¥50 per *tan*. Mushakôji and his colleagues consequently purchased land in Ishikawauchi, Kijô Village, Koyu County, Miyazaki Prefecture; cf. Chronology, 1918.11. Hills surrounded their flat plot, and the Omaru River flowed through it. Photographs of the area attest to its rugged, striking beauty. Mushakôji's Eden seemed safely remote from civilization and the city. The New Village opened on 14 November 1918, the birthday of the sculptor RODIN, whom Mushakôji and many SHIRAKABA colleagues deeply admired for his artistry and HUMANISM. In addition to the traditional Japanese New Year, villagers from the outset also celebrated the birthdays of the Buddha (April 8) and Jesus. Later they added TOLSTOY'S birthday (August 28) as well.

Aside from the joys of self-reliance, work, and camaraderie, good intentions [*zen'i*] provided the living mortar that cemented New Village relationships. Laudable humanistic objectives aside, the project began and proceeded under at least three shadows: insufficient capital, a shortage of operating skills, and personality problems. The need for money drove Mushakôji to publish frantically, especially between 1918 and 1930. To the end of his life, in fact, he committed a part of his income to support the village. One wonders how it might have survived had it not been for his productivity, dedication to his dream, and at times even the generosity of his novelist friends. Money shortages resulted in part from a lack of careful planning and structure. Whatever the reasons, scarcity of necessities negatively affected morale. Even then, the associates seemed not to appreciate the urgency, importance, or power of institutional organization as a factor in guaranteeing harmony. Nor did the splendid ideals that created the village automatically transfer into concrete procedures to ease members through the realties of their day-to-day struggles. The paucity of management, economic, and organizational skills made it unlikely that the village might soon become a stable or self-supporting institution.

These deficiencies increased other tensions in the village. Strained human relations presumably also played a decisive role in Mushakôji's late 1925 decision to move to Nara, where his friend SHIGA NAOYA was then residing; cf. Chronology. Mushakôji feared that excessive reliance on his financial support and leadership would surely erode the village ideal of self-reliance. Some members nonetheless remained excessively attached to their private feelings, and others behaved at times like the indulged scions of privileged families. Youthful visionaries and literary-minded people reared and educated in Japan's paternalistic vertical society understandably found it challenging to evolve and sustain a democratic community. In addition to that, there were hostilities—some rooted in male-female jealousies or the endless petty tensions indigenous to Japan's age-graded, hierarchical polity. Moreover, most associates were urbanites unaccustomed to manual labor or physical conditions that by any reckoning were extremely harsh, even primitive. Apparently they had not considered making provision for such problems. That the village survived these adversities was indeed a miracle.

THE WORD LOVE [*ai*] surely appears more often in Mushakôji's verse than in the works of any Japanese writer, ancient or modern. In his verse, *ai* suggests an altruistic or pure love akin to *agapé*, which Christians describe as God's love for humankind. *Ai* has no kinship with romantic or sexual love [*ren'ai*]. Mushakôji knew more than enough about the Bible and Christianity to be familiar with *agapé*, one of the handful of classical Greek words expressing the varied nuances of love. Christians regard *agapé* the ideal manifestation of spiritual love, which means that it does not emanate from the creaturely or physical aspects of *Homo Sapiens*. The term refers to the nature of the Creator himself, the indescribable Being: "God is *agapé* • love" (I *John* 4:8). By associating *agapé* with God's redemptive plans for humanity, theologians define the term as far more than altruism or unselfish concern for the welfare of others. This definition relates *agapé* to the most noble form of love as embodied in the teaching that the Creator sent his son to redeem humankind. This definition of *agapé* consequently infuses the concept with nuances of sacrificial giving, unstinting response to the needs of one's neighbors, and helpfulness to others without expecting reward or repayment. In Japan, these values have customarily had, and continue to have, extremely low currency.

The early translation of *agapé* as "charity" emphasized the virtue of imitating God's benevolence, generosity, and acceptance. This demonstrates how theologians interpreted *agapé* as God's activities to touch his children where they live. Concerns for justice and fairness naturally derive from an understanding of *agapé* as the way God demonstrates his love for humans. This also explains why, since the beginning of the Christian experience, children of God have been identified as those who show love to others (I *John* 4:7). Similarly, people whose behavior reflects *agapé* reveal themselves to be disciples of Christ (*John* 13:35). These universals embedded in *agapé* immensely impressed Mushakôji, who came across the concept during his adolescence. It is difficult in Japanese to describe this kind of love short of the simple word *ai*. Other possibilities either connote Buddhist abstractions or become a manufactured, and thus an alien-sounding, Chinese compound. The word altruism in English is no more capable than *ai* in Japanese of conveying the shades of meaning embedded in *agapé*. If Mushakôji's usage reflects the perfect selflessness that *agapé* implies, one should not categorically rule out altruism as an appropriate English rendering of *ai* in certain contexts.

Reading Tolstoy, the Bible, and other Western works may account for much of Mushakôji's knowledge of and stress on selfless love. It is not necessary, however, to assume that he derived every nuance of this love from Christianity. Chinese philosophy may to some extent have inflenced him, if only to prepare or open his mind to the possibilities of a universal love—whether or not it was identical with *agapé*. All educated men of his generation had broad familiarity with the fundamentals of Chinese thought. They were well acquainted with the texts and concepts of Confucianism as well as with those of Taoism and other competing schools. The philosopher Mo Tzu (a.k.a. Mo Ti, ?470–391 B.C.)—a major thinker active between the death of Confucius and the birth of Mencius—mounted a paramount challenge to the Confucian way. The era in which Mo lived and taught resembled Lao Tzu's; cf. page 19. It was a time of barbaric cruelty and constant warfare. Hate, betrayal, revenge, and joyful destructiveness had virtually become institutionalized. Like Lao Tzu, Mo Ti devoted considerable energy and thought to the obvious question: how might human beings survive such turmoil? He perceived it his mission to teach people not only survival skills but how to overcome spiritual chaos and become fulfilled persons.

Mo Ti's teachings, unique in the history of Chinese thought, identified the ills of his era with Confucianism. Strict class and status gradations, Mo charged, caused many of the world's disorders because loving those nearby meant hating those afar. Thus he claimed that Confucianism turned citizens into xenophobes easily convinced to fight and subdue the despised alien. Social problems arise, Mo said, the moment people's concerns for others require variable standards: some that apply to family and others that apply to strangers. Confucianism's commitment to hierarchy, he preached, must be held responsible for the constant warfare and the reigning spirit of revenge and aggressiveness. Maintaining, as Confucius required, different behavior toward those who are superior and those who are inferior increased social strains. Mo thought that only a humane, non-hierarchical caring displayed equally for everyone might overcome those strains. Just as Heaven impartially loves all, Mo reasoned that all who would follow Heaven must impartially love others. Universal love alone, he said, could resolve the era's turmoil.

These teachings were unpopular because they ran against self-interest and the mood of the times. They muddled common sense, as well. Mo's corpus additionally lacked the quality to entice scholars to study or propagate his ideas. Academics claimed his writings were as short on wit and beauty of expression as they were deficient in imagery and vividness. Some literati regarded them repetitive, without authoritative force, and lacking in subtlety. In the practical realm of social action, however, Mo Ti's disciples went about doing good and selflessly helping people in need, often at personal cost. Though few, his followers' dedication gained admiration and sympathy. This promised to increase Mo's repute among the populace and so helped make Mohism subversive. Limited popularity notwithstanding, Mo Ti's emphasis on universal love radically challenged Confucianism. The orthodox imagined that his doctrine undermined native values. In fact, Mencius, the best-known disciple of Confucius, regarded Mohism serious ideological competition. The fear that Mo's ideas might undermine the foundations of Chinese society induced claims that Mo Ti did more than simply oppose Confucian teachings. Mencius, in fact, considered Mo Ti's stress on universal love a revolutionary peril. He claimed that Mo's ideal of universal affection threatened to abolish the weight of fatherhood and the rule of hierarchy. Universal love, he averred, would destroy China's polity.

Of course Confucianism expected people to love and respect each other, too. The weight of love and respect depended, however, solely on one's station in the polity. The father or ruler stood at the apex of the status pyramid, and so he commanded the deepest love and the most respect. The more distant from the family circle or national scene, the less necessary to show concern of any kind. Mo Ti's advocacy of a universal, horizontal ethic—antedating Christ's parable of the Good Samaritan (*Luke* 10:30 ff.)—rejected this obviously particularistic, vertical ethic. The two ideologies mixed as well as oil and water, absolutism and democracy. Despite many modern features, Japanese society remains largely under the dominion of Confucian emphases on hierarchy and a vertical or particularized regard for others. This makes Mushakôji's tireless advocacy of selfless, democratic love as potentially revolutionary as Mo Ti's. Stressing an all-embracing, beneficient love displayed equally toward "the sisters and the brothers" consists, at the very least, of a covert attack on Japan's intrinsically paternalistic Confucian order. Small wonder his countrymen did not flock to support the New Village movement.

Neither Japanese nor English can match classical Greek in expressing the nuances of love, particularly its spiritual aspects. To reiterate, Mushakôji had at his disposal only the word *ai*. The non-Christian English writer may be limited to altruism. Labels aside, texts that describe how Mushakôji exhorts people to show love • *ai* make better sense if read against the meaning of *agapé* and its ethical dimensions of charity, liberality, and acceptance of others—even if they differ from you. Mushakôji believed that people who act in the *agapé* way will "inherit the kingdom of God"; cf. pages 246 and 269. Love is one key to what he means when he claims he wants to qualify to enter that kingdom. He had in mind no "Elysian fields" that one reaches after death. Rather, he envisioned an Eden that we can create in the here and now; cf. page 28. In that earthly paradise, people will love each other, gladly work together, praise one another, and accept differences.

WORK

ORK ALONE

Work alone is my master.
Work does not exist for me.
I exist for my work.

FOUNDATION

A solid foundation has been laid.
Now let's build a family where,
since each member will be self-reliant,
all will cooperate with each other.
Beauty, love,
and truth
will thrive in this family.
It will likewise nurture each member
as an individualist who can say,
"I won't do what I don't want to do!"
If your response has grounds, no problem.
If it has no grounds, however,
suit yourself
—— you're not one of our kin.

PEOPLE OF THE PAST

Hear us, people of the past:
We are pleased
to make the most of your toil
—— the crystallized labors
you've left on Earth for us.
You lived successfully
through trying times.
You finished many tasks for us
on Earth
—— deeds one cannot accomplish overnight.
We renew our gratitude to you.
We do not intend to let your pains, your blood,
your toil, and love
fade meaninglessly away.

WE

We will bequeath
to people of the future
what we've received from people of the past.
We'll augment it with our spirit and our sweat.
We hope to enhance it as much as we can.

PEOPLE OF THE FUTURE *

– 1 –

Listen, people of the future,
you of all humankind will live the way humans should.
You'll not repeat our follies
but live happily.
You'll work
so that all may rejoice.

– 2 –

People of the future,
you will harvest what we've sown.
We'd like to use the best possible seed
and sow as much as we can.
Harvest it joyfully for us.

– 3 –

People of the future,
we don't think of you as strangers.
You alone
will complete great tasks for us
on Earth.
Work for the glory of humanity.
Rejoice in being human
—— you people
of the future!

PEOPLE COMPELLED TO WORK

I praise
people who feel compelled to work.

I praise
those who hope for the happiness of others. •

I praise
those superior in some art or craft.

I praise
the sagacious.

I praise
the saint.

Blessed are all
who earn my praise.

WHEN I'M WRITING POETRY *

When I'm writing poetry,
Shinko comes
crawling along the *engawa*.
She looks at me and smiles.
She sits on the threshold
banging it,
looks up at me, and laughs.
"What a darling!
I pray for your happiness."

DOING MY WORK

It's quite a trial
doing my work.
Since it's more fun
frolicking with Shinko,
I end up playing with her.
I get anxious about my work, however,
so I can't spend all my time in play.
Look after her for me.
When I finish my work
I'll return.
Somewhere in my heart lurks the desire
to play all day with Shinko.

IF THEY DON'T WORK

If they don't work,
farmers know very well
that they cannot eat.
City folks think

they can't eat
if they have no money.
If you don't work you're not to eat
—— how much like something
the owner of a factory might say.
And how typical of a religious person to claim,
"Of course you'll have food on your table
if you pray."

SEEK THE KINGDOM OF GOD *

Seek the kingdom of God
and of course you'll have food on your table.
That's the truth.
Truly seek the kingdom of God.
Work earnestly so you can inherit that kingdom.

OTHERS' SENSE OF INDEPENDENCE

Refrain from infringing on the independence of others
    and offer help when you can.
This I take to be the foundation
    of the new morality.
A clear understanding of this simple principle enables me
    to maintain my private views.

WORK

Most people work for pay.
I truly crave money, too,
but nonetheless prefer jobs that pay nothing
to jobs that pay.
Even if I'm told I'll be paid enough
for such-and-such an assignment,
I want neither to misrepresent myself
nor to sell myself short.

It would be another matter if I couldn't support myself,
and a different issue if I couldn't feed my children.
Otherwise, I always prefer jobs where I take no pay but do not betray my self
to jobs that pay but force self-deception.
It's distressing when debts accumulate,
and I fail to discharge my responsibilities.
Selling my integrity, however,
distresses me more.

AGED TOILERS

Many aged toilers are beautiful people.
They're alive. Their faces record the history of their striving.
Theirs are not spiritual faces but faces with substance.
The face of the toiler contrasts with that of the stockbroker.
A life of emptiness produces an empty face.

THE CANARY THAT FORGOT ITS SONG

The canary that forgot its song
wanted to sing.
Although he kept trying,
he simply couldn't make a peep.

Then one night
the canary had a sound rest.
A lovely dawn broke.
He naturally
raised his voice
and began to sing.

"Oh, I forgot my song," he said.
"That's right, but I wasn't aware at the moment
that I had."

WHEN YOU WANT TO DO TWO THINGS AT ONCE

I can't settle down
when I want to do two things at once.
Whoever conscientiously executes a single task is wise.

I can't settle down
when I want to do something I'm incapable of doing.
Whoever persistently works
within his capabilities is wise.

I can't settle down
when I come up with presumptuous hopes.
Whoever does what he should
and entrusts the rest to others is wise.

THE JOY OF WORK

Whenever I feel energetic, I'm in the mood to work.
When I want to work so much I can't contain myself,
I feel even more energized.
Energy wells up within
and drives my work.
Yes, I burst with energy
because I always feel like working.

When I get up in the morning,
I'm anxious to work on my manuscripts.
I feel like writing something
beyond my assignment.
When I tire of the manuscript,
I take a walk.
Then I feel like painting a picture.
I'm delighted to be doing something.
I somehow can't relax
if I have nothing to do.

Throughout my life I've been busy at work.
I don't know if what I've done
will amount to anything.
I'm simply delighted
to work
single-mindedly.

Vigor wells up in me,
and I become more and more charged with energy,
more and more fervent.
Under my gaze,
the lines I paint
increasingly take on life.

Energy from within,
energy from without.
They coexist
elbow to elbow.
I exist.
The other exists.
We exist together.
I find joy in that.

I work
wholeheartedly.
Sentence by sentence
I write wholeheartedly.

I paint lines
wholeheartedly.
I do my calligraphy
wholeheartedly.
I awake each day in high spirits,
anxious to work at these tasks.
—— What joy in being able to work
with the whole heart.

SESSHÛ'S *THUNDERBOLTS* *

The four celestial gods
make an all-out, concerted attack
on an earthly traveler.
The traveler,
however desperate,
does not give in.
He energetically walks on, step by step
—— his entire being focused.

"Just a moment more,"
said Lightning,
encouraging them all.
Thunder was engrossed in beating his drums.
Wind emptied on the traveler
his entire sack of gusts.
The Rain Dragon, too, was dauntless.
But the traveler would not submit.

Lightning had said,
"Just a moment more,"
but the traveler's stalwart presence
apparently fascinated her.
"Perhaps," she supposed,
"this fellow is authentic.
I'll try him out,"
she thought,
"I'll temper him."

The traveler knew nothing of her resolve, but he would not yield.
He was truly a stouthearted fellow.
Courage increasingly welled up in him, and he said,
"I'm never ever giving in!"
This man's name was Sesshû.
He was sixty-seven then.

THE MORE I PAINT

I rejoice when the more I paint
the more the beauty of the object I'm painting begins to glow.
As I paint, however,
I lose my grasp on the object's beauty.
When my hand alone is active I feel a sense of isolation.
I pull myself together and observe the object,
but by then I'm weary
and lack a fresh sense of its beauty.
I toss aside my brush and collapse.
Then I timidly get up.

The world is replete with things of beauty.
The world is replete with animated things.
They're fresh, unadulterated, intensely vital.
I'd like to paint them just as they are,
but I soon grow weary and lose my sense of freshness.
Indeed, my brush cannot paint what my eyes observe.
I deserve the death sentence,
but how might death overcome my lack of talent?
Oh, whatever shall I do with myself?

Day in and day out I paint tenaciously,
from morning to night,
so I think I should be getting slightly better at it.
The simple truth, however, is that I'm not.
I have the sense that my true self appears
at those moments when I just can't manage.
I'm second to none in falling down,
and also second to none
in scratching my way back up.
Whatever anyone says,
I'll walk my own path.

I plod along my far-off path.
I plod along patiently.
I have no choice but to move ahead.
One day I'll near my goal.

Where an artist ruins three pictures,
I ruin a hundred.
But I ruin three hundred pictures
in the time that others ruin three,
so for me the process becomes
three times as instructive as it is for them.

I don't know what others aim for,

but I aim for what will let me perfectly realize my self.
Absolutely becoming myself in whatever I paint
will fully realize my fundamental self, such as it is.
Perhaps that's impossible.
I'll show as well as I can, however, how to achieve this ideal.

A HEMP PALM *

I see a huge hemp palm
whenever I open the *shôji*
in front of the desk on which I do my writing.
Full of life, it stretches its fronds to their limit.
The tree produces sturdy,
unbending fronds.
They look truly vigorous.
Four or five years ago
the palm wasn't even visible,
but over the last three or four years it flourished,
grew rapidly to its present size,
and produced those sturdy fronds.
I wonder how the tree focuses
so much vigor
on such a small piece of soil.
Potent verve, indeed.
Unrelenting vigor!
Several years ago,
I had no idea a hemp palm would be growing
in such a place.
Once I realized it was there,
the tree amazed me.
Four or five years later,
the hemp palm had matured resolutely and robustly
into a large tree.
What animated growth!
It's alive.
The more I wonder how it manages this much vitality
on such a scanty piece of ground,
the more splendidly it sprouts its buds.
It has proudly grown into a tree so large
that transplanting might be quite a task.
"How about me —— I'm alive!"
I, too, think you truly are alive.
I admire you.

MY DESK *

When I was fifty-one
my brother in Berlin invited me to visit.
I therefore left for Europe and America.
After an eight-month journey,
I returned to Japan.
In those days I was renting a house
near Inokashira Park.
One day a stranger came by
and asked if I wouldn't like to buy two ancient figurines:
one a squatting Shintô deity, the other a standing Buddha.
I found them so appealing
I decided to purchase them on the spot.
Some days later
the same fellow returned with a small, black, antique desk.
He said he hauled it over
because I'd so agreeably bought the two figurines from him.
The moment I saw the desk I liked it, so I accepted his gift
and made it the site for writing my manuscripts.
It's truly a diminutive table,
but it pleases me.
Ever since then I've used it for writing manuscripts.
I'm more and more satisfied with it,
and bit by bit I've been thinking
there is no better writing table than this.
It's actually a nondescript little desk,
but it appeals to me.
Other desks do not.
Long ago, I suppose somebody donated this common desk to some temple.
It hasn't a single embellishment,
which truly pleases me.
I'm delighted with this desk.
I've been working at it now
for more than thirty-five years.
I'll never tire of its appeal.

DESK and COT

I set up a cot next to my desk.
When I'm weary
I immediately stretch out on it.
The moment I waken
I'm back at my desk.
I find joy in that.
Men are animals
fond of finishing tasks.

ON MY DESK *

When I see a yellow rose on my desk,
I feel more like painting a picture
than writing a story.
I like being composed and depicting what's before me
rather than straining to paint something that isn't there.
But let me tell you my fondest hope:
it's to move for two or three years to a mountain
and to grapple with it as I paint.
If I could do that, I'd naturally devote full time to my grappling.
I'd like to try wrestling with that mountain
till I drop.
Though exhausted and dejected,
I want to grapple endlessly with my adversary,
according him every respect.

AN OLD PAINTER

I'm an old man now.
Some five or six years ago
I gave up painting in oils.
I thought I'd aged
and figured that painting in oil
might be too taxing.
These days, however,
though I'm far too old for it,
I somehow want to try
using oils again.
Could I manage a more tranquil frame of mind?
I'm in the mood now where I want to paint leisurely in oils,
slowly and without haste.
Being in a tranquil mood
makes me imagine that I could focus on a single work.
I sense that I'll neither spoil my painting
nor feel rushed.
I might, in fact, concentrate on this work
till I finish it.
I now feel no need for haste.
I imagine I can remain calm
until I complete the work.

I no longer have the sense that I might die
while I'm at the easel.
I want now to work
with composure.
I want to work with a tranquil mind

free of haste.
It's not that I'm giving up some tasks because I can't do them,
but that I now sense I can paint in oil and still be tranquil.
In any event, I'll work calmly.
I suspect that's appropriate for an old man.
I'm interested now in working
without a sense of haste,
settling myself down,
remaining oblivious to time.

I've become quite old.
The older I get
the more I want to work with a tranquil mind.

I do my work
leisurely and calmly
without losing self-control.

With an attitude like that,
an old person
can apparently work serenely.

I've turned eighty-six.
It should be all right at that age to be hurried,
but I do my work
with greater and greater calm
without feeling harried.

I work
with a tranquil mind.

I'm an old man.
The older I get
the more serenely I want to work.

An old man
can do the work of an old man.
Even his mood becomes composed.
A person of ninety
can do work
befitting a person of ninety.
That's how I've come to feel.
Little by little I've become an old person.
Remaining composed,
I do work appropriate to my age.

I'm an old man.
I want to do work

seemly for an old man,
remaining composed
and working within my capacities.
I sense
that I can manage it.

I want to go on working casually,
remaining calm,
having both the mood of a young person
and the mood of an old man.
An old man
—— I surely am an old man,
so I want to go on working casually,
remaining calm.

Oblivious to how old I am,
whether I turn ninety
or turn one hundred,
I'll forget about age
and think
I'd like to do my work
with the sense that I'll live forever.
In practice, I'd like to pay no attention to my years
and be carefree about my painting.
I don't figure on dying soon,
but I casually put such things out of mind
and feel I'd like to continue
doing my work in a leisurely way.
In practice, I want to paint in oils,
heedless of age.
I have the notion
that oil paintings are heedless of age.
I'd like to paint them forever.

WITHIN ME

The life, the powers, the manhood
within me
desire to work at something.
Is there no other work for me
than to take up my pen?
Is there no other job that enables me
straightforwardly
to make the most of my talents?
I don't think there is,
and so I again take up my pen.

REVOLUTIONARY

I dislike the life of a revolutionary.
I like the lives of people
who move steadily ahead to finish their work.

A GOOD SCRIPT

Of course I'd like to turn out a good script,
but I haven't managed to come across appealing material.
If I find something that beguiles me,
and if I can get everything into the script that wants to come out of me,
the result should be quite good.
But, well, until I run into something fascinating
    that I want to write up,
I'm not sure what to write.
Nuts to doing a script!
It's far better to do nothing but look at a picture
and be leisurely self-possessed.
Deadlines . . . contracts . . . whatever —— nuts to them.
I'll savor my indolence with dignity.

AN ANGLER'S SOLILOQUY *

Light —— sparkling is enough!
Flowers —— blooming beautifully will do!
A destiny of talent is given to the talented.
Only a great man, moreover,
can reel in a great destiny.
I bide my time. I'm waiting for something.
I do not, however, simply bide my time.
Nor do I merely fish.
Only a *compleat angler*
can reel the world in.
However much they gad about,
fools can only hook what is foolish.
Those who bemoan their bad luck
are for the most blind to their lack of talent.
Those prodigal with talent bide their time. They harvest time.
They do not merely bide their time. They nourish their talents as they wait.
However small,
I make whatever takes my hook my own.
That is, however, not the totality of my toil.
    It's one small stone in the creation of a greater work.
Those ignorant of how to build a massive castle
leave the smallest stones untouched.

They know neither how to nourish their talent
nor how to enhance their personal worth.
Angling idly, they idly exult in their big catch.
See! Even when I do not fish, I overlook no opportunity
    to nurture my endowments.
I fashion them to reel in a lofty fate.
When fate bites, I'll not be so stupid as to let it off the hook.
Nor do I act like a fool drowning in fate.
No one can reel in the clouds till one becomes a dragon.
Nor can one do it if one isn't yet a dragon.
I'm becoming a dragon. I shall summon the clouds, I shall summon fate.
If the clouds do not come when called,
the caller's to blame.
That's my belief.
Even if people ridicule me for living this way,
I'll not curse my fate.
I'll condemn only my lack of talent.
There's a cruel fate against which a man is powerless.
    Should I meet that fate and die, I'll have no complaints.
I'll merely develop my gifts.
I'll just nurture my gifts to reel in a lofty fate and grasp it firmly.
I'll be satisfied with that.

A STROKE OF LUCK

When I was young,
I awaited a stroke of luck.
As long as I waited for luck to come, however,
it simply refused to materialize.
Good luck comes
unexpectedly
when one puts it out of mind.
Still, even if I try
I can't entirely ignore it.
I'd like to do my work
faithfully
without expecting "a stroke of luck."
Luck just doesn't happen.
I can, however, do my work faithfully.
As I matured,
I came to think that working faithfully
is actually the best possible stroke of luck.

THE SEEDS I SOWED

When the sower lamented,
"The seeds I sowed never sprouted,"
something puny at his feet said,
"We're coming up.
We'll mature when you're dead
and sow seeds throughout the world."
The puny one had spoken.

THE GIVER *

Givers receive the most.
Observe the sun. He gives the most.
He receives because he cannot help receiving,
and he gives because he cannot help giving.
If only he can be himself,
things will rush to him,
become a part of him,
plunge into his inner self.
They will then shine with him.
He can't help shining.
He can't help giving.
If only he can be himself,
he gives the energy of life to everything
from our vast planet to a tiny poppy seed.

Was he born to receive
or born to give?
He need only be himself.
The will of nature is to give him what should be given
and to take from him what should be taken.
Is the aim to give
or to receive?
Are both the same
or does one embody the other?
He alone is the ideal giver,
the ideal receiver.
He alone is the source of everything that lives.
But he has only to be himself.
Never a thought of giving,
never a thought of receiving,
his life
is to give life to everything.
He is sun —— the epitome of life.

IN THIS WORLD

There are all kinds of people in this world.
There are those who can do things I cannot.
There are those who gladly take on tasks
I do not wish to do.
How delightful.
How welcome.

I'm glad there are all kinds of people in this world.
Through their cooperation
we can live with our minds at ease,
and I can concentrate solely on my work.

I'd like to move on and discharge my responsibilities in a commendable way
by faithfully carrying out my private duties.
If I can do that, I'll be able to stand before everyone
as a splendidly accountable adult without feeling useless.

THREE COOKS

There were three cooks at my place.
I gave all three the same ingredients and told them
to make me as delectable a dish as possible.
The first cook looked dissatisfied and said,
"I can't make a savory dish with such niggardly ingredients.
If you want to eat something tasty,
please give me better ingredients. I need the ingredients . . . ."
The second cook accepted the ingredients without a word,
cooked a dish, and presently returned with it.
I ate it but couldn't say it was first rate. The third cook
      looked at the ingredients and said,
"I'm not capable of getting the most of these excellent ingredients,
      but I'll do what I can."
What he made for me was truly delectable.
When I complimented him, he said,
"I've a long way to go. Next time I make this dish,
      I think I'll be able to exploit the ingredients more effectively."

Having been given the same human life,
some complain,
some are nonchalant about their tasks,
and some make the most of what they have.
If, indeed, we all are born and all die,
I'd prefer that we get as much as possible
out of whatever we've received.

THE SONG OF A MOUNTAINEER *

– 1 –

I break away
from my companions,
who are weaker climbers,
and scale the mountain alone.
This is the lonely way,
but I find joy in it.
My energies naturally seethe.
And yet it is lonely.

– 2 –

At last someone comes to climb with me.
What joy.
Before long, however,
he leaves
and joins another group along the way.
I'm by myself again
and lonely,
though I do walk my own path.

– 3 –

As I stroll through the forest,
flower sprites appear from nowhere
and walk with me.
When I get thirsty, they fetch water for me.
When I feel hungry,
they bring me fruit.
When I feel like talking with someone,
they talk with me.
When I pause and want to flirt with them,
they're glad to indulge me.
How buoyant they make me feel.
The fearful forest is no longer fearful,
the lonely forest no longer lonely,
the long path no longer long.
I lose track of time, of space,
and happily sing songs of joy
as I climb on
. . . then before I know it
I'm at the edge of the forest.
The flower sprites have gone off,
and I feel lonely and wretched enough to weep.
But there's no one here to comfort me,
no one to dry my tears.

Though I'm thirsty,
there's no one to bring me water.
Though hungry,
I must fetch the fruit myself.
Nor is there anyone to eat with me.
I feel like returning to the forest,
and yet I must push on
by myself.
My life demands it,
time demands it.
There's no choice for me but to walk on
alone.

For the Mountain Climber

A man who loves mountains,
a man who dreams of mountains,
today again climbs a mountain.

He enjoys climbing mountains.
Whatever he thinks of,
whatever he feels
whatever he sees
—— fulfills his life
and he seethes with vigor.

The peak is far off
and he doesn't know
when he'll finish his climb.
His legs are weary
but he looks back.
"I've come farther than I thought!"
Silently he continues his climb.

I'm a Worker

I'm a worker.
I'll work till I die.
I'm a worker,
for no one can exist who doesn't work.
I'm a worker grateful to have been granted good health.
I work to my physical limits.
I like enjoying life's pleasures,
but I'll take what I'm provided
only when I've done what I should.
I'd feel ashamed
to pilfer these pleasures. •

I'm a worker
who honors God and humankind,
who moreover honors those one ought to honor.
Some say labor is painful,
but there is assuredly great joy
in work.
When we're spent, let's rest.
When we recover, let's get back to work.
If labor is an agony, let's at least work so we won't
        unduly inconvenience our brothers and sisters.
We'll also work for brothers and sisters
who are weak or sick.
And we'll work for those who ponder problems and do research for us.
We'll show that people can work without being compelled.
That will demonstrate our pride in being human.

I'm a worker.
I'm the ally of those who work.
In every sense I side with people
who've discovered how to serve our brothers and sisters
and who practice their discovery.
I can't associate with
the excessively lazy,
with those who encourage indolence,
or with those who esteem pleasure over truth.
They have no respect for their brothers and sisters.
But we'd better not be too rigorous.
It's best not to become enslaved to work.
We'll do the work we must
as independent human beings.
We'll work to keep from over-burdening others.
When we enjoy our leisure, we'll do it with the brothers and sisters.
To compensate for not feeling ashamed that I lack
both the ability and the wisdom to accomplish everything,
I do my work and then commit to others whatever tasks remain.
We'll honor those who contribute to the joys and liberties
        of our brothers and sisters.
We'll honor those who promote human values,
but we can't associate with any who neglect their work
for indolence and pleasure.

Brothers! Sisters!
Let's stand and renew our determination.
Let's not give those who hope for our defeat a cause to celebrate.
Pay no attention to those who hope to rejoice over
and exploit our defects.
We'll be wary, too, of those who want to diminish our unity.
Only our foes honor those who degrade diligence, love, and health.

Those who sully our autonomy are the enemy.
It's best to renew our resolve each day.
Our work will not be done
until justice and love rule every human being.
Let's work calmly and with perseverance.

We must become toilers for God,
toilers for humanity,
the pillars of a just society,
the bedrock of an impartial polity.
We must prepare ourselves always to stand
tirelessly and with determination
for what we believe.

We will work.
We must tarnish neither the honor of our ancestors
nor the honor of the human being.
A true human shows that he can live admirably
        without being dominated by others, and also
        that he can find true joy in living that way.
Show how joyous you are to be born a human.
Demonstrate it through your toil, your love, your wisdom,
        your justice, and your stamina.
Brothers and sisters,
we have a solemn mission.

AT THE WORKSHOP

Even when I toil at the workshop,
I want
the time and the space
to romp in the mud.
I'm a New Village toiler.

SLAVES OF TOIL

Many are slaves of toil.
When they win their freedom from it, many no longer wish to work.
No one in that state can possibly be freed of toil.
It's necessary for us to toil voluntarily.
Those who wish to make all people free
must first master toil.
Those who can toil without being compelled by hunger or violence
are fit to live in freedom's realm.

Toil (i)

However you look at it, toil is not easy.
Yet it's far more stressful not to work.
Let's summon the courage and engage in toil.
Praiseworthily, I accomplished another day of work!
I'm a commendably independent person
who like a warrior
relishes his sense of pride.

Toil (ii)

By conquering toil,
we humans
become its masters.

In concert

We can work in concert.
Though we've been at it less than a year,
we nevertheless know the joys of working together.

Fire from a single match

Fire from just a single match
is capable of kindling everything flammable in the world.
It's simply a matter of brothers and sisters the world over
becoming earnest and working together.

The talented

Let me praise everyone with talent.
You have on our behalf
given our society
beauty
and energy
in every possible form.
You are human
like us
and can work
on our behalf,
giving life to and awakening
our potentials.
You are us,
not strangers.

You give life
in every conceivable form
to whatever we would enliven.
I praise everyone with talent.

LUTHER BURBANK *

Luther Burbank
—— a contemporary I most esteem.
Though I don't know much about you,
seeing the smallest news item
that merely mentions your name
fills me with genuine respect.
Indeed, it's been our hope
that a person like you might come forth.
How beneficial for creating a new world
that a man like you
has appeared.
We'd like to have a person like you in Japan, too.
What a joy if you lived in our New Village!
Stories of the trees and plants you managed
through your labors
to produce on Earth
are indeed beautiful tales that brim with hope.
The beauty,
the splendor of your work
—— laboriously discovering, laboriously breeding, laboriously reproducing
trees and plants most beneficial to us all.
Each time I hear about you,
I feel I'd like to have our New Village share your discoveries.
That time, however, has yet to come.
I hope it will come soon.
Luther Burbank,
I glorify you
as an extraordinary exemplar of humanity,
a genius at producing plants for us.

I'M A STANDARD-BEARER

I'm a standard-bearer.
The fact of the matter is
I haven't the slightest ability.
I merely tell people:
Work together.
Get serious.
Aim for goals

throughout your life.
Do work that benefits humanity.
Walk the path you've the most confidence in.
You earn your liberty
only after discharging your responsibilities.
Work sincerely at self-improvement.
Make the most of yourself
so your brothers and sisters can do the same.
This is not an impossible task.
You'll find life's greatest joy
and greatest pride
in doing it.
So then, brothers and sisters,
let's work together for all people.
Together let's make the most of ourselves.
I say that with confidence
—— and at times
I pick up a hoe.

YOUR WORK

Your work
will be accomplished
only after you assimilate all the building skills
of every last person, of every single member of humanity.
Human beings give you life.
The entire history of humankind,
and every single expended human effort, gives you life.
These will beget you in this age
—— that gives you the advantage.
You are now
extremely small,
but I'm not perturbed
because I know the energies that begot you.
I believe your future
will be blessed.

A NEW YEAR

A new year comes
with new resolutions,
new hopes.

We hope it will be a good year,
but reality by no means conforms to our hopes.
We nonetheless persist

more tenaciously than fate
in wishing for a year of good fortune.

During our lives,
we advance step by step toward our goals,
never abandoning hope.

Working day after day,
our labors add up.
We hope to demonstrate gradual progress this year, too.
The new year brings fresh hope!

SIX SONGS OF WORK

– 1 –

Today again we gallantly discharged
our assignments.
Well, now, brothers and sisters,
set your minds at ease and savor your liberty.

– 2 –

Then, brothers and sisters,
we'll work courageously again
tomorrow.

– 3 –

We know the joy
of having carried out our assignments.
We can't help
but work.

– 4 –

Once we work voluntarily
and do what must be done,
our liberties will welcome us
as everyday fighters:
those who win their daily skirmishes,
those victorious in combat.
We warriors return triumphant
and enter the hall of liberties
with a sense of relief.
Our liberties then will welcome us
to a feast of joy.
"This is your banquet.
You are the special guests.

You work each day,
so you're welcome each day.
It's our job
to serve you."
Blessed are those
willing to work.

– 5 –

We work.
We work without being forced to.
We work indifferent to money.
We work to discharge our assignments.
We work for our brothers.
We work for humanity.
We work though it's arduous.
We work willingly.
We work self-reliantly.
We work out of pride in being human.
There's joy in work,
and so we work.

– 6 –

We do not sacrifice ourselves.
We work to make the most of ourselves.
We also work to eat.
We work, too, to clothe ourselves.
We work as well to have a roof over our heads.
We work to make a living
as much as to stay alive.
We work both for our brothers
and to realize our individuality.
We do not overwork.
Not only do we acquire liberty,
we remain studious.
We become people who are not only effective but just.
We live as human beings should.
People must make it their highest, their singular aim
to live as we do.
That's how we exist.

THINGS I CANNOT DO

How praiseworthy
are those
who do well what I cannot
and who have virtues I do not possess.

At the same time,
I respect those
who've made their qualities
ever more beautiful.
Having such people nearby
makes living
a joy.

WRITE · CULTIVATE THE LAND

Every day
I write, cultivate the land, read,
anticipate . . . .

DAILY RENEWAL

Daily renewal.
Daily resolve.
Daily ardor.
Daily study.
Daily growth.

WHEN I'M WORKING *

When I'm working
I want to look at the baby.
When I see the baby,
I want to pick her up.
She gives me that inviting smile of hers,
and I end up holding her.
When I hold her,
I once again feel like working.
Work and the baby
—— double masters.
How well they engage me.

WHEN HE WORKS

When he works
he truly works.
When he relaxes,
he truly relaxes.
I like the sort of man
who is both composed
and steady.

MY VISIONS

When I'm old
I'll gather children round me
and tell them fairy tales.

I'll create the kind of town I want
and put on plays
in its theater,
personally looking after the details.

I'll go to the factory, too,
and help everyone with their work.

I'll welcome brothers and sisters
visiting from abroad
and put on a party for them.

When we become
old men and old women,
we'll tell tales of days gone by.

I'll perfect
my art
and write up my last testament
for posterity.

I'll walk about teary eyed,
always giving thanks to all.
Wherever I look,
I'll think of everyone as my brother, as my sister.

I'll climb a high mountain and say,
"Observe the work of our brothers and sisters.
This is how people can conduct their lives."

The beauty of the town
—— early in the morning
I'll trudge up the hill and kneel
with a sense of gratitude.

I'll visit old friends
and ply them with my boasts.

I'll visit animals far-off
or nearby
and feed them. •

I'll die peacefully
obliged to wife, sisters, brothers . . . .
"Thank you all."

A WORLD OF COOPERATION

A world of cooperation
——— a world where everyone works together
to create a new society
——— a world where everyone comes together
and cooperates.

A world where ten, twenty, thirty thousand,
where ten thousand, where a million
come together and cooperate
——— a world that creates what's new.

A world that honors the will of all,
that esteems human life,
where the free will of every individual exists,
and where one can realize his mission and fulfill God's will.

If more of this world's cherished children
can get together and work together,
they'll create a new society:
a realm of independence and cooperation.

A realm of cooperation, cooperation, cooperation
——— a place where the strengths of all are focused
on producing a new society.
A realm where people work together,
where there is no need to push others aside.

A realm of cooperation where,
in the endless growth of our New Village,
a realm of cooperation will endlessly mature.
There self-reliant people
will appear
and live without a care.

IN HYÛGA'S HILLS *

We who live and work in Hyûga's hills
are full of vitality
and considerate of every brother and sister.
I want to work energetically,
second to none
——— proud of my humanity.

THIS MISSION

If we accepted this mission
hoping for fame,
it will crumble when people speak ill of us.
If we began this mission relying on money,
it will crumble when there are no funds.
If we launched this mission depending on others,
it will crumble when they desert us.
But this mission is rooted in the sincerity of humankind.
As long as sincerity survives,
our mission will thrive.

THE NEW VILLAGE (i) *

If the New Village does not grow,
it will disgrace our humanity.
That's why it will work.

THE NEW VILLAGE (ii) *

The New Village
is an assembly of those who wish to live like humans.
Those with that firm hope
must give birth to the New Village from within.
If you haven't the strength to do it now, await the proper time.
If only you're devoted,
you'll certainly be able to give it life.
A decade of patience.

THE NEW VILLAGE (v) *

New Village!
You must become the most civilized of villages, the most spiritual, and physically the best-equipped community that exists.
You must at once know your responsibilities and be attentive to your rights.
You must at once work for all people and make the most of the individual.
You must supply the most constructive model for human living.
You must illustrate through your living how humans ought to exist and how they ought to cooperate.
You must respect the person and individuality of every human being.
Ignore those fools who label the way you live "a life of seclusion."
You must aim to make the most of every jewel humanity has acquired.
You must be obedient to God. You must build your Tower of Babel using every shred of wisdom this world has ever acquired.
Our village may not be a sphere of luxury, but it must be a place where nobody

deliberately causes others to suffer.
All those living among you must be your beloved children.
All of you are now still young and maturing.
You're still small in numbers, weak but receptive.
And yet you have the proper goals.
May you all move ahead toward those goals and transform our village into a most civilized, most humane, wholesome, and joyous place.
You in the New Village, hear!

THE NEW VILLAGE (vi) *

The New Village
will grow despite having money.
It will grow without it.

If all it has is money, however, it will not grow.
Nor will it necessarily grow if it has none.

It will grow only
with earnestness.

THE NEW VILLAGE (vii) *

I'd like our New Village to be beautiful.
I'd like its beauty to materialize, however, without spending money.
    I don't want to create the kind of place people can build
    if only they have the money.
I don't want to create a village you can't make beautiful
    unless you hire outsiders. I'd like to beautify the village
    with the teamwork of our brothers.

FROM THE NEW VILLAGE

Good people,
energetic people,
those with strong growth potential
and earnestness
gather here.
They're giving birth to something.
It's gestating now . . . .

THE VILLAGE AIR

Something
in the village air
wasn't completely assimilated.
It has been now.
The village's digestive organs have become sound.
Our village will now
singularly
come to life.

ALWAYS IN THE VILLAGE

In the village we always had
a branch
that couldn't survive.
Once that limb was gone,
the vitality of the village
revived
from one end to the other.
People with resolve
have gathered here.
Rejoice,
rejoice!
They have harmonized with the spirit of the village.
We've created a community
that openly accepts every resolve
of any individual determined to live
in conformity with the spirit of the village.
Rejoice,
rejoice!
Renew your resolve
and rejoice.
Rejoice!

AT THE NEW VILLAGE

－ 1 －

I'd like us to be
a diligent,
modest,
and peaceful people.
This morning I think
I could be satisfied with that
. . . this bright morning.

– 2 –

A citizen at peace,
I possess the tranquil joys of daily life.
Somewhere in my heart I want to be a person
who works hard at his daily tasks.

– 3 –

Bit by bit I'm becoming a rustic.
I can't think that the profusion of people concentrated in the city is beneficial.

SOME DOZEN OF US

Some dozen of us
walk along a midsummer forest path.
Men and women. Some talking. Some silent.
Some walking fast. Some walking slow.
Each thinking his or her private thoughts.
We head, however, toward the same goal.
We now move toward a village
to the east.

THE VILLAGE DOCTOR

You study
with the dream of becoming
our village doctor.
I hope you'll be a good physician
and sustain the lives
of the beloved brothers and sisters in our community.
I believe that
your serving our village
will redound to your honor,
give you satisfaction,
and bring both renown and joy
to our community.
Do your best!
We'll be truly grateful
if you become the delight
of people around the village.

TWENTY-FIVE YEARS OF THE NEW VILLAGE *

November 14 marks exactly twenty-five years since the birth of the New Village.
Though still excessively immature,
it apparently has taken on certain adult characteristics.
Evidently it's developed some vigor.
From now on everyone can presumably get to work.
Our brothers and sisters look to be active
in every phase of village life.
I was thirty-four at its birth
and now I'm fifty-nine.
Here we greet the joyous 25th anniversary of the village,
loving, being loved by the brothers and sisters.
Many incidents occurred over these years,
but this much is clear:
year by year we've grown.
Perhaps we've grown too slowly.
Even so, we'd like to show we've become a tall tree.
We move ahead ever more filled with hope.
Intent on our goals, we travel various paths,
moving always and ever onward.
Long live the New Village! Long live our brothers and sisters!

THE NEW VILLAGE GREETS ITS FORTIETH YEAR *

The blood of the ancestors in our veins,
the blood of humankind in our veins,
the blood of the Maker . . . .

A world where everything can exist,
where there is no need to mistreat one another
—— even though it now seems an impossibility,
we move ahead,
driven by an irrepressible power,
until we arrive at that world.

A realm where I exist,
where you exist,
where all people exist
—— a realm where we are all friendly,
where we can praise one another.

A world where the Earth is boundlessly beautiful,
where people rejoice in true peace,
where we can boundlessly love and respect each other,
where one cannot help but rejoice.
One day that world will come about.

We move ahead with that in our sights.
Rejecting other people pains one's conscience.
Both sides can exist in a realm
where people love each other,
in a domain of boundless beauty.
We move ahead with that world in our sights.
Indeed, *Hurrah for the human race!*

SUNFLOWERS IN OUR VILLAGE *

Sunflowers that Van Gogh adored.
Sunflowers fully worth Van Gogh's adoration.
Not only Van Gogh's
but all people's adoration.
It makes sense to love sunflowers.
Whenever I see them,
I, too, am amazed by their splendor.
Is there another flower like it?

Sunflowers bloom in the New Village.
Brothers Arai and Watanabe Kanji
brought them here.
I was so thrilled I painted them.
I didn't do a very good job,
but the village brothers told me they wanted to use the painting
    on the cover of the 100th issue of *This Path.*
I gladly agreed.

GROWTH POTENTIAL

Colleagues with great growth potential
who fear nothing whatsoever
and who simply go on growing
are pioneers who open up
new paths in this world.
All you with great growth potential
—— never stop growing!

BUILD IT! *

Toilers,
work together
and build a new factory for us.
If you approach one million people
and get a yen from each,
you can build a factory worth one million yen.

Then build the kind of factory you want.
When you fashion
new structures,
the old naturally give way.

Build a one million-yen factory
each and every month.
Use the profits from these plants
to construct
yet another new plant.
You'll become
factory managers
and build as many plants as you like.
Welcome, then,
any who contribute
to these plants.
Love from afar
those who do not!

When you
achieve the ability
to build a true work place
and can then
give it a life
that matches your aspirations,
a new world will truly come about.
You can then become
new people
rather than make a fuss
for the foolish to observe.
Build it,
build it:
build the new plant,
a plant run by justice,
a plant that meets your demands.
When it's finished,
you'll smile and savor your triumph.

Work together,
work together!
Put an end to destructive schemes
and adopt constructive ones.
That's how to take sides with humanity.
In doing so, a new life will definitely spring up
and you'll discover paths
you never knew existed.

A new age has come.

The human race does not rejoice
in destruction.
Build it,
build it!
The new age is here.
Rather than hearkening to voices from the past,
submit to these cries
in the hearts of all people:
Build it,
build it:
build the new plant,
the new life,
the new world.

THE MAN WHO WORKS EARNESTLY

The man who works earnestly,
who works so earnestly
he can't get anyone to make sense of him,
is the man who cannot dissemble
———— the world regards him a fool.
Such a man can be only what he is.

EFFORTS

Day after day
the same existence.
I'm married to my work.
At times things go well.
Sometimes they don't.
At times I'm lucky.
Sometimes I'm not.
I don't make things up.
I keep tirelessly
at my work.
One of these days, though still unseen,
my efforts will little by little amount to something.
One year of silent effort.
Three years of effort, five years, a decade,
two decades, three decades of effort
———— efforts invisible to all.
But these efforts alone
will little by little make something of me.

THE UNOPENABLE DOOR *

– 1 –

A man stands before
an unopenable door.
From time to time he knocks
and listens carefully.
Silence!
The door stands stolidly as though to say,
"I will never open
for you."

– 2 –

What is the key to the unopenable door?
Self-training.
After the man had finally trained himself,
the door opened.
By then he was eighty-eight.
Beyond the threshold sits that man
with the scythe.

DAY BY DAY

Day by day passes.
When my last day has passed,
I'll finally die.
I don't want to die but I will.
Once dead there's no need to do a thing.
Till I'm dead, I'm driven to do something.
That's my fate.
I'm so extremely occupied by one task after another
that it hardly matters if I want to do good work.
I move ahead wanting to finish everything wholesale.
When I die
I may have a wastepaper shroud.
That's all right with me.
Well, I can say that whenever I worked I gave it my all.

IN EARNEST (ii)

If you don't push
this door
in earnest,
it will not open.

LIFE'S WORK

I'm a man of fifty.
I figure on doing my life's work
piece by piece.

THUMBLING *

Thumbling felt uneasy
about every word and every sentence
other people uttered.
Adults are oblivious to everything,
but he simply focuses heart and soul
on the immediate task.

MACHINES and PEOPLE *

Machines are machines. They're not people.
People are people. They're not machines.
Machines are expensive. People are cheap.
People easily reproduce themselves. You can't as easily make a machine.
People have a small amount of power. Machines have a lot of power.
But people are people, I say. They're not machines.

MY PRESENT WORK

My present work
encourages me.
When from time to time I become irresolute,
it encourages me.
No one is as important to me as I am.
No one will do my work for me.
That's why I need cheers.

MY WORK (i)

If in my work
I display the slightest touch of cleverness
—— horrors,
horrors,
I'm instantly penalized.
Persist
in standing for what you believe
even if it costs. •

Have you never been penalized
for trusting excessively in people?
Have you ever been penalized
for trusting excessively in God?

MY WORK (ii)

No matter what,
my work will not go over budget.
Should the whole world turn out the way I want,
you see,
it'll be included in my calculations,
and even if all others desert me,
that, too, will be within budget.
If I die tomorrow, that's within my calculations.
If I live to be a hundred, that's within budget.
Whichever way life goes, it falls within my budget.
I do whatever I can.
I'm prepared for anything.

MY WORK (iii)

I'm a man who arouses the sincerity
inherent in every heart.
I'm a man who makes the sincerity alienated from every heart
burst into a single flame.

MY WORK (iv)

My work
requires single-mindedness.
Women!
Keep far away from me.
Far away.

LIVING and WORKING

I know a man
who is myself.
Other than myself, in fact,
I really don't know anyone
—— though I can still love.

During younger days
I knew many people I disliked

and many worthy of hate.
As I got older, however,
I remember only those I love.

I can't think of anyone
I dislike
nor anyone worthy of my hate.
It's not that such people do not exist.
I simply put them out of mind.
I no longer have the leisure
to give them a thought.

Yet I do dislike those
who make others unhappy.
I feel contempt for them.
And disgust as well.
It's unbearable to think of their victims.
But I do not give too much thought to such people.
I think of those
worthy of my love.

When I think of them
I find meaning in life,
in work.
Hoping for their happiness,
I adore life, I adore work.

TASKS I CANNOT DO

Brothers and sisters
do for me tasks I cannot do.
What joy, what gratitude I feel!

ONE HUNDRED EGGS

I'd like to produce one hundred eggs every day.
And yet I can only manage a single one.
That's irritating.

In my mind
a thousand ideas itch for life.
But I'm able to enliven
only two or three of them.
That's irritating.

THE BEAUTIFUL WORLD WE DESIRE

– 1 –

We hope to build
a beautiful world
where everyone
is glad to work
and glad to live:
a world where people can love one another
——— that beautiful world for which everyone yearns,
a realm of joy.

– 2 –

Be aware that
angels of joy live here.
I'm glad to say I admire,
I so admire this realm,
that I'm happy to live here.
That's why I work heartily
and yearn with everyone for a beautiful world,
a realm of joy.

– 3 –

I thirst for a realm of profound vitality
where all people
live in happiness,
where they can perfect themselves
wherever they live.
I thirst for a realm where people can love one another
——— that beautiful world for which we all yearn:
a realm of joy.

FRIENDSHIP & LOVE

THE JOY OF FRIENDSHIP

When I talk with a friend
and our conversation catches fire,
the two of us merge flawlessly, flawlessly,
into a single mind,
and eyes moisten
—— one then touches a presence,
a presence . . . .

A FRIEND

Walking along the street,
I happened to recall a friend.
I felt a strange longing to see him.
Friend —— I hope you're contented!

WHEN I WAS AILING

I thought of an ailing friend
when I myself was ailing.
Surely he sometimes feels helpless,
sometimes painful,
sometimes restless.
Friend, life is a matter
of putting up with these feelings, isn't it?
I pray in earnest
for your happiness.
If only a miracle . . . .

MY FRIEND

Am I an agitator?
Agitators I detest.
I detest agitators
unconcerned about other people's fate.
I detest agitators
who would sweep people off their feet. •

Stand on your own two feet!
Hope surely burns in you.
Shoulder your fate
before concerning yourself with the fate of others.
If there are those who say,
"You stirred me up
and made me lose my footing,"
I'll say,
"Too bad!"
But I disdain such people
before I offer them
pity.

Don't allow yourself to be stirred up!
People who shoulder their fate
without condemning others
are free.
I respect them.
It's tragic
when an individual like that suffers.
Such a one is truly my friend.

You may feel alone
my independent friend,
but hold out!
If things go well for you,
smile
the victor's smile!
Stand up,
but if you cannot stand,
crawl,
and when you can stand on your own,
stand up!
My friend,
good friend,
—— arise,
just as trampled grass
insists on springing back!

Then laugh at the fact
that you were born.
When you die,
my friend,
however you may cling to life,
do not berate your birth.

SHIGA and I *

Our chairs facing,
Shiga Naoya and I
talk with each other.
I happen to think back on the old days.
Forty years ago
when we were still young
we talked together like this.
We both were green then.
Burning with aspirations,
we talked of literature,
of painting,
we talked of our hopes for the future.
In those days we both were students.
We also talked of love.

We're now old men past sixty.
But we converse as in the old days
without the slightest sense of having changed.
Our bodies tell us, however,
that we have already thoroughly aged.
Forty years have passed like a dream.
We now have children and grandchildren.
Putting age out of mind,
we energetically talk about this and that.
Forty years have passed,
but what have we accomplished?
What have we seen? What have we experienced?

As we sat there facing each other,
I happened to wonder
how we might feel if we'd filmed
the way our faces have gradually changed
over these four decades.
I wonder how often during these forty years
Shiga and I sat face-to-face talking like this?
Our friendship is the same now as it's always been,
but before we knew it
two youths had been transformed into two old men.
Gazing at Shiga's face,
I felt more than ever the handiwork of the years.

AS LONG AS I'M ALIVE —— Losing Shiga

When I heard Shiga had passed,
I don't want to say I was utterly distressed,
nor that I didn't think he might die.
Having lost him, however, I realize
we'll never again meet and laugh together.
If we could meet and have a laugh, that would take care of it,
but we can neither meet nor talk again.
We can never laugh together.
He was a good man,
an honest fellow,
but we can never talk again.
It's painfully obvious,
but we can never talk.
How delightful that he lived into his eighties.
He died, however,
too soon.
How nice had he lived a bit longer,
but life doesn't conform to our wishes.
I hope from this point
to live as long as I can
and do what I like doing.
But I can no longer
laugh together with Shiga.
That's life.
I intend to live as long as possible
and do more and more of what I like doing.
But I wonder how long I can . . . ?
There are still many, many people
whom I love.
I'd like to go on working
for them as well,
but I wonder how long I can . . . ?
Living as long as possible,
I'll try to write what I want to write.
As long as I'm alive, I want to do honest work.

WHY LOVE ONE PERSON

Why do you love one person,
yet find yourself unable to love another?
Why detest one person
and not detest another?

I don't know.
Ask someone who knows. •

Why are flowers lovely
but centipedes and millipedes loathsome?
Why are caterpillars disgusting
but butterflies beautiful?

I don't know,
I don't know.

THREE MEN and A GIRL *

Three men fell in love
with a beautiful girl.
One became her husband.
One became a libertine.
The other, a poet,
they called Dante.

SEXUAL DESIRE (i)

Sexual desire is overwhelming.
It has the power to make me powerless.
Steer clear of temptation!
And yet something within me anticipates temptation.
How exasperating!
Even so, you don't sound all that exasperated to me.
How exasperating!

SEXUAL DESIRE (ii)

The wisest transcend sexual desire.
The most human properly relish it.

SEXUAL DESIRE and LOVE

Sexual desire shows your partner no respect.
Love urges you to make your partner into God.
Sexual desire takes no thought of your partner's fate.
Love acts responsibly toward your partner's future.
    Love makes you believe
        that entrusting your companion to another
        will be torture.

ROMANCE and WORK

Though I don't want to cry, the tears come.
I hope she may be happy,
but I'd like to be happy, too.
It's so impossible, however,
that I don't expect it.
What I can do
is work —— work.
That's all.

AUTUMN HAS COME *

Autumn has come,
cool autumn has come,
lonely autumn has come,
the autumn of yearning for her is here.

I fell for her in autumn.
In autumn I confessed to mother that I was in love.
It was in fall, too, when my love moved far away.
Even if she hadn't left, fall is a lonely time.

Autumn has come,
the time of remembering is here.
Last year at this time I saw her every day.
This year I spend the fall unable to meet her.

FEELING LONELY *

I've lost faith in myself again.
I live a lonely, an empty life.

I've become unwilling to talk with others
because I abhor listening to meaningless chatter that misses the heart.
I prefer solitude. I would, however, like to see her from time to time.

I want to roam the lonely, lonely vale of tears.
There alone my heart feels at home.

I feel wretched when I think of her.
I want neither to kiss nor to talk with her now,
but I would like to get a glimpse of her.
I'd like to know how she's doing.
I yearn for that lonely feeling in our glance.

However, I do dread facing her.

Being face to face will not decide our fate.
But what if our meeting makes her miserable?
Should that spoil it for her, I don't want to make her feel bad.

These days I haven't a shred of manliness.
I feel depressed and lifeless.
Once beyond the grave, I'll tell Otei, Maki, and the others
    how lonely they made my life.
I want to tell them that was their greatest gift to me.
I'm not being sarcastic. Loneliness holds treasures. I feel at home with it.
I'm seasoned to the lonely mind.

I'm a lonely fellow,
a man who loves solitude.
Whatever lacks a tinge of loneliness
seems vulgar and trivial to me.
I'm the kind who courts loneliness in gaiety
and uncovers there a place he can call home.

I hadn't been aware of that till now.
It may be more miserable being unaware of it.
Or it may be more miserable becoming aware of it.
I'm unloved by the one I love.
The ability to live without taking action
—— I'm grateful I'm fond of feeling alone.

SPRING —— At Kugenuma *
As I walked along I thought,
It's spring, it's spring, it's really spring.
I adore spring.
Long ago I felt lonesome when spring came,
for it was spring when Otei left.
Now I adore everything spring-like: cherry and peach trees,
barley and mustard blossoms, even young girls' kimonos.
Spring! Though you muddle my mind,
I adore you.
I love committing myself
to your raptures.
I adore going into the garden,
digging in the dirt,
catching carp in the pond,
uprooting *bôfu*,
gathering herbs.
I also love a hearty laugh
—— how spring-like! •

People may be at war now.
My heart, however, accommodates to spring.
I want to chatter on, I want to sing,
youthfully, joyously.
My chatter may not please you,
but I want to raise my voice and sing spring's songs
the way all nature sings her songs.
It's spring, it's spring, it's really spring.

TO SOMEONE

The person who would cultivate
in someone
a heart that thirsts for a just life
is worthy of praise.

Teaching people
to go back to being
just
is worthy of praise.

Getting someone
to come around
to loving the brothers and sisters
is worthy of praise.

LEAN ON ME

Do you dread having everyone make fun of you?
My love,
lean on me.
I, too, am weak,
but if you lean on me
I shall be strong.

My love,
my beloved,
do you dread the world?
Lean on me.
Bury your face in my chest
and I shall be strong.
No one in the world will then master me.

TO BE LOVED

I have no intention of being dishonest
simply to be loved.
I want to be loved only by those
who will love me more
the more I become my true self.
For me, being loved is a gift.
And yet,
I'm truly grateful
for my many gifts.

A LOVE TRAGEDY *

I love you.
You love me.
You don't love him.
He doesn't love you.
Why, then, must you become man and wife?

TO A CHINESE BROTHER *

I hear that you
understand my language,
have read my essays,
agree with my thinking,
and have faith in the New Village.
I'm deeply grateful.
It's a joy for us
that someone like you exists in China.
We were most happy to get the letters
you forwarded from Chinese in Su-Chou who don't know Japanese
but who read what you wrote about our village.
How we rejoiced!

Germans accepted the English,
and the English accepted the French.
I thought it would be impossible for Japanese to accept the Chinese,
but I know it is possible, it's possible.
I know that, thanks to you, my brother.
I'm grateful.

Who can say that the New Village,
whether as *Atarashiki Mura* or *Hsin-ts'un*,
could not succeed in China
before it succeeds in Japan?

What a joy
if it flourishes in your country.
I'd consider it an honor
to have brothers in your land.

Japan has a poor attitude
toward your country.
But it is possible
for Japanese
to be on friendly terms with your countrymen.
We can become brothers.
We certainly can.
I know that, thanks to you.
I'm grateful to you for that knowledge.

Japanese outside our circle
say this project is impossible.
But you do not think that way.
Some have read your work
and rejoiced.
If you labor earnestly on this,
brothers will surely appear here or there in China.
How joyful we'll be
when that occurs.

I find the poor relations between your country
and mine
truly unpleasant.
I'd like to work together with you for humanity.
You no doubt think the same.
Whatever the country,
even if one state doesn't get along with the other,
I'm sure it's possible for the people to get on well.
Let's work to help each other.
Let's work for humanity.
What a joy to know
that in your country there are many
who are virtuous and just.

At this point we still lack power in a material sense.
But we have sensitive hearts,
and we have yet to surrender our human dignity.
Wherever you go you find genuine people,
real brothers and sisters.
Tell me,
don't you think we should cry out and try
        to the best of our ability to awaken them?
You are the first to work

for a New Village in China.
Awaken the brothers in China.
Surely, unknown brothers await our cries,
even in your country.
They are not just our cries.
They are the cries of humanity,
the cries of human beings,
the expectant cries of all people.

You know that.
You believe it.
I'm grateful to you.
We expect, moreover,
a good deal of you.
We fervently hope you'll live up
to our hopes.

To a Chinese

Since my first glance of you,
I regarded you warmly
and considered you a brother.
Throughout your life,
move ahead
to what you regard as just.
Doing that,
my brother,
will bear fruit.

The Chinese

I hear someone claims that the Chinese
have excessive confidence in our work.
It isn't that the Chinese have excessive confidence
but that the Japanese have an excessive lack of it.
It's all right to have as much confidence as you can.
We won't betray that confidence.
However much we restrain ourselves, our certainty grows.
We've only just sprouted small buds, but our roots sink deep enough
    to reach into past and present, East and West.
They will reach deep enough to merge with all humanity.
Those with confidence, have faith!

GOOD BROTHERS and SISTERS

Indeed, I have many
good brothers and sisters,
—— many indeed.
They live here and there.
Surely
I'd love to live in the same town they do
so I could see them when I want.
It's dreary being unable to see them
whenever I wish.
Certainly
I'd love to live in the same town
and meet every day
with my most beloved brothers and sisters.

WITH LOVE and GRATITUDE

When I look at things with love and gratitude,
I find our world
filled with beauty.
Dying, too, is beautiful.
This makes me grateful.

GENUINE and LOVABLE PEOPLE

Ah, genuine and lovable people!
I can believe you exist in this world.
The happiness of humanity,
a world where everyone can truly make the most of themselves.
That's my honest, my earnest hope.

LOVABLE PEOPLE

Whatever else you may say, we love people, we love nature,
    we love this world.
There are truly many lovable people here.
I am a human, I love humans.
The way I write is assuredly inept,
but I love this world, I love all people.
I think I was lucky to have been born a human.
I love people.
I hope you'll allow me to say
that I'd like to rejoice with others born here.

SOMEONE LIKE ME

"The fact that you cannot love
and cannot forgive
someone like me
proves your lack of love."
To such a person I say:
"That's correct.
My love is not so magnanimous
that I can tolerate
a person like you.
I abhor those who wring from me ideas
that do not well up in my mind.
I equally abhor those who wring love from me
that does not well up from my heart.
In short, I resent
all who presume on me."

COMICAL COUPLE *

Here you can encounter
comical couples, carefree couples, enlightened couples, the new couple.
The narrative of the Marquis and the Marchioness Chaplin.
The pair of them
self-indulgent.
The Marquis hotheaded,
the Marchioness obstinate.
Each an excellent squabbler
who must have the last word.

A knight
comes on the scene.
Loyal and inflexible,
he is the favorite of the Marchioness.

The knight adores the Marchioness,
who is his amulet in battle.
If he goes out to joust in her name,
no foe shows up to face him.
That puts the Marchioness in high spirits.

Marquis Chaplin becomes intensely envious.
However much he tries to control himself,
his heart bursts with jealousy.
The Marchioness then falls ill.
Again and again and again
they're not sure whether she'll live or die.

The Marquis Chaplin,
no doubt solicitous of his wife,
becomes absolutely agitated
and vows
he'll surrender his inconsequential life
if God will only save his spouse.
She thereupon instantly recovers.

The wife concentrates on recuperating.
The Marquis concentrates on his work.

While the Mrs. is away,
a lady of the court
assumes the responsibility
of looking after the Marquis.
The lady's excellent job of caring for him
puts the Marquis
in high spirits.
He says he feels exceedingly lonely when the lady isn't around.
The lady takes as good care of him as his wife did.
Now the Marchioness succumbs to jealousy.

After difficulties
of one kind or other crop up,
the tactful foursome
manages to get along smoothly.
The wicked prosper, the virtuous prosper.
Everything ends propitiously.
At that point, the movie ends. *Clappity clap.*

STARS IN THE HEAVENS

Stars in the heavens,
flowers on Earth,
love in people.

TO A FRIEND

One of my friends is cantankerous.
I've been unable to become cantankerous in return,
so I act as though his behavior makes no difference to me.
That's because whatever side of himself my friend displays
falls within my calculations.

AFTER A FIT OF ANGER

I'm morbidly susceptible to fits of anger,
but once my anger passes
I'm flooded with a spring of love.
Eyes brimming with tears,
I feel like extending the hand of reconciliation.
And I feel like weeping together.

THOSE I CAN'T DESPISE *

I can't despite those I can't despise.
I love those I have no choice but to love.
If asked why I don't despise someone, I say I have no choice.
If asked why I love someone, I say I have no choice.

HIS CHILDREN

Marx would no doubt be furious
were his children made the property of the state.
It's all right if it's for propaganda,
but who wouldn't be furious if it actually happened?
If it occurs, that alone
will suffice to do the radicals in.
Take care!
When people are no longer in a bind to eat,
they think of their children.

IN THE KINGDOM OF GOD (ii) *

In the kingdom of God
people will live complete lives.
Those people who now appear unclean
will then truly be made clean and become radiant.
Fire will purge everything impure.
Love will ply directly from heart to heart,
and people will laud each other.
Intellect will develop to the utmost,
and Earth will become a paradise.
Heaven exists not in the past
but in the near future.
The kingdom of God in us
will come about on Earth.
Even then, those who lack the mind of God
will be cursed.

LOVE (i)

Love
comes from heaven.
Blessed are those who
with the help
of angels
can live here below.

LOVE (ii)

I've been loved by my woman.
She's taken care of me.
We're in love.
I think this is true
happiness.
Even now
I'm not oblivious to that love.
She, too, has been satisfied with her life.
We regard it our good fortune
to love each other.
I feel we haven't had a care
in the world.
I can't neglect such love.
There's never been the slightest unhappiness between us.
We've loved each other.
This surely is infinite love.
It's nothing more
and nothing less than that.
We thought of nothing except our love.
We grew old,
but our minds have been at ease.
And content.
We believe heartily in our love.
Whether growing old
or getting sick,
nothing takes precedence over love.
Even now the two of us trustingly love each other.
I think that's beautiful
—— a couple's perfectly-trusting love.

PART III

ART & POETRY

There is no greatness where there is not
simplicity, goodness and truth.

— Leo Tolstoy —

To every poet, to every writer, we might say:
Be true, if you would be believed. Let a man
but speak forth with genuine earnestness
the thought, the emotion, the actual
condition of his heart.

— Thomas Carlyle —

PART III presents poems that deal with Mushakôji's poetic · aesthetic; cf. page 363 ff. Many convey his ideas about or joys in painting, others offer his attitudes toward critics, still others sketch his approach to spontaneity. In general, the prefatory comments immediately below expand on information in the Introduction or Notes. Mushakôji's dedication to suppress the "artificialities" of intellection in favor of "natural" intuition and spontaneity encourages emphasis on his attempts to mimic nature or reality. I consequently append a brief comment on mimesis.

✦   ✦   ✦

SPONTANEITY defines the genuine artist. Although Mushakôji wrote many more poems about his experiences as a painter than about himself as a poet, either art illustrates his notion that spontaneity alone creates a faultless work. He believed that the ideal artist was, in truth, also the ideal person. He describes this person in various ways, but his portrayal invariably centers on being open to the dictation of the Muse, the inner self. Spontaneity similarly characterizes Taoism, the non-intellectual strain of ancient East Asian thought; cf. page 18 ff. The ideal artist or the ideal man knows how and when to detour the conscious intellect and rely on the intuitions of the heart. Indeed, the heart or *kokoro*—the fundamental nonverbal self that transcends verbal description—is the controlling principle of spontaneity. This concept is so central to Mushakôji's thought that his poetry consistently implies the contradictory injunction: Be spontaneous!

Nobody can will spontaneity. One can only be prepared to let it "happen." Mushakôji opened himself to its happening by cultivating enthusiastic absorption, inner focus, and silence. Enthusiastic absorption involves avoidance of self-conscious control of writing or painting. Absorption in spontaneity disinclines the creator from interest in false objectives. First, absorption allows one to write unaffectedly and unpretentiously. Mushakôji wants all poets to be as natural as the hen that produces eggs day after day without worrying about how many she has laid, which ones might hatch, or who will eat them. Those liberated from preoccupation with the processes and results of creativity escape the curse of self-consciousness. That the gives them the candor necessary to create honest works. The state of mind necessary to achieve complete absorption resembles that of the Zen archer who, to the observer, appears to shoot arrows at a target. In reality, his archery is only an exercise in self-discipline and focus. He needs such practice to pierce the wall of ego that separates him from his true self and thus from a fulfilled life. That wall, not the bull's eye, is his real target. In the same way, the poet's intensely self-less involvement in the creative process becomes its own end, far exceeding in importance his "hitting the target"; cf. page 225.

Once poets achieve a Zen-like state of concentrated, egoless involvement, they stand on the threshold of spontaneity. They do not wait for inspiration, however, but go out to engage it, for no genuine Muse takes pleasure in inertia. Once engaged—and then driven by a state of consciousness that opens the writer to spontaneity and facilitates becoming a poet unawares—the product rises to a new dimension. Writers accessible to inspiration will not be conscious of the moment

177

intellect surrenders control and makes impromptu expression possible. Passionate engrossment and openness to inner, non-rational control of writing will, very simply, expose poets to the voice of their *kokoro*. The moment they interact with the pure experience of the inner self, they will produce extemporaneous verse. Mushakôji regards such spontaneity a function of the artist's mental disposition. It has little to do with objective criteria of excellence, judged by the presumed worth of the artist's product, and everything to do with the poet's human qualities. Only inner intensity freed from an anxiety-ridden compulsion to produce a specific result liberates writers from conscious controls—controls that falsify the pure emotions of the *kokoro*. Mushakôji describes this freedom metaphorically as crossing a threshold in response to opportunity. He suddenly realizes a door he imagined shut was not locked. He then opens it and nonchalantly enters; cf. page 67. By contrast, the poet who writes according to external formulae, conscious effort, and volition will not produce genuine poetry. Creation must always be a happening of the heart.

Spontaneity also requires inner focus. This second state of consciousness, which assumes that poets will direct wholehearted attention to their deepest feelings, enables spontaneity to "happen." The self unblocks, as it were, and opens a pathway to the *kokoro*'s pure experience. The unblocked experience—whether the solemn joy of living, a sense of loneliness, or whatever—bubbles up as naturally as a spring. Poets then happily share their feelings with others. Spontaneity "touches," it is clear, only when artists reach into the innermost self. Responding to the voice of the heart wakens the Muse. A clear inner focus also enhances single-mindedness and integrity. If absorption keeps poets from being swayed by false objectives such as impressing others with their brilliance, inner focus makes them rigorously honest in presenting experiences exactly as the *kokoro* dictates. Honesty compels artists to direct attention to feelings and to ignore the expectations of others. Artists betray themselves principally when they produce work alien to their sensibilities. To keep from blurring inner focus, poets must therefore train themselves to respond single-mindedly to the inner voice and to no other.

Unless sharply attuned to the *kokoro*, poets will very likely find themselves incapable of resisting the influence of critics. Even if an artist momentarily gives in to third-party norms, however, having a clear focus at length obliges return to the honesty of the heart. The *kokoro* alone assumes no poses and has no persona—no mask representing the calculated intellectual pose of the self-conscious individual. Poses may fool the critic. They do not fool the inner self, the *kokoro*. Masks also make spontaneity impossible. In the end, true artists must rely solely on their natural, authentic selves. As long as they maintain a lucid inner focus, they can tap into the *kokoro* and avoid doing what they do to please others. They can be their true selves. Those with this well-honed inner focus share their selves freely with others because single-minded integrity is the epitome of selflessness.

Sharing, however, never implies compromising commitment to inner values. Mushakôji describes the ideal sharer in two poems about the traditional metaphor for a poet: a flute player; cf. page 221 ff. Because this flutist is an authentic artist, he neither plays to the crowd nor requires an audience. Oblivious to what others think, to criticisms of ineptness, even to whether others enjoy his tunes, he plays because he must. The flutist cares nothing about talent and everything about playing with his whole being, for inner necessity drives him. He continues at his pace, grateful to share the joys of his *kokoro*. Of course, he rejoices when others choose to share his joy. Nevertheless, his playing does not depend on how—or whether—others respond. This is precisely the attitude that Mushakôji so admired in THE AGED REMBRANDT; cf. page 207. An artist does not paint to win fame, friends, or worldly goods. The urge to share one's *kokoro* shields the poet against all such external objectives. If the artist covets the approval of anyone, it must be that of the true critic who alone can probe beneath surface techniques to contact the artist's essential, dedicated self. As Mushakôji writes, "Well, I can say that whenever I worked I gave it my all"; cf. page 154. Constant dedication defines the artist whose enthusiastic absorption maintains a sharp inner focus on his *kokoro*.

Silence is the third state of consciousness necessary to spontaneity. Absorption helps prevent the intellect from taking over the creative process. Inner focus then allows communication with the *kokoro*. That results in a stress on feeling, the language of the heart. The heart's dialect is, of course, the language of silence. Poets who realize the imperfection of words as tools for expressing feelings have the proper mindset for spontaneity. Again, Mushakôji illustrates this in the familiar poem where he asserts that silence is closer than words to his true self; cf. page 8. He claims his poems stand as mere shadows of a truer self, implying that the silence between the words embodies more of his *kokoro* than the words themselves. This concern notably roots itself in his invisible spirit, not in the visible words of the poem. He believes that the poet's inner being, his *kokoro*, thrives in the "spaces" between—perhaps even in the infinite spaces beyond—the words.

Respect for silence enables poets to avoid giving undue attention to the vocables that express their feelings. They know words are but vehicles, not ends in themselves. That's why, in the manner of Taoists or Zen practitioners, poets must resist getting too attached to words. Mushakôji can write as though his poems contain no words because he is not nailed to the medium of his expression. Poets unconstrained by their medium stand on the verge of spontaneity and are unlikely to be seduced by the desire to impress others with verbal pyrotechnics. Mushakôji writes "I'd like to write a poem / that makes people think that spring has come"; cf. page 230, #2. His basic concern nevertheless remains to communicate the feelings in his heart. Disengagement from the tyranny of words exhilarates emotions. That invites spontaneity, which transcends silence's burdensome requirements. Vocables are particularly troublesome to poets, for words serve as the primary tools of their craft. Silence can be equally onerous to readers because it demands that they approach the poem with the heart rather than the head. Spontaneous poetry requires readers, too, to have a *kokoro* that resonates with the silent "spaces" between the poet's words. They must also have an openness and ability to enter those spaces and respond imaginatively to the feelings contained in their stillness. For Mushakôji, the burden for poet and reader is thus the same: non-attachment to the medium of expression. Once aware that communication occurs only between *kokoro* and *kokoro*, poetry will flow spontaneously between poet and reader. A verse resulting from the poet's absorbed inner focus on the silences of the heart will be spontaneous and so evoke in the reader an instantaneously absorbed response.

Absorption, inner focus, and silence are merely inferred labels attached to states of consciousness that in my view Mushakôji believes necessary to spontaneity. He often implies the existence of these states, although he does not discuss them systematically. Nor do these notions ever relate to each other linearly in his poems like causes to effects, for Mushakôji studiously avoids systematic, discursive logic. They rather resemble ingredients in a recipe. This is especially so in his verse where pure spontaneity reigns. Although many of his poems deal with the configurations and characteristics of the "ideal artist," Mushakôji's prime concern is "ideal existence," the way human beings should live and conduct themselves. Genuine being for him originates, then, not in the self that thinks but in the self that feels, a view Japanese have shared for centuries.

MIMESIS is the mimicry or copying of the sensed real world. Self-consciously or intellectually altering sensual input does not mime reality but manufactures it. Spontaneity assumes such mimicry. Imitation of life or mimesis becomes an essential attribute of Mushakôji's art. In poetry, his objective is to depict the ungarnished reality of the feelings that exist in his *kokoro*. In painting, it is to depict the beauties of nature exactly as he perceives them. For him, creativity is not the result of analysis, nor is it is usually a process of discovery in the sense that his painting may end up differing from the object he copies. Nor does Mushakôji interact with his ideas or his brush lines quite in the manner of the artist who regards creativity a freewheeling interplay between the self and the imagination. The "accidents" that frequently happen to the artist open to this dialectic are not likely to happen on a large scale to Mushakôji. He deals with what he can see before him, or with what he can dredge up directly from his heart's reservoirs. He expends no energies trying to funnel the media and his inspiration into preconceived directions. Rather, he prefers his brush to capture, say, the dimensionality of a potato. In pursuit of that goal he paints pictures of potatoes year after year after year. He could not possibly end up with a painting not recognizable as a potato; cf. page 183 ff. The same applies to his poetry. In poem after poem he tries to imitate his sense of joy as a human being who attempts to live an authentic and spontaneous existence.

✦   ✦   ✦

The arrangement of works in this section is largely topical. Selections in the painting category offer remarks about Mushakôji's art or art in general. Then follow works that consist of observations on painters, first from East Asia and then from Europe. I arrange these chronologically by the age of the painter. The next section groups Mushakôji's views of critics. Following are several poems that deal first with Japanese and then with Western poets, again arranged chronologically.

ART & THE ARTIST

Ⓟ AINTING VEGETABLES

Someone may ask,
"What do you get out of painting such things?"
Since painting them is a delight, however,
and since some people enjoy my pictures, I have no choice.

I venerate foods raised for human beings
—— those joys for humanity,
those gifts
from nature.

Do you know the beauty of vegetables?
Do you know the beauty of tubers?
I find great satisfaction in knowing their beauties.

Look at potatoes
to see how much nature values tubers.

When I look at a pumpkin
I'm amazed that in six months a small seed
so easily gets so big
and serves as human food.

I love what fills life.
Things that fill our lives are beautiful.

Nature makes all sorts of things.
It even makes outlandish objects.
It makes marvelous things.
It surprises us with lovely things.
It makes foods with rich flavors.
It makes superb items that look commonplace.

Humans are good at making the most of nature's gifts.
Nature and man working in concert
—— that's the merit of the human being.
Whenever I observe vegetables, I sense that merit.

When I view nature's masterpieces,
I admire them, laud them,
and humbly sketch them.
That's a delight.

181

DYING TO PAINT A PICTURE

I'm dying,
simply dying to paint a picture.
I go to a nearby greengrocer's,
buy some apples, paint them.
Somebody asks, "What do you get out of painting apples?"
Do such people know
what you "get" out of living?
I'm simply dying,
dying to paint something.
If I paint a picture,
I'm satisfied with that.
If I'm satisfied,
isn't that enough?
Since it's enough for me,
I'm satisfied — that's sufficient.

SQUASH and POTATO *

At this moment the artist
is about to paint
three squash and five potatoes.
He has several kinds of squash:
red, green, yellow,
smooth skinned and rough skinned.
The painter combines them
in various ways
because it's the grouping that lends interest.
In front of the squash sit the potatoes,
each the same color
but each with contrasting contours.
The painter picks them up one by one.
Then he tries placing them in various positions.
Finally he decides where to locate
each squash and each potato.
Sitting next to the ones they should sit next to,
they form a pleasant harmony.
Each displays its specific features —— quite lovely.
The artist picks up his brush
with a satisfied smile
and tells himself,
"This time I'll make it work."

POTATO (i) *

A potato lies on the straw mat.
The artist observes it.
As he watches the potato,
it rounds full
and appears to take on depth.
Observing that gives him the urge to paint it.
If only he could capture that sense of solidity!
When he takes his brush and starts to paint, however,
the potato's cubic solidity takes flight.
He lays down his brush
and looks again at the rounded potato.
He thinks, then, "If only I could paint this potato's depth!"

POTATO (ii) *

The potato says,
"I'm satisfied with myself.
Wherever I sit,
I am myself.
I'm not ashamed of that.
I'm grateful
to the one who made me.
It's all right for me to be me.
Wherever I sit,
there's nothing greater
and nothing lesser than I.
That's where I want to sit,
forgetting everything but myself."

IN PRAISE OF POTATOES

Potato! Potato!
You grit it out in the ground.

You persistently
soak up the soil's delicacies.

You do not exist to be praised,
you exist to live.

You live on.
Your flowers are lovely,
but in that respect many surpass you.
I can't even recall
whether your blooms bear fruit. •

But your tuber alone
brims superbly with taste.

Child of the soil,
you reproduce your offspring in the soil.

Thanks to you,
I've learned the knack of painting.

Innocent objects
teem with life.

Each single existence
no more than what you are,
your shapes of infinite variety,
but each of you
substantial.

I gaze at you.
I gaze calmly without painting.

You become more and more rounded
and beautiful.
Teeming with energy,
your lines acquire increasing interest.
Potato,
I adore you.

ON A PAINTING OF SOY BEANS

On a painting of soy beans:
"One grain, a hundred fold."

THE PAINTER

The painter
concentrates on depicting yams.
Once a friend told him
he'd never seen a good representation of a yam,
so whenever the artist saw a yam he felt like painting it.
Since nobody had managed to do it,
he figured he would try.
With that in mind,
that painter concentrates on depicting yams.

A FRESH PAINTING

I've been alive
for eighty-six years.
At eighty-six I'm an old man.
I wish, however,
I could be smarter.
I'm still too immature.
I want to be acquainted
with more and more beauty
and ceaselessly
paint objects of beauty.
There are many beauties in nature.
I observe them,
but I just can't depict them properly.
Painting them well is a challenge.
I'd like to become more self-possessed
and paint something without a misstep.
I see many wondrously stimulating objects.
Yesterday I saw an onion
with a sprightly appearance.
It was indeed freshly invigorating.
It didn't have an especially marvelous face.
I admired rather its fresh
and ordinary hue.
It was much too common,
yet its extraordinary freshness
astonished me.
However often I observed it,
I found its freshness amazing.
Perhaps if I tried to depict it
in oils
just as I see it,
I could produce a vigorous painting.
I haven't tried to paint in oils for the last four or five years,
but I thought about trying to do one.
I think I'll try to paint a fresh picture
—— this old man of eighty-six.

WEARY FELLOW

The fellow resigned himself to longing for the leisure
to paint what he liked.
When he won the leisure
he fell asleep
rather than paint what he liked.
He was too weary.

SILENCE (ii)

Whenever I see you
I want to paint you.
You want to be painted.
You fall silent.
I fall silent, too.

STILL LIFE

After painting children,
I welcome doing a still life.
The objects do not move at all.
They're perfectly composed.
They'll sit calmly
till their bottoms rot.
I can paint then to the limit of my ability.
I can paint till I'm exhausted.
But it's a pity I lack the stamina.
Since I simply have no place to file my complaints,
I just paint silently on.

TITLING A SKETCH OF AN APPLE

I'm a single entity.
I'll live beautifully until I wither.
When I do, I'll leave my seeds on the ground.
I'm satisfied being
a single entity.

GENIUS and ARTISTE

Is there genius without authority?
Never!
Except the artiste.

THE JOY OF SEEING A FINE PICTURE *

To what can I compare the joy of seeing a fine picture?
Eyes welling, I walked back and forth
through a room of Titian's paintings.

The joy of seeing a fine picture,
the joy of touching the most lovely of hearts
—— I quiver tearfully with the joy of communicating with that heart.
Ah, the joy of the famished heart

communicating directly with a heart like his
fills me with tearful gratitude.

I learned first-hand
that all fine pictures derive from
a devastated soul.
They derive from what searches for that soul.

SELF-ADMONITIONS WHEN I PAINT *

Be loving.
Take chances.
Move over the ground till you sprout wings.
Walk your singular way.
Be deaf to what others say.
Plod on along the path of confidence.

THE MAN PAINTING A MOUNTAIN *

A painter
observes the mountain.
Though he feels
somehow
that he'd like to paint
its contours
to his heart's content,
he lacks the expertise
and cannot paint them skillfully.
The more he observes it,
the more solemnly the mountain
stands snow-capped.
The mountain's folds are, moreover,
rather fetching,
truly intricate, and impressive.
Although he wishes he could somehow paint them,
by no means can he realize his hope.
He engages in a staring match with the mountain.
However often his glare flags,
he looks all the more yearningly,
renews his determination,
takes his paintbrush,
and grapples with the mountain.
The mountain more and more sternly and forcefully
lays claim to its existence.
In the end the painter admits defeat.
"You bested me this time,
but one day

I'll show you
that I can capture your splendor
intact on my canvas."
The mountain as usual looked solemnly down
on the painter.
Though he had laid down his brush,
he was still gazing at the mountain.
He told himself,
"One day I'll show everyone I can paint you!"
Dusk approached
and the mountain,
bathing in reflections
of the setting sun,
cut an even lovelier figure.
The painter could not abandon his hopes
—— he still had tomorrow and the day after that.
Before dying,
he'd try to make something of his opportunities.
With that in mind,
he gazed devotedly at the mountain.

MOUNTAINEERING

"What will you get out of climbing that mountain?"
I don't know.
I merely want to try climbing it because nobody's done it yet.
I want to try climbing it because it's difficult.
If somebody else can do it,
let him,
but I want to try
because nobody's been able to climb it.
Since I'm hardly up to the task,
I plan to spend a lifetime trying.

OBJECTS I'D LIKE TO PAINT

I'd like to paint
a number of scenes.
There are many I wish I had painted.
But there's a mountain I'd dearly love to paint,
one I've even seen in my dreams.
I don't know where the mountain is, but it exists somewhere.
There are truly wonderful mountains in China.
I suppose you can find splendid mountains in Japan, too.
The mountain in my dream perfectly suits my skills.
In the dreams I sometimes have about that mountain,

I'm in a hurry to sketch it.
Then, the next time I see it, the mountain's appearance has changed.
That discourages me.
I hope to encounter a mountain,
an actual mountain,
that doesn't change however much I observe it,
a mountain I'd like to paint so much I can't bear it.
If I run across that mountain,
I'd like to build a small cabin there
and paint it till I'm pleased with my work.
If I could do that, I feel I could become a genuine artist.
I'd like to encounter such a mountain
and paint till I'm pleased with my work.

IMPAIRED PAINTER

I'm indeed an impaired painter.
Perhaps I cannot call myself a painter.
I'm simply a painter who can only paint what he's observed
exactly as he observed it.
In compensation, as a painter I find that what I've observed
gradually becomes more and more beautiful.
I then admire it and want to paint it.
I'm a painter who feels solemn joy
in painting with unparalleled fidelity.
I'll be happy if my paintings give people a taste of that solemn joy.
I'll be happy if I can convey to everyone
how I feel when I paint a picture!
As a painter I'm impaired
but in bliss.

THE JOYS OF PAINTING PICTURES

I paint shellfish.
Though I'm depressed,
they are not.

A friend brings
some tomatoes
he grew.
I do not blush
as I paint the green ones and the red ones,
and yet the painted tomatoes
gradually redden.

I paint pictures
while I still can see,

while my arm can move.

Have you experienced
the joy of painting?
I know
that joy.

THE POEM OF AN OLD PAINTER

An old painter takes a stroll.
Everything in sight he finds lovely.
Whatever he sees is beautiful.
Little by little the old man becomes delighted,
absorbed,
agitated.
He and the universe merge.
Everyone becomes his brother, his sister.
He feels they all want him to paint.
Life's spring overflows.
I laud them all,
they all laud me.

AN ARTIST and A FROG *

An artist told the frog he was sketching,
"One of your ancestors
jumped on a willow tree
and made Michikaze the patron saint of calligraphy.
Later on, another of your ancestors
once jumped into an old pond
and made Bashô the patron saint of haiku.
Well, then,
sit still
and make me the patron saint of painting."
But the frog unpredictably
hopped off
and disappeared.

I'M A PAINTER —— Poem by the Chief of Fools *

I'm a painter.
I'm the one who observes,
not the one observed.
Some laugh at me,
saying my face,
my attire, and such are odd.

That nevertheless
does not concern me.
If I can observe an object with care
and paint it
wholeheartedly,
I'll die in peace.

PAINTING PICTURES

Painting pictures is to grapple with nature.
Nature is not likely to yield.
It exerts a force
in response to the force you apply.
People can wrest from nature
only what their strengths permit.

IN MY TINY ROOM *

In my tiny room I now have artifacts of great value:
a Grecian terra cotta vase,
a Rodin sculpture,
one of Ch'ên Chung's dragons,
a painting by Shih-t'ao . . . .

Immersed
in the high-toned atmosphere
of these works,
I feel grateful for having been born a human.
I also feel I want to continue
doing solid work.

Daring to move ahead
come what may,
not making the slightest concession
—— the demeanor of these artists was superb.
Their beautifully-composed attitudes
reached beyond where they were able to reach.

I want to do the same.
I'd like to reach a level beyond my reach,
beyond my capabilities
—— a level I can claw my way to.
I don't think I can possibly become enlightened
until I manage that.

A man cannot die
without having done the best he can.
I'd like to go on creditably

doing the best work I'm capable of.
I'd also like to continue doing work that grows on people:
the more eminent people observe it
    the more they will admire and appreciate it.

It's no use casting my lot
with the brainless,
the heartless.
I want to persevere in doing work that most profoundly affects
the finest brain,
the peerless heart.

A FINE WORK OF ART

Whenever I see a fine work of art,
I truly want to buy it.
I go crazy for it.
If I had the money,
I'd like to buy a number of pieces.
Never satisfied even if I buy them,
I keep thinking I'd like to buy another one, too.
You know, however, that I'll forever be dying to acquire more.
Why do you think that happens?
I suppose it's because art becomes food for the soul.
Those who treat works of art as luxury items
are absolute dolts.
After all, for their kind
the fact that people have souls
is chiefly a frill.

ONE OF MY PAINTINGS SOLD

One of my paintings sold.
My painting sold.
Someone bought my painting.
I'd painted a picture nobody appreciated.
Somebody showed up who appreciated it and liked it.
Apparently I'm at last on my way to becoming someone
who paints pictures for other people,
not just for himself.
The world where I proudly paint pictures,
where I can proudly go on eating
—— that world has been opened to me.
It's too early to rejoice,
but it is possible to say that there's hope.
I want to paint pictures more and more charged with sincerity. •

I'll go to my grave painting, painting, painting.
Who in a millennium will see my paintings and rejoice?
I send that person my ardent love
and accept his or her ardent love.
Regardless of what anyone says,
my sincerity will survive.
I don't care how many people mistrust it,
I trust it —— I trust sincerity alone.
For those who do not trust it, death is the end.
Those who trust in sincerity live beyond death.
Posterity will accord them the ardent love due sincerity.

I don't think those who find me a fool
are wise.
It's enough if I go on living completely fulfilled.
I can't abide the hollow heart.
I go on living by steadily using my brush to make the most of my sincerity.
I can't manage it by having others help me.
I can, however, do it on my own.
I'm grateful for the mental poise
that persists in moving my brush with sincerity.

I'm a happy fellow.
What would it mean
these days
if a person could go through life with mental poise
and not be happy?

Fools exult in bad-mouthing others,
but they cannot achieve mental poise.
Because they can't, they make more and more of a fuss.
The proof of their foolishness
is that they think they can achieve mental poise
without actualizing their sincerity.
Those who don't even realize they are seeking mental poise
. . . oh, how talk of them in the same breath?

Those I adore, those I love,
are silent,
but in truth they live in complete fulfillment.
I paint heartily and adore the self-sufficient
who stretch their limbs to the full.
I'm happy being able to spend my days glorifying them.

At no time do I live with a more devoted sense of humility,
or with a greater sense of awe,
than when I'm painting.
If I'm just slightly inattentive, my brush makes a slip.
I love living with that awareness.

Because I can earnestly experience this awareness,
I figure it's all right to regard myself a painter.
If someone in daily life can experience this awareness,
such a person is certainly a saint.
I am no saint. I'm a painter.

Whenever I'm painting
I'm forced to be honest,
unassuming, earnest,
and to walk my singular path.
In this way, I'll succeed bit by bit.

Today a beautiful stranger
brought me some lovely flowers.
She said somebody asked her to do it.
I wonder if there's a God-like person
in this world
. . . a person fit to be an angel
came on this errand.
I gratefully accepted the flowers.
My hand trembled as I took them.
My heart trembled even more.

WHEN I PAINT

When I paint,
I once figured it'd be ideal
to do serene and static objects
at a leisurely pace,
making my mind ever more placid and calm.
My mind was overly eager.
And yet these days
when I'm about to paint,
it seems that the object to be painted
is indeed firmly
composed
and waiting for me
to paint it leisurely.
For my part,
I feel I'm too composed
and too expectant
to be able to paint more deliberately.
I've come to the point where I paint slowly
by composing my composed feelings
to a greater degree of composure.
Apparently the impatience is not in me.
Rather is what I'm painting
agitated. •

Which is the proper approach?
Little by little I've come to wonder whether
getting into a composed mood,
remaining calm,
and painting the picture
is the best way to get into the proper mood,
or whether it's better when I've come to think about it
in my own way.
It makes no difference
whether I'm dead
or alive.
Is it proper to do my work
becoming more and more composed,
working very, very deliberately?
A great-grandchild born this year,
not yet two,
is always in a flurry
trying to learn every possible word.
Have I bit by bit become the opposite,
and bit by bit attempted to become too calm?

I don't know
which is proper.
Is it proper
to live to the hilt,
wrack my brains,
retire,
and then end up doing nothing?
I don't know.
Is it proper that all creatures work to the hilt,
and then retire
when they no longer work?
I don't know the answer to that.
To the extent that one lives in this world, however,
is it proper to work until you're dead,
leave what you cannot do
to others,
and then retire?
I don't know the answer to that.
It may be proper
to work just as much as one wishes
and then retire.
Shall I decide, however, first of all
to work as much as I can
with composure and,
when the time comes to rest,
absolutely to rest? •

Doing a tolerable job at life,
do I live as long as I can
and then stretch out calmly?
Or do I do a tolerable job of living calmly
and then take it easy?
People living in this world
aim for a tolerable degree of happiness,
and so I think it's no mistake
to work as much as one can
and move leisurely on.

I'll do a tolerable job of moving leisurely on.

I won't feel flustered and wait for death
but all in all work slowly and go on living.
I'm a happy-go-lucky fellow.
Life is long
and there are too many tasks to be done.
To begin, I'll calmly go on living
and leisurely do my work
in this world.

NEO-IMPRESSIONISTS *

When Neo-Impressionists and Cubists
go well beyond imitating nature,
they hasten their downfall.
They take a dogmatic view
and habitually observe objects in a monotonous manner.
It's the fate of this method that people become bored.
If others get bored, that's far better
than if they get bored themselves —— and that's the end of that.
The person who gets sick of what he should get sick of, however, is wise.
I suppose such individuals will move on to paintings
that maintain their interest.

CHINESE PAINTING *

Whenever I view a Chinese painting,
I see a lighthearted fellow
—— a man leaning against a crag and gazing upward
as though he's forgotten
whether he belongs to the universe
or the universe belongs to him.
This beguiles me.

LIANG K'AI *

Liang K'ai!
I truly adore you.
How many pictures did you paint?
It's certainly regrettable that
perhaps more than ninety percent of your works
have vanished from the Earth.
Luckily, however,
a number of the pictures you painted
are preserved in Japan.
Having seen them with my own eyes,
I've positively come to adore you.
You perceived the truly unlimited profundities in every-day life.
Hui Nêng, the Sixth Patriarch, chops bamboo. In your picture
        he eternally chops bamboo. He chops on and on . . . .
I have the euphoric sense
that you managed to depict so expertly
that portrait of innocence,
that figure intently chopping bamboo, having forgotten all else.
The scene appears to be about nothing at all,
but the patriarch actually accomplishes a supreme and peerless task.
He's chopping bamboo wholeheartedly, having cleared his mind of everything.
Perhaps he's also forgotten that he's chopping bamboo.

The young Li Po you painted
also strides on eternally
—— you've delineated his gallant figure perfectly
and with unprecedented skill,
an expression beyond euphoria.
You were possibly content with it, too.
Viewing it delights me.

Proof that a man like you once lived,
that the spiritual strength you once displayed
when you painted these pictures
has survived till now
—— these touch our hearts.
I can't possibly offer an adequate accolade!

VIEWING LIANG K'AI'S *DANCING HOTEI* (i) *

Hotei! Hotei!
What are you so joyous about?

"I've altogether forgotten
what made me joyous, so joyous,

so very joyous I can't control myself.
Joyous, joyous,
just to be alive is joyous.
And even death is joyous."
Isn't that what you're thinking?
An odd fellow, aren't you?
"Joyous, joyous,
I've forgotten what caused my joy,
but I'm joyous, so joyous I can't control myself."

Viewing Liang K'ai's *Dancing Hotei* (ii) *

Hotei walks down the road
jumping with joy.
He's not in the least aware
that everyone is watching him.
What does he find delightful?
He's forgotten.
He's simply delighted.
He's forgotten time and place,
his poverty,
his mortality,
his being laughed at.
He's merely delighted.
He jumps with joy
—— just as the life in him decrees.

Hotei, Attributed to Mu Ch'i *

"Hotei, Hotei,
how come you have
such a good-natured air about you?
Given our present world,
I can't imagine
being able to make a face like yours.
Aren't you aware
of the loathsome events occurring here,
the cruelties being perpetrated?"

"I'm aware of them.
All too aware.
But I've struck a spring of joy and love of life.
Before I knew it,
love and joy
flowed from it into my heart.
That's why when I'm alone
I end up with this look on my face.

An artist once drew my face
when it looked like that.
The painter, too,
was a man who'd struck a spring of love and joy.
He apparently had good insight into my feelings and, so to speak,
he then depicted them in his painting,
just as you see."

A spring of love and joy.
The pure joy
that wells up from that spring.
The expression of a man whose heart is sated with love and joy.
The picture painted candidly with nothing added, nothing missing.
Viewing it,
I felt the urge to write this poem.

WU CHUN'S *HOTEI* *

Wu Chun depicts Hotei,
who has flung down both staff and sack
and worships the moon.
Wu writes,
> *The moon in far-off skies*
> *flows white into our confines. He views it,*
> *but it puzzles him.*
Wu says Hotei observes the moon but cannot comprehend it.
It's natural it was a puzzle to Hotei,
but lack of understanding doesn't affect his worship.

Wu has become Hotei
worshipping the moon.

I'm not interested in this painting
because Hotei worships the moon.
The painting dumbfounds me
because its honest, straightforward depiction and calligraphy
are incomparable.

A man who conducts his every-day life with such spiritual strength
—— when the time comes,
such a spirit will naturally emerge,
and the man will have nothing to worry about.

The man has already graduated from questions of life and death
and lives on with a focused mind
—— he will, moreover, be committed
to the laws of the universe
and be self-composed. •

This picture is not something a mere artist painted.
It's something a true individual sketched.
That authentic person
is quite a human being.
What a delight that I can now view this painting
that would not exist if such a great person hadn't created it!

LIANG K'AI'S *HARPIST UNDER A PINE* *

This high-minded gentleman forgets about playing his harp
and listens to the sounds of wind
in the pines.

The artist Liang K'ai,
whom I most respect,
painted a miniature picture
of that scene.

But the profundity of the heart
concentrated in it
creates a state of mind
enabling the artist to paint
only after he has identified with nature.

Liang's super-human ability with the brush!
How can he paint such lines?

Liang K'ai is the only painter past or present, East or West,
capable of drawing the lines of this garment.

He went where he was destined
and left indisputable proof of his skills.

The proof is a verity.
Viewing that verity,
I am more and more attracted
to the painter's mental powers and state of mind.

Yes, such a person
once existed,
and in his paintings he left
a part of his heart.

His work actually allows a glimpse
of the most human super-human.

𝕀 PRAISE MU CH'I and LIANG K'AI *

I praise these two.
I don't know how many thousands,
how many tens of thousands
deserve praise.
I don't know how many thousands,
how many tens of thousands there are past and present, East and West.
Today, however, I begin by praising these two,
Mu Ch'i and Liang K'ai:
mighty painters,
great human beings,
genuine men.

They drew marvelously
wonderful pictures.
It's amazing
yet not amazing
how they could produce such fine paintings.
Moving ahead steadfastly,
painting honestly
what they wanted to paint,
finishing their pictures before they knew it.
It's obvious that they could do it.
It's as though a pine cone
had grown into a huge fir.

Liang K'ai realizes Liang K'ai.
Mu Ch'i realizes Mu Ch'i.
What's the mystery in that?

There's one of Li Po strolling.
Another of a striding crane.
However could they paint
such pictures?
They did it because they could.
They could paint them
because they had the abilities.
And yet their skills are awesome.

In truth, the world has seen some great ones.
Their powers naturally increased
until ultimately they could produce such pictures.

Their spirits were animated.
Their perfectly tempered spirits
became animated.
They were enlivened because their time had come.

The ability to develop that level of skill
is awesome.

Hotei dances.
The Sixth Patriarch single-mindedly chops bamboo.
The black-cloaked priest, an idiotic look on his face,
obsessed with a cock fight.
These, too, are engrossing.
Truly engrossing.
They give me pleasure.
I suppose they also gave pleasure to Liang K'ai who painted them.
Can you comprehend
his pleasure?
If you grasp
this joy
given to humankind,
you'll begin to dance
like Hotei.

A tiger appeared.
A dragon came along.
Fearful tiger, fearful dragon:
good companions.
Both will be bested.
Mu Ch'i painted them
with all his powers focused.
It's a marvelous picture.
Mu Ch'i observed his work and said,
"You see, don't you,
the merit of this painting?"
Pleasantly surprised, the Japanese monk said,
"I see, I see.
Please let me have it."
"If you see its merit, I'll give it to you,
for you've understood it the best.
This certainly is
a good painting."

"It's more than a good painting.
It's a great one.
It's a wonderful picture.
They'll rejoice throughout Japan when they see it.
Even if you asked me to return it,
I won't give it back."

"Don't worry,
I wouldn't think of asking for it back.
I'm not as stingy as that.

Anyhow, I can draw any number of far better ones.

"I saw a crane striding today.
On a treetop were a long-armed monkey and her baby.
Between them I saw a vision of Kannon.
I'll be able to make a good picture out of that."
"When you finish it, give that one to me, too."
"You're a greedy fellow, aren't you?"

Each picture Mu Ch'i paints has its own magnificence.

Liang K'ai and Mu Ch'i
—— two magnificent men
who drew splendid pictures.
Both men extraordinary painters.
Both excellent. I like them both.
They painted quite different pictures,
yet either style is fine.
I acclaim them both!
Such superb men!

In China Mu Ch'i *

In China Mu Ch'i
ignored tradition
so they apparently regarded him
a barbarian.
But Japanese
properly understood
Mu Ch'i's most eminent aspects
by apprehending them directly.

If you have him paint the powerful,
he does dragons, tigers, lightning-fast warriors, and the like.
Along stylish lines
he paints birds, persimmons, wild geese, and such
—— hardly a barbarian.
He knew how to concentrate his skills on the harp,
and also how with his fingertips to make the instrument
        positively sing with tenderness and beauty.

ONE REED LEAF *

Rendering a single reed leaf
exhausted Mu Ch'i.
He momentarily rested.
Those observing him attributed his exhaustion to age.
Mu Ch'i laughed and said,
"To paint this single leaf
I exerted in one second the skills acquired over thirty years of discipline.
Because I've got the knack of it,
I can now consider myself an artist,
and I can keep smiling
no matter what anyone says.
That's why
I've studied for thirty years."
Observers were amazed
to hear Mu Ch'i boasting.
In the end, however, they couldn't comprehend
how he had managed,
however skilled,
to draw that single line
with a sharper edge
than a master swordsman could cut.

MU CH'I'S PICTURE OF PERSIMMONS *

Seven persimmons lined up.
You saw them
and painted them using only India ink.
That's all there is to the picture.
But the profound ravine of your peerless mind
lives unaccountably in that fruit.
I imagine that even unrivaled world-renowned masterworks
will blush before this piece,
but your face is composed.
The deepest profundity reveals itself
by putting on the most ordinary face.
If I asked, "How could you draw such a picture?"
I suppose you'd smile and say,
"I don't really know."

TESSAI *

Tessai, who lived to ninety and completed his work,
apparently vented everything he had to.
That's precisely why I can say he finished his work.
It's beautiful when someone continuously makes the most of his life on Earth.

LEONARDO DA VINCI'S LILIES *

This is certainly a painting of lilies.
And I'm sure it's a Leonardo da Vinci work.
Many lilies are in bloom,
but Leonardo is alone.
If the goddess of beauty saw this picture
she'd be pleased to say,
"This man truly grasped my feelings
when I created the lily.
There are some extraordinary human beings, aren't there?"

VIEWING A TITIAN PAINTING *

The painter boldly
viewed the model.
The model boldly
lay on her side,
stretching out
stark naked.

The greatest painter
nature created
gazed at the greatest masterpiece
nature created.
He then boldly
took his paintbrush.

Look! This is how
a painting of the greatest beauty
gradually took shape
on canvas.

TITIAN'S *GIRL IN A FUR* *

A voluptuous young woman stands wearing a fur. She looks demurely at the painter. But her eyes and mouth reveal her charm. One breast partially exposed. The fleshiness of her bare arm —— oddly beautiful. A wholesome beauty.

The painter closely observes his model.

Having chanced on a subject that perfectly matches his skill, he gladly paints the picture. The painter was no doubt gratified that he was able to paint this model. I suppose, however, that the woman he painted was even more gratified. You can find beauties in every age. But you cannot say that geniuses exist in every age.

Much less a genius like Titian.

You must call a woman fortunate to be painted by a genius.

It's a once-in-a-lifetime experience.

The canvas displays every aspect of the woman's beauty.

REMBRANDT (i) —— On viewing one of his self-portraits. *

Rembrandt!
You're on your feet,
standing restrained, restrained
—— alone like a monarch,
hat tipped back,
hands on your hips, defiant.
Rembrandt!
You're on your feet.

REMBRANDT (ii) *

Ah, Rembrandt,
I think of you often these days.
I'm not sure I admire everything
in your work.
But the way you worked
appears ideal to me.
Indeed, your skills
are worthy of praise.
I don't care to imitate your fate,
but just to imagine
you at work
gives me strength.
Perhaps I'm a small mountain
looking up at a big one,
but Rembrandt,
how amazed we'd be
if present-day Japan produced a man like you.
I'd like to bring two or three of your masterpieces
to Japan.
If you have a mind to
make the effort,
let us witness the influential excellence and quality of your painting
—— and let us die of shame.
Then allow us to scratch our way from there
to your renown.

REMBRANDT (iii) *

It was more than Rembrandt
could handle.
He was nevertheless the lion king.

THE AGED REMBRANDT *

The aged Rembrandt paints intently.
Not a soul grasps what he's doing,
yet he paints intently.
He has no intention of seeking appreciative friends
or of boasting.
He has no desire to make money,
nor has he other expectations.
He just paints intently.

TITLING REMBRANDT'S PAINTING OF A BEGGAR *

Leaning on his crutch, an aged beggar walks down the street.
An old painter sketches him.
Before he's aware of it, the old painter
senses he's turned into the beggar.
The two merge.
The beggar becomes the painter
plodding wearily along
—— an aged and lonely monarch in a procession.
Though poorly dressed
and trembling with solitude,
his gait exposes regal force.
I don't know the beggar but I know the painter.
He is Rembrandt himself, of whom I'm very, very fond.

THE RETURN OF TOBIAS —— On viewing Rembrandt's painting *

Warming himself by the fire,
the blind Tobit sat absorbed in thought.
You're probably thinking of your son, Tobias,
who should have returned by now.
You've been thinking about him as you wait day after day.
And yet it was not Tobias who knocked at your door
but some stranger,
so I suppose you're depressed.
Just now
you hear your son's cheerful voice, don't you?
So you stand up.
You stumble into and knock over the spinning wheel,
but how could that matter?
Tobias has returned.
You excitedly grope for the door.
Welcome home —— well done!
Tobias has safely returned.

Besides, guarded by an angel,
he's carrying the huge fish he caught.
It's fortunate to have someone
coming back home.
How unfortunate to have a child who doesn't return
however long one waits.
That's why I say killing is evil.
Isn't that right, Tobit?
I suppose you think that way as well,
for you've truly experienced the anxiety of waiting for a child
and the joy of his return.

REMBRANDT'S ETCHING OF FAUST *

Whenever I see it, I can't help admiring Rembrandt's depiction of Faust.
His vision is truly animated. A revelation of some sort appears in it.
The etching glistens
—— a flashing revelation that glows in a moment of our life.
The picture conveys the sense that in this world something exists beyond us.
That feeling manifests itself as a sensation.
I have the sense as I view the etching
that we share that revelation with Faust.
The treatment of black and white, of light and shadow,
      truly brings the vision vividly to life.

HENDRICKJE! *

Hendrickje!
Don't laugh
and tell me my paintings don't sell
or that no one praises my work.
Don't laugh if the old man next door sneers at me.
Regardless of what anyone says,
I have no choice but to paint.
And then, if I sketch something,
I have no choice but to sketch what pleases me.
You see, there's no more reason to draw
than there's reason not to draw.
Don't laugh
even if I call myself the best artist in Holland.
Don't laugh if I tell you that
sooner or later they'll pay fancy prices for what I've painted.
After all, I can't imagine otherwise.
Sleeves rolled up, I paint on and on
till I personally have no choice but to feel satisfied with my work.
There's no way I can shortchange myself
to satisfy others.

COURBET *

I'm quite fond of Courbet.
I don't especially care for his artistic principles, but I like his forcefulness,
his expressions, his exactness, the way he grapples with objects.
His waves are stunning. So are his still lifes. And his nudes are remarkable, too.
Both his woods and his human subjects are superb.

DAUMIER *

I really like Daumier, as well.
His oils are magnificent.
I'm happy he painted a number of pictures of Don Quixote.
The Third-Class Carriage is splendid.
His impressive energies
—— vibrant as a waterfall.
Whatever he confronts he does so in a grand style.

DELACROIX *

I bend my head to Delacroix.
His lions and tigers are fearful.
How about the back of the boatman who poles the craft
carrying Virgil and Dante, a picture he painted at twenty-five?
Mountains, cliffs, clefts in the hills.
His powers awe me.

VIEWING A RENOIR NUDE *

"Your painting costs ¥15,000,
mine less than ¥100.
But my painting is costly and yours is not.
Rather than buy 150 of my paintings,
I'd rather buy one of yours.
I'm an elementary school pupil,
you're a genius.
Though your paintings employ a hundred,
a thousand times the intellect and sensitivity as mine,
they are not costly.
Sorry, but my works cost more."
That's how I felt.
"Let me do my best!
I, too, have inner strengths.
I need only apply them.
I'm just extremely short of ardor."
That's how I felt.

VIEWING A BOURDELLE PAINTING *

Left hand raised,
a woman stands in the wind,
her dress fluttering.

She seems on the verge of speaking.
I can't guess
what she wants to say.

I know only that the roughly sketched posture
of this woman
is lovely.

She
expands
our minds.

Like her,
we, too, want to address
some unknown friend . . .

 . . . just as she wants to bare
to everyone
the mind of Bourdelle.

With capaciously-composed hearts,
we, too, desire to speak
to everyone.

VAN GOGH *

Van Gogh,
you blaze with will!
Whenever I think of you,
I seethe with energy.
Seething energy drives me to the summit.
Seething energy drives me to my limits.
Oh, yes, I seethe with the energy
that drives me to my limits.

VAN GOGH'S PAINTING OF AN OLD MAN *

The old man in Van Gogh's painting weeps.
The woman in Millet's painting weeps.
What are they weeping about?

VAN GOGH'S DRAWING OF A FOUNTAIN *

Van Gogh sketched the fountain
in the insane asylum.
Its water doesn't fall
but appears to climb straight into the skies.
It never stops climbing on its direct path to heaven.
No doubt this points to some meaning.
Thus did Van Gogh ascend to heaven.

HODLER *

Hodler, mighty loner!
Whenever I think of you,
I gain poise
—— I throb with inner strength.
You are spiritual serenity incarnate.

READING HODLER'S BIOGRAPHY *

When I read Hodler's biography
I indeed seethe with energy.
He's a self-confident man
who absolutely made the most of himself
—— a pleasing fellow.
In whatever I do,
I want above all to fulfill myself.

MUD

"Mud!
My, you're filthy."
"But look at my hair,
look at what I've produced.
Perhaps certain of my products are filthy,
but I've also given birth to incomparable loveliness.
Not only that. Look carefully
at the beauty of my hues,
the magnitude of my mass.
Those who know about them know well.
You don't know, do you?
Your ignorance is no blot on me,
but doesn't it blot you?"

TWO MEN

Two men
went into the same art museum.
One sought out the most famous paintings in the collection
and came out filled with admiration.
The other viewed, however, the most insignificant paintings
    and came out indignant.
Both were honest men,
but I'd rather be the one who appreciated what he saw.

Since I was born a human being,
I want to communicate with the most beautiful human minds.
And I want to rejoice that I was born a human.
Whatever you say, humans are mortal,
yet as long as I'm alive I want to love them.
The person who lives and despises humanity
may be honest,
but I prefer to love people while I'm alive.

AN INCOHERENT PICTURE

Having myself painted incoherent pictures,
when I see a picture I don't care for I tell the artist,
"You have no comprehension of what a painting is."
What a brazen fellow I am.
(That's that.)

WHATEVER I OBSERVE

I get the urge to paint whatever I observe.
I paint whatever I have the urge to paint.
I paint wholeheartedly with undiminished attention.
I'm oblivious to time, to place, to the people watching me.
I'm oblivious to money or the fact that I'm alive.
The joy of painting makes me oblivious to everything.

CRITICS & WRITERS

CRITIC and PAINTER

A critic
made this comment
about a picture:
"Do you think an artist
painted this?
Isn't this by a consummate amateur?
Anyone can paint something like this.
It's irresponsible to paint such things
and claim to be an artist."
When the painter who painted it
heard that
he said,
"Still, I did the very best I could.
Of that at least I'm confident.
You know, I figured I could paint something you never see amateurs try.
Yet it took me about a day to do it."
Then he smiled a smile
brimming with pride.

BIG TREE

Say, kid,
when you look at a big tree,
focus on the whole.
Don't hunt just for its crinkled leaves.

ARTIST and CRITIC

In response to a critic's request,
I put on various masks
and showed them to him.
Not a one pleased him.
I then took the mask off.
If you don't like my face as it is,
you can lump it.

LUDICROUS FOLKS

Weary after finishing an important assignment,
I went out for a stroll.
One of those ludicrous folks
came mincing by
and said to me:
"What's happened to you lately?
Your recent paintings are lifeless.
Don't you know that turning out such work
will be the end of you?
I figured you might achieve
more than you have.
If you soon do not mend your ways,
you'll never get back on track."
Being told that
didn't particularly upset me.
On the contrary, I couldn't suppress
a self-satisfied smile,
because I was thinking
that if he saw what I'm doing now
he'd no doubt feel ashamed of his pronouncements
and curl up in a hole.

When I ran into this fellow
a year later, however,
I felt for him
—— wondering what he might say by way of apology.
I felt exultant when I met him,
but he put on airs
as though he were
some five or six notches above me,
and said,
"You're painting well
these days.
It's admirable
that you took my advice.
No doubt
your work may amount to something
if you continue
in this way.
Don't be discouraged.
Keep at it."
I couldn't keep my jaw from dropping.
Running into such a fellow
was revolting.

GO MASTER *

I was gargling when these lines came to mind:
Whatever the kibitzers say,
the *Go* master
calmly places his stones where he believes he should.

Whatever the kibitzers say,
the master, aware of his destiny,
calmly follows the path he believes he should take.
After all, he perceives precisely
what the kibitzer cannot.

ONE PAINTER

One painter
told a fussy critic:
"Say whatever you please.
I'm hard of hearing.
After all, I've chosen the only path
—— the one that's natural, that's inevitable,
that's proper
for me.
There's no way I can make appropriate changes
and meet your demands."

CRITICS' DISDAIN

I dread
the critics' disdain.
I dread as well their not disdaining me.

ONE CRITIC

One critic
asked a painter,
"What do you hope to achieve, painting such pictures?"
The painter looked earnestly into the critic's face
and burst out laughing,
"Ridiculous peculiarities
exist everywhere, you know.
It's just like nature to be brazen
and to create the kind of works
I cannot contrive."

DEVOTED CRITIC

A. Is this writer friend or foe?
B. He's foe.
A. Really . . . ? Well, then, I guess it's all right to badmouth him.
B. But of course.

TO CRITICS

Let the critics babble on.
The true artist spends his life
tirelessly treading the path of certitude.

TO THE CRITIC

I don't go to the right because you say, "Go right," you know.
I go to the right because I want to go to the right.
When I want to go to the left, I'll go to the left.

ONLY TO THE RIGHT

"Spread your roots only to the right.
It's despicable spreading them to the left."
"Nincompoop!
I don't mind spreading my roots
to the right or left, front or back.
I take whatever provides nourishment.
I'm no parasite
but an independent tree."

I SIMPLY

– 1 –

You know, I simply
ignore the critics.
I have yet to learn a single thing from them.
They attempt to portray me
as someone untrue to himself.
But I am true to myself.
I think I'm true to humankind and nature, as well,
but I have no intention of being true to critics
who grasp nothing that has depth.

– 2 –

Critics make various demands on others.
In sum, what they do is pointless,
you see.

LOTS and LOTS OF POETS

Lots and lots of poets
express what I cannot
in language I'm unable to manage.
I admire that.
I tip my hat to them
and listen humbly
to their rhetoric.
Yet I am myself
and have my own "voice."
I express myself
in ways that they cannot.
I let out
whatever wants to pour from me.
I speak up
whether or not anyone listens.
I do not intend senselessly to dampen the energies
that bubble up from within.

THIS SMALL POETRY COLLECTION *

May this small poetry collection
end up in various homes
and become a companion to people's hearts,
to those who go into the hills and fields
——— a good companion on the journey of life.

THIS BOOK *

I wrote this book.
Its text and pictures prove my existence.
Neither would have existed
had I not produced them.
Regardless of what people think when they see it,
the fact is that I exist in this book.
Even when I'm dead,
people who see this book
will know I once lived.
They'll know what sort of person I was.

This book will be in the libraries
of people who can love me.
I suppose from time to time
they'll open it and look at it.
At such times I'll send these persons my love.
I don't know
what parts of this book
might appeal to readers,
but I think I'd like to produce books
worthy of the reader's love.
Perhaps many
will find them trivial.
I believe at least a few of my books are worth
someone's love.
That belief has urged me
to make this book with my whole heart.
Those who see my work
will experience sincere delight and,
beaming with smiles,
laugh that I so persistently wrote about
the commonplace.
At the same time, however, they're likely to sense the warmth
in what's been written here.
I love what I wrote
in this book.
I intended to write it
whole-heartedly, soberly, and without malice.
Those who sense that
are likely to love this book.
I publish this book
filled with my dreams,
and so I hope that people who love it
might pick it up and from time to time read it.
I made this book dreaming that dream.
I dedicate this book to those who love me
—— it's one small bouquet
that vindicates my life.
I am, after all, such a simple-minded man.

THINGS I'D LIKE TO WRITE

The joy of being able to write what I want!
Almost fifty,
I make a living with my pen.
Commercial magazine editors tell you again and again that,
if you submit something to them,
you have to rewrite it

until it becomes salable.
I wasn't born to be a commercial writer,
but I'm a man who exists by producing manuscripts.
My wife and children must eat.
If I didn't write I'd be penniless,
and I'd have nothing but debts.
The tax collector shows up without fanfare.
Because there's nothing I can do about that,
I write half in despair,
can't turn out good work,
and then they won't accept what I do.
So again it's, Rewrite! Rewrite!
Vital time and energy
haplessly depleted.
Twenty-nine days out of a month
eroded.
What's left
but shame?
At least for a single day
I'd love to write something I want to write.
Oh, the joy of being able to write what I want!

WORK WITH MY PEN

I don't make a point of boasting
that I work with my pen.
I chose this field
because I can't do anything else.
I chose this field
because there's no other work I'm capable of doing.
In this endeavor, I'll be happy
if I can be of use to my brothers and sisters.
If not, I'll feel ashamed.

PREFACE POEM *

Whatever else you may say,
it's a fact that in life
we experience
beauty, love, and joy.
While you may object that there's more to life than these,
I don't think you can deny
that life involves all three.
Without making a conscious point of it,
I've been glorifying this trio from the outset.
Even if I do make a point of it,

I'd like to continue glorifying all three.
Beauty, love, joy
—— these three stars
glisten in life's sky.
How beautiful!
Looking up at them,
travelers through life
will from time to time
shed tears of joy.
If these three stars
did not brighten my life,
how desolate
it would be.
Yes, three stars
—— beauty, love, and joy.

SUBSTITUTE FOREWORD

"Is it an essay?"
"No."
"Is it a story?"
"No."
"Is it a poem?"
"No."
"What is it?"
"I don't know what to call it."

"Why publish something like that?"
"Because I feel most confident writing such things."
"Pieces like this . . . ?"
"That's right."
"You talk far too much about yourself."
"That's right. I talk, however, only about that single individual
    most familiar to me."

"What you say is full of contradictions, you know.
Which statements would you say are true?"
"All of them."

SORDID POEM *

A flock of birds landed
on a white birch
where they took turns leaving their droppings.
The more sordid the mess, the prouder they felt.
"Look at my droppings!

You may be a white birch,
but haven't you had enough?"
All laughed with glee.
The white birch made a sour face
but told itself,
"I appreciate your mess of guano.
Thanks to you, I've got my vigor back."

WHEN PAN PLAYS HIS PIPES *

When Pan plays his pipes,
men and women, young and old, begin to dance.
That's because the life in them
begins to dance.

PLAYING THE FLUTE *

Someone
plays his flute.
No one comes.
He plays
and one comes.
He plays on.
Two come.
He plays on.
Ten come.
He plays on.
A hundred come.
He plays on.
He plays his flute,
oblivious to all.

MAN ON THE FLUTE *

He doesn't claim
to be very good at it,
but a man plays his flute.
He pipes tirelessly.

Playing the flute eases his mind.
He thinks his piping can give others pleasure.

He pipes serenely,
improvising the melody.
Though no one dances to his airs,
he plays the flute. •

He pipes modestly.
He plays on
—— undisturbed by anyone,
and so regards himself
a happy man.

I'm delighted.
He's delighted.
Even if few are delighted,
he plays his flute.
He has no choice
but to play.

Yes, a man on the flute!
He pipes when he's lonely,
he pipes with tears blurring his eyes.

He pipes when he's joyful
and when he's vexed.
He finds comfort in notes
even if they contain no beauty.

When only those who wish to hear
gather round,
he gladly plays his flute.

Some call his performance trifling,
some wonder why he pipes,
but though he's no longer young,
he's absorbed in playing his flute.

He's ashamed
that he has no other skill.
He plays his flute sincerely
in his personal style.

Yes,
a man on the flute!
He pipes today, too.
He simply plays to his heart's content.
It doesn't bother him in the least
whether there's anyone to listen
or whether they delight in his piping.
He's just grateful
he can play his flute.

He's the sort of man
who'll play his flute till he dies.
He's a man who'll pipe even after he dies. •

For that which gives him life
lives in others as well.

Yes,
a man on the flute!
He pipes whether or not others get pleasure from it.
He would, of course,
prefer to please everyone.
He regrets only that he lacks the talent to delight them.
Pushing that from his mind,
he plays on.

WITH ANOTHER'S FLUTE *

Blessed are those who can dance to another's flute.
Even more blessed are those who can dance to their own flute.
Cursed are those who, to dance,
must have someone play for them.

SKYLARK

Skylark!
You fly
so very
high.
Your vigorous chirruping
isn't just to attract a mate, is it?
You sing because you want to soar through everything you can
in tune with the rhythms of life.
I, too, want to sing perfectly in tune
with the rhythms of life.

POET OF THE SEAS and THE SKIES

Someone laughed at me and said,
"You're just a teeny poet from a teeny isle . . . ."
"Have you never seen the vast sea?
I'm a poet who sings his songs
standing on the shores of a vast sea,
shouting noisily at the Pacific's surf.
Don't you know those sounds,
the sounds of swells, of crashing waves?
I know them.
Though I live on a teeny isle,
I want to be a poet of the seas and the skies."

GOOD INSTRUMENTS

It's foolish to think that if only you could produce a good instrument
you'll beget talent.
But it is true that if you have a good instrument
you're more likely to inspire it.

HOWEVER FINE THE INSTRUMENT

However fine the instrument one may play,
if your ears are assaulted from morning to night
by someone who can't play it well,
you couldn't possibly regret
being born with an ear for music.
The more the musician
makes those with the best ears
miserable,
the less welcome he'll be as a good musician.

MUSICAL INSTRUMENT

How you play the instrument
you've been given
depends upon your skill.
But the instrument given you
is exceptionally choice.

STONE BY THE WAYSIDE *

You wanted so much to see the poet,
but you'd fallen by the wayside.
A fellow came along
and heard your silent words.
He then picked you up
and took you to the poet.
You were silently delighted.
Then you mutely asked the poet
to thank the person who'd taken you to him.
At last you'd come to the poet.
Finally you acquired a beachhead on peaceful existence.
A thousand years will change you into a precious stone.

EXPERT ARCHERS *

Many expert archers gathered to shoot at the bull's eye.
Three hit it with their first arrow.
Four hit the bull's eye with their second arrow.
Seven hit it with their third.
Others, for the most, hit it after twenty or thirty tries.
One man, however, failed to hit the bull's eye however many arrows he shot.
The others left, but he stayed and shot arrow after arrow.
In the end he never made a hit.
At length he broke into tears.
Even a decade later, he still hadn't amounted to anything. He nevertheless did not lose hope. Nor did he weep again.
He began to take aim at what others would not aim for.
It was another decade before he amounted to anything, but nobody knew what he'd achieved.
After he died, people saw an arrow that had so deeply penetrated a tree in the valley that nobody could pull it out. Who shot that arrow with such force? People looked at it in amazement. This fellow's name was carved on the shaft. For the first time, they realized he'd been a master archer with no peer.

THE ARROW SHOOTER

Watch the arrows I let fly.
The first one missed
The second one missed, too.
The third one also missed.
The fourth and the fifth missed as well.
But don't laugh.
I won't always be missing.
I've been shooting arrows
every day, day after day,
for more than a decade,
each time thinking, This one's it.
This next one will connect for sure!
Even assuming I'm not yet an authentic archer,
I have occasionally hit the mark.
Look!
I'll show you that now
I can put this large arrow
into the center of the human heart
—— an arrow you can't remove!
Watch the arrows I let fly.

WHAT YOU WRITE

Someone asked, "Is what you write poetry?"
It makes no difference.
As long as my heart lives in it,
it makes no difference.

BECAUSE HE WROTE A POEM *

Because he wrote a poem,
are Michelangelo's sculptures now inept?
Because he worked in many fields,
are Leonardo's paintings empty now?
Because he became an actor,
are Molière's works trivial now?

CREATIVITY

Am I the one who creates?
Creativity, however, doesn't happen at will.
What clears my head
makes me creative.
Brains! Get healthy soon.
The bubbling spring won't flow
when it's blocked.
The spring of my brains
is clogged.
Creativity doesn't bubble up as I'd like.
Creativity, hurry and spurt!
Hurry and revive my brain, my brain.

A GIANT'S CALLIGRAPHY

Sometimes I note
a giant's calligraphy
or a picture he painted.
The vastness
of his so solidly built realm
fills me with awe.

KINOSHITA! *

Kinoshita!
Have you died?
You so abhorred dying,
but at least now
I hope you're at peace.
Flowers in the garden
of your life work
will always bloom,
exude fragrance,
enrich people's minds.
Your amiable heart!
Kinoshita,
my friend,
now that you're dead
I don't suppose you find death unpleasant.
O noble spirit who struggled mightily
through solitude,
sleep in peace.

TO SENKE *

I read your verse
whenever I felt lacking
in inner strength.
Strength then surged up in me.
Reading you exhilarates me
and cleanses my heart.
I'm beholden.

Your poetry
gives strength.
It purifies
even the defiled heart.
It restores hope
to those who've lost it.
In your work
they'll also re-discover beauty.
You are a poet.
I'm beholden.

SENKE MOTOMARO *

He was indeed a poet,
the "Poet of Paradise,"
though in this world a destitute bard.
Those along the way looked scornfully on him
as he passed by.
He loved and adored
every creature on Earth
and thought he lived in Paradise.
He applauded everyone of genius,
and now he has joined them.
He entered the temple of beauty and radiated light.
He leisurely frequented realms
that the achievers in society could not.
He, indeed, is a genuine bard:
"Poet of Paradise."

MOTOMARO'S DEATH *

Though three years younger than I,
Senke died before me.
I hoped he might be around much longer.
I wanted him to live.
I thought that he would soon achieve a secular victory
and win acclaim
as a poet of the world,
as a representative Japanese bard.
Senke left us, however, before that could happen,
departing in a manner worthy of the man.
Senke not only lived like Van Gogh or Rembrandt,
you can say he died the way they died.
As Senke's friends, we'd like to show the world
his true merits.
We'd like to tell people about
his unbounded love,
his matchless ardor.
He was indeed a poet,
a poet not easily replaced:
a friend to the poor,
a man who applauded nature, beauty, and talent.
He was truly a poet
in the realm of the imagination.
He's dead now,
but he'll live eternally
in the realm of imagination.
Senke Motomaro, *Banzai!*

WHITMAN (i) *

Whitman,
dauntless libertarian!
Whenever I think of you, I surge with hope,
a hope affirming the existence of all that is.
You overwhelm me with a sense
of vital force.

WHITMAN (ii) *

Whitman
walked gallantly,
unruffled.
Could he be a Marxist?
If so, I admire him.
If not,
he's a fool.
Whitman
walked in silence.

WHITMAN (iii) *

Whitman,
Blake,
Rembrandt,
and 13,600 more,
too many to mention by name
—— what splendid individuals there are.
Whatever difficulties we meet,
we remain true to ourselves and,
without losing heart,
continue moving steadily on
to perform tasks of unrivaled solidity.
Another decade!
Day after day,
I will work on and on,
doing my utmost.
I have nothing to do with fools.
My mind focused,
I attend only to those
able to love devotedly.
I'll keep moving on, keep struggling till the end.

LOST TITLES

- 1 -

I'd like to write a poem
and never tell anyone about it.
I'd love to write a poem
that nobody can understand,
then put it away
without showing it to anyone.

I'd like to write the sort of poem
that someone will read
years and years after I die,
and then file it away
without showing it to anyone.

- 2 -

I'd like to write a poem
with the fragrance of a plum.
I'd like to write a poem
that makes people think that spring has come.

I'd love to write
a warm poem
that streams from the self-evident,
that's aromatic.

I want to do
what can't be done.
I want to make a stab
at what is not allowed.

- 3 -

I'd like to paint
a tiny, tiny picture.
I'd love to paint a picture that sparkles
lovely as a gem.

- 4 -

I'd love to paint a picture
that's artless,
that's honest,
that's nothing to look at
—— and yet the longer you look
the more you like it.

WORTHLESS POUCH

The pouch is disintegrating
but the gem it carries glitters more and more.
Such is the man who lived for truth.

TWO ON A MOUNTAINTOP

No one knew
what the two on the mountain top
were talking about.
At that moment, their life metamorphosed whole
into a realm of poetry.
Nobody knew
it had occurred.
Realm of dreams, realm of beauty, realm of love.
No one knew
that two people were living there.
Nobody knew it but they.
When they died they found that their present life
had become a realm of poetry.

PEOPLE WITH TAILS

I dreamed that people with tails
had gotten together and were talking.
I was surprised at the way
all their tails began to wag
when the food arrived.
Everyone's tail again began to wag
the moment a young woman came in.
When she talked in a friendly way
with one of the men,
his tail wagged in a curious manner.
At the same time, the other tails stopped wagging.
If a slight earthquake had surprised everyone at that moment,
every tail would have drooped.
And, when the quake was over,
every tail would start wagging again, wouldn't it?

One fellow among them,
a self-important look on his face, his tail still,
assumed an air of aloofness.
I intuitively perceived
that this fellow
was a writer.

When I went up to him
and said,
"You really do splendid work,"
his tail instantly began to wag.
He tried at that moment, however, with feigned aplomb to still its wagging.
It was both pathetic and comical to notice
that his tail was predisposed to wag.
That's when I realized
how fortunate I was
to have no tail.
Having your tail instantly start wagging on you
over a mere trifle
is a bit annoying, isn't it?

I DARE

I dare to stay calm.
If it isn't something I want to write,
I just won't write it.
As long as I'm not in the mood,
I simply do not write.

PART IV

GOD & COUNTRY

Neither heavenly nor earthly, neither mortal
nor immortal have we created thee, so that thou
mightest be free according to thy own will and
honor, to be thy own creator and builder.
To thee alone we gave growth and development
depending on thy own free will. Thou bearest
in thee the germs of a universal life.

— Giovanni Pico della Mirandola —
Philosopher and Humanist
(1463–1494)

That which shows God in me, fortifies me.

— Ralph Waldo Emerson —

PART IV contains poems dealing with what is greater than the individual: the Maker or Creator, who is God [*kami*, defined in NOT GOD], and the state or nation. After surveying Mushakôji's views of the Maker, I emphasize or re-emphasize several essentials of what I perceive to be the nature of his religiosity.

✦   ✦   ✦

MAKER · CREATOR · GOD—terms I use interchangeably—identify the being whom Mushakôji believes to be the absolute. In many works the poet states that men are the offspring of a supernatural being, but he does so most often, most insistently, and most elaborately in verse written between ages 79 and 80 (1964–1965). These verbose and diffuse works explore the significance of this belief through dialogues with the Creator · Maker [*sôbutsusha* · *zôbutsusha*]. This being invested people with special gifts. Above all he gave them the capacity to love one another; cf. *agapé*, page 114 ff. God hopes that humans who live authentically [*hontô ni ikiru*] will honor truth and permit love to characterize their behavior. Another gift granted to those who carry out the Creator's will [*tenmei*] is freedom from the fear of death. Philosophers universally recognize this attitude as a primary quality of the authentic person. Freedom from general anxieties also characterizes those who submit to God's rule, while insecurities indicate insufficient submission.

Most revelations of God's will occur when the poet imaginatively meets and converses with the Creator. These meetings sometimes result from the poet's desire, sometimes from the Creator's desire, to talk. The deceptively simple-minded nature of these impromptu, intimate chats systematically conceals the degree to which they deal with significant moral problems. Mushakôji depicts a Creator who, like himself, frets about human beings, their relationships, their behavior, and their future. His depictions contain neither fuzzy abstractions nor arcane concepts—nor anything approximating a coherent, systematic, or consistent theology. No doubt Mushakôji presents his stray impressions in the form of dialogues to fend off expectations for system and consistency. The dialogue's strategic value is naturalness. He reports these imagined talks verbatim without reworking or "correcting" them. Since even minor editing would gain notable improvements, most will wonder why Mushakôji lets his rambling repetitions stand. Aside from the usual argument that uncorrected signifies *sincere*, he does regard himself a teacher of ethics. Because he also knows as well as any preacher how to communicate with those in the pews, as it were, he uses his "pulpit" to tell them what they should hear about the Maker and his love for us. He tells them. Then he tells them what he told them.

Fatherly, relational, pursuing, concerned: this caring Creator will sound familiar to those in the Judeo-Christian tradition. A major difference lies in the extent to which Mushakôji's Maker acts on the world or gets involved with his creatures. His God is more deistic than theistic. In general, he waits for humans to realize their divine potentials to love and care for each other. Yet he does at times enter the human dimension, at least to chat with a believer. Those who, like Mushakôji, rely on divine help in times of need he favors most. The poet always does his best and leaves the results to God; cf. pages 64 and 276. At times Mushakôji's God appears to be a theistic being willing to deal aggressively with events on Earth. But Mushakôji never expected miracles. If there were waters to part, he knew he must part them; cf. page 131. When he had "done his utmost" and still cannot solve his problem, he prayed, "Lord! / this is all I can do"; page 261. This crisis management technique reflects the Taoist *wu-wei* approach; cf. page 20 ff.

Conversant with the frailties of his crowning glory, the Creator acknowledges human potentials. His expectations hence remain as lofty as Mushakôji's, whose writings constantly display his intense hopes that humans might soon realize their promise. Similar expectations flavor his conversations with God. The biblical record describes how positive values represent ideals the Creator planted in the human heart. The record asserts, too, that God imbued people with his qualities, thus making them in his own image. That, too, is Mushakôji's belief. These qualities reveal the kind of people the Creator likes or dislikes. No human trait is more fundamental than appreciating the gift of life and relying on "The Giver"; cf. page 131. If people realize they are but stewards, they will be more submissive to God's will that we love one another. Those who trust in God and have faith in him also will trust in other people and have faith that they will eventually choose to work toward realizing the potentials of the race. The Creator approves of such individuals and of those who live and die without anxiety. He loves, in short, the authentic person. God does not approve of any who live anxiously for themselves, which is the height of inauthentic existence. Nor does he favor those who, thinking themselves as important as their Maker, have forgotten both God and their own mortality. Only inferior people take the self as the measure and manipulate others in their grope for success, selfish satisfaction, or power.

Reliance on the giver of life includes imitating his nature—an obvious requirement for those made in his image. Mushakôji's version of "In the beginning was the Word [*Logos* • Tao]" (*John* 1:1) is "In the beginning was emotion [SINCERITY • intuition]." That is, since humans act properly when they rely on the innate tendencies of the heart, feelings must be the guide to human relations. These tendencies the Creator planted in us Mushakôji calls *honshin*, heart of hearts, the core of human values. From the *honshin* emanate beauty, love, truth, and sincerity—at once the qualities of God himself and Mushakôji's favorite nouns. Not only are the emotions that arise in the *honshin* reliable, God approves of those who act according to them. He disapproves of people who deny the *honshin* and trust instead in logic and rationality. Anyone committed to intellect unfortunately becomes enamored of words, the more convoluted the better. As a result, artifice overwhelms art, the complex and the snarled overshadow the commonplace and the simple, and human will subverts God's will. This Creator, a tolerable reflection of Mushakôji's most cherished values, also expects others to live harmoniously with their fellows. Those who follow the *honshin* readily serve others and work for their happiness. Ideal individuals generously love and show concern for others. Since all who act according to their *honshin* intuitively know how to balance individuality with relatedness, few tensions develop between their egos and the needs of the group. This is not true of those who make private desires the measure. They serve themselves, pursue personal gain, and distrust, manipulate, even abuse others. They also denigrate sincerity and show little hesitation to cause suffering and misery.

The Creator assumes that humans who follow their *honshin* eventually will live up to his ideals. God made people to be good, to love others, and to make the world a happy, fruitful, beautiful place—a paradise. Being loyal to their *honshin* helps them realize that paradise. They also must live like genuine humans [*hontô no ningen*] and trust and respect each other. Too few follow their God-given bent to do good, yet the Creator nonetheless optimistically hopes that the number of such people will increase. These hopes prevent neither doubts nor reservations about his creation. God worries, for example, about the human's persistent self-serving smugness and cocksure attitude. Or he wonders about the wisdom of having given human beings free will and wide powers over all the creation. At times the persona consoles the Creator with his optimistic views of life on Earth. Mushakôji's Creator not only dispenses but requires consolation. Frustrated expectations for improved behavior do not, however, entice the Maker to interfere in history.

These chats illustrate Mushakôji's rhapsodic views: he honors heart over head, intuition over intellect, and feelings over facts. These views mock the scholar's attempts to explain life's mysteries using elaborate jargon and ponderous logic. Although totally alien to the theologizing or philosophical mind, the rhapsodic approach taps into ancient and deep-rooted indigenous sensibilities, some of which resonate with the qualities of the Creator revealed in diverse sacred records.

RELIGIOSITY or a sense of worshipful perspective cultivated Mushakôji's self-effacement and sense of responsibility before God. Religiosity has no connection with cults, dogmas, or systems of worship. Rather, it entails feelings of awe or reverence for and a desire to have relationship with the absolute. Being "religious" means acknowledging one's place in the creation as a humble reflection of the Maker's person. That attitude will stimulate people to discharge their duties.

Spiritual perspective assumes faith in a power beyond the self. Belief then prescribes taking a modest pose in God's presence. Mushakôji began there. Although he remained open to every reality and belonged to no organized sect, he nevertheless nurtured a robust, old-fashioned, naive faith. Those so certain they have all the answers they do not bother with faith tested his restraint. He was furthermore impatient with institutionally-certified believers. Their immodest assurances revealed to him that they had, in effect, abandoned belief. For them faith was no longer "the assurance of things hoped for, the conviction of things not seen" (*Hebrews* 11:1) but pseudo-scientific certitude. Nor did Mushakôji display much interest in the exegesis of sacred texts. His scripture was humanity, his gospel the fulfilled human life. Religiosity without that perspective he rejected. His faith also committed him to the universal priesthood of believers, a notion that lets people approach God without intermediaries. No priests, no dogma, no rituals, no organization—certainly no institutional church—for him. The heart was enough. He remained always a guileless man whose blind but steady faith linked him with his Maker. Mushakôji might nonetheless be considered a camp follower whose interest in Christianity was as intense as his loathing for Christendom. His respect for a

God who made individuals with free will obliged him to reject orthodoxy, which he thought theologians designed to create conformity and prevent human beings from being authentic. He was certain that perfect personhood cannot be achieved short of grace, over which institutions have no control.

Religiosity compelled Mushakôji to love others responsibly. That called for creating an environment that makes loving relationships possible. He accordingly regarded himself an evangelist announcing the "good news" of a radically new way to interact with others in his vertical society: love them. He thought it necessary to balance love for me and my group with love for you and your group, a revolutionary stance in Japan; cf. page 116. Altruism's horizontal relations challenge Japan's paternalistic, vertical polity. His message, like *agapé* (cf. page 114), called for taking the initiative: filling new skins with new wine. From at least his early twenties, Mushakôji was committed to the idea, "If you know these things, blessed are you if you do them" (*John* 13:17). He rejected any who stopped at "blessed are you," for he knew that action—not inert knowledge—receives the benison. Mushakôji's religiosity uniformly assumed a concern for responsibility, HUMANISM, and universal love in a culture that makes them all but impossible to realize. Readers with a Christian background will see that Mushakôji's dedication to love verifies the assertion that God has left all people with "some clue to his nature" (*Acts* 14:17).

A society that honors altruism will encourage people to love each other. To create such a polity—a heaven on Earth—requires one to challenge socio-cultural conventions. Remember that Mushakôji's heaven contained no trace of traditional Confucian dogmas that designated it the abode of the ancestors; cf. page 28. His paradise had as little to do with the past as with future rewards beyond death. Nor did he worship the ancestors or accept their standards as normative. He simply expressed gratitude for the heritage people of the past bequeathed him. Because his view was always dynamic, he dedicated himself to improving what he had received. He regarded it his duty to give the next generation not a stagnant legacy but one etched with his personal efforts, private style, and unique improvements; cf. page 117 ff. Human history he considered a constant flux where people and time interrelate and interact. He thought that each individual must feel responsibly committed to augmenting the tradition. In short, Mushakôji deals with cultural conventions in a vigorously pragmatic, instrumental, and dialectical manner.

Japanese intellectuals, totally convinced that religion and literature relate like fire and water, reject these views. Predictably, they relegate religiosity to the cultural wastebasket. Their radical repudiation of faith blinds them, however, to an arresting fact. Both literature and religion aim to confront human beings with the truths of the human condition. Worse, Mushakôji's stance implies that he thinks poets should be teachers of humanity and morality as well as writers who communicate love and truth. He therefore commits several unpardonable sins, for most critics reject all such "religious" beliefs, shun ethical issues, and avoid questions like the existence of God or humanity's mission on Earth. Deliberate disinterest in these issues demonstrates the impoverishment of the intellectual's dedication to improving human life. That's why Mushakôji's devotion to a primitive, basal humanity wins critical neglect but merits attention. Those blind to the importance of returning the heart to the state it enjoyed before corruption are too insensitive to understand the need for love. To reclaim that state of primal purity, Mushakôji adopted the highest thoughts of Socrates, Buddha, Confucius, and Christ. Unfortunately, the resulting potpourri alienates orthodox adherent and scholar alike. This did not distress Mushakôji, for he chose to focus on respecting the religiosity of the sincere individual. That, he thought, was infinitely more meaningful than either the manufactured dogmas of the theologian or the fabricated literary theories of the self-important academic. In this, too, his principles required subordinating the self to the feelings of the heart, never to dogma, logic, or ratiocination.

The perspective he achieved once he overcame his dread of death strengthened his religiosity. Death did not distress the mature Mushakôji, as indeed it should not distress the authentic person. He wrote again and again how he wanted to discharge his responsibilities or finish his work. Yet he stood ready at any moment to cross the Styx. This readiness endowed him with a pliability and optimism that irritates critics, who seldom tire of knocking him down. Time after time he bounced back like a Daruma or tumbler doll. Mushakôji invites such treatment, particularly from any who adore the pompous, because he excels at oversimplifying the extremely complex and then stating it in an extremely transparent manner. As a result, his obvious and commonsensical statements escape notice. Even when he deals with profound human problems—why fear death? why suffer death's agonies?—he does so in his customary non-intellectualizing and unself-conscious manner; cf. "Two Human Types," page 246. Not only does he avoid objective analysis and difficult terminology, the simplicity of his surfaces entices the reader to disregard the import or depth of what are often insightful and enlightening utterances.

＋　　　　＋　　　　＋

The four talks with the Maker • Creator total an excessive 800 lines that stultify as poetry. Anyone interested in understanding Mushakôji Saneatsu, however, must assuredly be familiar with the values these works present. Spontaneous though meandering, these pieces become interesting and meaningful, I believe, if read simply as intimate, informal chats that expose Mushakôji's views about God and humankind. Even where the poet appears foolish or absurd, keep in mind his tenet that the disclosures of the child-like heart are pure and hence worth sharing.

Several patriotic selections clarify Mushakôji's attitude toward his country and the Pacific War. His military poems expose the heinous extent of his "war crimes." He later confessed that his unqualified support of Japan's armed adventures in East Asia and the Pacific constituted naive nationalism and misguided, "cracked" patriotism. But how is it possible that a man who loves his country might wish it to lose the war? How can a loyal if imprudent patriot be guilty of criminal behavior merely by urging fellow citizens to support their army and honor the fallen brave?

WITHOUT GOD *

I can exist without a woman
but not without God.
God is my life,
my joy,
the ground of my being,
my bone and my marrow.
I stand firm
and do not stray,
for God is here to lead me.

HOW DESCRIBE GOD?

How describe God?
He is the spirit that pervades the universe,
the spirit that pervades humanity,
the purest spirit
within the self
—— one who lives eternally
and bonds with the eternal.
Though humans perish,
though the Earth perish,
he will never perish.
When I'm at one with him,
I have no cares.

DOES GOD EXIST? (i)

Does God exist?
From my view,
those who debate such questions
will even wonder whether they are living or dead.

DOES GOD EXIST? (ii)

I don't know if he exists.
If, however, I commit my life to God, I can feel secure.
    There is no other path to peace of mind.
That's why I think you are here for me.

DOES GOD EXIST? (iii)

Does God exist?
I simply do not know.
But there is a being to whom with peace of mind
I can commit my life.
That is God.

ONE WHO SAW GOD *

I'd strayed into a world of giants.
I felt so very small, so scrawny, so ugly.
The giants spoke to each other without restraint.
Shrinking in fear, I listened silently.
Heeding what they said gave me courage.
But I felt ashamed whenever I reflected on myself.
Why had I come?
Just then God inconspicuously entered.
No giant was aware of his presence.
God seemed to be searching for someone,
but no giant paid attention to him.
God stood without a word,
looking them over one after the other,
beginning with the largest.
Not a one took note of him.
God looked at each and every giant.
Not one paid attention to him.
Just as he was about to leave,
he took one final look around.
That's when he noticed me
kneeling in tears
and worshipping him.
When he walked over to me,
I thought I'd pass away.
He stood silently before me
and touched his right hand to my forehead.
"My beloved son!
Toil for me."
Stretched out before him in tears,
I finally found the strength to say:
"If there's anything the likes of me can do . . . ."
When I recovered,
God had disappeared.
The giants were still talking,
but I was no longer afraid.
I felt determined:
I've no choice but to live what I believe.

STRINGLESS HARP *

The stringless harp.
The unwritten tale.
The silent speech.
The sage transformed by non-action.

AN OPTIMIST MEETS THE OPTIMISTIC CREATOR

I was strolling through the realm of the imagination
when I met an old man.
I knew that this old man
was the Creator.

The Creator said to me,
"I knew you'd come.
I know you're filled with admiration
that I made humankind.
I know many splendid people,
but not one matches you in believing without qualification
in the humans I created.
That's why I wanted to see if I could meet you,
and that's why I called you here.
You do believe in me, don't you?"

"But of course.
I'm nothing but
a human being.
I rejoice that I was born a human
and that it's my ideal to live like a true human being.
Even when present-day people are able to exist like humans,
they take pride in living in a fashion
that opposes your will,
taking no confidence in the way you made them."

"You're right. I'm aware of that.
They figure they're greater than I am.
Unsatisfied with the way I made people,
they want to make others morbid."

"That's certainly true.
They've gone astray
and don't know how to get back on track.
They figure it's wiser to go farther and farther astray."

"That's correct.
They make simple things complex.

Even when they're aware they've left the highway,
they don't want to return to the road.
I gave them reason,
but they disdain listening honestly to reason.
They make everything difficult,
consider acts sinful that are not sinful,
and all along somehow rationalize and justify
what is sinful.
If their hearts ache,
they try to cover up their pain
in the most unnatural ways."
"They've lost their sense of modesty,
and they've misinterpreted your will.
They imagine they're being clever
to conceive of everything in complex terms.
They furthermore do not grasp
what is most obvious.
They conceive of wisdom in the most convoluted terms possible.
They scorn whatever is clear."

"I made the universe so that even a star
will be vividly visible as a single light
tens of thousands of light years in the future.
I made both water and air colorless and clear,
tasteless and odorless.
Though I'm capable of making such things with no trouble,
humans lack trust in me.
Instead, they make everything in a disorderly way
and then feel complacent.
I made people in such a way that they could think about matters,
not so that they could make them convoluted.
But it looks as though I've somehow erred in the way I made them.
I placed too much trust in humankind.
Apparently the last animal I made
somehow lacks acumen.
These days I'm wondering whether I should create a creature above humans
and let it rule this world.
Everything people have produced is far too rooted in human standards,
so from my view too much of it fails to delight me."

"Please put off making a creature above us to rule our world.
Present-day humankind meanders about, but we're still in process.
People have, however, at last become aware of man's mission.
I think we've finally become attentive to the question,
How can we live authentically?
The human's makeup is certainly not mistaken.
Even those who at this moment live in confusion
aren't at all satisfied to exist that way.

I'm sure they'll soon come to their senses and all will live in harmony."

"I did not create humanity
for the sake of humanity.
I made them because I wanted to make Earth more beautiful,
and because I wished to turn Earth into a paradise.
But people think too highly of themselves,
increasingly make the world colorless,
and more and more vulgarize their minds.
There's a possibility that everyone will soon become mad.
Up to now I've had confidence in people,
but I can't trust them completely any more."

"If the one who created humans can no longer trust us,
     we'll become discouraged, too.
However, I prefer not to look at it that way.
Since I'm a human being, I'm acquainted with people.
There are exceptions among us.
Some are morbid,
but they're the exceptions.
The great majority
are truly good-natured people who deserve to be loved.
Please consider those
who are gentle, charming, and amiable people.
Whenever I see such people rejoicing,
I'm easily moved
to tears.
That is, you know, the most beautiful sentiment
you created in human beings.
You observe people externally.
You cannot directly experience the goodness
you have created in us.
I've had direct personal experience of it
and demonstrate in my person the goodness of your handiwork.
Surely we humans have been wonderfully made,
but the excellence of your handiwork has not yet revealed itself.
When it is,
you'll be amazed."

"I'm hoping that might happen.
When I became competent to create humans,
I told everyone,
'Look at the human being I just fashioned!
This certainly is the noblest creature I could make.'
They all looked at the person I'd fashioned and laughed.
'You made this
—— this is your noblest creature?'
'That's right,' I said, proud of myself.

'Look at this creature's offspring.
They'll develop beyond your imagination
and rule the Earth,' I told them.
They all laughed.
But I looked confidently on the creatures I'd made
and said, 'Wait and see!'
And yet, whenever people seemed about to make something of themselves,
they always fell short.
Then came an undreamed-of outcome:
humans adore opting for evil.
That certainly wasn't what I had in mind for them.
I've been patiently watching over them, awaiting the outcome with pleasure.
But they just don't seem to make anything of themselves.
They all laughed at me and called me an optimist.
But I had faith in the way I made human beings.
I definitely still have that faith.
Aside from myself, however, nobody has confidence in humanity's future,
and they wonder how I can still have faith in people.
When I was in that frame of mind
I heard that you trusted in me,
so I wanted to see if I could meet you.
You do believe in humanity's future, don't you?"

"Of course I do.
The way you made people is truly splendid.
It's just that humans have yet to display on Earth their true selves.
It's a fact, however, that people in various areas have now
        started to display their genuine selves.
Beyond that, my intuition tells me the truth of man's splendid makeup.
Humans will soon show their natural selves and know the true meaning
        of the subtleties of harmonizing independence, freedom, and cooperation.
All will display their original selves, praise each other, love each other,
build on Earth a kingdom of beauty,
and realize here their self-made, unlimited will.
That's my belief.
Your expectations for humankind are not misplaced."

The Creator smiled at that, I thought.
That's when I returned to reality.
The reality was just as it had always been.
I am, however, grateful there are many people in the real world
whom I should love.
I laud the labors that genuine people have accomplished in the past.
When I observe a painting
that must be termed a true index of humankind's achievements,
I laud the more those humans
who have honestly given life to humankind's spirit.
Human beings deserve our trust!

IN THE KINGDOM OF GOD (i) *

I want to keep myself, mind and body,
qualified to live in
the kingdom of God.

PEOPLE *

Create a state where people can work
willingly and with enjoyment,
and it will develop into the kingdom of God.
A kingdom of God
unable to accept people who work with their hands
is a realm of fleshless jack-o'-lanterns.

IN EARNEST (i)

When I can work in earnest,
I'm happy
because I then feel that God loves me.
When I can't work,
I'm vaguely apprehensive
because I feel that God may loathe me.

TWO HUMAN TYPES

When I met the Creator,
I mentioned my displeasure
that humans have been given a dread of death
and suffer excessive agonies when they die.
The Creator
then said to me,
"Oh, I am aware of that.
We debated that problem
when I made humankind.
As a result
I tried to fashion two human types.
To the one I gave an intense degree of death's dread and its agonies.
I made the other type so it would not intensely feel
either the dread or the agony of death.
The latter type to be sure
always lived cheerfully.
These people seemed to have a pleasant time.
Compared to that,
the former type always felt depressed.

It distressed me to see them.
I then figured I should have made everyone like the latter type,
and I repented having created the former.
At that moment, however, I became aware of another factor:
when life becomes a bore,
all those who have no fear of dying
find death pleasant
and die without a struggle.
That means the survivors
were those who find death fearful
and who are bewildered by death's agonies.
That's the only type that will go on living in the world.
However agonizing the times,
they at any rate do go on living.
That's how it was."
The Creator smiled regretfully as he spoke.

WHEN MY HEART IS PURE

When my heart is pure
I have the feeling
someone is watching over me.

I'M A BELL *

I'm a bell.
Won't one of you drive out my innermost tones?
Everyone just touches me gently.
Human life is —— "I'm a Bell."

MY PRAYER *

"Here I am again!"
said the Creator, sitting next to me.
"What are you writing?
Humans accept many inconveniences.
Speech is indispensable
for communication."
"I wonder who made us like that . . . ?"

"I made people so that heart-to-heart they could understand each other
without using words.
I made them so they could love each other as well.
But, you know, people still have many defects.
Apparently they can't just keep their thoughts only in their hearts.

They then fashioned this inconvenience called language.
People are absolutely thrilled, you know, being able to speak their words.
They attach words to everything!
By now they can no longer communicate without them.
They need words even to think.
They no longer come to understand through silence
what each other wants.
In the old days two people would meet and smile at each other
     —— that'd be enough.
After language came about, it's talk, talk, talk
—— but, forgetting to talk about what's true,
and unaware of distinctions between fabrication and truth,
they let the words tumble out haphazardly.
It's talk, talk, talk.
They don't know for sure what they're talking about.
In the end their expressions do not match their feelings,
and they dash about —— the world in chaos.
In this age where people imagine they can accomplish everything,
they put my will completely out of mind.
What's happened is that
'In the beginning was the Word,'
and in the end was the human.
Human foolishness has developed without limit.
They've forgotten about me.
They've completely forgotten the true way to live as human beings.
They've even forgotten that they've forgotten.
You alone in this society remember me.
I've come to think that idle curiosity
drives many people in this world."

"It's just as you say.
People have utterly forgotten you.
Though they occasionally refer to you
and adore you as *The Lord God,*
they forget that they're your dear children.
They've also forgotten
that they're fools unworthy of being called sinners.
It would be ideal if they could live blamelessly.
Though capable of living guileless lives,
their existence is filled with evil intent.
It disgusts me when they call themselves sinners,
but those who complacently call others sinners
disgust me even more.
Why can't people rejoice more innocently,
delighted to be born on the Earth as humans,
delighted we are all human beings?" •

"That's right. If only humans lived the way they should
they could rejoice in that,
but people are not living the way humans should.
They look at a person, think he's a thief,
and believe they'll be killed if they aren't careful.
They mistakenly regard people as bloodthirsty murderers.
I truly feel sad
both when I wonder how the people I created
    could possibly turn into such creatures,
and when I look at these idiotic, bloodthirsty murderers.
Sometimes I think giving people so much free will was a mistake."

"Some people are truly disgusting
and do not deserve to be called human.
But those are the exceptional exceptions.
Among humankind
are truly wonderful people.
However much you love them, you cannot love them enough.
You'd like to make a vast number of people like them truly happy
—— people interested in helping those who suffer.
Although I have neither the time nor the energy to do so,
I'd like to get together with such folks.
The truly good people in this world outnumber the bad."

"Don't get so serious.
I'm aware of those you can't love enough
regardless of how much you love them.
Indeed, I'm troubled that there are so many of them in the world.
I desire a world
where all such people can achieve happiness.
For the most, I've surely given people that spirit."

"You have. That's why it's worth fretting over.
Being on in years, I've known many such people.
I pray for their happiness and feel sad that I have so little ability to help them.
I know, however, the meaning of the truth
that people have been given one life, not two.
I must above all make the most of myself.
That is my greatest duty. I wish to grow as much I can
and perfect myself as much as I can,
making sure my thoughts are in order.
I will learn the true way to live for humankind,
put this way into practice, and make it a reality.
I'd like to become a person who can then die without misgivings.
I think that is your will.
I'm no doctor,
only a mere human being who wonders:
What is the authentic way for a mere human to live?

How should we live to please you?
I want to live staking my life on this quest.
I have faith in you
rather than in what men of the past have said.
I haven't the slightest interest in the tenets of any single religion.
I think it's quite enough
if I can follow your will and make as much of myself as possible.
Then I'll be free of all anxiety
—— a life where my heart is perfectly composed.
I'm hardly the incarnation of righteousness.
I'm only an ordinary person
who respects the instincts you've given me,
a man who would gladly live, aptly capitalizing on what you've given,
and one who hopes with utter honesty to make the most of himself.
I don't want to be anything more than a mere human,
but I trust my heart the most.
Other people's criticisms and views are none of my business.
However much I'm praised, I feel impotent without confidence.
However much I'm slandered, if my heart is serene I can be content
to walk the path I regard the authentic way to live.
That, in short, is the life you expect of me.
Satisfaction comes from compliantly carrying out what you expect.

"When people are truly human and act authentically,
there will be no problems.
I find unjust the behavior of those
who hinder someone trying to live authentically.
People living such a life couldn't be genuine humans
if their hearts did not ache.
They would be unenlightened savages,
uncultured, or incapable of being fully human.
The more all people earnestly make the most of themselves, the better everyone
      will get along well together.
In that world we can respect each other.
That world will be composed of authentic people.
That's the world for which we long.
My belief is that
you made us
hoping that's how we might behave.
And, to the extent that humankind is humankind,
I think that, wherever human beings are human,
this idea is definitely common to everyone.
An idea that hinders the life of anyone living authentically
is not a legitimate ideology
and can't be called an ideology for humans.
Nor is thought that denigrates the sincerity of a single human being
an ideology fit for people.
An ideology only temporarily popular,

or one popular only among a single group,
is not authentic.

"I believe this
because I haven't the slightest doubt
that you've created men hoping this is how they might behave.
I do not believe those who dare to say the most pompous things
and who would blithely warp the life of a single individual.
Such people deprecate man's makeup.
You have not made people to cannibalize each other.
I think what made you the happiest when you created man
was that you were then able to believe
that the time for rapport between independence and cooperation would come.
You knew the secret to the way all can move ahead in harmony without strife.
Your creatures could at last surmount a brutal age
        where the powerful were victorious.
You knew the joy of having fashioned in this world a creature with reason.
I sense the joy
you then felt.
I'm proud that I was one of the first
truly to have sensed it.
Thus could humans initially overcome the rule of tyranny and brute force,
survive the age of barbarism,
and enter an era where they can be authentic humans.
We haven't yet been able to advance to our limits
but still live with one foot in barbarism.
Though countless tragic victims continue to exist in our world,
however, the barbaric age is at last nearing its end.

"The time is coming when I and others, when all people,
will live not under the dominion of violence
but under the dominion of reason.
The splendid bugle call sounding 'Forward March'
is the sound of humanity's joy at being able to enter wholly
        the realm of humankind.
I've been able to meet with you because I could hear the bugle call.
The joy of a human in being a human
is not a matter of living for myself.
In this life if only I do everything I must do,
you will love me.
Your wishes fill my heart with hope.
My commencement as a human starts with my mind at ease
and with faith in humanity.
As a human I will discharge my duties with a sense of justice
and without prejudice.
With your sanction, I'll discharge my duties as a human without regrets.
I'll trust in the future of humanity and live as long as I can,
hoping those I love enjoy every possible happiness.

Beyond that, worry free, I leave it up to people of the future.
My task is simply to pray that all might be happy.
I have no reservations about leaving everything up to those who are wiser
    and more talented than I.
This one life that has been given me in stewardship
I will fulfill and make the most of.
I'll continue to live an unhurried existence and follow your will.

"I'm so composed these days people wonder if I'm an idiot.
I go on living with gladness and joy,
holding nothing back as I make the most of the various gifts
you deigned to grant me.
Enthused to do what I choose to do,
I endeavor to make something of myself, forgetting the passage of time.
I'll forge ahead till I die.
I simply use to the hilt everything I've been given.
Being moreover serene and free of indecision,
I follow my conscience,
the inner voice you gave me,
rather than what others say.
I hope from afar for the happiness of those I love,
and without fettering their freedom
or having mine fettered,
I take the way allowing my single-minded advance.
I continue on the way that affirms an authentic way of life for all people,
    a path where no one needs to lose his way.
It's a way that causes no one the slightest unhappiness,
a way where one can walk with tear-filled eyes,
a way that's most spectacular, a way of independence that, moreover,
    somehow pervades the heart.
Though a solitary road, it matches the feelings of all people.
The joys of being able to walk this path
—— a way where everyone loves one another,
a way where I have supreme composure and where my eyes mist with gratitude
as I serenely take this path
—— a way where I can rejoice with everyone
—— a way where even after I'm gone
all will be empowered with greater and greater happiness.
Children, grandchildren, all those I love!
Those now alive, those yet to be born,
people who live in compliance with your will
—— I pray for your happiness.
It's truly a pity there are so many people these days
    who still can't enjoy perfect happiness.
After death, they'll find a realm of supreme innocence.
That's why I sincerely pray that people might be happy
    and live like true humans now.
I pray for that vigorously, my eyes moist."

GOD'S LOVE (i)

Just once in my life
I'd like to write a play
that makes God's pure love
absolutely echo
through the human heart.
I'd like to convey the reality of God's love
abundantly to the hearts of those who view the play.
When I can do that, I'll be ready to die.

GOD'S LOVE (ii)

He is blessed who truly knows the joy
of being able to accept God's love.
He is blessed
who through God alone
can communicate his love to all.
He is blessed who leaves everything up to God
and tirelessly does what he should.

LOVED BY GOD

I'm unbeatable
so long as I think God loves me.

LOVE THAT CONQUERS DEATH

Death is not the end.
Love has the power to overcome death. Love alone guides us.
But love laments the immensity of unhappiness in the world and wonders:
    When will unhappiness vanish from the Earth?
When will a host of courageous people multiply on Earth
    and sing the praises of love?
The dominion of love is imminent.
Surely love will soon bind heart to heart
and link us all together.
Surely the love that transcends death will move far into the distance
to free me from my self
and lead me to the kingdom of God, to the realm of beauty.
I glorify love.
May my love move unassumingly ahead.
May the love that loves me unassumingly enter my heart.
Though I am powerless,
my love reaches out.

Love that has reached out
will return again with much love.
Oh, when will that beautiful realm materialize
where people will love and help each other?

NATURALLY *

If I can lead a life of compliance,
I'll naturally
gain enlightenment.

THAN THIS PATH *

There is no path other than this
where I can fulfill my self.
This is the one I'll take.

ONE MORE STEP

On every occasion I think,
"One more step."
Now is truly a vital instant of time.
One more step.

RIVERS FLOW

I like watching
rivers flow.
I'd like to watch them forever.
They're alive, they're alive
—— frightfully alive.
Rivers rejoice.
They can flow to the sea.

A TEARDROP *

I awoke during the night
and thought:
The next time I run into the Creator,
this is what I think I'd like to tell him:

"I'm satisfied being a human.
I'm hoping, however, that I'll be able to live
as an authentic person.

It's rare in our society that a person
can live authentically.
Most people do not live like humans.
Some are not well-intentioned
and cannot live as a human should,
but many can't live authentically because other people
        have corrupt objectives.
I sympathize with these people.
I hope everyone might be able to live authentically.
When we are truly able to live as a human should,
we shall for the first time be able to enjoy how we've been constituted.
Those who do not live the way a human being should
will not appreciate how God made them.
Certainly humans
still lack wisdom
and almost intentionally make themselves miserable.
Of course, if we were prepared
much better than we now are,
I suppose many more would be capable of happiness.
People mutually plant the roots of unhappiness
and make themselves miserable.
There are, to be sure, miseries we can do nothing about.
If, however, people were somewhat wiser
they could perhaps avoid
such miseries.
Though I trust our human make-up,
I do not suggest I can live each day without a care.
I intend to exist in a truly cautionary manner,
fearing that misery may come
but being as prudent as possible
and leading a diligent life.
I will also feel grateful
that every day I can be healthy
and get my work done
without incident.
That's to feel joy that the matter-of-fact
is matter-of-fact.

"In our society, however, are many unfortunate circumstances,
an endless continuum of events one cannot squarely face.
Just as every human being was born,
every last one will die.
One rejoices when someone dies
after living his natural span,
but those who die before their allotted time
are a hundred out of a hundred,
a thousand out of a thousand.
It's doubtful that even one in ten thousand will live his full time.

Almost everybody
experiences a heartbroken end.
Everyone is heartbroken
but none merit our hate.
I cannot, however, abide those
indifferent to distressing others.
Yes, these unbearably cruel people
at times make others suffer.
Compassion cannot assuage
the feelings of the victimized.
Yes, let every tale of cruelty disappear from the world.
I'm sure that the Creator does not will them."

The Creator then appeared
and distinctly told me:
"Of course, I do not will cruelty.
I suppose, however, there's a flaw of some sort
in the way I constituted humans,
but I definitely gave them
the ability to correct that flaw.
When I created people,
I made concern for others
their primary characteristic.
I intended to give a sense of compassion
that humanity's many other passions could not negate.
So that people might endure in this world, however,
I at the same time endowed them with the capacity
to go on living though others may die.

"Had I not done so, everyone would die when a loved one dies.
Had I created people in such a way that when the parents die
      their children would also die,
humankind would cease to exist,
and the means for humans to come into this world would vanish.
The husband dies, so the wife dies.
The wife dies, so the husband dies.
If that happened, what would become of the children?
However unbearable it is to lose a loved one,
you must have the strength to survive even that loss.
It is very difficult
to achieve a balance between, on the one hand,
hoping your loved one might live forever,
and, on the other, having the strength when you lose a loved one
to survive the loss with fortitude.
Average people maintain their equilibrium
and somehow survive—that's how I created them.
A slightly morbid individual, however,
or a person facing excessive difficulties in trying to make the most of himself,

won't be able to survive a tragedy unless he gives more thought to himself
than to others.
Overly zealous about realizing himself,
he is no longer considerate enough to think of other people's griefs.
I don't know what such a person might do about this problem.

"Beyond that, there's another difficult task I had to perform:
creating sexual passion.
No doubt humans must have libido.
If they lack it, they would definitely become extinct.
Their erotic drive for self-preservation must be
the most powerful factor
enabling humans to attain their present-day glory
and survive various epochs
of unimaginable historical events.
Every animal has managed to survive because I provided each
        with appetites for food and sex.
Because I made humans so they'd be especially clever,
I went to great lengths to create libido
and its seductiveness.
I dare say that I took great pains to make passion so bewitching
that nobody, not even angels, can resist it.
But if I made its charms excessively lewd, children would be created irresponsibly.
That would result in the mass production of inferior beings,
which I feared most of all.
If it's only a matter of childbirth, that's as simple as hatching fish.
But having a baby and raising it
to become a splendid adult is daunting.
A good mind in particular is vital.
A human child requires a long period of nurture
before it can stand on its own.

"At that point this thought occurred to me:
If I furnish them only with libido, people will irresponsibly
produce children, and that could cause problems.
Thus, thinking I'd have to do something about it,
I first infused passion with a sense of shame
and made people so they'd take care about letting passion swamp them
and not love each other in an irresponsible way.
On the other hand, I provided them with romantic love
and arranged it so that the couple might together raise splendid children.
A smile of satisfaction spread over my face for the first time
when I was able to give humans the sentiment of romantic love.
This is wonderful, this is wonderful, I thought to myself.
I figured that humanity would become more and more impressive
—— an animal matching my ideals.
But things do not work out as one hopes.
It is indeed preferable

to find your ideal partner through love
and bear ideal children
rather than produce them only out of passion.
When neither individual is an ideal man or woman, however,
and when two who are not ideal
seek ideal partners,
one readily ends up with comedy or tragedy.
This situation may also become farcical.

"I've been waiting patiently for the reality where one aspires to realize ideals.
Such patience among humans is taboo,
but I'm patiently looking for people to improve.
Their forward progress falters,
but humans do continue to move ahead.
They become more beautiful, wiser,
and come to value each other's existence.
By no means is this adequate,
yet it's rapid progress if I consider how things once were.
All humanity
has become aware that people everywhere are human beings.
They no longer see foreigners as the enemy.
Long ago people considered foreigners mortal foes
and determined that war with a foreign country was a nation's fate.
They thought no one greater than the brave warrior,
who was also the most highly respected person in society.
At present, most respect the children of truth.
But it's too early to rejoice.
I can't feel great optimism
about the future of the race.
People living in today's world
have certainly suffered many tragedies.
Human efforts, however, will gradually eliminate
all such intolerable conditions.
Humans are capable of doing that.
I'd like to see evidence that people get along peacefully and live like humans
as they make the most of the various abilities I gave them.

"I don't consider passion sinful.
Much rather do I personally admire the way it's constituted.
I feel inwardly satisfied because I'm aware of its positive and negative aspects.
One facet of this problem, however, makes me speechless:
those who've forgotten what's vital in life and become
         captive to sex.
I blush thinking from time to time that this was my blunder.
But when I see those who, rejoicing innocently,
         discover in sex the joys of life,
I think everything is all right.
I'm proud of having created affection between the sexes,

though when I see men or women languishing over lost love
I honestly can't help feeling deplorable.
The level of affection is what's difficult, but nothing comes of
    having too little love.
Whenever I see parents lamenting a lost child,
I can't help wondering whether I'd given them excessive parental love.
It is, however, because I gave humanity so much love
that people are able to live as human beings.
One's depth of affection reflects the depth of human life.
It's a fact that,
many people remain foolish and incorrigible.
Yet, as you know,
there exist good people, lovable people
—— people you can't possibly love too much.

"Beyond everything mentioned lies beauty.
It incessantly allures the human heart.
Truly very few know the secrets of such beauty.
Those given to argumentation
will not grasp its secrets.
Beauty, it seems, is involved in the harmony of the universe.
You can see traces of that
here and there throughout the Earth.
Only God
knows the essence of beauty.
Traces of that God exist
in your hearts.
When you touch on that beauty
you shed tears.
People who know the taste of such tears
are aware of my heart.
The haughty,
those who no longer remember to love me,
are not aware of what is immortal.
I pity the empty-heartedness
of all who render service to what decays:
people who simply exist
without experiencing the joy of living,
people who lack the slightest connection with the secrets
    of an eternally changeless love,
people who, when everything has perished, leave nothing in their wake,
people with nothing to dedicate themselves to,
people unable to shed a tear in the temple of beauty.
These people I call The Vacant.
They merely wear human skin.
Temples of beauty exist everywhere throughout the universe:
these eternally-unchanging temples sustain something
that communicates with the human heart:

the beauty of immortality.
Invisible beauty then becomes visible.
It is the way that traverses the deepest and most mystic aspects of our hearts
—— sincerity, truth, love, and beauty.
Those who have achieved harmony,
those one can't help loving,
those who return to where they belong,
those who can exist here as genuine people, carrying out the will of heaven
—— these are only people who can know
what I expect from humans.
Sooner or later,
some centuries, some thousands of years, or some eons hence,
people will know how they were created.
Though it resides there, however much you search the flesh
you'll never discover the essence of life, the spirit.
You can say that God exists in his temple,
but the temple is by no means God.
Someone has said
'God is love.'
Many others have said it, too.
Someone who truly sheds tears making that confession
has perhaps perceived that God of love in his heart.
Yes, only the one who knows the taste of such tears
has touched the mystery of human life."

A teardrop glistened in my eye
as the Creator spoke these words.

NOT GOD *

Do I have within me something that is not God?
I don't know for sure,
but it appears I do.
In that, too, however,
if you positively uncover it,
you may find it derives from God.
Sexual desire, sufferings, the fear of death
—— these are life, and life is of God.
Death, too, is of God.
For those who can devotedly kneel before him,
even sinfulness appears to be of God.
Be fearful, but not excessively so,
of committing sin!
Certain crimes can't be revoked
before the law.
That's not the case with God.

GOD (i)

God is like water.
When your heart is humbled
and you empty yourself of self,
he naturally comes
and replenishes your emptiness.
God is like water.

GOD (ii)

When I've done my utmost,
I pray to God:
"Lord!
this is all I can do.
I leave the rest to you."

GOD (iii)

God isn't a rigid fellow,
nor is he a zoo keeper.
God will be magnanimous
so long as we do not violate our love for our brothers and sisters
—— he'll be truly magnanimous.

It's fine if God's children
can live without guile
and lead compliant lives.
God detests
rigidity.
It's all right to live compliantly.

Aware of that,
I live compliantly,
not inconveniencing others,
though I freely accept their favors.
God rejoices when I live like that.

ONE CALLED GOD

Though God may not exist,
I stand in awe . . . .

Buddha's Gospel *

You'll find these words in the Buddha's gospel:
"Discharge this truth: your brothers are your flesh.
Take the path of righteousness
and you'll realize when death comes
that your immortality lies in truth."
Three thousand years ago you said
what I want to say
in a voice louder and clearer than mine.
Buddha! I bend my knee.

Buddha and Jesus

If Buddha and Jesus
had said it's all right to kill,
I couldn't have even a tenth
of the respect I now have
for them.

Rather Than People *

Love God more than people.
Love truth more than people.
Love righteousness more than people.
Don't even think of defying any of these
just to gain someone's favor.
If you do, may your work be cursed
and collapse like the Tower of Babel.

Being True to God

Being true to God
is being true to your brothers
and being true to your self.
Unless we are true to God,
how can we be true to our brothers, to our selves?

God and Humankind (i)

God and humankind
exist within us.
Their unflagging flames and energies
spur us on.
God and humankind do not surrender,

they stand on truth.
No one but they quicken our wills.
Be attentive to the mission they've assigned us!

GOD and HUMANKIND (ii) *

Is God a human being
or something other than a human?
Was God begotten by humanity,
born from the sincere hearts of all?
The person who has seen God says,
I'm ready now to die.

FORGETTING GOD

Blessed are those who, having forgotten God,
can enjoy themselves.
Return to yourselves, however, when the time is right.

PURE PEOPLE *

I again felt like meeting the Creator.
Fortunately, he then appeared.
When I said, "I wanted to see you,"
the happy-go-lucky Creator said,
"I came because I wanted to see you."

"There's no longer anything for me to do," he added.
"I've already done everything I could.
Now it's a matter of awaiting the outcome.
Having transferred this world into people's hands
means I feel relieved.
There are, however, many more foolish people than I imagined,
so from time to time I do worry.
Still, there's not yet the need for a *deus ex machina.*
I intend to observe a while longer how humans manage.
They'll somehow make do, I suppose.
I'm sure people have at least that much wisdom.
There are nevertheless many brazen fellows
who figure they are greater than I.
They forget the most significant tasks
I assigned them
and imagine that nobody is quite as great as they!
They nonchalantly sow seeds of calamity
and are dumfounded when the seeds take root and sprout.

I assume they had it coming,
but it wasn't supposed to turn out that way.
They are the losers.
When the Grim Reaper appears,
such people become so upset
that their behavior draws laughter.
Only individuals like that
will forget their own deaths.
Those who indifferently make others suffer are ridiculous
and yet get upset over their own misery.
That's their just reward, I'd say, the divine punishment
they brought on themselves.
Those who live carefree, having left everything up to me,
gratify me when they appear,
but such people are rare."

"Well, then, you do care for me, don't you?"
"Don't be so smug!
I can't say for certain that you perfectly comprehend my love.
Down deep you still have traces of insecurity.
There is no reason you'd feel like that
if you truly lived according to my will.
As long as even a few
traces of anxiety survive,
I can't say you've been thoroughly enlightened."
"But little by little
I no longer feel insecurities.
I'm simply apprehensive
that I may become insensitive, a fool
——— just an old man who grins constantly."
"You can't be serious.
I'd admire you
if you became a grinning old man."
"Even if I'm a fool?"
"It would be a problem if you became a grinning fool.
If you get truly wise, thoroughly wise,
and can always grin,
you'll be absolutely authentic."
"Well, however authentic I may be, merely grinning like that
would be a problem for me."

"If you're truly wise,
if you grasp everything as it is
and truly understand how to live authentically,
and if you live and work
on the basis of that understanding,
I'll admire you.
Even in modern times

if such people truly live authentically,
they will without fail
cast the light of truth and the light of love
into the hearts of those who have not yet lost their purity.
The true niceties of the Zen expression
to attain enlightenment through inaction or *wu-wei*
will radiate from such a person
and infiltrate people's hearts."

"Even then will there be unhappy people?"
"There will. Regrettably, there will.
Those who have pure hearts, however,
will through word and act
come into contact with the minds of authentic people
and sing songs that praise humanity.
I think it's no problem for those who are already dead.
I want the living,
at least while they are alive,
to be genuine people.
I want them to be expressions of the human heart
so boundlessly beautiful
that we cannot help loving them boundlessly.
Such love alone
sows seeds of pure love in everyone's heart
and testifies to a person capable of living.
I recognize and feel misgivings
that actual life comprises various circumstances.
However, those who can make the love I bestowed on human hearts
flower in a truly beautiful way
are people
who more than others genuinely touch my heart.
Having bestowed on people the most beautiful and human of gifts.
I wait for them to come to life on Earth."
"I roughly understand how you feel."

"Your eyes glisten with tears
so I know you're telling the truth.
At all times,
never forget to love humanity.
And keep in mind that I hope
every single person
will become an authentic human.
An authentic human being
is infinitely beautiful.
Those who dare to make the human being inhuman
are certainly the most frightful people
who do not understand how exquisitely humans have been made.
Listen! Get an ever clearer grasp of how beautifully people are made

and work for all humanity."
My eyes on the verge of tears, I looked around for him
but the Creator was gone.

OH, GOD (i) *

Oh, God,
everyone thought you were dead,
but you're certainly not dead, are you?
You exist with such refreshed sovereignty
that one wonders if you're a new God.
It's simply that you're not visible
to the semi-enlightened.
None are more truly abhorrent
than the vaguely aware.

OH, GOD (ii) *

Oh, God,
however merciless and irrational
your actions may seem,
I have no choice but to depend on you:
grateful that I can positively feel you're with me.

GOD'S WILL *

"Not even a sparrow dies
if God does not will it."
This passage, somewhere in one of the Gospels,
is anathema to me.
If we accept these words as truth,
then murders, wars, death sentences, and deaths from starvation
must all be God's will.
It's inconceivable that such a God exists.
This passage is anathema to me.
I'd find it far more pleasant
to be told,
"A human's death is beyond my concern."

DEDICATED TO GOD

We are fires that do not fade.
Our supply of firewood is meager,
and yet we never completely burn it up.

New firewood
materializes from nowhere
and the fire becomes increasingly intense.
Praise be to God!

GOD and SATAN

Those who sow love reap love.
Those who sow hate reap hate.
God and Satan resolutely sow
and each reaps what he sows.
Delighted with his abundant harvest,
Satan looks at God and scoffs,
"You have quite a bountiful harvest, don't you?"
Not responding, God gazes at his harvest
with tear-filled eyes.
Unguardedly he says,
"People —— what beautiful creatures!"
Satan snickers, "You say people are beautiful . . . ?"
God then looks at Satan and says,
"How enamored you are of emptiness!
What you have reaped is worthless.
It will simply vanish.
People at times become your pawns,
but your power over them is bound to fade."
Satan says, "How's that possible?"
But look! The higher Satan's harvest piles up the quicker it vanishes.
The harvest that God reaped, however,
glistens more and more.
At that point a human being passes by.
When God sees him he says with delight,
"Your children have again managed to hand down such splendid work.
You simply continue to grow and grow.
Soon you may outstrip me."
The human says respectfully,
"What can I say . . . ?"
Seeing that, Satan remarks with resentment,
"Listen human, take a look!
Can you feel proud of this
and claim it shows that people have grown?"
"Look at what?"
"At this."
"I don't see what you mean."
"It's this."
"I don't see anything.
Whatever doesn't benefit my life is invisible to me.
Even if I see it, I immediately forget it exists.

You're a fool to make such efforts for emptiness,
and yet I care about you, too,
for at times you give us people pleasure.
It's a bit unfair that humanity still only has the Lord God to serve."
Satan didn't understand, however, what that meant.

WHERE IS GOD?

Where is God?
He exists in our petitions.
The being we wish to become, we call God.
We say the wisest person is as wise as God.
We say the most beautiful person is as beautiful as God.
The most desirable country we call the kingdom of God.
God exists in our petitions for perfection.

ON THIS DAY JESUS WAS BORN *

On this day Jesus was born.
On this day, Jesus was born.
On this day a God-like person was born.
His life was short.
It's said he completed his work in three years.
But he of all people
had a pure heart,
a gentle heart,
and he sought
the kingdom of God and its righteousness
like someone famished, like one whose throat was parched.
No one is exempt from seeking
the kingdom of God with any less fervor than he.
He sought the kingdom of God
as intensely as anyone is allowed to seek it.
He was fearfully pure.
Observe him!
This person was surely
the most perfect individual on Earth.
He trod the path of suppressing the flesh and giving the spirit life.
Living thirty-three years on Earth,
his life was short,
but during those years there was no limit
to the depth of his vital devotion.
Yes,
that man was born this day.
He died having made
absolutely the most of his devotion,

and from start to finish he sought the kingdom of God and its righteousness.
He was born this day.
Our light and our hope
—— Jesus was born this day.
We should rejoice,
we should give thanks,
that he was born on Earth,
that he was born on Earth.

To LIVE IN THE KINGDOM OF GOD *

The least suitable disposition
of any who hope to live in the kingdom of God
is that of the malcontent.
Root out the discontent in yourself
and simply take joy
in doing whatever you do.
Loving justice
does not mean being discontented.
Helping the weak
does not mean being discontented.
Only milksops flaunt their discontent.
They are the least appropriate to inherit the kingdom of God.

Every heart
harbors a malcontent.
Unless you overcome that tendency
and your heart is like a cloudless sky,
you cannot inherit the kingdom of God.

The malcontent's problems are that
he views other people's faults with a microscope
and cannot perceive their virtues.
He fixes his attention only on what disturbs him.
Jesus was most concerned about such people.
I'd like to tell them,
"You must learn to disregard the speck in your neighbor's eye
by becoming sensitive to the beam in your own."

Than THE MALCONTENT *

There is, however, a more sordid type
than the malcontent.
That's the person who says,
"Can't you overlook the beam in my eye?"
—— then struts around boasting of it.

TO THEIR WORK *

Long live those devoted to their work.
Long live those who build a foundation so firm that future generations
     will be able to build on and expand it.
Long live those who invent devices to make life convenient.
Long live those whose discoveries contribute to progress,
     whether in the human spirit or the material world.
Long live those who produce things of beauty.
Long live those whose contributions help bring people together.
Long live those who teach humans how to live.
Human beings must in every area head gradually toward perfection.
Long live those who work so they might in mind and body
     be fit for the kingdom of God.
Long live those, too, who with self-denial help in these tasks.
Hurrah! Hurrah!
Long live those loved by humankind.
Long live those who do not deny the existence of a single person's life.

IN THE VILLAGE *

Some frigid feelings
heavily infecting the villagers
had burgeoned
beyond our notice.
They enabled one individual to become
even more cordial
than a real brother.
What a boon!
That's precisely what our village is about.
Move ahead with this spirit.
God will certainly keep you.
Move ahead with this spirit.

THE SELF-RELIANT

We are the self-reliant,
the determined,
those who work for the brothers and sisters,
those who on this Earth
intend to carry out humanity's will,
intend to carry out God's will.
We're not starving,
but even if we were
we would move ever onward,
never losing sight of our goals.

NEW VILLAGE (iii) *

Brothers and sisters,
it's appropriate to love the New Village
more and more.
I believe that
loving the New Village
will make God and humanity rejoice.

NEW VILLAGE (iv) *

The New Village
consists of a polity
living under God's defense.
Our polity resolves not to tread a path
that God will not defend.

DÜRER'S *ST. JEROME* *

Dürer's picture of St. Jerome.
Everything in the room sleeps:
both the dog and the lion,
and every ambition
in Jerome's heart.
He simply devotes himself
unconditionally and fervently
to translating the Word of God.
St. Jerome's demeanor will survive
as long as human beings exist.
The demeanor of St. Jerome,
who steadfastly pens the Word of God,
will survive as long as human hearts beat.

ARTISTS

Artists
devote their lives
to beauty.
Humanitarians
devote their lives
to humanity.
Religionists
devote their lives
to God.
Blessed are those who have something

to which they wholeheartedly devote their lives.
I'd be glad to devote my life
to all three,
but I'd like to enjoy my leisure time
in a somewhat carefree mood.
That's a difficult
as well as an interesting issue
—— that's being human.

I wonder if it's possible to find a way to be idle
without impairing my strength.
If it's bound not to be,
I'll resign myself, of course.
But, you know, I have a slight reservation.
I know that these secular pleasures
of which God approves
exist somewhere.
Each person who has that secret
is certain to shine all the more on me.
I don't wish now to write more on this.

LISTENING TO THE PIANO

Last night I found myself
watching a young French pianist
performing
on television.
Musically I'm illiterate,
but as I listened to his playing
I somehow felt joyful.

The rhythms of the piece . . .
carried away by the rhythms of the piece,
I ended up in a most joyous mood.
I haven't experienced such a pure and joyous mood
for some time.
I suspect the intently-performing pianist
was also in a most joyous mood,
so I, too, could end up with pure feelings
—— this pure mood
given to humankind.

This world is full of noise,
of impurities,
and it is in truth rarely possible to feel the purity I felt then.
The nature of the human being's true self, however,
is not the impure but the pure. •

Last night as I listened vaguely to the music,
not giving a thought to such issues,
I somehow ended up in an affable mood.
To call people absolutely ignorant
of this affable
"human" realm
makes me feel a modicum of regret
before the One who made us.

JESUS and ST. FRANCIS *

Jesus and St. Francis take a stroll.
Jesus receives some food and nonchalantly eats it.
    St. Francis sprinkles ashes on his and eats it.
Amazed, Jesus says, "Do you like ashes?"
"The food tastes too good to me."
Jesus couldn't quite grasp what St. Francis meant.
He thought, "What an odd fellow!"
St. Francis thought, "Jesus is indeed the son of God."

THOSE ABLE TO ENTER HEAVEN *

Those qualified to enter heaven
get there step by step.
Do we meander about the Earth
to make ourselves eligible for entry?

LEAVE EVERYTHING TO GOD *

Leave everything to God.
Do only what you ought.
Even if others offer only a small amount of oil,
don't let it bother you.
Be concerned about whether you personally have given too little oil
for God's lamps.
Don't let it bother you
that some might steal
oil dedicated to God.
Merely offer more and more oil.
God's glory will light the hearts of such people
and kindle in their breasts
an imperishable fire.
You who believe this
will inherit
the kingdom of God.

TO FATE

Crushed by fate,
crushed by sickness,
crushed by poverty and anguish.
—— I can't bear to think that such things might befall me.
I praise people
who go on with life
and despite bitter experiences
believe all the more in heaven.
Noble, hardy folk.
Stout pillars of humanity.

THE PATH TO TRIUMPH

Even in death,
I believe in the triumph of man.
Truth must always triumph.
Love has no foes.
Humanity must survive.
Living together
is the path to triumph.

JAPAN BRIMS WITH HOPE *

I acknowledge no grounds
for looking pessimistically at today's Japan.
I find present-day Japan
a most fascinating land.
Over the next fifty years,
Japan will be able to make a great strides in philosophy.
That's my belief,
that's what I feel.
Now is the time for Japan to produce
a Goethe, a Schiller,
an Emerson, a Whitman,
a Dostoyevsky, a Tolstoy,
an Ibsen, a Bjørnson,
a Maeterlinck, a Verhaeren.
A young nation,
an awakening land,
a nation without despotism
—— such a polity will be a delightful place to live.

AMERICA'S WILSON *

America's Wilson:
Unless you're a hypocrite and a liar,
you probably know that a foe much more fearful
than Germany or Japan exists in your America.
The entire world fears that foe, Wilson
—— President of the land of the world's mammon!

JAPAN HAS BEEN LEFT BEHIND

Japan has been left behind.
Let's be on our guard!
If the situation remains as it is,
dreadful times lie ahead!

What do you mean, "Let's wage another war . . . "?
Ignoramuses!
Dreadful things will occur.

If you don't believe me,
try starting a war
with America.

TO THE DENTIST

People go to the dentist because they have bad teeth.
People go to the oculist because they have bad eyes.
I'm happy that those who gather at my place
have pure hearts.
They have tremendous capacity for growth.
They're seekers.
They say that people everywhere are seeking their fortunes.
Beauty, mystical beauty,
exists everywhere.
I can see from the train window
the characteristic loveliness
in every rugged silhouette.
The mountains' ever-changing contours,
their grand and lovely bearing,
utterly impress me.
I've come to feel, moreover, that I'd like to reconsider with regret
my notion that Japan's scenery
and the beauty of her islands and seas,
is trivial.
Take the mystical contours of islands in the Inland Sea:

I think Japan shouldn't regard them inferior
even to the isles of Greece.
The beauties of islands and mountains
that exhibit various forms, guises, relationships . . .
if only you have the eye for it,
you'll find a surfeit of beauty
even in a single tree.

To Japan

Isn't the fact that Japan has the New Village a matter of national pride?
It's a national disgrace that Japanese are so unenthusiastic
        about whether or not our village thrives.
We cannot, however, let this indifference, this contempt, get the better of us.
We are certain to despair when we place excessive trust in others.
        We must increase and fortify our capacities.

I'm a Patriot

I'm a patriot.
At least I disparage those
who disparage Japan.
I myself, those I love, my friends
—— each and every one of us is Japanese.

Even in Japan

Even in Japan we have formidably excellent paintings.
The Japanese are remarkable.
Foreigners are remarkable,
but Japanese are remarkable, too.

I'd like to give thought to the ways in which
the national characteristics of the nations of the world
might cooperatively move ahead
by setting the eminently eminent art works of foreign countries
along side Japan's eminently eminent works of art.

I'd like to inform people that in the name of truth
we ought to move cooperatively ahead.
Whatever the realities,
I believe that sooner or later,
abiding truth will win out.
I'll demonstrate that when various countries work together
we can create the perfect human.

TO AMERICA *

We Asians
leave America's problems
for Americans to handle,
and yet I wonder why
America can't leave Asian issues
for Asians to handle.

We're content to let Americans
manage America's wealth,
and yet I wonder why
America cannot be content
to let Asians manage Asia's wealth.

Do you intend to loot Asia's wealth
even if it costs a million lives?
Don't you Americans have a single righteous person among you?
Why can't you let Asians manage
Asia's problems
the way we let Americans manage
American's problems?
Think about that.
Think about it.

WE'RE A MASS OF STEEL

We're a mass of steel.
We're substantiality itself.
We want to live solidly.
We hope to avoid being vacuous.
We wish to be substantiality itself.
You understand that feeling, don't you?

SURRENDER OF SINGAPORE *

Singapore! . . . Singapore!
"If only Singapore falls,
we can drive British power from Asia,
and then the real Asia will be born."
We were told that since we were children
and we believed it.
That's the Singapore that has at last capitulated.

The very Singapore
they called impregnable

finally capitulated today,
a mere seventy days
since the onset
of the Great East Asia War.

A wild dream
has become reality.

Japan resolutely executed
its grand mission
and honored the Imperial directive.
Japan has equipped itself
to liberate Asia
from Anglo-American rule.
The time had arrived for this nation to take a stand.
Since we initiated action,
we by all means had to subdue Singapore.

We rose to the occasion with that resolution
and at last carried out this noble task.
The assignment entailed grave difficulties.
Our soldiers efficiently overcame them.
We're grateful to our Imperial Army,
feel proud of it,
and wish to rejoice greatly in its victory.
We also intensely wish to rejoice
with those we've liberated.

At the same time, however,
we must make a significant determination.
We must bring about an Asia so noble that neither American nor Britain
will again be able to corrupt her with their influence.
Asian culture
must shine radiantly.
Severing these baneful influences over Singapore
will enable the valiant birth of a liberated Asia.

World history will be rewritten here.
The events of this day
must be written for the future, for eternity,
in huge burning letters:
"Singapore finally capitulated. At that moment a new Asia was born."

YEAR TWO OF THE GREAT EAST ASIAN WAR *

We greet the spring of the second year
since the beginning of the Great East Asian War.
The fighting has become progressively grim.
Our determination also becomes successively resolute.
It must become resolute
and we must triumph.
If the enemy becomes more and more serious,
we must become even more serious.
We will beat them, beat them, beat them soundly.

This is not a struggle we can lose.
There's no struggle
we must win more than this one.
This struggle shoulders the fate of all Asia.
Those who would betray Asia to America and England are exceptions.
Those who desire the co-prosperity of Asia
must force America and England to regret their outrageous greed.
They must prudently pull back
to where they ought to be.

America and England do not appreciate Asian peoples
yet feel qualified to exercise sovereignty over Asia.
They must repent their extravagant ambitions
and humbly apologize for their offenses.
Military might alone, however,
will bring them to realize the need to do so.
We will beat them, beat them, beat them soundly.

The might of our victory.
The achievements of those who toiled for decades to cultivate that might
have gathered and at this moment
beautifully bear fruit.
With a single stroke we freed East Asia of Anglo-American influence.
But the Americans and British will tenaciously
cling to their ambitions
and try to suck up the last drops of Asia's tasty broth.
They fear the strengthening of Asian peoples.
They're thinking how nice if only Japan were weak.
We must not give them cause to rejoice.
We must bring divine punishment on them
for their offensive objectives.
That is Japan's mission.
Though discharging this mission will not be easy,
    we must consider it an honor to do so.
Thus must America and Britain withdraw from East Asia,
return to East Asia its plundered wealth,

surrender their ambitions to subjugate East Asia,
and go back to where they belong.
Justice expects as much.
The world and humanity expect as much.
East Asia's guardian deities expect as much.
Having once sipped our choice broth, however,
America and Britain will not meekly relinquish East Asia and withdraw.
They want by all means to lap up our appetizing broth more completely,
so of course they'll resist
with all their might.
This year and the next may be the most intense.
But we have greater allies on our side.
Justice is our ally, humanism is our ally, humanity is our ally,
        the gods are our allies.
Those in the right must eventually be victorious.
They must return East Asia to East Asia.
Countries like America that possess vast expanses of land not yet fully utilized
are enormously audacious to meddle in East Asia.
Americans must repent of their behavior.
We will beat them, beat them, beat them soundly.

On the dawn after we've won the war,
the peoples of East Asia must sponsor a joyful celebration.
Then, harmoniously pooling our strengths
and defending the new world order,
we must make the wealth of East Asia the joy of East Asian peoples.
America and England will not in the least be able to hinder that.
Nowhere will there be the need to fawn over them.
The world's wealth must be fairly divided,
and we must more fully advance East Asian culture.
The realm of East Asia will then become the center of human culture,
and the peoples of the world will regard it life's supreme joy
        to come to East Asia as peaceful guests.
Feeling that life is worth living,
they will realize it was preferable to entrust East Asia to East Asian peoples.
We must move ahead with that objective.
To accomplish that we must first wrest East Asia
from the hands of the Americans and the British.
Then we must chastise them
until they are no longer able to have designs on us.
To do that we must first win the war.
We will beat them, beat them, beat them soundly.

OUR WARRIORS ADVANCE ON ATTU *

If you want a realistic idea
of what energies will be unleashed
when Japanese determine to lay down their lives
and advance against the enemy,
imagine our warriors on Attu.
Here the spirit of the Japanese
existed in an ideal way.
The same flower that earlier bloomed at Minatogawa
bloomed again on Attu.

Our Attu warriors
took no delight in pity.
They existed in a sublime realm
diametrically opposed to such sentiment.
The warriors declined reinforcements.
They thought not about themselves
but about Japan.
Our Attu warriors were most apprehensive about their country
and talked exhaustively by short wave,
passing on every shred of data
they thought necessary to defeat the Americans.
"We have no regrets.
It is regrettable only that the incomparable loyalty and valor
of your men may remain unknown to you.
But praise them.
Each is a Japanese warrior.
There's not a coward among them.
I rejoice
that I can die with men who,
regardless of how much, how very much you praise them,
cannot be praised enough.
Can there be a happier ending
for a warrior?
Rejoice with me!"

Thus did that death-defying band of soldiers
solemnly begin their charge.
When they reached the enemy lines
they attacked like frantic demons
and quickly breached the defenses.
The warriors glanced at one another with smiles of satisfaction
and continued to rush the enemy's positions.
Our warriors' ordered visible advance
soon turned into a formless invisible advance of the spirit
against which enemy forces stood powerless.
Till Japan secures the final victory,

thus will continue our spiritually focused and most sublime advance.

Our warriors' assault inspires us
—— giving one hundred million citizens a single mind.
We must swear
before the souls of the Yamazaki Unit warriors
that we will complete the course to victory.
May their sacrifice lead us
on the path of triumph.

A poem is the very image of life
expressed in its eternal truth.

— Percy B. Shelley —
A Defence of Poetry

Poetry is at bottom a criticism of life.

— Matthew Arnold —
Essays in Criticism: Second Series

Poetry is man's rebellion against being what he is.

— James B. Cabell —
Jurgen

What must be practiced—assiduously, infinitely and
without the slightest pause—is anti-servitude,
noncompliance, and independence.
Poetry is the other face of Pride.

— Odysseus Elytis —
1979 Nobel Laureate in Literature

SUPPLEMENTARY

Chronology • 287
Notes • 309

Appendix I: Chronological Listing of the Poems • 349
Appendix II: Views of Mushakôji's Work • 359
Appendix III: Mushakôji on His Poetry • 363
Appendix IV: Poetry Collections • 371

English Index • 375
Japanese Index • 385

Yakusha Offerings • 397

CHRONOLOGY

Most data derives from *Mushakôji Saneatsu kyûjûnen* [Mushakôji Saneatsu: 90 Years], edited by Watanabe Kanji (Kaibisha, 1995), 91 pages. Mushakôji's youngest daughter Tatsuko provided a copy. Chronologies that Nakagawa Takashi compiled and other sources provided further details. When inconsistencies occur, I defer to Watanabe. Appendix IV, page 371, presents details on the poetry books, including graphs. I omit almost all painting exhibitions. Small caps refer to an entry in the Notes and ❹ marks information on the population of the New Village. SA for Saneatsu clarifies and simplifies referents to Mushakôji. *Kyôgen*, which often poke fun at authority, are short farces inserted as comic relief between Nô plays. The following abbreviations I adopt from Nakagawa:

D	Drama	LN	Long novel
DC	Drama collection	MN	Mid-length novel • story
E	Essay	NA	Novella
EC	Essay collection	SS	Short story
IC	Impressions and • or comments	SSC	Short story collection

DATE   EVENT

1885   **12 May:** Born in Motozono, Kôjimachi (now Chiyoda) Ward, Tokyo, the eighth and last child of Viscount Saneyo (born 1852; descendant of Kyôto aristocrats) and Naruko [variant reading of Akiko] née Kadenokôji (born ca. 1854; descendant of farmers). By 1885, five siblings had died. Only sister Ikako (then 6) and brother Kintomo (born 1882, then 3) survive.

1887   **27 October:** Father Saneyo dies of pulmonary tuberculosis at age 35. The government chose him to spend the years 1871–1874 studying in Germany, where he acquired an extensive library of books on law, literature, and philosophy—all destroyed in the fires following the 1923.09.01 Kantô Earthquake. After his return from Germany, Saneyo worked as a diplomat. He was reputedly one of the two or three most brilliant individuals among Japan's younger aristocrats.

1888   **July:** Until ca. 1895, SA spends the summers in Kamakura with his family. They usually stay at the Kômyôji, a Pure Land [Jôdo] Buddhist temple founded in 1243. It lies ca. 1.25 miles south of Kamakura Station. The family doctor wanted tuberculosis-prone Ikako and SA to breathe the sea air for their health.

1890   Attends kindergarten for at least a year. Mother Naruko begins making efforts to modify SA's short-tempered, peevish nature.

1891   **September:** Enters the elementary division of the Peers' School (the Gakushûin). People constantly compare SA negatively with his older brother Kintomo, who compiled a distinguished academic record before going on to Tokyo Imperial University. Mother Naruko constantly calls SA lazy and shiftless. His favorite subjects are reading and math, his least favorite are music, drawing, and composition. SA is especially inept at singing, which he thoroughly detests.

1895   **July:** The family begins spending summer vacations with mother Naruko's younger brother, Kadenokôji Sukekoto (dies 1925.06). Having failed in an enterprise and gone bankrupt, Sukekoto retreated to the agrarian setting of Kaneda on the seashore of Miura Peninsula. Sometimes SA helps out with farm chores— background that later facilitates his adjustment to NEW VILLAGE life (1918–1926). Sukekoto, who introduces SA to the Bible and Tolstoy, becomes one of the consequential early influences on SA's life and thought.

DATE EVENT

1897 July: Graduates from the primary level of the Gakushûin. Because SA is physically inferior to his classmates (he usually comes in last or second last in foot races), he detests sports, especially the martial arts. SA excels in debate and math. September: Enters the Gakushûin middle school. SA continues to let his hot temper get the better of him. His eyesight deteriorates so he can no longer read the blackboard. Begins to study German, which he continues for seven years.

1899 12 December: Sister Ikako dies at age 21 after six months of illness, very likely of pulmonary tuberculosis. Before falling ill, she had been married for less than six months to a son of the Hirata family in Wakayama. SA dearly loved Ikako and later writes *Shi* [Death] about her passing (cf. 1914.08).

1900 April: Meets Shimura Otei [the graph for *tei* can also be read *sada*], 12–13 years old at this time. She is his first crush. Prior to that SA reputedly had a secret homosexual relationship with a classmate. SA later makes Otei the heroine of his story, *"Hatsukoi"* [First Love, retitled from *"Dai ni no haha"* (My Second Mother; cf. 1914.06)]. SA refers to her in several early poems (e.g., page 165). Otei is in the capital from Ôsaka to study at a finishing school. She stays with an aunt in a tenement near the Mushakôji mansion in Kôjimachi.

1902 In his sixth year of middle school SA meets SHIGA NAOYA (1883–1971), who had flunked several grades. They become life-long friends. At higher school, SA spends time talking with Shiga about literature. Lacking confidence in his physical ability, SA decides to make his mark in writing. He religiously practices composing and, deciding also to nourish his courage, begins to study Zen and Wang Yang-ming [1472–1528; known as Ô Yô-mei in Japan], the great Ming Confucianist and father of Tokugawa ideological orthodoxy. SA had long been fond of reading on the sly the *Sun Tzu* and other books on the warrior's art. Around this time, uncle Sukekoto encourages him to read Tolstoy, e.g., *What is My Faith?* (1883–1884; in Japanese translation, *Waga shûkyô* [My Religion]).

1903 March: Otei finishes her schooling and returns to Ôsaka. She largely ignored SA. He assuages his disappointment by determining to dedicate his life to writing and literature. SA requires a decade to get over this infatuation. July: Graduates from the Gakushûin Middle School. During summer vacation on the Miura Peninsula, SA voraciously reads his uncle's collection of Tolstoy's works in Japanese translation. September: Advances to the higher school. Brother Kintomo enters the elite law course at Tokyo Imperial University.

1904 January: Buys a paperback containing German translations of Tolstoy stories and spends a month reading a story of more than 30 pages, the first time SA has read anything but text books. He gains a reputation for earnest behavior, eschews vulgar language, and becomes more active in public speaking and debate. February: The Russo-Japanese War breaks out. SA sympathizes with those who oppose the conflict and expresses anti-war sentiments.

1905 March: Kintomo marries Kazuko, the sixth daughter of Duke Môri. The statesman Inoue Kaoru (1835–1915), then financial adviser to the Mushakôji clan, acts as go-between. August: At his uncle Sukekoto's home, SA reads in translation a section of Tolstoy's 1877 masterpiece *Anna Karénina* as well as a number of short stories by Maksim Gorky (1868–1936). September: The Russo-Japanese War ends. SA becomes enamored of Tolstoy's essay on Christ's expression, "The kingdom of God is within [some authorities prefer 'among'] you" (*Luke* 17:21). Because of his attempts to emulate the great novelist, classmates begin calling SA "Tolstoy." With friend Shiga, SA visits the famed translator Ueda Bin (1874–1916). They ask Ueda about European literature and learn of Count Maurice

DATE   EVENT

Maeterlinck (1862–1949), the Belgian dramatist, poet, essayist, and 1911 Nobel laureate in literature.

1906   **23 March–10 May:** Copies out in notebooks a German biography of Tolstoy. One volume of this work is preserved in the Tokyo Metropolitan Museum of Modern Literature. **April:** During spring break, takes a "pauper's trip" with friend Shiga Naoya. **25 May:** SA notes in his diary the death of the Norwegian playwright Henrik Ibsen (born 1828), whom he credits with teaching him how to achieve his goals. **July:** SA graduates from Gakushûin Higher School, fourth from the bottom of his class. **September:** Enters the Sociology Department of Tokyo Imperial University. Joins friends from the Gakushûin—novelist Ôgimachi Kinkazu (1881–1960), tanka poet KINOSHITA RIGEN (1886–1925), and novelist Shiga—in planning a literary magazine. SA becomes increasingly involved with European literature, reading translations of Bjørnson, Carlyle, Dostoyevsky, Goethe, Gorky, Gerhart Hauptmann, Heine, Ibsen, Nietzsche, and Turgenev. SA believes that universities are sites where the useless or absurd [*kudaranai mono*] gather. **20 November:** Inspired by Tolstoy, SA writes up a dream about an ideal society that reflects what he later describes about the NEW VILLAGE (cf. 1918.03).

1907   **January:** First visit to the novelist Tokutomi Roka (1868–1927) to ask about his talks with Tolstoy. **8 February:** Recently-married Otei visits her aunt and cousins in Kôjimachi. SA sees her before she leaves. **14 April:** First meeting of the *Jûyokka kai* [14th Club]—formed with friends Kinoshita, Ôgimachi, and Shiga—scheduled to meet monthly on the 14th to study literature and criticize each other's works. **4 June:** Gives at the Gakushûin a speech titled *"Ningen no kachi"* [Human Values] in which SA asserts that the military doesn't comprehend values related to the peace of humankind. The principal of the school, retired General Nogi Maresuke (1849–1912), was in the audience. SA reads a German translation of Maeterlinck's *La sagesse et la destinée* [Wisdom and Fate] (1898). **July:** Kintomo graduates from Tokyo Imperial University and enters the foreign service. **August:** From his uncle Kadenokôji's place on the Miura Peninsula, SA writes Kintomo—legally the house head and thus *in loco parentis*—saying he wants to drop out of college. SA says the meaningless lectures bore him. Instead, he wants to focus his energies on literature. He receives a telegram of approval. **September:** Drops out of the university. **14 October:** At the 14th Club meeting, the four friends continue to discuss and plan a magazine. They decide on the name *Shirakaba* [White Birch] and determine the layout of the cover and the illustrations. Various problems force them to postpone publication.

1908   **26 January:** Birth of Kintomo and Kazuko's first child, daughter Yoshiko. **3 April:** SA publishes his first book, *Kôya* [Wilderness] using money from Kintomo. *Wilderness* contains stories written after 1906, reflections, and poetry. **25 June–13 July:** Visits Arishima Takeo (1878–1923) in Sapporo, Hokkaidô, where he teaches at the Agricultural College. **19 July:** Through a go-between, SA proposes to Hiyoshi Taka, but is told she is "too young." He persistently but unsuccessfully pursues this girl for some four years. **22nd:** Kintomo assigned to the Japanese Consulate in Shanghai. Around this time, SA becomes enthusiastically interested in the German painter and sculptor Max Klinger (1857–1920). **22nd:** The 14th Club issues No. 1 of the private magazine *Bôya*, the immediate progenitor of *Shirakaba* (1910.04). **August:** Writes *Perushajin* [The Persians]. **7 September:** Kintomo's daughter Yoshiko dies. **10th:** SA substitutes for Kintomo at the funeral. **23rd:** Writes the story *"Yoshiko,"* appearing 1911.11 in *Shirakaba*. SA regards this his "virgin" work. **23rd:** Kintomo returns to Japan. **16 October:** Kintomo takes

DATE   EVENT

wife Kazuko to his post in Shanghai. SA becomes more familiar with the work of
Emerson, Goethe, Klinger, Nietzsche, and Walt Whitman.

1909   **April ff.**: SA becomes involved with his three friends and some dozen others in
planning the *Shirakaba* magazine (renamed from *Bôya*), which they plan to pub-
lish in 1910. **October**: Writes the three-act play, *"Aru katei"* [A Family Affair],
SA's first drama. It later appears in the second issue of the *Shirakaba* (spring
1910). His reading includes the works of Dostoyevsky, Emerson, Victor Hugo,
Ibsen, Maeterlinck, Nietzsche, Tolstoy, and Whitman. Becomes intensely inter-
ested in the sculpture of Auguste RODIN.

1910   **5 January**: Birth of brother Kintomo's first son, Sanemitsu. **February**: Writes
"Omedetaki hito" [Simple-Minded Fellow] (NA). **April**: Arishima and his brother,
the painter Ikuma (1882–1974), join in the venture to publish the inaugural
edition of *Shirakaba* (issued by Rakuyôdô), which carries "Simple-Minded
Fellow." For this edition SA also writes a complimentary review of the novel
Sorekara [And Then...] by Natsume Sôseki (1868–1916). Sôseki invites him to
write something for his literary column in the *Asahi Newspaper*. The SHIRAKABA
associates wonder whether they might sell 200 copies, but from the outset readers
buy around 700 copies a month. Most reactions are positive. **July**: Goes to visit
Sôseki, hospitalized with stomach ulcers. It is their first meeting. **7 November**:
Tolstoy dies. **14th**: The special 236-page issue of *Shirakaba* commemorating
RODIN's 70th birthday carries SA's *"Rodan to jinsei"* [Rodin and Life]. SA becomes
acquainted with the novelist Nagayo Yoshirô (1888–1961).

1911   **February**: Rakuyôdô issues *Simple-Minded Fellow* (SSC) (cf. 1910.02). **March**:
Shirakaba carries *"Kojinshugi no dôtoku"* [The Ethics of Individualism]. SA has his
first sexual experience with a former maid in the Kôjimachi mansion. **April**: At the
end of the month, SA leaves for Sapporo, Hokkaidô. **May**: Spends all month in
Sapporo with his fellow *Shirakaba* writer Arishima Takeo. SA also takes a trip to
Otaru to visit the now-married Otei, on whom he had a crush when she was 12–
13. This is the last time SA sees her. He writes a dozen or so poems while in
Sapporo. **June**: Early in the month returns to Tokyo. **22 December**: Arrival of
three small bronze statuettes that Rodin sent as thanks for the *ukiyoe* prints the
Shirakaba associates had sent him in June. This year SA becomes acquainted with
the Western-style painter Kishida Ryûsei (1891–1929).

1912   **January**: *Shirakaba* carries *"Nochi ni kuru mono"* [The One who Comes After
(Me)], words of John the Baptist referring to Jesus (*Matthew* 3:11). Also publishes
"Kôki inshôha ni tsuite" [On the Post-Impressionists]. **March**: The one-act play
"Aru hi no yume" [A Dream], based on SA's visit to Otei in Otaru, appears in
Shirakaba. **12–13 May**: Twice in a row SA runs into Hiyoshi Taka (whom he'd
been trying to marry since 1908.07.19). **24th**: Takeo Fusako (born 1892.03.10)
comes to visit him. They begin corresponding. **1 June**: The two go to Kugenuma
together. **July**: Mother Naruko approves of SA's marrying Fusako. **12 August**:
Visits Fusako and her mother in Fukui, capital of Fukui Prefecture on the Japan
Sea (NNW of Nagoya), a city known especially for its silk weaving industry.
September: Writes the one-act play, *"Futatsu no kokoro"* [Two Minds • Souls].
October: *Shirakaba* carries *"Kosei ni tsuite no zakkan"* [Stray Thoughts on Individ-
uality]. **November**: *Shirakaba* carries the play, "Two Minds." SA publishes *"Gohho
no ichimen"* [One Aspect of Van Gogh] (IC). **14th**: Rakuyôdô publishes *"Seken
shirazu"* [Ignorant of the Word] (NA) and *"A no tegami mittsu"* [Three of A's
Letters] (SS). SA sets up in the Motozono, Kôjimachi family mansion a household
with Fusako, but there is no reception or official announcement of their marriage.

DATE EVENT

Continues to receive an allowance of ¥30 per month. During this year SA becomes acquainted with the poet Senke Motomaro (1888–1948).

1913 **February:** Writes reminiscences about Otei, *"Dai ni no haha"* [My Second Mother]; cf. note for "Rhapsodizing on My Birthday" ②. **April:** Publishes in *Shirakaba* the one-act play *"Aru hi no Ikkyû"* [Ikkyû—Once], the 15th century Zen monk; cf. 1937.06. Later publishes two more one-act plays. **September:** Brother Kintomo and family return from service in Germany. **November:** Writes the play *"Washi mo shiranai"* [I Don't Know Either]. **21 December:** Rakuyôdô issues *Kokoro to kokoro* [(Between) Heart and Heart] (IC). On the 25th issues *Seichô* [Growth] (IC). SA deepens his friendship with Kishida, Nagayo, and Senke.

1914 **1 January:** In two to three hours SA writes the one-act play *"Nijûhassai no Yaso to akuma"* [Jesus at Twenty-eight and Satan], then spends the New Year holidays in Fukui with Fusako and her family. *Chûô Kôron* carries "I Don't Know Either" (D), a piece said to mark SA's development as a playwright. **February:** *Shirakaba* carries his play, "Jesus at Twenty-eight and Satan." **March:** *Shirakaba* publishes *"Tsumi naki tsumi"* [Guiltless Sin]. SA formally registers his marriage to Fusako. **May:** SA leaves the family mansion in Motozono, rents a two-room home in Kôjimachi for ¥15 a month, and with Fusako sets up an independent household. Allowance from SA's family increases to ¥50 a month. **June:** *Ego* carries *"Hahaoya no shinpai"* [Mother's Concerns] (D). *Shirakaba* carries *"Dai ni no haha"* [My Second Mother. later retitled *"Hatsukoi"* (First Love)]. **7 July:** Brother Kintomo's wife Kazuko is admitted to the Red Cross Hospital where she dies of complications associated with pregnancy. **11–25 August:** Encouraged by Sôseki, the *Tokyo Asahi Newspaper* publishes SA's novel *Shi* [Death] in 14 installments (cf. 1899.12). **September:** After Japan decides to participate in World War I, *Ego* tries to publish SA's article *"Mata sensô ka"* [War Again?], but censors disallow it. **November:** Because SA's younger cousin, Kadenokôji Yasuko, had lost her husband, there is talk of adopting her daughter Kikuko. Fusako and SA take to the girl (then ca. 4). **November–December:** *Shirakaba* publishes *"Kare ga sanjû no toki"* [When He (i.e., I) Was Thirty], in which SA describes his home life and association with friends Nagayo, Kishida, and Senke. **31 December:** SA and Fusako adopt Kikuko, then look for a roomier house to rent. During this year, friends Nagayo and Shiga marry and Kishida paints SA's portrait (preserved in the Tokyo Metropolitan Art Museum).

1915 **January:** Moves from Tokyo to Kugenuma in Kanagawa Prefecture, near Fujisawa and Sagami Bay. *Shinsekai* publishes *"Chiisaki sekai"* [A Small World] (SS), which features recollections from middle school. **February:** Writes the one-act play *"Minôryokusha no nakama"* [Incompetent Companions]. **March:** Shirakaba Books publishes *Kare ga sanjû no toki* [When He was Thirty], which includes three other short stories. *Shirakaba* publishes *"Sono imôto"* [His Little Sister] (D). **June:** *"Washi mo shiranai"* [I Don't Know Either] (D) staged at the Imperial Theater, the first performance of a SA play. Invites Natsume Sôseki to see it on the third day. Sôseki takes him and Fusako to dinner. **September:** Publishes *Himawari* [Sunflower], which contains seven plays and one short story. *Chûô Kôron* carries *"Akumu"* [Nightmare] (D), publishes another one-act play. Moves from Kugenuma back to the capital, where SA lives in Sendagaya, not far from Kishida. Fusako's younger sister, just out of girls' school, has come to Tokyo to study, so she stays with them. **October:** After five years, *Omedetaki hito* [Simple-Minded Fellow; cf. 1910.02] sells 1,000 copies and is re-issued. **November:** Publishes the one-act play *"'A' to gen'ei"* ["A" and Illusions]. *Shirakaba* publishes *"Happyakunin no shikei"* [800 Sentenced to Death], in which SA describes an incident on Taiwan

DATE	EVENT

that involved 903 individuals who opposed Japan's rule. Shintomi Theater stages *"Futatsu no kokoro"* [Two Minds • Souls; cf. 1912.09].

1916	January: *Chûô Kôron* carries *"Aru sôdan"* [A Proposal] (D). Publishes *"Chiisaki unmei"* [Trivial Fate] (D). *Shirakaba* carries *"Zakkan"* [Random Thoughts]. February: Writes the one-act play *"Aru hi no dekigoto"* [An Incident] and *"Ane"* [Big Sister] (SS). Shinchôsha publishes *"Sono imôto"* [His Little Sister] (NA). *Shirakaba* publishes an article dealing with SA's reactions to the *Analects* in which SA says he has deeper respect for Jesus than for Confucius. After being burglarized again, SA moves to Ishikawa (now Bunkyô) Ward. March–November: *Shirakaba* serializes *"Aru seinen no yume"* [A Young Man's Dreams] (D). April: Through Shinchôsha, SA publishes *Chiisaki sekai* [Small World], an anthology of seven plays and seven dialogues. July: Publishes *Chiisaki izumi* [A Tiny Spring] (IC). October: *Shinchô* carries *"Atarashiki ie"* [The New Family] (SS). November: Publishes *Chiisaki unmei* [Trivial Fate] (EC). 12 December: Attends the funeral of Natsume Sôseki (who died on the ninth of stomach ulcers; cf. 1910.04). 20th: Moves into the house built on the banks of Lake Tega in Abiko, Chiba Prefecture, close to friends novelist Shiga Naoya (1883–1971), fine arts scholar Yanagi Muneyoshi (1889–1961), and the British potter Bernard Leach (1887–1979). From about this time, SA is designated a "popular writer."

1917	January: *Chûô Kôron* carries *"Yamatotakeru no Mikoto"* [Prince Yamatotakeru (81–113)], third son of Emperor Keikô and legendary hero known for suppressing the Kumasô rebellion at age 16. Through Shinchôsha issues *The New Family* (SSC). *A Young Man's Dreams* comes out as a book. 30 March ff.: Akasaka Rôyarukan stages *"Sono imôto"* [His Little Sister] (D). 5–6 May: The Ushigome Geijutsu Kurabu [Art Club] stages *"Akumu"* [Nightmare] (D). Shinchôsha issues *Atarashiki ie* [The New Family; cf. 1916.10] (EC). July: *Shirakaba* publishes several children's plays, including *"Kachikachi yama"* [Crackle-Crackle Hill, based on a folk tale]. Writes the one-act play *"A to B"* [A and B]. August: Writes *"Aru chichi"* [A Father] (SS) and *"Aru haha"* [A Mother] (SS). September: Publishes *Zakkan dainishû* [Stray Thoughts, Volume Two]. October: Writes *"Haha toshite no waga haha"* [My Mother as a Mother] (SS). *Shirakaba* carries SA's essay, *"Bijutsukan o tsukuru keikaku ni tsuite"* [On the Plan to Build an Art Museum] and asks for donations to support the project. December: Hears about the 17 November death of Rodin at age 77. Writes *"Aru chichi no tegami"* [A Father's Letter] (SS). Life in Abiko—where SA lives with Fusako, adopted daughter Kikuko, two maids, and two dogs—is said to be filled with visitors and visiting.

1918	January: The *Chûô Kôron* publishes *"Nojima Sensei no yume"* [The Dreams of Professor Nojima] (D). March: The *Ôsaka Mainichi Shinbun* [Ôsaka Daily News] carries the first part of *"Atarashiki mura no taiwa"* [Questions and Answers on the NEW VILLAGE]. Spring: Announces plans for the Shirakaba Bijutsukan [Shirakaba Art Museum]. May–June: *Shirakaba* carries parts two and three of "Questions and Answers on the New Village," initially titled *"Atarashii seikatsu ni hairu michi"* [The Path to a New Life]. July: To publicize the project establishes the organ *Atarashiki Mura* [NEW VILLAGE]; cf. prefatory remarks to Part III, page 177 ff. August: Shinchôsha publishes *Atarashiki mura no seikatsu* [Life in the New Village]. September: *Shirakaba* carries *"Aru kyakuhonka"* [A Playwright] (NA). 14th: First public lecture series on the village held in Tokyo's Hongô district. 15th: Interested parties gather at SA's home in Abiko to discuss possibilities. 23rd: The land search committee leaves Tokyo. Along the way, SA gives speeches at Hamamatsu, Nagano, Matsumoto, etc. 30th: They arrive in Kyôto. October:

DATE   EVENT

Gives speeches at Kyôto on the 1st, at Ôsaka on the 2nd, at Kôbe on the 3rd, at Fukuoka on the 7th. **10th:** The group arrives in Totoro, Kyûshû. **14 November:** SA and 19 others decide on a piece of land for *Atarashiki Mura* [New Village] in Ishikawauchi [NB: Professor Iida verified this reading with officials in the Kijô Town Hall. Reliable authorities alternately offer Ishikawachi and Ishigawauchi], Kijô Village, Koyu County, Hyûga, the ancient name for what is now Miyazaki Prefecture. ◀ They open with some 12 individuals. They rent a house in Ishikawauchi and commute by boat to their land. **December:** Genbunsha publishes *A Playwright* (DC).

1919   **January–June:** In *Shirakaba* SA serializes *Kôfukumono* [The Happy One] (LN), new title of *Jibun no shi* [My Teacher]. **Mid-March:** To Tokyo to celebrate the tenth anniversary of the *Shirakaba*. **April:** Publishes an anniversary edition of 550 pages with 30 pages of pictures. Friend and poet SENKE MOTOMARO joins the village in mid-month, making SA ecstatic, but leaves after a few days. Shiga helps sell SA's Abiko home, bringing over ¥4,000 into the village. **1 May:** Senke apologizes for his abrupt return to Tokyo saying he couldn't bear being so isolated [*sabishii*]. **12th:** SA celebrates his first anniversary at the village. First structure finished. SA writes the one-act play *"Shin Urashima no yume"* [Dream of a New Urashima, the Japanese Rip van Winkle], performed at the village. **7 July:** Chou Tso-jên (Japanese read Shô Sakujin [born 1885]; TO A CHINESE BROTHER) visits from China. *Kaizô* carries *"Hen na genkô"* [Strange Manuscript] (SS). **August:** Begins to serialize *Yaso* [Jesus] in *Atarashiki Mura* (to 1920.06). Shinchôsha publishes *Jiko o ikasu tame ni* [How to Make the Most of Oneself] (IC). Publishes *Dai ni no haha* [My Second Mother; cf. 1913.02 and 1914.06], containing the novelette and two plays. **September:** Sôbunkaku publishes *The Happy One* (MN). **October:** Kintomo (37) marries 26-year-old Fujiko, the second daughter of Baron Itô Yoshigorô. **16th:** The *Ôsaka Mainichi Shinbun* [Daily News] serializes *"Yûjô"* [Friendship] (NA) (to 12.21). SA writes the dialogue, *"Yûshi to seijin"* [Heroes and Holy Men]. **November:** Publishes *Hitotsu no michi* [A Single Path] (SSC).

1920   **Late February:** Completion of SA's new 12 *tsubo* house (area equals ca. two 9' x 12' rooms), used also to hold meetings, the only structure still remaining in the New Village Hyûga. **March:** In a nearby community, they set up Kôyasha as the village print shop. Shinchôsha issues *Atarashiki mura no rôdô* [Labor in the New Village] (IC). Sôbunkaku issues *Ningenteki seikatsu* [Human Existence] (IC). **26th–30th:** Five performances at the Imperial Theater in Tokyo of *"Nijûhassai no Yaso"* [Jesus at Twenty-eight; he began his ministry at 30]. **April:** Kôyasha publishes the first issue of *Atarashiki Mura* [The New Village], official organ of the village. *Kaihô* publishes *"Tochi"* [Land], a brief record of the founding of the New Village. **Mid-month:** Shiga Naoya visits the village, then SA tours sites on the Inland Sea with him. Shinchôsha issues *Ippon no eda* [A Branch] (SSC). ◀ Six move into the second village, just established nearby. Ibunsha issues *Friendship*. **May:** Publishes *Jibun no jinseikan* [My Views of Life] (EC). **July:** SA writes two more one-act plays and issues his first poetry collection, *Zatsu sanbyaku rokujûgohen* [A Miscellany of 365 (Poems)]. **September:** Kôyasha issues *Atarashiki mura no shinkô* [The Faith of the New Village] (IC). **September:** Kôyasha publishes *Yaso* [Jesus], a critical biography. **5 September–9 October:** Lecture tour to publicize the village includes Kôbe, Ôsaka, Kyôto, Niigata, Shinshû [Nagano Prefecture], and Tokyo. SA returns to the village at month's end. **5 November:** "Two Minds" (cf. 1912.09 and 1912.11) performed at the Shintomi Theater. Writes two new short stories and a one-act play. The first imported Van Gogh oil painting, one of his

DATE   EVENT

"Sunflower" pictures, arrives in Japan (lost to fire during World War II).

1921   **January:** *Shirakaba* begins to serialize *Dai san no inja no unmei* [The Fate of the Third Recluse], originally titled *Detarame* [At Random] (ends 1922.10). Through Kôyasha issues *Tochi* [Land] (SSC). **27th:** Fire destroys the main structure in the village, which housed bachelors, the library, bath, kitchen, and meeting hall. **February:** Publishes *Uzumorete ita mono* [The Obscure] (IC). **12 February–19 March:** Gives talks in Tokyo, etc. **9 March:** Lectures at Keiô University. Writes *"Aru tokai"* [A City] (SS) and *"Yuda no benkai"* [Judas's Defense] (SS). Shinchôsha issues *Ikin to suru mono* [One who Would Live] (DC). **April:** New Village Publications establishes the magazine *Seichô suru hoshi no mure* [Throng of Expanding Stars], later retitled *Hoshi no mure* [Star Throng]. **May:** Has a friend purchase in Paris a small Rodin sculpture titled "Little Sphinx." This 25.3 cm. (ca. 10") tall piece features a voluptuous kneeling nude with a lion-like face—contrasting with the Egyptian original that has a male face and the body of a lion; cf. page 191. For a photograph, cf. *Daini no tanjô—Kishida Ryûsei to Saneatsu* [Second Birth—Kishida and Saneatsu] (Chôfu: Mushakôji Memorial, 1995), page 21. **June:** Beginning of the month, wife Fusako develops a high fever and in a delirium says things that adversely affect their relationship. Shinchôsha issues *Companions of the Incompetent* (cf. 1915.02) (DC). **July:** Starts giving thought to using water to generate electricity for the village. Begins serialization in *Kaizô* (over 19 issues to 1923.11) of his autobiographical novel *Aru otoko* [A Man]. Kôyasha issues SA's collection, *Enzetsu futatsu* [Two Speeches] (IC). **August:** Rodin's "Little Sphinx" arrives. SA dreams of an art museum in the village. **14 September:** Leaves on a lecture tour, which includes stops at Fukuoka, Ôita, Shimonoseki, Okayama, Kôbe, Ôsaka, and Kyôto. Picks up Fusako in Fukui and they go to Tokyo, where SA gives talks. **October:** Lectures also in Yokohama, Sendai, and Shinshû. **11 November:** Returns after more speeches along the way. ◀ At its 3rd anniversary, village membership reaches 40. **December:** Kôyasha publishes *Zakkan* [Stray Impressions]. Shinchôsha publishes *"Dôwageki sanpen"* [Three Children's Dramas] (D), cover and 33 illustrations by artist friend Ryûsei (cf. 1911.12).

1922   **January:** Ryûsei designs covers for the New Year editions of *Shirakaba, Hoshi no Mure,* and *Atarashiki Mura*. SA writes *"Chichi to musume"* [Father and Daughter] (SS). Publishes *Aru seinen no yume* [A Young Man's Dreams] (SSC). **February:** Issues *Gendai sanjûsannin shû* [Thirty-Three Contemporaries] edited by Arishima Takeo and Shiga Naoya to help pay for the electrification of the village. **Late February–Late March:** In Tokyo on family business. Fusako remains in the capital. **March:** Kôyasha publishes *Moyuru hayashi* [Burning Grove] (DC). **June:** Publishes the one-act play *"Kami to otoko to onna"* [God • Man • Woman]. **22 June–9 July:** In Tokyo. **25th:** SA attends an unsatisfactory performance of one of his plays at the Yûraku Theater. **August:** Shinchôsha publishes *Aru kyakuhonka* [A Playwright]. **September:** *Chûô Kôron* carries *"Ningen banzai"* [Hurrah for Humanity!] (D–*kyôgen*). **21–22 October:** Yûraku Theater, Tokyo, presents *"Atarashiki mura no tame no kai"* [Convocation for the New Village], including a performance of SA's play, "God • Man • Woman" (cf. June). SA had become attached to Igô (variant of Iikawa) Yasuko (born 1900.09.06 in Shizuoka City, her family lives in Ôsaka), the first daughter of Yasunobu and Kiyo. She had graduated from the Hitotsubashi Girls' Occupational School and was studying Japanese-style painting under Kaburagi Kiyotaka (1878–1972). **November:** Yasuko observes her first year in the village. SA marries her this year (not registered until 1929.12.18). SA says he divorced Fusako because she had not been a wife to him since the summer of

DATE EVENT

1921. She later marries Sugiyama Masao, and both remain ardent supporters of the village (cf. 1929.12, 1932.01, 1935.10, and 1976.11). **December:** Yûraku Theater puts on another of SA's plays.

1923 **January:** *Chûô Kôron* publishes *"Hideyoshi to Sorori"* [Hideyoshi and Sorori] (D– *kyôgen*). Toyotomi Hideyoshi (1536–1598) was Japan's military dictator, and Sorori Shinzaemon was a comedian or jester whom Hideyoshi often summoned to entertain him. Serializes (to July) *Risôteki shakai* [The Ideal Society]. **April:** *"Hideyoshi to Sorori"* performed at the Imperial Theater. *Chûô Kôron* carries the play *"Kusunoki Masashige"* [Kusunoki Masashige (?–1336)], SA's first tragedy (cf. "Our Warriors Advance on Attu," page 281 and Note). **5 April ff.:** Initial advertisements appear for a 12-volume series of SA's *Works*, to include 9,000 pages and cost ¥50. **End of the month:** Spends ca. two weeks in Tokyo. Introduces pregnant Yasuko to mother Naruko. **May:** Geijutsusha starts to issue the *Works*, one volume per month. **12th:** Issues *The Fate of the Third Recluse* (cf. 1921.01). **9 June:** Friend Arishima Takeo commits suicide with his lover. **July:** Leaves at month's end to lecture in Kyôto. **30th:** Gives a talk in Kôjimachi. **August:** SA finishes writing *Aru otoko*. Publishes what ends up being the last issue of the *Shirakaba* magazine. **19th:** Returns to the village. **1 September:** Kantô Earthquake. Post-quake fires destroy the publishing house that printed *Shirakaba*. **2nd:** SA returns to the capital with four others. Finds his Kôjimachi home devastated, all contents lost in the fire, but his mother and other relatives are safe. **October:** *Fujin Kôron* publishes *"Jibun no koto, sono ta"* [Personal Matters, Etc.], in which SA says that family matters consume 20–30% of his time away from the village. **12 November:** Writes the *kyôgen*-style play *"Daruma"* [Daruma, the first Zen patriarch, one of the gods of good fortune] cf. page 336. **1 December:** First daughter Shinko born—the *shin* means "new," echoing the New Village. **11th–13th:** Ushigome Kaikan in Tokyo puts on SA's play *"Nojima Sensei no yume"* (cf. 1918.01). **18th:** Sees Shinko in Ôsaka for the first time. **22nd:** Mother Naruko meets her granddaughter. SA returns to the village at month's end.

1924 **January:** Publishes in the *Chûô Kôron* the one-act play *"Daruma."* Kôyasha issues *Chichi to musume* [Father and Daughter] (DC). **31st:** Over four days writes *"Aru otoko no hanashi"* [Tale of a Man], which describes SA's relationship with Yasuko. **February:** The Azabu Minami Theater puts on a SA play. **14th:** SA takes his family to Yasuko's home in Ôsaka, visits his home in Tokyo, etc. **March:** Issues *Atarashiki mura no seichô* [Growth of the New Village] (IC), *Ningenteki shakai* [A Humane Society] (IC) and *Onna no hito no tame ni* [For Women] (EC). **April:** Several *Shirakaba* fellows (SA, Shiga, Senke, Kinoshita, and Kurata) put out the first copy of the literary arts magazine *Fuji* (lasts 27 issues to 1926.07). Kôyasha issues *Atarashiki mura no kongo* [The Future of the New Village] (IC). Shinchôsha issues *Sôgen* [Prairie] (IC). **6th:** Returns with Yasuko and Shinko to the village. **May:** Kôyasha issues *Kyakuhon itsutsu* [Five Plays] (DC). Shinchôsha issues *Tôgen nite* [At Tôgen (Peach Root)] (DC). **4th:** Leaves to visit Shiga in Kyôto, the ailing Kinoshita, and also his mother in Tokyo. **13th:** SA views a performance of his play "Daruma" (cf. 1923.11 and 1924.01). **19th:** Returns to the village. **June:** Kôyasha publishes *Jibuntachi no shimei* [Our Mission] (IC) and *Kensetsu no jidai* [Age of Construction] (IC). **June:** Announces satisfactory progress for the village. **July:** Shinchôsha issues *Mahiru no hitobito* [Midday People] (SSC). Goes to Kôbe to greet brother Kintomo, returning after some four years abroad. **September:** Kôyasha publishes *Sanhômen* [Three Aspects] (IC). **October:** Kaizôsha publishes *Fude no muku mama* [Following My Brush] (EC). **2–20 November:** Goes to

DATE EVENT

Tokyo to visit his sick mother Naruko, etc. *Fuji* publishes *"Rakuen no ichigû"* [A Corner of Paradise] (D).

1925   **January:** *Fuji* carries *"Unmei to Go o suru otoko"* [The Man who Plays Go (i.e., Gambles) with Fate]. Leaves in late January, gives lectures to early February, hears that Kinoshita is failing, visits him in Kamakura. **15 February:** Friend and Shirakaba associate Kinoshita Rigen • Toshiharu (cf. 1906 and Note) dies. **25th:** Second daughter Taeko born. Atene Shoin publishes *Izumi to kagami* [Fountains and Mirrors] (IC). **March:** Involved in setting up a printing shop to supplement village income. **April:** Complete the structure for the print shop. *Fuji* publishes a special issue on the death of *Shirakaba* co-founder Kinoshita. **May:** SA travels in midmonth to the capital to see off his brother Kintomo, appointed ambassador to Romania. Mother Naruko's deteriorating health makes parting difficult. **18 June:** Uncle Kadenokôji Sukekoto dies at 66 (he is seven years younger than SA's mother). **July:** Shinchôsha publishes *Jinsei o kaku kangaeru* [How I Think of Life] (IC). **September:** Early in the month travels to Tokyo. Shinchôsha publishes *Unmei to hitobito* [People and Fate] (DC). Atene Shoin issues *Izumi to kane* [Fountains and Bells] (IC). **Ca. 20th:** Returns to the village. The print shop issues SA's poetry collection, *Shi hyakuhen* [100 Poems]. Until its demise in 1940, the shop issues 15 volumes related to the village. **October:** Early in the month leaves Tokyo, giving talks along the way. **December:** After seven years, SA decides to leave the New Village, hoping to further its objectives and offer support from the outside. Looks for a house to rent in Nara where friend Shiga Naoya then resides. Among his reasons for leaving the New Village, SA gives his mother's health, his two children, and concern for the independence of the villagers, who rely excessively on his leadership and financial support.

1926   **7 January:** Moves to Nara, but Yasuko and the children remain at mother Naruko's place in Ichigaya, Tokyo. *Kaizô* publishes *"Aiyoku"* [Desire] (D). SA writes *"Aru inu no hinpyôkai"* [A Dog Show] (D–*kyôgen*). **February:** From the tenth, the Tsukiji Little Theater offers SA's play *"Seimei no ô"* [The Master of Life]. Shinchôsha issues *Shizen • jinsei • shakai* [Nature • Life • Society] (IC). **March:** Kaizôsha issues *Desire* (DC). Late in the month SA visits the village, remaining until early April. **May:** Shinchôsha publishes *Yaso* [Jesus]. **July:** First performance of *"Aiyoku"* [Desire] at the Tsukiji Little Theater. Shinchôsha issues *"Nanatsu no yume"* [Seven Dreams] (D), first performed at the Tsukiji Little Theater. **Late Summer:** Takes family to Wakayama to visit. **August:** Kaizôsha issues *Bungaku ni kokorozasu hito ni* [To Those Determined to Go into Literature] (IC). **September:** Kaizôsha issues *Kodoku no tamashii* [The Lonely Soul] (DC). **October:** Shunjûsha issues *Seimei ni yakudatsu tame ni* [Helping People Live] (P). **November:** Shinchôsha publishes *Ren'ai • kekkon • teisô* [Love • Marriage • Chastity] (IC). **December:** Moves further east to Wakayama. **10th–16th:** Stays in the village, where on the 12th they belatedly celebrate the eighth anniversary of its founding. Shinchôsha issues *Kimagure nikki* [Whimsical Diary].

1927   **January:** Iwanami Shoten publishes *Jinrui no ishi ni tsuite* [On Mankind's Will] (IC). Sôbunkaku issues *Wakaki hitobito* [Young People] (LN). **February:** *Kaizô* publishes *"Aru chôkokuka no dôtokushin"* [A Sculptor's Sense of Morality] (SS). Iwanami Shoten issues *Unmei to go o suru otoko* [The Man who Gambles with Fate] (DC•SSC); cf. 1925.01. Moves to the village of Koiwa on the northern outskirts of Tokyo (now in Edogawa Ward)—living again near the capital after almost a decade. **22 February–9 August:** The *Asahi Shinbun* [Morning Sun Newspaper] serializes *Haha to ko* [Mother and Child] (LN). **April:** With former *Shira-*

DATE EVENT

kaba colleagues begins the magazine *Daichôwa* [Great Harmony; printed by Shunjûsha], which lasts through 19 issues to 1928.10. **June:** Shunjûsha issues *Bungei zakkan* [Miscellaneous Views on the Arts] (IC). This month the first New Village Exhibit opens at Isetan in Shinjuku, Tokyo (sponsored by the Kinokuniya Book Stores). **September:** Shinchôsha publishes *Heiwa na tami* [Peaceful Subjects]. **October:** Kaizôsha issues *Mother and Child* (LN). Moves to Ushigome Hachiman, now in Shinjuku Ward. **November:** Kaizôsha publishes a collection of SA's work in its series on modern Japanese writers.

1928   **January:** SA moves to Kôjimachi to be near his ailing mother. **February:** Creates the Tokyo Atarashiki Mura Kaijô [New Village Hall] near Yûrakuchô Station, which each month sponsors an exhibit, lecture, play, or specific cultural activity. **May:** *Chûô Kôron* issues *"Korosareru hitobito"* [Murder Victims] (D). **3 June:** Public lectures on the New Village held at Yomiuri Hall. **13 July:** Public lectures on the New Village held at Asahi Hall. *Daichôwa* begins serialization of *Torusutoi den* [The Biography of Tolstoy]. **September:** *Kaizô* carries *"Sado no Nichiren"* [Nichiren on Sado Island] (D). Nichiren (1222–1282) was the celebrated monk who founded the militant Buddhist sect named after him (sometimes called Hokkeshû). Nichiren had been banished to Sado from 1271 to 1273. *Daichôwa* dedicates this month's issue to Tolstoy's birthday. **October:** Last issue of *Daichôwa*. **November:** Renames the journal *Daichôwa* (cf. 1927.04; published by Shunjûsha) *Dokuritsujin* [The Self-Reliant], which lasts through 1931.06. **1 December:** Mother Naruko dies at 75 of liver problems. **4th:** Third daughter Tatsuko born during Naruko's funeral. *Dokuritsujin* publishes *"Nobunaga to Hideyoshi"* [Nobunaga and Hideyoshi] (E). Oda Nobunaga (1534–1582) was a famed warrior who helped quell civil wars and unify the country. For Hideyoshi, cf. 1923.01. In mid-month, SA to Hyûga to celebrate the 10th anniversary of the New Village.

1929   **January:** *Kaizô* publishes *"Unmei no tawamure"* [Fate's Flirting] (D). **February:** *Kaizô* publishes *"Ninomiya Sontoku"* [Ninomiya Sontoku (1787–1856)] (E), the beloved Edo era paragon of diligence and hard work. **April:** Moves to Shimo-Ochiai, now in Shinjuku Ward but then outside the city limits. **24 September:** The New Village Players perform *"Detarame"* [At Random; cf. 1921.01] at the Imperial Theater. **October:** *Chûô Kôron* carries *"Hen na mura"* [Strange Village] (D). **November:** Moves to Soshigaya on the outskirts of the capital (now Setagaya Ward). **9 December:** SA officially registers his divorce from Fusako (cf. 1922.11), who at the time was living in Kamakura with her new husband, Sugiyama Masao, and adopted daughter Kikuko. **18th:** Legally registers his marriage to Yasuko (cf. 1932.01). **20th:** Friend and painter Kishida Ryûsei (cf. 1911.12, 1914.11, etc.) dies in Manchuria of complications from stomach ulcers. He is only 37.5. Establishes in Omote Sarugaku, Kanda Ward, the Hyûgadô, an art store.

1930   **January–March:** In Nagaoka Spa, Izu, to write and recover from neuralgia. **February:** Hyûgadô issues its first book, *Jibun no jinseikan* [My Views of Life]. **March:** The Hongô Theater performs a SA play. **5 April:** Visits the village in Hyûga for the first time in ca. 18 months. **April–November:** The *Fujin Kurabu* serializes *Toge made uruwashi* [Even Thorns are Lovely]. **June:** Hyûgadô issues *Geki gohen* [Five Plays]. **September:** *Bungei Shunjû* carries *"Gankô na otoko"* [Obstinate Fellow] (D). **October:** *Kaizô* publishes *"Sanetomo no shi"* [The Death of (Minamoto) Sanetomo], 1192–1219, the third and last Minamoto Shôgun, whose nephew assassinated him at a temple near Kamakura. **December:** Hyûgadô issues *Even Thorns are Lovely* and 1,000 copies of SA's personally-edited *Shishû* [Selected Poetry]. Kôdansha publishes *Ninomiya Sontoku* (cf. 1929.02).

DATE   EVENT

1931   **January:** Hyûgadô publishes *Seiun* [Nebula • Star Cloud] another Shirakaba jour-
       nal. It lasts only nine issues through September. **March:** Hyûgadô publishes *The
       Death of Sanetomo* (cf. 1930.10) (DC). **April:** SA appears with the New Village
       Players in *"Damasukusu e"* [To Damascus] by the Swedish playwright Johan
       August Strindberg (1849–1912). **June:** The Players perform in Tokyo SA's
       "Unmei to go o suru otoko" [The Man who Gambles with Fate]; cf. 1925.01 and
       1927.02. **24 June–1 August:** *Jiji Shinpô* serializes *"Ihara Saikaku"* (1642–1693)
       (NA), the Edo novelist of merchant mores. **July:** Moves to Kitami in the village of
       Kinuta on the outskirts of Tokyo, now in Setagaya Ward. **August:** *Bungei Shunjû*
       carries SA's *"Bokuryû chûshingura"* [My Version of The Treasury of Loyal Retain-
       ers] (re the famed 47 *rônin* [masterless samurai]). SA writes "wooden [*boku*]
       dragon [*ryû*]," which Professor Iida points out puns on "*bokuryû* • my style."
       September: The last issue of the journal *Seiun*. **14–18 November:** Visits Hyûga to
       celebrate the 13th anniversary of the New Village.

1932   **23 January:** Former wife Fusako wants to use the Mushakôji name, so her
       husband Sugiyama Masao is formally listed in the Mushakôji *koseki* [family regis-
       ter] as the adopted son of SA and Yasuko (cf. 1929.12). **19 February:** Masao
       officially marries Fusako and then converts his "adopted son" status so he can be
       the independent householder Mushakôji Masao. He continues using the name
       Sugiyama as a writer, etc. **June:** Kôdansha publishes *Ôishi Yoshio* (1659–1703),
       the chief of the 47 *rônin* (cf. 1931.08). **30 September–8 October:** Travels to Kan-
       sai, stopping to see Shiga in Nara, etc. before arriving at Hyûga. ✦ Eleven males,
       six females, four children, and four babies now live in the village. **October:**
       Iwanami Shoten issues *Rongo shikan* [My Views of the Confucian *Analects*].
       August: *Chûô Kôron* carries *"'A' sensei no ikô"* [Posthumous MS of Professor "A"].
       November: *Chûô Kôron* carries *"Tetsugakusha Ramê no shi"* [The Death of the
       Philosopher Ramée]. This refers to the French humanist philosopher and reformer
       Pierre de la Ramée (a.k.a. Petrus Ramus; 1517–1572), killed in the St. Bartholo-
       mew's Day massacre. With *Shirakaba* colleague Nagayo Yoshirô (1888–1961)
       issues the magazine *Jûkô*, which lasts 22 issues (1932.11–1934.10).

1933   **January:** *"Aiyoku"* [Desire] (D) performed at the Tsukiji Theater. **February:** The
       Kabuki Theater puts on another SA play. **March:** Reissues the monthly magazine
       Atarashiki Mura [The New Village]; 33 issues appear through 1940.01. **July:** The
       New Village Players give seven performances of *"Shijin no musô"* [A Poet's
       Visions]. **November:** Celebrates the 15th anniversary of the founding of the New
       Village. Sponsors a "New Village Festival" at the Sankai Hall in Akasaka. **14–22
       December:** Stays at the village in Hyûga. Considers resurrecting the *Shirakaba*.

1934   Through 1935 SA writes a number of biographies of famous men for Kôdansha's
       mass-readership magazine *Kingu* [King], which hopes to become the monarch of
       monthly magazines (published between 1925.01 and 1957.12 and renamed *Fuji*
       between 1943.03 and 1946.01). **January:** The widow of Ryûsei (cf. 1929.12.20)
       offers to rent SA her home. He then moves to Tsuruyamakôji in Kichijôji, now in
       Musashino, a western suburb of Tokyo. **April:** *Kingu* publishes *"Miyamoto
       Musashi"* (1584–1645), an essay on the famed swordsman. **June:** Yamamoto
       Shoten issues *Kûkai oyobi sono ta* [Kûkai (774–835) and Others]. Kûkai is the
       monk who imported Shingon Buddhism from China. **July:** *Kingu* carries *"Kuro-
       zumi Munetada"* (1780–1850), the founder of the Kurozumi Shintô sect that
       accords special honor to the sun. **August:** *Kingu* publishes *"Saigyô to Tenryû no
       watashiba"* [Saigyô and the Tenryû Ford]. Saigyô (1118–1190) was the famed
       monk-poet-recluse-wanderer. The Tenryû River, known for its fierce rapids, is in

DATE EVENT

Shinano, now Nagano Prefecture. **October:** Kôdansha publishes *Shaka* [Buddha]. **November:** Celebrates the 16th anniversary of the village. **7–14 December:** Visits the village in Hyûga. Moves to another house in Kichijôji.

1935 **5 February ff.:** Holds an exhibition of SA's paintings in Kôjimachi. **Spring:** Five paintings displayed in the 14th annual National Art Exhibition. **April:** Becomes a member of the *Kokugakai* [National Painters' Club]. **May:** *Kingu* publishes SA's *"Kuroda Josui"* [a.k.a. *Yoshitaka*] (1546–1604), the Christian general from Kyûshû. Begins serialization in *Atarashiki Mura* of letters written to him at the village between 1919–1925. **June:** Yamamoto Shoten issues *Nihon no sugureta hitobito* [Outstanding Japanese]. **July:** *Kaizô* publishes *"Saigyô suketchi"* [Sketches of Saigyô (cf. 1934.08)]. Publishes *Jinrui no ishi ni tsuite* [On Human Will]. **August:** SA avoids the summer heat with his children in Mito on the Izu Peninsula (south of Numazu on the Pacific). A case of sunstroke results in a high fever and a severe case of neuralgia that confines him to bed for almost a month. **October:** *Chûô Kôron* publishes *"Yowai"* [Age]. Former wife Fusako, husband Sugiyama [Musha-kôji in the family register] Masao, and adopted daughter Kikuko return to Hyûga to live in the New Village after an absence of eight years. **November:** Gakugeisha publishes *Jinsei • shûkyô • bungei* [Life • Religion • Literature], comprising 45 essays written over the last decade.

1936 **January:** *Chûô Kôron* carries *"Kare no nichijô seikatsu"* [His (i.e., My) Daily Life]. **March:** Issues *Shiga Naoya no tegami* [Letters of Shiga Naoya], for which SA writes a preface on his relationship with divorced wife Fusako and life-long friend Shiga, who donates his royalties to the village. **April:** Kôdansha publishes 800 copies of SA's biography of Tolstoy. **27th:** Leaves Yokohama on the Hakusan Maru, bound eventually for Berlin to visit brother Kintomo, Japan's Ambassador to Germany. **7 June:** Arrives in Marseilles. Soon thereafter begins to send regular reports—based on journal accounts of numerous rich and varied experiences—to magazines like *Bungei Shunjû, Chûô Kôron, Gendai,* and *Tabi,* as well as to newspapers such as the *Tokyo Asahi Shinbun* and the *Tokyo Nichinichi Shinbun.* These earn income to support SA's family, supplement the village budget, and provide travel funds. Newspapers, for example, send him ¥200 monthly (ca. $100 U.S.). SA's articles present his reactions to the Berlin Olympics (which open on **1 August**), European art museums, scenic spots from Berlin and Vienna to Naples and Pompeii, and the art of specific painters. SA also publishes interviews with Pablo Picasso (1881–1973), Henri Matisse (1869–1954), Georges Rouault (1871–1958), and André Derain (1880–1954). **6 November:** SA leaves London and boards a German ship. **14th:** Reaches New York. SA sees the sights for three days, then goes to Washington, D.C. where Ambassador Saitô Hiroshi (MANY HARDSHIPS) shows him around. After three days in Washington, SA travels to Chicago to visit the art museum. He then crosses the continent by train to San Francisco. **27th:** SA boards the Asama Maru. **12 December:** Arrives as scheduled in Yokohama.

1937 This year in *Bungei Shunjû, Chûô Kôron,* and other journals SA publishes reports or reminiscences of his experiences in the West and evaluations of European painters and their work. **3–6 March:** Visits the village in Hyûga. **June:** Moves to Mure in the western Tokyo suburb of Mitaka. Since daughters Taeko and Tatsuko are enrolled in Myôjô Gakuen, SA wishes to live near the school. He becomes a member of the Japan Academy of Arts [Geijutsuin]. Publishes essays on three his-torical figures: *Ikkyû • Sorori • Ryôkan.* Ikkyû (1394–1481), famous for populariz-ing Zen, was a painter, poet, and Rinzai Zen monk of the Daitoku Temple in Kyôto. Sorori was a comic; cf. 1923.01. Ryôkan (1758–1831) was a poet, calligra-

DATE   EVENT

	pher, and Sôtô Zen priest of the Kôshô Temple in Kyôto. **July:** For the first time in ages, SA is able to turn out 100 pages of creative writing. **October:** Kôdansha publishes *Kusunoki Masashige* (?–1336) (LN), the tragic samurai general defeated at Minatogawa; OUR WARRIORS ADVANCE ON ATTU; cf. 1923.04. **26th:** SA tells Shiga that he likes this book on Kusunoki the best of his recent publications.
1938	SA's interest in painting intensifies. Has exhibitions of his work in January, February, May, and October. **February:** Publishes in *Shônen Kurabu* a story about the blind farm-boy-turned-scholar, Hanawa Hokiichi (1746–1821). **September:** Announcement of dam and hydroelectric plant construction near Takajô in Miyazaki Prefecture. This project will cause the loss in Hyûga of ca. 75% of an acre of the very best New Village paddy land. Search begins for replacement property near Tokyo. **November:** Ikuseisha publishes *Aijô no sho* [Book of Love] (DC). Iwanami Shinsho [Library] publishes *Jinseiron* [Views on Life] (IC), written at the personal request of the founder of Iwanami Shoten. During this year SA also publishes a book on the beloved rebellious anti-hero Saigô Takamori (1827–1857). **4 December:** Visits Hyûga and on the **9th** confers with the governor of Miyazaki Prefecture concerning the displacement of villagers.
1939	**March:** Kôdansha publishes a collection of SA's essays. **July:** *Nihon Hyôron* carries *"Ai to shi"* [Love and Death] (NA). **September:** The novel's excellent reception results in Seinen Shobô issuing *Love and Death* as a book. Determination made to establish the New Village East on the Kantô Plain, so associates purchase ca. 4,000 *tsubo* (some 3.25 acres) in Moroyama, Iruma County, Saitama Prefecture, west-by-northwest of Tokyo Station. Moroyama—situated between the towns of Hidaka and Ogose—lies in the southwest section of the prefecture, slightly north of Hannô. **17th:** A ceremony commemorates the beginning of work in Moroyama at the *Higashi no mura* [New Village East], officially called *Higashi dai ichi atarashiki mura* [East New Village #1]. **October:** Kôchô Shorin publishes *Ihara Saikaku* (cf. 1931.06). The first structures appear at Moroyama. **30 November:** Work on the Moroyama village meeting hall begins. ♦ Two families remain at the New Village in Hyûga. Two other families plan to move to the Kantô area.
1940	**January:** *Kaizô* carries *"Aru hanazono"* [A Flower Garden] (D). **January–October:** *Fujin Kôron* serializes *Kôfuku na kazoku* [The Happy Family] (LN). **February:** Kôchô Shorin publishes *Rakuen no kora* [Children of Paradise]. **March:** Chûô Kôronsha issues *Katatsumuri no hitorigoto* [A Snail's Soliloquy]. Shares the Second Kikuchi Kan Prize for *Love and Death.* Plans to visit Moroyama the fourth Sunday of every month. **June:** Kôchô Shorin publishes a collection of articles about SA's 1936 trip to the West. **September:** With help from Yasuko's father, SA buys a large house in the village of Mitaka (west of Tokyo) and moves again. This is the first time since leaving the village in 1926 that he has lived in his own home. **October:** Chûô Kôronsha issues *Kôfuku na kazoku* [The Happy Family]. **November:** Kawade Shobô publishes a collection of SA's writings in a series on the *Shirakaba.* **December:** Shôchiku makes *The Happy Family* into a movie.
1941	**January:** The People's New Theater stages *"Shichifukujin"* [Seven Gods of Luck] (D–*kyôgen*). SA publishes *Kôshi* [Confucius]. **January–December:** *Shinjoen* serializes *Utsukushiki kokoro no monogatari* [Tales of a Noble Heart] (LN). **April:** Publishes *Musha shishû* [The Musha (literally, wheel-less, but a pun on his name) Poetry Collection]. **May:** First issue of the New Village monthly organ, *Bareisho* [Potato] appears. **28 August:** On the birthdays of Tolstoy and Goethe, sponsors readings and lectures at the Imperial University in Hongô. **8 December:** Pearl Harbor and the onset of hostilities with America. SA joyously supports the war but

DATE EVENT

later regards his rapture over Japan's victories as irrational and barbaric.

1942 **March:** Issues *Gashû to garon* [Picture Collections and Views on Painting], a limited edition of 300 copies. **April–September:** *Fujin Asahi* serializes *Akatsuki* [Dawn]. **May:** Kawade Shobô issues *Daitôa sensô shikan* [My Feelings on the Greater East Asia War]. Appointed chair of the literary drama section of the Patriotic Literary Association [Bungaku hôkokukai]—an honorary post sans responsibilities. Sakurai Shoten publishes *Musuko no kekkon* [The Son's Marriage]. **June:** *Jitsugyô no Nihon* issues *"Bijutsuronshû"* [My Views on Art] (EC). **August:** Sets up an art store and a village office in Jinbôchô, Kanda. **October:** First daughter Shinko marries Kimura Ryûzô, employed by NHK, the Japan Broadcasting Company. An only child, Kimura is not a candidate for adoption by SA. **November:** SA lectures at the Greater East Asian Literary Conference held in Tokyo. **December:** Bungei Shunjûsha issues *Bijutsu o kataru* [Talks on Art]. During this year, SA publishes 21 new or re-issued books.

1943 **January:** *Bareisho* [Potato] publishes a special issue on Ninomiya Sontoku (cf. 1929.02 and 1930.12). **February:** Publishes *Akatsuki* [Dawn], a collection of short stories and conversations. Sponsors through 1944.01 regular lectures on the village in Kanda. **1–3 April:** Attends the Sino-Japanese Cultural Society Conference in Nanking. Visits Beijing, Manchuria, and the New Village branch in Seoul. **9 August:** Adopted daughter Murata Kikuko (cf. 1914.11–12)—whom Fusako and Sugiyama had raised—dies at 33 from an ulcerated stomach and duodenum. SA attends the Greater East Asian Literary Conference held in Tokyo, where he meets with Chinese writers. **September:** Kôchô Shorin issues *San shônen kuni o mamoru* [Three Lads Defend their Country]. **10 October:** Daughter Shinko has her first child, Tsuneyo, SA's first grandson. **14 November:** Celebrates the 25th anniversary of the New Village at Kyôiku Kaikan in Tokyo. **December:** Chôbunkaku publishes *Jinsei to seinen* [Life and Youth].

1944 Despite air raids and shortages, SA does not alter his work habits. **May:** Atago Shobô publishes *Yasaisan* [In Praise of Greens]. **July:** Akashi Shobô publishes *Hô Taikô no tegami* [The Letters of Imperial Adviser Toyotomi]. This was the title of the warrior chief Toyotomi Hideyoshi, 1536–1598; cf. 1923.01 and 1928.12. **October:** Koyama Shoten issues *Sanshô* [Three Smiles] (DC). Writes several works in support of the war effort, including in **December:** *"Tôa bungakusha taikai ni okuru ji"* [Address to the East Asian Writers' Conference] published in *Bungei Nippon*. SA visits northern Honshû and considers the Akita area suitable for escape from the capital (cf. 1945.05). At year's end SA discovers that, if the war continues, American military planners anticipate 20 million Japanese will die of starvation. Even the Japanese military predicts the number could rise to 10 million. SA begins to wish the war would end.

1945 SA decides to evacuate Tokyo and retreat to Akita, but since the area is remote he must wait till travel becomes convenient. **March:** Third daughter Tatsuko marries Mushakôji Minoru, the adopted son of a collateral family. He teaches history at an Army officers' school. Starts writing *Wakaki hi no omoide* [Recollections of Younger Days]. **April:** Taking wife Yasuko, second daughter Taeko, and grandson Kimura Tsuneyo (father Ryûzô cannot leave his broadcasting job; cf. 1942.10), SA moves from a hotel in Ôhito (south of Mishima) on the Izu Peninsula to Sanjô in Niigata Prefecture. **12 May:** SA celebrates his 60th birthday in Tokyo with ten others (immediate kin and New Village members). **13th:** Leaves the capital for Sanjô. **23rd:** The family removes to Inazumi Onsen, a hot springs near the city of Akita in northern Honshû. **15 August:** Japan surrenders. At the end of the month,

DATE   EVENT

SA returns to the capital. **November:** Writes General Douglas MacArthur arguing the need to keep the Emperor system to guarantee a peaceful future. **14th:** Celebrates in Inokashira Park (MY DESK) the 27th anniversary of the founding of the New Village. **December:** Holds the first postwar lectures on the village.

1946   **January:** SA publishes in *Shinsei* his November 1945 letter to General MacArthur. **22 March:** Imperial appointment to the House of Peers. SA may attend sessions only if he cares to, in which case he will be chauffeured to and from the Diet. Kensetsusha publishes *Shin Nippon no kensetsu* [Building the New Japan]. **April:** *Recollections of Younger Days* (LN) appears. **May:** Kawade Shobô publishes *Gusha no yume* [A Fool's Dreams]. **July:** Purged as a minor "war criminal," SA is forced to resign appointments to the House of Peers and the Geijutsuin (cf. 1937.03). **August:** Seikei Shunjûsha issues the novel *Niji* [Rainbow]. **September–October:** Travels through Hokkaidô with the Western-style painter Nakagawa Kazumasa (1893–1991; cf. page 47). **October:** Publishes *Mokkei to Ryôkai* [Mu Ch'i and Liang K'ai], a study of the Chinese Ch'an [Zen] painters (cf. Notes). Travels to Kyûshû, giving lectures along the way. **November:** Publishes the article *"Warera wa ika ni iku beki ka"* [How Shall we Live?]. Publishes 27 books during the year. ◆ The population of New Village East increases to 17 people representing three families. In Hyûga are two families numbering 11 people.

1947   **January:** Edits the magazine *Himawari* [Sunflower], meant to be a monthly. It publishes only three issues before being discontinued in January 1948. Hyûga Shokan publishes *Inazumi nikki* [Inazumi Diary; cf. 1945.05]. **23 February:** First visit to the New Village East in several years. **23–30 May:** The Tokyo Metropolitan Art Museum holds the first New Village Art Exhibit in Ueno. **June:** Rôdô Bunkasha publishes *Ai to jinsei* [Love and Life]. **August:** Issues the poetry collection *Kanki* [Joy]. **September:** Holds at a Ginza salon the first exhibition of SA's calligraphy (22 works). **November:** Kyôritsu Shobô issues *Utsukushiki jidai* [The Noble Age]. **December:** Kyôei Shuppansha publishes *Shin-ren'ai to kekkon* [Marriage and the New (Style) Romantic Love].

1948   **January:** Last issue of *Himawari* [Sunflower]. **February:** Koyama Shoten publishes *Kishida Ryûsei* (1891–1929), about the renowned Western-style painter and friend who died of complications from ulcers (cf. 1929.12). Publishes *Gei ni ikiru hito-bito* [People Who Live by Art]. **March:** Wakei Shoten issues *Renburanto* [Rembrandt]. The New Village East is legally set up as a foundation (juridical entity). **14th:** Friend and poet Senke Motomaro dies of pneumonia (cf. 1912.11 and 1919.04). **April:** Second daughter Taeko marries Ataka Kanzaburô, who takes the Mushakôji name. **1 July:** SA and more than 40 other mature writers, artists, and scholars band together to support publication of the first issue of the literary journal *Kokoro* [The Heart • Soul]. With a minor interruption or so, it has appeared monthly. *Shôsetsu Shinchô* publishes *"Kare no senbô"* [His Envy] (SS). **September:** Publishes *Kyôdai* [Siblings]. **October:** Celebrates the 30th anniversary of New Village. **November:** Publishes *Bakaichi* [Chief of Fools]. Wakei Shoten publishes *Bi wa doko ni mo* [Beauty Everywhere].

1949   **January ff.:** *Kokoro* begins two-year serialization of *Shinri sensei* [Professor Truth] (LN). **April:** New Village East begins to publish the monthly journal *Atarashiki Mura* [New Village]. **May:** Stays two nights in Moroyama. **September:** Celebrates the 10th anniversary of New Village East.

1950   **April:** Shorin Shinkôchô publishes *Kôda Rohan* (1867–1947), novelist and scholar of Japanese literature. **May:** New Village members set up the Chôwasha to publish collections of SA's work. The first stage includes 12 volumes. **7–30 June:** Trip to

DATE   EVENT

Kyûshû. Spends two nights at Hyûga New Village, SA's first visit since 1938. December: Last installment of *Professor Truth*.

1951   March: The Folk Players perform *"Sono imôto"* [His Little Sister] (D) at the Mitsukoshi Theater. April: To raise funds for new structures, New Village Publications issues *Fue o fuku* [Playing the Flute], a self-selected collection of his poetry. 6 August: Officially released from the purge. 3 November: The Japanese government confers on him the Order of Cultural Merit [Bunka Kunshô]. The city of Mitaka (a western suburb of Tokyo) makes him a Distinguished Citizen [*meiyô shimin*]. December: The Kadokawa Library decides to include *Shinri sensei* [Professor Truth] in its series. It becomes a best seller.

1952   April: Re-elected to membership in the Geijutsuin (cf. 1946.07). People purchasing SA's paintings increase noticeably from this time. May–December: Sôgensha issues a six-volume collection of SA's works. June: *Bungei* carries *"Atarashiki mura wa ikite iru"* [The New Village Survives]. October: *Chûô Kôron* carries *"Shiawase na otoko"* [A Happy Man], the final chapter of *Bakaichi* [Chief of Fools], the series on the fictional character Sanya Gohei.

1953   January: Kawade Shobô issues *Chief of Fools*. March: Kaname Shobô publishes *Waga dokushoron* [My Views on Reading Books]. April: *Kaizô* carries *"Shizen wa erai"* [Nature is Wonderful]. May: Kadokawa Shoten publishes a selection of SA's works as Volume 12 in its survey of Japanese literature published since 1926. June: Shôchiku makes a movie of *"Sono imôto"* [His Little Sister; cf. 1915.03, 1916.02, and 1951.03]. July: Kaname Shobô issues *Waga jinsei no sho* [The Book of my Life]. October: Seirin Shoin publishes *Waga shôgai o kaerimite jinsei o kataru* [Reviewing my Existence—Speaking of Life]. September: *Bungei* carries *"Shiga Naoya"* [cf. Note]. 14–15 November: At the New Village East in Moroyama, SA observes the 35th anniversary of the village. Critics at last begin to concede the success of the New Village. Kawade Shobô publishes *Kûsô sensei* [Teacher of Dreams]. Shinchôsha makes plans to publish a multi-volume collection of SA's work. December: Publishes *Nonki na hitotachi* [Easy-Going People].

1954   January: Starts serialization in *Kokoro* of Sanya Gohei stories, later a long novel, which continues through 1956.03. *Chûô Kôron* issues *"Nihonjin no ketten"* [Shortcomings of the Japanese]. From this year on, SA has a January exhibition of his art work. March: Kaname Shobô issues *Waga jinsei to shinjitsu* [My Life and Truth]. May: *Bungei Shunjû* carries *"Watashi no kenpô sôan"* [My Draft of the Constitution]. Kadokawa Shoten publishes *Hana wa mankai* [Flowers in Full Bloom], SA's collection of 17 recently-written but unpublished works. July: The Takarazuka Kagekidan performs *"Ningen banzai"* [Hurrah for People!]. August: Shinchôsha publishes *Tsurezuregusa shikan* [Personal Views of the *Tsurezuregusa*]—the classic *Essays in Idleness* by Yoshida Kenkô (1283–1350). October: Radio Tokyo dramatizes *Ai to shi* [Love and Death; cf. 1939.07 and 1939.09]. SA buys 1,000 *tsubo* of land (ca. 80% of an acre) in Iruma Machi, close to Sengawa Station on the Keiô Line in the western suburb of Chôfu. The land contains a spring and pond around which SA will build a house. November: Shinchôsha begins to issue SA's works in 25 volumes (the project ends 1957.03). Ikeda Shoten sets about issuing a limited edition of 1,000 copies of three books dealing with SA's views on life. Radio Tokyo broadcasts a dramatization of *"Ikkyû to jigoku tayû"* [Ikkyû and the Chief Steward of Hell]. For Ikkyû, cf. 1937.06.

1955   January: Kawade Shobô issues *Bakaichi banzai* [Long Live the Chief of Fools]. *Gunzô* carries *"Nihiki no nezumi"* [Two Rodents]. Bungei issues *"Aru nôka de"* [At a Farmhouse]. March: Publishes *Jiko o ikasu tame ni* [To Make the Most of One-

DATE EVENT

self]. 12 May: On SA's birthday, Chikuma Shobô issues a volume about him in its series *Bungaku arubamu* [Photo Albums on Literary Figures]. The company also issues a collection of SA's work as Volume 19 in *Gendai Nihon bungaku zenshû* [Collected Works of Contemporary Japanese Literature]. June: NHK (the Japan Broadcasting Company) airs the drama *"Musume no tenki yohô"* [The Girl's Weather Report]. July: *Shinron* carries the essay *"Sôri daijin ron"* [Views of the Prime Minister]. 21st: Celebrates the framing [*jôtôshiki*] of SA's new Chôfu house. August: *Bungei* issues a Mushakôji Saneatsu Reader. This special edition is titled, *"Waga jinsei—shi o tôshite mita boku no naimen seikatsu"* [My Life—My Inner Life Viewed through Poetry]. 3 October: Essayist and editor Kawashima Denkichi (born 1897) dies. He lived in the New Village for 27 years. 20 December: SA moves into his new home in Ogino, Iruma Machi, Chôfu City—in an area called Sengawa—where he lives 20 years till his death. The house and grounds in Wakaba Machi are now preserved by the city as Saneatsu Park.

1956 January: One-man painting exhibition at the Isetan Department Store, Shinjuku. February: Chikuma Shobô sponsors a film series lasting 30 minutes each, the first of which features SA painting at his new home in Iruma. The film also depicts the New Village lifestyle. March: Kawade Shobô publishes *Sanya Gohei* (hero of the *Bakaichi* series; cf. 1952.10 and 1954.01). Shinsei Shobô publishes *Medetashi* [Auspicious] (D & IC). 2 April: Friend and colleague, the poet-sculptor Takamura Kôtarô (born 1883), dies. 13 July: NHK airs another historical drama. 14th: Gives the lecture *"Renburanto no ningensei"* [Rembrandt's Humanity] at the Asahi Auditorium. 16th: NHK broadcasts his talk, *"E to chôkoku no bi ni tsuite"* [On the Beauties of Painting and Sculpture]. September: *Kokoro* carries *"Hitorigoto"* [Soliloquy], which again clarifies his 1923 divorce from Fusako and her marriage to Sugiyama. October: Shinchôsha publishes *Waga jinsei* [My Life]. November: Yomiuri Shinbunsha publishes *Jibun no aruita michi* [The Path I've Trod].

1957 January: Some of Senke's remains (cf. 1948.03.14) interred at New Village East. February: *Kokoro* celebrates its 100th issue. March: Sôgensha publishes *E o kaku yorokobi* [The Joys of Painting]. Shinchôsha publishes the last of the 25 volumes of SA's *Works*. April: Begins serialization in *Kokoro* of *Hakuun sensei* [Professor Whitecloud], which ends 1959.03. *Atarashiki Mura* publishes a special issue on Senke Motomaro (cf. 1948.03). July: NHK broadcasts SA's radio drama, *Shiawase na baka* [Happy Fool]. August: Nichizô Bijutsu Shuppansha publishes *Mushakôji Saneatsu gashû* [A Collection of Mushakôji Saneatsu's Paintings]. November: Celebrates in Chiyoda Hall the 39th anniversary of the New Village.

1958 January: *Atarashiki Mura* serializes *"Boku no kobijutsukan"* [My Little Art Museum] over four issues. These consist of pictures and explanations of SA's private art collection. February: Chiseisha publishes *Ikiru koto wa subarashii koto da* [Life is Wonderful!] (IC). October: Chiseisha publishes *Kô ikiru no ga shinjitsu da* [This is Living the Truth]. On the 40th anniversary of the New Village, Kadokawa Shoten publishes *Kono michi o aruku* [We Take this Path], which gathers four decades of essays on and reminiscences of the New Village. 13 November: Celebrates at the Kudan Kaikan in Chiyoda Ward the 40th anniversary of the village. SA reads his poems and comments on his art slides.

1959 January: Begins serialization (to June) in the *Fujin Kôron* of *Nippon Tarô* [Nippon Tarô] (LN), for children. 19–31: NHK broadcasts the 12 installments of *Professor Truth* (cf. 1949.01 and 1950.12). March: Completes the 21st installment of *Professor Whitecloud*. April: Kadokawa Shoten publishes *Professor Whitecloud* (LN). July: Nikkatsu makes a movie of the 1939.07 novella *Love and Death* (cf. 1939.07,

DATE   EVENT

1940.03, and 1954.10), re-titled, *Sekai o kakeru koi* [Love Spans the Globe]. **September:** Serializes in *Kokoro* (to 1960.04) *Baka ichi no shi* [The Death of the Chief of Fools], later retitled *The Life of the Chief of Fools.*

1960   **April:** Lectures at the village in Moroyama. **May:** Changes journal name *Atarashiki Mura* [New Village] to *Kono Michi* [This Path], issued by the New Village. *Kono Michi* serializes (to 1961.04) *Dôtokuron* [On Morality] (EC). A show of his oils honors SA on his 75th birthday. **17 December:** Death at 79 comes to fellow *Shirakaba* founder Ôgimachi Kinkazu (born 1881); cf. 1906.09.

1961   **January:** NHK Educational TV broadcasts SA's play "Daruma"; cf. 1923.11 and 1924.01. Jitsugyô no Sekaisha issues *Aru otoko no zakkan* [One Man's (i.e., My) Stray Thoughts]. **March:** Ikeda Shoten publishes *E to fumi* [Paintings and Books]. **7–12:** The Nihonbashi Mitsukoshi Department Store sponsors a showing of SA's art and calligraphy. **May:** Kadokawa Shoten publishes *On Morality* (cf. 1960.05). Older brother Kintomo suffers from softening of the brain. **September:** NHK presents readings in nine installments of *Omedetaki hito* [Simple-Minded Fellow]; cf. 1910.02 and 1915.10. **29 October:** Novelist, dramatist, friend, and Shirakaba colleague Nagayo Yoshirô (born 1888) dies at age 73. **December:** *Kokoro* publishes *"Nagayo Yoshirô ni shinarete"* [Losing Nagayo Yoshirô].

1962   **January:** Ikeda Shoten publishes *Watashi no kaigara* [My Shell], which consists of paintings, prose, and poetry. **8 April:** The Seventh Artists' Festival presents him with a commendation for distinguished service to art. **21st:** Brother Kintomo dies at age 80. NHK (Japan Broadcasting Company) TV presents SA's novel *Yûjô* [Friendship]; cf. 1919.10. **May:** *Kono Michi* serializes (through July) *"Watashi no jijoden"* [My Autobiography]. **June:** Invited to meet Crown Prince Akihito and wife Michiko (Emperor and Empress from 1989.01). **July:** Writes reminiscences of Kintomo in this and the next five issues of *Kokoro*. **November:** *Kokoro* carries *"Aru rôjin"* [An Old Man]. SA lectures at the Tolstoy Memorial Festival.

1963   **January:** Gives a lecture, *"Ichi Nihonjin toshite"* [As a Japanese]. **April ff.:** NHK–TV starts broadcasting the year-long serial dramatizations titled *"Akatsuki"* [Dawn]. This is not the famed play of that name but a pastiche of various compositions. **May:** Kadokawa Shoten publishes a collection of essays on famed painters. Shinjusha issues *Rokunin no gendai gaka* [Six Contemporary Painters]. **August:** The Hyûga New Village officially registered as a legal entity. **5 November ff.:** With third daughter Tatsuko takes responsibility for the agony column (like Dear Abby) in the *Asahi Newspaper*. **13th:** celebrates the 45th year of the Hyûga New Village at the Kyôritsu Kôdô in Tokyo.

1964   **January:** Doctor cautions him about overwork, for it brings on dizzy spells. SA appears in NHK's serialized production of "Dawn"; cf. 1963.04. **April:** Yamato Shoten issues *Shishû* [Poetry Collection]. **May:** Seidôsha begins to issue a 12-volume set of selected SA writings (finishes 1965.10). **June:** Writes *"Atarashiki mura to kane"* [Money and The New Village] for *Kono Michi.* **August:** Records *Friendship* (cf. 1919.10) and *Simple-Minded Fellow* (cf. 1910.02) for an Asahi sonorama series of modern authors reading their works. **October:** Haga Shoten publishes in six volumes *Mushakôji Saneatsu 80-sai kinen shuppan* [Commemorative Publication of Mushakôji Saneatsu's 80 Years]. **10th–24th:** The XVIII Olympiad held in Tokyo. SA, no fan of athletics, took special pleasure in the opening and closing ceremonies because they suggest universal friendship and cooperation among the 94 participating nations.

1965   **January:** SA publishes *Sanya Gohei kanpai* [The Overthrow of Sanya Gohei]. **February:** NHK broadcasts *Shinpen zakki* [Miscellaneous Personal Notes]. Chûô

DATE   EVENT

Kôronsha publishes an English translation of *Ai to shi, sono shi* [Love and Death, Her Death] in *Nihon no Bungaku* [Japanese Literature]. **3 May:** On the eve of SA's 80th birthday, the Tokyo Metropolitan District makes him a Distinguished Citizen [*meiyô shimin*]. **12th:** Birthday party at the Seiyôken in Ueno attended by more than 500. Through Kadokawa Shoten, SA privately publishes *Nonki na otoko to nonki na zôbutsusha* [An Optimistic Fellow and the Optimistic Maker; cf. page 242 ff.], which he sends to all who attended his party. The evening edition of the *Tokyo Shinbun* [News] serializes through 23 July *"Omoide no hitobito"* [People I Recall]. **October:** *Gunshû* carries the essay *"Gonen mae no koto"* [Five Years Ago].

1966   **January:** Publishes *Omoide no hitobito* [People I Recall] and *Gusha no yume* [A Fool's Dreams]. **February:** The Mitsukoshi Department Store in Nihonbashi, Tokyo, sponsors *"Waga aisuru shogaten"* [An Exhibition of My Favorite Paintings and Writings]. Shûeisha's *Nihon bungaku zenshû* [Collection of Japanese Literature] devotes Volume 23 to SA's works. Kôdansha issues *Jinsei ronshû nanakan* [Collected Essays on Life in Seven Volumes]. **March:** *Gunshû* issues *"Honki ni natte kakeru koto"* [Being Able to Write Earnestly]. **15 May:** The 102-year-old Tsue Ichisaku visits from Miyazaki (cf. the 1972 poem "Two Callers, " page 99, and the Note on this work). **August:** *Sono imôto* [His Younger Sister] (cf. 1915.03, 1917.03, 1951.03, and 1956.06) performed at the Actors' Theater. *Kono Michi* carries *"Atarashiki mura no mokuhyô"* [Objectives of the New Village]. **November:** Publishes *Rôjin no nikki* [An Old Man's Diary].

1967   **January:** Begins serialization of three novels in *Shinchô*, including the autobiographical *Hitori no otoko* [A Man (i.e., Me)], which appears over 24 issues. **March:** *Ueno* starts serializing through 22 issues *Watashi no bijutsu henreki* [My Artistic Pilgrimage]. **July:** Lectures on the 20th anniversary of the journal *Kokoro* [The Heart]. **October:** Kawade devotes Volume 15 of its series *Nihon bungaku zenshû* [Collection of Japanese Literature] to SA's work. **14 November:** Illness forces him to miss the 49th anniversary celebration of the founding of the village.

1968   **January:** Publishes *Tenmei* [Fate], *Atarashiki mura no mirai* [The Future of the New Village], and *Aru hi no kaigô* [A Meeting]. **February:** Issues *Ikite iru toki wa* [While I'm Alive]. Holds a 50th Anniversary Festival for the New Village at the Bunkyô Kôkaidô. **8 April:** At the New Village East in Moroyama, Saitama, establishes a kindergarten for children living in and near the village. **14th:** SA dedicates a poetry stele commemorating the 50th anniversary of the founding of the village. **July:** Interviewed on the NHK–TV series *"Kono hito to kataru"* [An Interview With...]. **August:** The Mitsukoshi Department Store in Nihonbashi sponsors an art exhibition commemorating the 50th anniversary of the New Village. **November:** Celebrates the village's 50th anniversary. Sets up a poetry stele in Hyûga.

1969   **6 January:** Channel 12 in Tokyo broadcasts the program *"Watashi no Shôwashi • Atarashiki Mura gojyûnen"* [My History of the Shôwa Period • 50 Years of the New Village]. The new meeting hall at the village is completed. **March:** Kaibisha issues the poetry collection, *Jinsei no tokkyûsha no ue de hitori no rôjin* [An Old Man on the Superexpress of Life]. **July:** Tokyo TV Channel 12 broadcasts *"Hito ni rekishi ari"* [People with Histories], which treats several decades of village life. **August:** Issues his 60th chapter on the fictive adventures of Sanya Gohei.

1970   **January:** SA spends the month in bed recovering from a cold caught late in 1969. **September:** Issues *Jisen shigashû* [My Favorite Poems and Paintings]. **December:** Last installment of his autobiographical, *A Man;* cf. 1967.07 and 1921.07.

1971   **February:** Publishes *"Mishima-kun no shi"* [The death of Mishima (Yukio; 1925–1970)] and *"Mishima jiken to watashi"* [My Views of the Mishima Incident]. **1–30**

DATE EVENT

May: The Tokyo Metropolitan Museum of Modern Literature sponsors an exhibition of SA's works. June: Shôchiku makes a movie of *Love and Death* (cf. 1959.07). August–September: Publishes *A Man* (cf. 1970.12) in two volumes. 21 October: Life-long friend SHIGA NAOYA dies at 88. November: *Shinchô* carries what ends up being SA's final story, *"Aru rôgaka"* [An Old Painter].

1972 January: The 100-year-old wood sculptor Hirakushi stops by; TWO CALLERS. May: *Kono Michi* devotes a special issue of essays by 66 writers to honor SA's upcoming 88th birthday; cf. page 95 f. June: Publishes *"Kawabata Yasunari no shi"* [The Death of Kawabata Yasunari (1899–1972)], the 1968 Nobel laureate in literature. 13 July: Interviewed again (cf. 1969.07) on the NHK–TV series *"Kono hito to kataru"* [An Interview With...]. Writes an essay for the special issue commemorating the 25th anniversary of *Kokoro*. October: Publication of *"Mushakôji Saneatsu • kono hito • kono michi"* [Mushakôji Saneatsu • The Man • His Path] in the collection of NHK (Japan Broadcasting Company) recordings.

1973 January: An exhibition of SA's art work commemorates his 88th year. February: One of his granddaughters participates in the performance of SA's poem, *"Fue o fuku hito"* [Flute Player], set to music and choreographed for ballet. May: *Kono Michi* publishes a special issue commemorating SA on his 88th birthday. June: Wife Yasuko enters the hospital. September: A remission allows her discharge in mid-month. November: A special issue of *Kokoro* features SA's essay, *"Motto hatarakitai"* [I Have More Work to Do].

1974 3 January: *Shirakaba* colleague, novelist Sonoike Kin'yuki (born 1886), dies. 4–8th: An exhibition of SA's art works at the Matsuzakaya Department Store in the Ginza area. February: Tokyo University Press publishes Ôtsuyama Kunio's 423-page study (which ends in 1918 with the founding of the New Village), *Mushakôji Saneatsu ron* [On Mushakôji Saneatsu]. May: *Kono Michi* offers a special issue commemorating SA's 89 years. August: Issues *Watashi no bijutsu henreki* [My Artistic Pilgrimage] that he had serialized for some months. This is SA's last new book. November: The journal *This Path* (cf. 1960.05) re-named *New Village*. December: Completes his last oil painting.

1975 8–9 January: NHK–TV broadcasts a program honoring SA's 90th year. 11–21st: Matsuzakaya Department Store sponsors an exhibition of his paintings titled, "Truth and Harmony." 23rd: Wife Yasuko again admitted to the hospital but discharged in late March. April: The Archive of Modern Japanese Literature sponsors an exhibit featuring Shirakaba authors. 29 July–3 August: The 28th New Village Exhibit. Summer: SA suspends almost all his serializations. 6 December: Yasuko's health deteriorates and she again enters the hospital, but family members keep her true condition from SA. He writes a preface of five manuscript pages for the posthumous work of a friend, the final piece he writes.

1976 25 January: Visits Yasuko, whom doctors list in critical condition. Returns home and suffers a cerebral stroke. 6 February: Yasuko dies peacefully at 75. Family members decide not to inform SA of her death and funeral. 8th: Her remains interred at the New Village East. SA's condition deteriorates but he remains alert. 22 March: Enters the hospital. 9 April: Passes away a month short of turning 91 without having been informed that Yasuko had died. 24 April: Non-religious funeral rites held at Aoyama Cemetery, Tokyo. 16 May: SA's remains interred with Yasuko's at the New Village in the Hall of Great Love. August: SA's will bequeaths his house and property in Wakaba to the city of Chôfu, which names the complex Sengawa Park. SA gives his library and art works to the New Village and the Tokyo Metropolitan government. November: An exhibit held in Kichijôji

DATE EVENT

titled *"Jinsei no shijin* • *Mushakôji Saneatsu"* [Mushakôji Saneatsu • Poet of Life]. ⚫ The population of the Hyûga New Village consists of former wife Fusako and her husband Sugiyama plus a bachelor. Moroyama has 14 families with 41 individuals and 14 unmarried people (total: 55).

1977   October: The Tokyo Museum of Modern Literature sponsors an exhibition on SA's work. December: NHK–TV broadcasts a dramatization of *Yûjô* [Friendship]; cf. 1919.10 and 1962.04.

1978   12 May: Chôfu honors SA's birthday by opening Saneatsu Park. November: Major exhibition of SA's works held at the Japanese Museum of Calligraphy.

1979   April: The remains of Yasuko and SA re-interred in the family plot at the Central Cemetery, Hachiôji. The painter Nakagawa Kazumasa's epitaph (cf. page 47) is carved on the memorial tablet. 12 May: Kaibisha publishes a collection of photographs spanning SA's life. 9–14 November: A memorial exhibit on 60 years of the New Village held in Urawa, Saitama. December: *Kokoro* publishes daughter Tatsuko's record of her parents' final days. ⚫ This year the Village East population reaches 60—13 families with 40 people and 20 unmarried individuals.

1983   Tatsuko publishes a volume of reminiscences about her father.

1986   2 September: Nakagawa Takashi, the noted SA bibliographer and curator of the Saneatsu Library, dies at 80. 8 December: Oldest daughter Kimura Shinko dies at 63 from a heart attack.

1987   November: Shôgakukan issues the first of 18 volumes of *Mushakôji Saneatsu zenshû* [The Works of Mushakôji]. Plans to issue a new volume every third month.

1988   14 November: New Village East at Moroyama celebrates the 70th anniversary of the movement. ⚫ Eleven families consisting of 31 people and 18 unmarried individuals (total: 49) live there. Two families (four individuals) reside in Hyûga.

1989   17 September: New Village East celebrates 50 years of existence. 10 December: The *Tokyo Asahi Newspaper* introduces the New Village in an eight-column article that attracts many applicants, but only two manage to qualify.

1990   6–18 February: An exhibition of SA's India ink drawings at a Ginza gallery marks the 80th anniversary of the publication of *Shirakaba*; cf. April 1910.

1991   10 April: Shôgakukan publishes the last volume of the *Works*.

1992   12 May: Watanabe Kanji edits *Atarashiki mura no tanjô to seichô* [The Birth and Development of the New Village].

1994   May: Chôfu opens a ferro-concrete, two-story archive associated with the Mushakôji Memorial. 12th: Publication of *Ningen rashiku ikiru tame ni* [To Live Like a Human], a volume about the New Village that Watanabe Kanji edits.

1995   12 May: Chôfu joins with the New Village East to celebrate the 100th anniversary of SA's birth.

NOTES

Entries appear in ABC order, omitting initial articles. A pointing finger ☞ indicates a note (in small caps) or a poem (in quotation marks followed by the page number) in *Long Corridor*. MSZS refers to Mushakôji's *Works*; cf. page 373. A down-slanting arrow ↘ indicates further or gratuitous information on the item. A five-pointed star ★ denotes a major shift in topic. A bullet • either separates a series or introduces alternate readings, meanings, etc. I hope that certain items might satisfy the curious reader who lacks the necessary time, a handy reference shelf, or the language skills to investigate the sources. Some information may cast light on or supplement the poetry, but dieters beware: these annotations are not fat free.

❖　　　　❖　　　　❖

AGED REMBRANDT—For details ☞ REMBRANDT (i) • (ii) • (iii), and HENDRICKJE!

AMERICA'S WILSON—Using *omae* for "you" in this 1918 work, Mushakôji addresses Wilson with undisguised contempt. ★ Thomas Woodrow Wilson (1856–1924) was the 28th President (1913–1921) of the United States. He studied political science and jurisprudence at Johns Hopkins University (Ph.D. in 1886). In 1890 he became professor of jurisprudence and political economy at Princeton, where in 1902 he was elected to the presidency of the university. He resigned in 1910 to enter politics. He then won election to the governorship of New Jersey, where he instituted many progressive policies. Two years later he ran as a Democrat and won the presidency. ↘ Wilson sought to maintain neutrality during the early years of World War I. During negotiations after the war, he tried unsuccessfully to obtain more humane treatment of the vanquished than the vindictive victors wanted. He was also a driving force behind and a vigorous supporter of the League of Nations, one of his long-standing dreams. ↘ It is difficult to understand Mushakôji's animosity toward Wilson or to grasp his reasons for depicting him as a rabid foe of Japan. ★ Mushakôji uses the rare word "mammon"—the Aramaic word for money • wealth • riches, which I assume he learned from the Bible. Modern versions of the Japanese New Testament render this word *tomi* • wealth. ↘ Jesus says in *Matthew* 6:24 that no one can serve both "God and mammon." In *Luke* 16:9–13, Jesus first talks of the stewardship of life and then repeats the sentiment reported in *Matthew*.

ANGLER'S SOLILOQUY— ① The Japanese title of this poem is *"Urashima no dokuhaku"* [Urashima's Monologue]. Since Urashima was a fisher, I alter the title to convey the sense. Every Japanese schoolchild knows this story. ↘ Urashima Tarô not only exemplifies the "compleat angler," he resembles our Rip Van Winkle. Urashima is so much a part of Japanese culture that the *Nihongi* [Chronicles of Japan, 720 A.D.], one of the nation's oldest records, offers the date 478 as the year he left Japan for the Dragon Hall • Undersea Palace; ☞ DRAGON. Legend states he returned in 825. ↘ Dragon Hall is the magical undersea kingdom where Urashima spent nearly four (some versions say three) centuries. ↘ As a youth, he saved a turtle, symbol in East Asia of old age. Later, when out fishing, he met the creature he had saved. As they talked, he discovered the turtle was the daughter of the Dragon King of the Sea. After she transformed herself into a beautiful young woman, Urashima went with her to the Dragon Hall. They soon married.

② After a short while (one version says three days), Urashima wanted to inform his family of his good fortune and make sure his parents were cared for. His bride objected till he firmly promised he would return. She then gave him a lacquered (some accounts say jeweled) box tied shut with a silk cord. She told Urashima that if he opened the box he would never see her again. She then led him back to shore (in some versions, he takes the trip alone). ⊀ On returning home, he hardly recognized the area. Shocked to find that his parents had been dead for centuries (a day in the Dragon Hall is a century on earth), he returned to the beach, where, curiosity drove him to open the box. When he did, all the years that had passed leaked out. He immediately grayed and died.

③ "The compleat angler" (line 9) means to suggest the import of Mushakôji's Taikô Bô (the Japanese reading of the Chinese for T'ai-Kung Wang), the East Asian symbol of Piscator, the perfect fisher. In East Asia, fishing has long symbolized man's search for wisdom, solitude, quiescence, and perspective. ⊀ For comparison, ☞ the masterpiece, *The Compleat Angler* (1653), a literary treatise on fishing by Sir Isaak Walton (1593–1683) that describes the ultimate angler. ⊀ T'ai-Kung Wang, king of the Chinese state of Chou, lived in the early 12th century. He was also known for unifying the country through his superlative knowledge of military strategy, which survives in a treatise ascribed to his authorship. ☆ The East Asian symbol of the ☞ DRAGON [*ryû* • *tatsu*] is sufficiently complex to merit a special entry.

ARTIST AND A FROG—This work proves that not every Mushakôji poem is a dour and humorless sermonette on morality. ☆ Historians regard the Heian era master Ono no Michikaze (some read Dôfû; 894–966) the patron saint of calligraphy. Thinking he had reached the limit of his ability, Michikaze once felt defeated and discouraged. One day during a walk along the river he noticed a frog persistently trying to jump up on a willow branch. Refusing to accept defeat, the frog finally succeeded. ⊀ This both encouraged and embarrassed Michikaze. He realized that he must keep striving to improve and that he had given up too soon. The frog thus spurred him to work harder at his craft. Since this story appeared in all pre-1945 Japanese grammar school readers, everyone educated in that milieu was familiar with it. Professor Iida supplied this information. ☆ Matsuo Bashô (1644–1694) is regarded the "patron saint of haiku" (a 17-syllable poem) because he so refined and expanded the art. The haiku in question, which every literate Japanese knows, is: "*Furu ike ya / kawazu tobikomu / mizu no oto.*" This might be rendered, "An ancient pond / A frog jumps in / Sounds of water."

AT EIGHTY-EIGHT—*Beiju* [rice age] or *yoné no iwai* [the celebration of rice] relates to the fact that the graph for [unprocessed] rice [*bei* • *komé* • *yoné*] can be viewed as a stylized way of writing the number 88. ⊀ East Asians place immense significance on double numbers. For birthdays, this is especially true for 77 and 88. These years mark major family celebrations and call for the presence of as many relatives as can attend.

AUTUMN— ☞ I ADORE FALL for the universal symbolisms associated with autumn.

AUTUMN HAS COME—Mushakôji here refers to his first love, a 12–13 year-old girl called Otei (the graph for *tei* can also be read *sada*). She apparently never showed much interest in him. This 1909 work refers to the fall of 1904 when Mushakôji was 19; ☞ FEELING LONELY, RHAPSODIZING ON MY BIRTHDAY, and the Chronology, 1900, 1903, and 1911. ☆ Otei came to the capital from Ôsaka to attend school. She stayed in Kôjimachi with an aunt who lived not far from Mushakôji. Otei returned to Ôsaka in the spring of 1900 after she finished her schooling (Mushakôji was then 15). After marrying, Otei moved to Otaru, Hokkaidô, where Mushakôji visited her in 1911; cf. page 94, top.

BEAUTIFUL WOMAN—Professor Iida points out that Mushakôji's basic idea in this work is to suggest that men are attracted to beautiful women because they want to possess them.

In reality, however, since men only rarely realize this desire, their failures make them miserable [*sabishii*]. To overcome their misery, nature fashioned men to struggle for all they're worth to achieve their objective(s) and be successful. This drive becomes the soul or spirit of the male's existence. Nature thus makes beautiful women a means of spurring men to act and realize their aims. ⋆ Familiar ideas lurk in Mushakôji's homespun "theory" of the parallel between the sex drive and the urge to achieve. This view agrees with the ancient Greek concept—later appropriated by Freud and other psychoanalysts—of Eros, which in classical Greece suggested aspiration for the good. Eros drives the human instinct for self-preservation and symbolizes the life force. Some believe the spiritual aspects of Eros imply "the upward striving of the human spirit towards the divine." ⋆ It is not clear whether Mushakôji acquired these ideas from his reading or discovered them on his own. It is clear, however, that poets through the ages have appropriated these insights without having read Plato, Freud, or anyone else. ⋆ For Mushakôji on libido, ☞ "A Teardrop," first full stanza, page 257.

BECAUSE HE WROTE A POEM—Separate entries exist for ☞ MICHELANGELO and Leonardo, ☞ LEONARDO DA VINCI'S LILIES. ⋆ French playwright Jean Baptiste Poquelin Molière (1622–1673) created French high comedy with his many sophisticated plays. These include *The Misanthrope* (1666) and *The Bourgeois Gentleman* (1670). He had an exquisite gift for exposing through farcical humor the foolishness and hypocrisies of his society. Mushakôji would surely adore a playwright who lampooned the affectations of fashionable intellectuals. He would also sympathize with other behavior that did not endear Molière to the critics. ⋆ Molière, incidentally, was intimately involved in all phases of the production of his plays, not only as playwright but as director, actor, and stage manager. He died, in fact, while performing the title role of his last play.

BUDDHA—This Sanskrit word means "he awakes • the enlightened one • the awakened one." Any person who has achieved spiritual enlightenment may be called a Buddha. Additionally, Japanese regard the dead as Buddhas [*hotoke*], presumably because they no longer suffer the desires, hungers, and humiliations of the life of the flesh. ⬥ Buddha refers also to Siddhartha Gautama (563?–483? B.C.), a royal prince and heir to the kingship of the Sakya clan, which lived in the foothills of the Himalayas. Sakyamuni, one of his titles, means "sage of the Sakyas." He is the Indian mystic who founded Buddhism after achieving enlightenment at the age of 35.

BUDDHA AND JESUS—For the historical Buddha, ☞ BUDDHA, above.

BUDDHA'S GOSPEL—For the historical Buddha, ☞ BUDDHA, above. ⋆ Mushakôji uses the Christian term for gospel [*fukuin*, literally, "good • happy news," the original meaning of gospel]. I understand that Buddhists do not use this term to describe their preaching, scriptures, or doctrines. ⋆ The "you" in the last line is the familiar *omae*, which Japanese customarily use toward inferiors. Mushakôji probably equates *omae* here with "thee." This usage also appears in several 1920 poems addressing God; ☞ for example OH, GOD. In 1965, when he speaks to the Creator • Maker (☞ page 235 ff.), however, he invariably uses *anata*, the far more polite and respectful (but distant) "you."

BUILD IT!— ☞ NEW VILLAGE. In 1921 ¥2 roughly = $1. Because the New Village commune (☞ page 111 ff.) intended to be self-supporting, it required workshops that produced the community's daily necessities, including pottery. Actually, Mushakôji had to dedicate a part of his income from writing to keep the project afloat.

BURBANK, LUTHER— ☞ Luther Burbank.

CHINESE PAINTING—The man unsure of whether he owns the universe or the universe owns him may refer to the famed dream illusion of the Taoist philosopher Chuang Tzu (a.k.a. Chuang Chou; 369–286 B.C.?), familiar to all educated men of Mushakôji's generation (☞ page 22). The philosopher could not tell whether he was a butterfly dreaming he was Chuang Chou or Chuang Chou dreaming he was a butterfly.

CLAY FIGURINE—*HANIWA*— ① The magazine in the text is the *Geijutsu Shinchô* [New Waves in Art]. ☆ These fired-clay figurines became a part of Japanese history after the entry of Buddhism. In antiquity, the death of a highly–ranked Japanese meant that the lord's soldiers and servants, as well as his and the retainers' weapons, equipment, and the like, must be buried with him. Two notions supported this custom: a retainer could serve but one master, and in the next world the master required vassals to serve and protect him. Included in the burial were horses—symbols of leadership—and related gear. Later items included replicas of buildings. ☚ Legend states that this practice ended 2,000 years ago under the mythical 11th Emperor Suinin, said to have ruled 100 years. Suinin—his legendary dates are 29 B.C.–70 A.D.—ordered earthen or clay *haniwa* figurines made and buried in place of live sacrifices. Others aver that humanistic Buddhist thought, which entered Japan several centuries later, encouraged the Japanese to end this barbaric custom of sacrifice. Thereafter they interred *haniwa* with deceased Emperors and other persons of high status. Thus *haniwa* also symbolize the affirmation of life.
   ② Saitama is the prefecture immediately to the north of the Tokyo metropolitan area. Kumagaya, on the Ara River in the northwest sector of the Kantô Plain, is not far from the northern border of the prefecture. Kumagaya is 64.7 kilometers (39 miles) from the heart of Tokyo and now takes about one hour from Ueno Station by train on the Takasaki Line. ☆ The poet-sculptor Takamura Kôtarô (1883–1956), a sometime SHIRAKABA admirer, believed that the simple, sparse charm of *haniwa* characterizes the individuality of Japanese-style beauty. He also implies that some of Mushakôji's works exemplify the simple, stark refinement of the *haniwa.*

CLOSING MY EYES—After he turned ten, Mushakôji spent many summers in the rural setting of his uncle Kadenokôji Sukekoto's farm on the Miura Peninsula. There he also participated in agricultural work that prepared him for life in the ☞ NEW VILLAGE; cf. page 111 ff. He consistently preferred to live on the outskirts rather than in the heart of the city. ☆ In 1930 Mushakôji counted this one of his favorite poems; ☞ page 365.

COMICAL COUPLE—Because this is a 1923 poem, Mushakôji is obviously not writing about a talking movie. ☆ Aristocratic rankings from lowest to highest are: baron, count, viscount, earl, marquis, and duke. In short, Chaplin's aristocratic rank is near the top.

COURBET—The French painter Gustave Courbet (1819–1877) is remembered for his depictions of everyday scenes and for resisting all vested authority, aesthetic or political. His formal schooling in art consisted mainly of copying masterpieces in the Louvre. ☚ The "artistic principles" to which Mushakôji refers could be Courbet's commitment to frankness, vigor, and realism. The bourgeois critics of his day demeaned his work as aesthetically and politically offensive. They found it ugly, shocking, audacious, and even blasphemous. Such scathing criticism is sufficient to gain Mushakôji's interest, if not his enduring respect. ☚ Courbet's best-known works include *Burial at Ornans* (1850), *The Meeting—Bonjour Monsieur Courbet!* (1854), and *The Atelier* (1855). ☆ In describing Courbet's work, Mushakôji uses *suteki* [wonderful • stunning • superb] four times.

CUBISM • CUBIST— ① The non-objective Cubist school of painting and sculpture developed in Paris around 1907. By 1918 it had become a bona fide movement. ◄ Cubism constitutes a focused rebellion against most artistic shibboleths. The revolt began by obliterating the requirement of realistic duplication or mimicry of nature; ☛ mimesis, page 180. Cubists rejected in particular the sensual appeal of tints, textures, and realistic figures. ◄ Another concern behind the cubist revolt is an obvious if basic problem: how can the artist represent three-dimensional reality on a two-dimensional canvas? Cubism is the story of how some painters and theorists went about trying to give a modern answer to that question. Pablo Picasso (1881–1973), doubtless the best-known cubist painter, illustrates in his works the way(s) he sought painterly solutions to these philosophical problems. ☆ Dealing with such puzzles requires analysis, intellection, and conscious experimentation—all of which represent a level of intentionality that can only make spontaneous and intuitive painters like Mushakôji feel very uncomfortable.
  ② In general, the French painters tried to reduce and fragment natural forms into abstract structures. Frequently these become geometric shapes that the painter renders as separate planes. That often gives the appearance of simultaneity or multiple representation of an object—views of the same object from various angles. This allows the viewer to appreciate dimensionality (like a holograph) and multiple views without reverting to mirror reflections. Simultaneity creates a host of new problems, however, not the least of which are distorted objects and relationships that become extremely difficult to grasp. ☆ The cubists appear to exult in avoiding centrality. Every item in their pictures is as important as everything else. Here, imitation of nature—in fact, all mimesis—becomes passé. Many a convenient or cliché touchstone of "beauty" falls like mimesis by the wayside. The entire surface of the canvas has literally been sacrificed to the very self-conscious conceptual aesthetic that cubism became.

DAUMIER—The French caricaturist, lithographer, painter, and sculptor Honoré Daumier (1808–1879) is best known for his bitterly satirical lithographs of scenes from bourgeois society. Drawing cartoons for an opposition liberal newspaper earned his bread and a six-month jail sentence for caricaturing the emperor. He also joyfully lampooned bourgeois banalities and pretensions. ◄ Daumier, who worked from memory rather than use models or view nature, produced some 4,000 lithographs but only 100 paintings, many famous for their "exceptional intensity and sense of modernity." His primary interest is in what was happening around him—events and people he frequently portrayed with fluid power, vitality, insight, and spontaneity; ☛ page 177 ff. For a century he has given common people the sense that he stands on their side. ◄ Daumier painted at least two oils on wood (☛ DON QUIXOTE and Sancho Panza). One critic praises these versions, which date from his last years, as illustrations of his "prodigious powers of synthesis and evocation.... These veritable symbols of the universal human condition unite the grotesque with the sublime and reveal the variety of Daumier's talents." Small wonder these paintings impressed Mushakôji. ◄ The Third-Class Carriage (ca. 1862), a watercolor, is now in the Metropolitan Museum of Art, New York City.

DELACROIX—French painter [Ferdinand Victor] Eugène Delacroix (1798–1863) is best known for his grand, dramatic canvases and exuberant use of color, as in Liberty Leading the People (1831). Some critics consider him the foremost painter of the romantic movement. Others condemned his ravishing colors and intensely disliked his propensity to depict violence. ◄ Despite being uncommitted to religion, Delacroix painted many religious scenes. He is also the painter of the celebrated and haunting 1838 portrait of Frédéric François Chopin, with whom he spent several summers at the home of the novelist George Sand (pseudonym of Amandine Dudevant, then Chopin's lover). ◄ Paintings that depict animals include Tiger Attacking a Horse (1825–1828), Horse

Devoured by a Lion (1840), *Lion Devouring a Wild Boar* (1853), and *Lion Devouring a Rabbit* (ca. 1856). Delacroix had viewed lions and tigers in zoo cages, but he had never witnessed the imaginative scenes he depicts—with what some describe as majestic power, verve, and accuracy. ✦ He painted the *Bark of Dante* at age 24 and in 1822 submitted it to the Paris Salon, which accepted it for display. This painting pictures Virgil • Vergil and Dante on a small craft being poled through the underworld by a naked and muscular boatman. Wicked Florentine men and women attempt unsuccessfully to climb aboard the boat. ★ Most Delacroix's masterpieces feature interpretations of scenes from human or animal subjects rather than landscapes.

DON QUIXOTE— ① Refers to Don Quixote de la Mancha, whose antics Miguel de Cervantes (1547–1616) burlesques in *Don Quixote*, a world-famed classic. The gentle Don is a dignified and lovable country gentleman whose simple-minded immersion in chivalry led him to believe his mission was to achieve justice for all. He consequently sets out with his rustic squire Sancho Panza to redress the wrongs of the world. ★ Customary interpretations of Cervantes' famed anti-romance portray Don Quixote as a metaphor of the power of illusion to transform behavior. Critics also see in him the tragic consequences of a simple-minded idealist locking horns with the real world. Thus our association of the word "quixotic" with the impractical, visionary pursuit of unattainable goals. ✦ Like Quixote, Mushakôji and his ☞ SHIRAKABA colleagues believed both that the power of an idea can transform behavior and that ideals are possible to realize in the real world. They never imagined their goals were unobtainable.

② The obverse aspect of Don Quixote's quest applies more accurately to Mushakôji. The critic Harry Levin sees the quixotic principle as "a register of development, an index of maturation. Its incidental mishaps can be looked back upon as milestones on the way to self-awareness." Quixote, a common person with uncommon dreams, focused on self-discovery. Cervantes has him say, "I know who I am and who I may be, if I choose." The Don longed to know his strengths and weaknesses so he could realize his full potential as a human. In no other way could he become an individual. That is precisely Mushakôji's agenda. ★ Countless thinkers and writers taught that man is the architect of his fate. Scholars point out, however, that only Aristotle and Cervantes linked the power of free will with self-knowledge. There is no other route to psychic wholeness. Quixote teaches each of us how to become an individual, a genuine person. This describes, in short, the process of individuation. Mushakôji aimed for no less.

DOSTOYEVSKI'S FACE— ① Russian Novelist Feodor Mikhailovich (1821–1881), born and raised in Moscow, is a towering figure in world literature. His alcoholic father, a military surgeon, was so harsh and despotic that his serfs brutally murdered him in 1839. Some think this event conditioned Dostoyevski's preoccupation with murder. ✦ He soon abandoned a career as a government draftsman and devoted himself to writing. His first story earned applause when it appeared in 1846. In 1849 he was arrested as a socialist and condemned to death. A last-moment reprieve reduced his sentence to four years' hard labor in Siberia and four years in the Army. ✦ By the time Dostoyevski resumed writing after 1858, he had begun to suffer epileptic seizures. A compulsive gambler, he constantly escaped creditors by taking up residence in Germany, Italy, or Switzerland. When he returned to Russia in 1871, he had already acquired some fame and prosperity. ★ Mushakôji agreed with Dostoyevski that beauty might save the world.

② Much of Dostoyevski's work deals with psychological duality. His stories tantalizingly weave a tapestry of profound psychological insight, compassion for the downtrodden, and religious mysticism. He was also skilled at exposing the evils of power and authoritarianism, though he dealt with injustice and suffering from a psychological rather than a social viewpoint. ✦ These concerns poignantly affected Japanese readers,

few of whom had ever been exposed to works with such psychological impact or philo-
sophical subtlety. All Dostoyevski's finest stories and novels have long been available in
Japanese translation. His best-known works are *Crime and Punishment* (1866), *The Idiot*
(1868–1869), *The Possessed* (1871), and *The Brothers Karamazov* (1879–1880).

DRAGON— ① Despite several points of similarity, the dragon of East Asia [in Chinese, *lung*;
in Japanese, *ryû* or *tatsu* in the zodiac] differs notably from that of the West. When
Mushakôji says he wants to become a dragon, we must understand that his wish has
little to do with becoming evil, threatening, or fearful. ✣ Differences between East and
West become especially poignant if we consider the negative references to the dragon in
the Bible. These associate the beast with evil and thus with Satan, "the great dragon"
(*Revelations* XII:9). People of the Middle Ages made the dragon a metaphor of sin and
paganism. In fact, many legends in the West depict the winged serpent as mankind's
primordial enemy. ✣ From the Greek Apollo through prehistoric British knights, to
Siegfried in the Teutonic legends, the hero must combat and slay the dragon to prove
his mettle. Many fables, moreover, depict Christian saints, including several females, as
having slain dragons. This act symbolizes overcoming chaos (even that of the uncon-
scious) and ordering one's world. A psychiatrist might see the dragon as a symbol of the
instincts or whatever is difficult to overcome. This could include, for example, an
attachment to, or an incestuous desire for, one's mother. The winged serpents of the
West also often signify some sort of plague on humanity or a threat to our well-being.
      ② In China, by contrast, the dragon symbolizes the rhythms of life. It possibly also
suggests happiness, for it can make the potion that gives immortality. Furthermore,
dragons have long been associated with warding off evil spirits and with maintaining
Earth's fecundity (through rain, for example). This mirrors the function in Greek myth
of the dragons that lived deep in Earth's interior. Generalizing on the dragon's cosmic
effects in Chinese myths is complicated, for there are various types. Some inhabit the
Earth, others the seas or the skies. Those inhabiting the skies—Mushakôji presumably
has the celestial dragon in mind—represent a higher spirituality than terrestrial or
thalassic dragons. ☆ After 1500 B.C., the dragon motif appears on Chinese bronze
vessels, objects of art, and the like with increasing frequency. Before the beginning of
the Christian era, the celestial dragon in China became the symbol of the power and
wisdom of Heaven. By the beginning of our era (the Han dynasty), it stood as the
official symbol of the emperor, who sits on the "dragon throne." ☆ In a similar
manner, the dragon became a sign of royalty in England. It had long been a symbol
used on the war standards of ancient Britons and Welsh.
      ③ The dragon is, furthermore, the fifth sign of the East Asian zodiac. It personifies
the east, the rising sun, and the spring rains. Those born in the year of the dragon
[*tatsu-doshi*] (Mushakôji is the cock [*tori*], the 10th zodiac sign) are entitled to the best
fortune. They are destined to be honest, brave, and sensitive, as well as short-tempered
and stubborn. They nevertheless attract people's love and admiration, advance to the
top of their fields, usually enjoy uncommon success—and uncommon failure as well. ✣
As a symbol of life and growth, the dragon supposedly conveys such blessings as virtue,
longevity, harmony, and riches. All these relate to the poet's uses of the term dragon.

DÜRER'S *ST. JEROME*—Albrecht Dürer (1471–1528), son of a Nuremberg goldsmith, was
the first painter and engraver to gain considerable fame outside Germany. His self-
portrait at 13 reveals the drafting skills of a prodigy. ✣ Dürer's works and theories,
which show acute awareness of individuality, had a wide influence. He supplemented
keen powers of observation with a rationalized system of perspective and the ability to
express fantasies and visions of terror as well as realistic scenes. ☆ The full title of the
picture is *St. Jerome in His Study* (1514). As a young man, Jerome (ca. 347–420?)

renounced his classical learning and fled to the desert to study scripture and learn Hebrew. He was later acclaimed for his exposition of the Scriptures. Jerome revised the majority of the Latin translations of the Bible, wrote commentaries, and translated from Hebrew such prophets as *Isaiah*, as well as *Kings, Psalms,* and *Job.* His texts became the root of the Vulgate he was commissioned to edit. He is buried in Rome. ★ Dürer paints a lion in St. Jerome's study because, according to legend, the beast was forever loyal to him after Jerome pulled a thorn from its paw. The watchful lion lies at the entrance to the study, and a curled-up dog sleeps next to him. ↖ Jerome is hunched over a writing stand on his desk. Though he is busy with a pen, it is hard to imagine that he could be translating anything, for his desk is clear of everything but the writing stand.

EGGSHELL—For data on Tolstoy, ☞ TOLSTOY'S WORDS.

EVE—Mushakôji reflects on his reading of *Genesis,* the early chapters of which contain the Hebrew creation myth. Having just decided that Adam needed a partner, God took one of Adam's ribs and fashioned from it a female helpmate. When God brought her to him Adam said, "This is now bone of my bones, and flesh of my flesh: she shall be called Woman, because she was taken out of Man" (*Genesis* 2:23). ↖ After eating the forbidden fruit and being cursed—but just before God expelled the couple from the Garden of Eden—the legend reports that "Adam called his wife's name Eve, because she was the mother of all living" humans (*Genesis* 3:20). ★ Mushakôji not only imagines the scene where God presents Eve for Adam's evaluation. He infuses it with an erotic dimension that does not exist in the *Genesis* account.

EXPERT ARCHERS—Archery provides a metaphor for the intuitive "no sweat" Zen approach to the arts and other activities, that is, to *wu-wei*; ☞ STRINGLESS HARP and page 20 ff. An archery master's objective was to hit the bull's eye by aiming with his inner eye. Presumably, he could succeed in this even in the dark or wearing a blindfold. ★ Hitting the bull's eye also symbolized driving through illusions to find the true self.

FEELING LONELY—For Otei, ☞ AUTUMN HAS COME, RHAPSODIZING ON MY BIRTHDAY, and Chronology, 1900, 1903, and 1911. Works to his "lost love" often sound forced. Mushakôji required more than a decade to get over being smitten by Otei, who never apparently regarded him very highly. ↖ Maki presumably refers to one of the women who interested Mushakôji before he married Takeo Fusako in 1912 when he was 27.

FROM MY THREE CHILDREN—This poem dates from early 1936 when, between April and December, Mushakôji took a round-the-world trip. His daughters were then 13 (Shinko, born 1923), 11 (Taeko, born 1925), and eight (Tatsuko, born 1928). ↖ Older brother Kintomo, then Ambassador to Germany, invited him to attend the summer Olympic games in Berlin. Mushakôji also interviewed many artists and visited museums, theaters, and famed scenic spots. In late fall he sailed to New York, visited Chicago and then San Francisco. There he boarded a Japanese ship bound for home; ☞ Chronology, 1936. ★ For related works, ☞ "Time Passes Fast" (page 82), and "Many Hardships" and "On a Train to San Francisco" (page 83).

GIANT (i) • (ii) • (iii)—Mushakôji's references to giants imply people with extraordinary skill or ability. Giants also have much in common with the ancient Chinese confidence in the moral power of the great man or "true gentleman," the *chün-tzu* (Japanese read *kunshi*). Ancient Chinese philosophers at times identify this morally or spiritually superior man as a "great • big person" [*ta-ren*, the modern Japanese compound for adult, *otona*].

Regarding the correlative, the "small person" or *hsiao-ren*, who is morally inferior, ☞ MALIGNED. ✫ Mushakôji may have in mind the ideas of the British historian Thomas Carlyle (1795–1881), whose works students in his milieu knew and admired. Carlyle thought that the "great man" makes a difference in a nation's history.

GIANT APPEARED, GIANT MOVES AHEAD, GIANT'S CALLIGRAPHY, GIANT'S FOOTPRINTS, and GIANTS ONLY WALK—For details on the significance of giant, ☞ GIANT above.

GIVER—The standard Taoist metaphor of effortless effort [*wu-wei;* ☞ page 20] with maximum effect is ☞ WATER. Simply by submitting to gravity in its search for the sea, water manages to cut gorges through mountains. It must only be itself to achieve these feats. This poem suggests the sun as a metaphor for ideal human behavior.

GO MASTER—*Go* is often rendered checkers, a notably less complex game. ✫ "Kibitzer" freely renders Mushakôji's *"hebo"* [= *heta*], meaning inferior or unskilled players—like students unaware of how little they know. ◥ The game itself, dating from antiquity, has simple rules. Two players take turns moving black or white stones on a lined *Go* board. Since each contains more than 300 possible locations, the game's boundless possibilities make it even far more complicated and challenging than chess. The aim is to surround and thus "capture" enemy stones, which must be removed. ◥ *Go* is a pleasant pastime for many Japanese, but professionals regard it a consuming and demanding art.

GOD AND HUMANKIND (ii)—Mushakôji likely refers to Simeon's famous statement in *Luke* 2:29 ff., the *Nunc dimitis* [now dismiss (your servant)], which has for centuries been used in the Christian liturgy. ◥ This righteous and devout old man was told that he would "not see death before he had seen the Lord's Christ [savior]." When Joseph and Mary brought the infant Jesus to the Temple in Jerusalem, Simeon recognized Mary's child as the promised Messiah said: Lord now let your servant die in peace, for I have seen the salvation you have prepared for all nations (paraphrase).

GOD'S WILL— ① The verse in question is *Matthew* 10:29: "Are not sparrows two for a penny? Yet without your Father's leave not one of them can fall to the ground" (New English Bible, NEB, 1961). The King James Version (1611) stays close to the Greek and says simply that not a sparrow shall "fall on the ground without your father." The Revised Standard Version (R.S.V. 1946 [NT] and 1952 [OT]) extrapolates "without your father" to "without your father's will." ✫ Other translators resolve the lacuna in this verse by rendering the passage to harmonize with a parallel reference in *Luke* 12:7. Luke stresses the idea that God does not even *forget* a single sparrow, for humans are worth far more than birds. Thus in his 1952 translation of the Gospels, J. B. Phillips renders the passage, "without your father's knowledge," and the 1961 NEB cited above uses "father's leave." This echoes but considerably tones down the R.S.V.'s notion of "your father's will." The Catholic Confraternity Edition, incidentally, uses "father's leave."

② The Reverend Satô Kunihiro, General Secretary of the Japan Bible Society, assures me there is no Japanese translation of this passage that matches Mushakôji's citation. In support of his contention that Mushakôji "created the phrases," Pastor Satô provided copies of the text in the seven Japanese translations issued since early Meiji. Mushakôji could have referred to but four of these. The 1880 version offers *chichi no yurushi* [our father's leave • permission], in 1901 it is *chichi no mune* [our father's mind • heart • will], in 1910, *chichi ni yorazu* [(not) by • without our father], and in 1917 again *chichi no yurushi*. ✫ I conjecture that Mushakôji's poem reflects his mis-reading of the 1901 or 1910 Japanese translations. Another possibly is the poet's defective comprehension of the passage in English. *Allowing* (an echo of "causing" in Japanese) a bird to die is not to *will* its death, which is how Mushakôji seems to understand this passage.

GOSSIP—This title constitutes an unusual rendering of the word *seken* [society • the public at large • the world]. In Japan, *seken* is the sphere where human beings live, interact, and maintain their "face" or reputation. It is, in short, where public opinion (often in the form of gossip) helps to condition conformity. It is not other people or society but the threat of their rejection or censure that terrified Mushakôji's mother.

GOVERNMENT OFFICIALS— ① Between 1871 and 1947, Monbushô [the Ministry of Education] exercised stringent control over educational institutions. Monbushô directives especially affected compulsory education, grades 1–6. Instructions issued from Tokyo might even prescribe which pages of which textbook should be taught on which day of each week. ✎ The paternalistic autocrats who created a maze of regulations never imagined they were engaging in censorship. After all, the aim of all state-supported education, including the national universities, was to produce "obedient subjects." ✎ ☞ ② below for an example of the police or the Naimushô [Home Ministry] banning an "offensive" play. From its 1885 founding, the Naimushô was involved in thought control and censorship. ✎ Ultra-conservative bureaucrats doubtless also had the customary antipathy to any but traditional dramas, Kabuki, Nô, and Bunraku [puppet theater]. Like haiku and tanka, these were "safer" than modernist free verse and theater. Officials associated modern theater with both social protest (the objective of the loathsome socialists) and the license or "perversions" often associated with Hollywood.

② One incident of shutting down a play occurred in 1912 during the early days of ☞ SHIRAKABA activity. This incident clearly illustrates the questionable effectiveness of the government's drive to control public morality. After eight days of sold-out performances at the Yûrakuza in Tokyo, the police (an arm of the Naimushô) suspended production of the 1893 play *Heimat* [Homeland, *Kokyô* in Japanese translation] by the Prussian playwright and novelist Hermann Sudermann (1857–1928). ✎ Police claimed the heroine Magda's opposition to her mulish army father undermined Confucian values of obedience to the patriarch. In a showdown, Magda so resolutely rebukes her father for his unyielding attitudes that he has an apoplectic fit and dies. So, daughters must be submissive—regardless! The 41-year-old Waseda University professor translator managed to get the suspension lifted by adding a scene: a kneeling Magda confesses to God her responsibility for her father's death. ★ This ill-advised effort to "preserve public morals" gave nation-wide free publicity to the play. It also broadcast the courage of a daughter who criticized a tyrannical father's intransigence—with which many girls in Japan could identify. This vastly increased the popularity of the female lead.

GROWTH—The Chinese classics, with which people of Mushakôji's generation were uncommonly familiar, contain many Taoist (or Zen-like) sayings that relate to the point of this poem: You cannot force nature. Be patient. The time will come and you will be ready. ★ The best-known example in the Chinese classics of the need to allow nature to take its course describes a silly farmer eager to help his rice crop mature. He went out into his paddies and pulled on the plants to encourage their growth, thus killing them all.

HEMP PALM—The hemp palm [*shuro*], a member of the coconut palm family, grows from 8'– 18' in height and flowers in early summer. Haiku poets have long referred to its small, pale-yellow blossoms as signifying the onset of summer. The plant's firm, fan-shaped fronds, extend—like all typical palms with stems or fronds but no proper branches— from the crown of the tree. These grow up to 2' in length and droop at the ends, almost like claws. They are used for making brooms, summer hats, and over-sized hand fans [*uchiwa*]. *Shuro* wood is used for making trays and utensils. ★ *Shôji*—uniformly-sized sliding dividers paneled with translucent rice paper—invariably face the corridor (☞ *engawa* described under WHEN I'M WRITING POETRY) running along the southern exposure in traditional homes throughout Japan. In general, *shôji* separate living quarters from hallways. They sometimes serve as interior window coverings as well, similarly separating living space from a corridor. ★ On the desk Mushakôji refers to here, ☞ "My Desk," page 126 and Note.

HENDRICKJE!—Hendrickje Stoffels (1626?–1663), originally hired as a maid, served after 1650 as a model for ☞ REMBRANDT (i) • (ii) • (iii). She later became his mistress. Some have claimed that she was illiterate. Rembrandt's wife Saskia died of tuberculosis in 1642, but he did not remarry, presumably because of a clause in Saskia's will that could have caused him to forfeit an inheritance from her wealthy father. ⬥ Hendrickje, who also apparently died of TB at around 37, was the fetching model for such paintings as the nude *Bathsheba* (1654), the *Woman Bathing* (1654), as well as *Flora* (ca. 1657). ★ Flora, the Roman goddess of spring, vines, and flowers, was traditionally depicted as a courtesan. In his rendition, Rembrandt achieves a plain solemnity. Mushakôji interestingly makes the painter the persona of this poem. ⬥ After Rembrandt declared bankruptcy in 1656, Hendrickje and his son Titus, then age 17, formed a corporation to protect the painter from creditors—not bad for an illiterate! Their umbrella company handled his art works and paid Rembrandt a salary that his creditors could not garnish.

HODLER—The painter and lithographer Ferdinand Hodler (1853–1918) was a central figure in modern Swiss art. While trying in his late teens to make a living by painting portraits, scenes, and signs, a benefactor taught him the principles of proportion, symmetry, rhythm, and the like. These lessons deeply affected all later work. ⬥ Hodler expressed his mystical search for the ideal in the manner of the symbolists. French symbolism initially attracted him, but he soon developed parallelism, his personal means of expressing himself. A high level of draftsmanship and classical clarity define his best work, which especially impacted the Impressionists; ☞ NEO-IMPRESSIONISTS.

HOTEI—ATTRIBUTED TO MU CH'I—On the identity of Hotei, ☞ VIEWING LIANG K'AI'S *DANCING HOTEI* (i) • (ii). For the painter Mu Ch'i, ☞ IN CHINA MU CH'I; also ☞ I PRAISE MU CH'I AND LIANG K'AI and MU CHI'S PICTURE OF [6] PERSIMMONS.

HUMANISM • HUMANIST—Renaissance humanism is too complex to allow succinct generalizations. In several ways, however, this humanism differs radically from Mushakôji's. Traditional humanists were elitist artists and scholars with no interest in the common man or his welfare. They were hero worshippers who honored talent but regarded as a vulgarity the notion of prosperity for all. Though they rebelled against authority, their values were hardly libertarian, nor could they possibly fit any modern definition of democratic. Most distrusted eccentricity in any form. An open mind in Mushakôji's sense would surely have struck them as an alien concept; ☞ page 29 ff.

I ADORE FALL—This poem is a coffer of clichés about autumn. Fall is the time of yearning and loneliness, for self-reflection and mulling over past and present, for thinking of the future and connecting the death of the year with one's own mortality, for becoming nostalgic for one's spring and summer days, and so on.

I'M A BELL—Mushakôji refers to bells at Buddhist temples which, unlike those in church belfries, have no clapper. One "rings" them by pulling back and releasing a log-like striker suspended in two places from a rafter attached to the structure that supports the bell. The intensity of the sound depends on how hard it hits the bell, the striker's size, and how far from the bell one releases it. ✮ This explains "drive out my...tones."

I PRAISE MU CH'I AND LIANG K'AI—For Mu, ☞ IN CHINA MU CH'I and MU CHI'S PICTURE OF [6] PERSIMMONS. For Liang, ☞ LIANG K'AI. ↘ Liang K'ai's portrait of the famed T'ang era poet Li Po (a.k.a. Li Tai Po; ca. 700–762) now hangs in the Tokyo National Museum. ↘ The striding crane doubtless refers to the 70" high left panel of a Mu Ch'i triptych titled *Crane in a Bamboo Grove*, which is done in ink on paper with muted colors. ✮ Liang K'ai's *Hui Nêng, the sixth Ch'an [Zen] Patriarch Chopping Bamboo at the Moment of Enlightenment* is an ink-on-paper hanging scroll some 29.25" high. ↘ ☞ DRAGON. ↘ Kannon is the Buddhist goddess of mercy (and namesake of Canon products). ✮ On Hotei, ☞ VIEWING LIANG K'AI'S *DANCING HOTEI* (i) • (ii).

I'M A PAINTER—"Die in peace" attempts to register *jôbutsu suru*, which also can suggest "enter Nirvana" [a blessed, careless state after death], "become a Buddha" [after death one is free of longings and attachments], or to "be enlightened" [attain Buddhahood]. ↘ "Chief of Fools" [*Bakaichi*] also titles a 1953.01 book; ☞ Chronology, 1948.11. ✮ This scene reminds of Van Gogh, who in Arles painted with a candle attached to his head.

IN CHINA MU CH'I—Mu Ch'i (Mokkei in Japan), the religious name of the Chinese painter Fa Ch'ang (Hô Jô in Japan), was born in Szechwan. This late Sung (middle 13th century) figure was a Ch'an [Zen] monk famed for his landscapes, still lifes, studies of flowers, and particularly his works on Ch'an Buddhist themes. The style of his best work, unappreciated and unrecognized by the academics of his day (☞ LIANG K'AI), demonstrates an "economy of means, inspired brushwork and deep spirituality." His *sumie* [black ink on white paper] paintings deeply influenced Japanese painters. ✮ Traditional East Asian artists did not paint in oils. Thus they never re-painted or dubbed over their work. The traditional Chinese and Japanese painter rather painted over from scratch a work that did not please. Any effort to touch up the work disqualified it as art. Emphasis on spontaneity (☞ page 177 ff.) and immediacy has always been the approach to calligraphy, too. ↘ This is why X-rays of the works of traditional Chinese or Japanese painters cannot possibly reveal anything like the small, furry dog that Thomas Gainsborough (1727–1788) painted out of the lower right-hand corner of his best-known work, *The Blue Boy* (1770). Also ☞ *HOTEI*—AFTER MU CH'I, I PRAISE MU CH'I AND LIANG K'AI, and MU CH'I'S PAINTING OF [6] PERSIMMONS.

IN HYÛGA'S HILLS—Mushakôji and his colleagues founded the ☞ NEW VILLAGE in Hyûga, the ancient name for Miyazaki Prefecture, in the southeast quarter of Kyûshû. This region boasts the 5,165' high Takachiho-no-Mine on which legend claims the ancestors of Japan's first Emperor—the mythical Jinmu, assigned the dates 660–585 B.C.— descended from the plains of heaven. ↘ Hyûga, naming one of the seven major cities in Miyazaki, lies near the eastern coast in the northern half of Kyûshû, where it serves as the distribution point and entrepot for an agricultural hinterland.

IN MY TINY ROOM— ① Terra-cotta, an Italian word meaning baked earth, is a form of pottery that first gained importance in classical Greece. The Greeks used terra cotta to make statuettes and vases as well as to decorate structures. Some vessels were a natural red-brown, some were glazed, and still others were painted. ✮ For the famed French sculptor, ☞ RODIN. The sculpture is the ca. 10" high "Little Sphinx"; for a description, cf. Chronology, 1921.05. ✮ Mushakôji writes Ch'ên So-wêng [Japanese read Chin Sho-ô], possibly a pseudonym of the Sung painter Ch'ên Chung • Jung, active between 1235 and 1260. Ch'ên, an eccentric fellow who served as a government official and a poet, is known as China's premier ☞ DRAGON painter. One of his most famed productions is titled the "Nine Dragons Scroll." This work, which art historians acknowledge as the superlative surviving picture of Chinese dragons, is now owned by the Museum of Fine Arts, Boston. ☆ Only the Emperor was allowed to wear clothing that contained nine dragons. The city Kowloon • Ku-lung, incidentally, means "Nine dragons."

② Shih-t'ao (1630–1717; a.k.a. Tao-chi, Sekitô in Japan), is the pseudonym of an early Ch'ing painter famed for his exquisite landscapes. It was prudent to become a priest after the Ming fell because he was related to a Ming emperor. Shih-t'ao visited every famous mountain in the land. Eventually, legend claims, he felt that he had become a soaring mountain. The reason his landscapes, executed in ink and pale colors, are so outstanding derives from the myth that he had become a living part of nature. ↖ Aside from a fascination with mountains, some of Shih-t'ao's artistic tenets echo Mushakôji's. For example, he wrote, "I am always myself and must naturally be present [in my work]." He also said, "I am beholden to no school, but paint in my own style with nature my only master"——reason enough to guarantee that the academic critics of his day would refuse to acknowledge his work. Japanese connoisseurs fortunately rescued Shih-t'ao from obscurity. Critics in the West and in Japan now rate him the most original and revolutionary figure of the 16th and 17th centuries—a giant in the history of Chinese painting. ↖ The last line in stanza 4 uses *jôbutsu*, which means become a Buddha • be enlightened • enter Nirvana; ☞ I'M A PAINTER and NATURALLY.

IN THE KINGDOM OF GOD (i) • (ii)—On Mushakôji's use of God [*kami*], ☞ NOT GOD. On the kingdom of God, ☞ LIVING IN THE KINGDOM OF GOD.

IN THE VILLAGE— ☞ NEW VILLAGE.

JAPAN BRIMS WITH HOPE— ① The world-acclaimed poet Johann Wolfgang von Goethe (1749–1832) was also a noted scientist who conducted research in botany and other fields. He was, as well, a statesman who held several high government positions. A master of drama and the novel as well as verse, he is now ranked as the founder of modern German literature. Goethe is especially famed for his two-part dramatic poem *Faust* (1808 and 1832). ☆ The dramatist Johann Christoph Friedrich von Schiller (1759–1805) is also a primary figure in German literary history. Most critics rank him second in importance only to Goethe. A leading romanticist, Schiller is best known for historical plays like *Don Carlos* (1787), which some see as pleading for political liberty and opposing excessive idealism. Schiller is furthermore famed for his long, didactic poems and for the "Ode to Joy," which Beethoven used in his ninth symphony.

② The philosopher Ralph Waldo Emerson (1803–1882) became the central figure in the American transcendentalist movement. He preferred, however, to regard himself a poet, not a philosopher. Scholars regard his poems, orations, and especially his essays (such as *Nature*, published anonymously in 1836) as landmarks in the development of American thought and literary expression. ☆ For Whitman, ☞ WHITMAN (i). ☆ For Dostoyevsky, ☞ DOSTOYEVSKI'S FACE. ☆ For data on Tolstoy, ☞ TOLSTOY'S WORDS. ☆ Henrik Ibsen (1828–1906) is the international-minded Norwegian playwright whose realistic masterpieces broadly influenced the development of modern drama. Ibsen was especially successful in both exposing the empty traditions to which people loved being enslaved and revealing truths his society preferred to ignore. His depictions of the tensions many 19th century women felt with social expectations display his rebellious spirit and feminist attitudes. In this he was well ahead of his time. ↖ His major works include the poetic drama *Peer Gynt* (1867), *A Doll's House* (1879), *Ghosts* (1881), *Hedda*

Gabler (1890), and *The Master Builder* (1892).

③ Bjørnstjerne Bjørnson (1832–1910), a major figure in Scandinavian literature, was a national-minded (some think chauvinistic) Norwegian poet, dramatist, and novelist. He was also a brilliant journalist and political leader who championed the rights of the oppressed and urged a parliamentary democracy. Japanese regard him the "people's poet." Bjørnson also sought to revive the literary language and character of his country as well as to free Norwegian drama from its "Danish yoke." ◆ His works include the novel *The Fisher Girl* (1868), the epic poem *Arnljot Gelline* (1870), and the play *A Gauntlet* (1883), which "attacked the blindness and hypocrisy of authority." He urged the liberation of the human spirit from prejudice and religious dogmas. Bjørnson won the 1903 Nobel Prize for literature.

④ Count Maurice Maeterlinck (1862–1949) was a Belgian writer of poetry and symbolic dramas, including notably *Pelléas et Mélisande* (1892), which Debussy turned into an opera (1902). Maeterlinck also wrote a wide-range of essays. The symbolists and mysticism, particularly through Novalis and Emerson, had a deep influence on him. ◆ Maeterlinck's works have not survived their milieu. At least they have lost much of the appeal they held for his contemporaries. Japanese, however, have long held in highest regard the play *L'Oiseau bleu* [The Blue Bird] (1909), an allegorical fantasy for children. Maeterlinck won the 1911 Nobel Prize for literature. ☆ For the Belgian writer Verhaeren, ☞ SENKE MOTOMARO, toward the end. ☆ "Despotism" (line 2 from the end) interprets Mushakôji's *"ôsorichî"* [authority], one of his rare uses of an English word, particularly in a poem as early as this (1911). Here he means "authoritarian." Very likely he uses the English word to call special attention to and thus underline his point.

JESUS AND ST. FRANCIS—One of the greatest Christian saints, St. Francis (1182–1226) was born Giovanni (John) Bernadone in Assisi, a town in central Italy where he also died. He founded the Franciscan order of friars, a new kind of order of itinerant preachers who worked to support themselves. He was especially known for his humility, love of poverty, and devotion to mankind. His religious fervor drove him to wander the countryside preaching. He also visited Spain, France, and Palestine.

JOY OF FRIENDSHIP—The word joy [*yorokobi*] appears in the titles and lines of dozens and dozens of Mushakôji's poems. Along with beauty, truth, and love (cf. page 41), joy is doubtless one of his favorite terms. ◆ When Mushakôji mentions the word "friend" with no specific referent, he often refers to his life-long chum ☞ SHIGA NAOYA. ☆ "Presence," my subjective interpretation, assumes that Mushakôji's *nanimonoka* [something] implies an indefinable something that is holy, mystical, or numinous.

JOY OF SEEING A FINE PICTURE—For data on Titian, ☞ VIEWING A TITIAN PAINTING.

KINOSHITA—Toshiharu (1886–1925)—graphs pronounced in the Chinese way as Rigen give his pen name—was a tanka poet born in Okayama Prefecture. Adopted at age four, he was taken to the capital and in 1891 entered the primary level at the Gakushûin [Peers' School]. There, in 1902, he became friends with ☞ SHIGA NAOYA and Mushakôji. He graduated in 1911 from Tokyo Imperial University with a B.A. in Japanese Literature. ◆ In 1910 Kinoshita joined with Mushakôji, Shiga, and Ôgimachi Kinkazu (1881–1960) in founding and editing the ☞ SHIRAKABA magazine; ☞ page 29 ff. Following the journal's demise after the 1923.09 Kantô Earthquake, he continued to be involved in producing similar humanistic magazines. ◆ In his personal life, Kinoshita was no stranger to tragedy. He lost all three of his children in their infancy. After several bouts with pleurisy, he succumbed to pulmonary tuberculosis.

LEAVE EVERYTHING TO GOD—For Mushakôji's concept of God [*kami*], ☞ NOT GOD.

LENIN'S EMBALMED REMAINS—Vladimir Ilyich [Nikolai] Lenin (1870–1924) was the founder of the Bolsheviks, leader of the 1917 Russian Revolution, an indispensable Communist theoretician who produced volumes of essays and speeches, and the first head of the U.S.S.R. (1917–1924). ✭ Mushakôji refers to Lenin's mummified remains—visible under a glass-topped sarcophagus—displayed in the Lenin Mausoleum (on the Kremlin wall, the west side of Red Square in Moscow); ☞ Chronology, 1936.

LEONARDO DA VINCI'S LILIES—The work of the Italian painter, engineer, musician, and scientist Leonardo (1452–1519) opens the gate to the High Renaissance. Leonardo's notebooks overflow with engineering and scientific observations that justify the claim that he was the most versatile genius of the Renaissance. Scholars now realize that many of Leonardo's ideas were centuries ahead of their time. ✭ As a painter, he was already receiving important commissions at the age of 26. His work gave fresh impetus to portraiture (note, for example, the *Mona Lisa*, 1503+) and landscape painting. Leonardo attempted to integrate landscapes into his pictures by detailing natural elements like foliage, plants, and the like. ✭ I have not been able to identify the picture to which Mushakôji refers. Lilies, however, have long been associated with the death and rebirth theme of Easter. ✭ The "goddess of beauty" doubtless refers to Venus, customarily considered the goddess of physical beauty who serves also as the goddess of sexual love.

LIANG K'AI—This Sung era Chinese priest-painter (Ryôkai in Japanese) flourished ca. 1210. Liang began as a successful and rewarded traditional academic painter but later became a Ch'an [Zen] Buddhist priest. Once he turned his back on court life and accepted styles, the Establishment no longer accepted his work. ✭ Fortunately, most of his best-known pieces—which date from his Ch'an period—survive in Japan. His minimalist style, described as "abstract shorthand," features inspired brush strokes. Liang is credited with producing "some of the most evocative and profound paintings in the entire pictorial history of China." ✭ Hui Nêng (638–713; Japanese read E-nô) was the sixth Ch'an [Zen] Patriarch. For Hui and Li Po, ☞ I PRAISE MU CH'I AND LIANG K'AI.

LIANG K'AI'S *HARPIST UNDER A PINE*—For Liang K'ai, ☞ above entry. A ca. 3″ x 2″ reproduction of this miniature appears with the poem, ☞ MSZS:XI:170. Mushakôji purchased this work in 1947. It is now in the Mushakôji Saneatsu Memorial Museum.

LIKE A TORTOISE—The point of possessing a sturdily "armored" sense of self dominates the poem. Having a strong retreat helps the artist survive Japan's often suffocating conformist society. ✭ Since all Japanese are familiar with Aesop's hare and tortoise fable, it is difficult to ignore the nuances and implicit lesson(s) of that tale.

LONELINESS (i) • (ii)—The word "loneliness" is the least imaginative rendition of *sabishisa*. This subjective word has a surprisingly broad horizon that describes the way situations cause the persona certain unpleasant or empty feelings. These include the sense of being alone, feeling cheerless, deserted, desolate, dreary, empty, forsaken, lonely, melancholy, miserable, and missing somebody—or experiencing sadness for any of these reasons.

LONG CORRIDOR—For an explanation of why I use this poem as the title of this collection, ☞ page 16. ✭ No doubt Mushakôji's family mansion contained several long hallways (aside from the *engawa*, ☞ WHEN I'M WRITING POETRY). In finely-made Japanese houses, all such corridors were usually made of resonant wood that allows an echo chamber effect similar to that of a Nô stage. It is all but impossible to clomp down any corridor in the usual Western house and experience the same satisfying reverberations.

LOVE TRAGEDY— ① This 1908 verse criticizes the Japanese family system, in particular *miai kekkon* [arranged marriage]. The propertied classes held that families not individuals got married. Clan elders thus viewed unions in terms of long-range familial stability, not short-range romantic or sexual attraction. ✦ Possibly because members of the aristocracy stood above the Confucian caste system, their families often displayed less rigidity on this point. In most instances, however, elders understandably had a vested interest in the marriage partner of the heir, usually the oldest son (these strictures would, in any event, not normally apply to a second surviving son like Saneatsu). The larger the property involved, the larger the folly in surrendering the choice of the bride to hormones.

② Educated Japanese of this milieu knew the novel *Hototogisu* [Cuckoo] by Tokutomi Kenjirô • Roka (1868–1927). This work appeared serially in the *Kokumin shinbun* [Citizens' News] between 1898.11.29 and 1899.05.24 and was issued separately as a book in 1900. ✦ *Hototogisu* focuses on the heartless manipulation of women in Meiji Japan. The hero and heroine, Takeo and Namiko, become symbols of the tragic way that parents, by claiming the family comes first, can arbitrarily (and legally) separate a married couple who love one another—thus causing the love tragedy that Mushakôji mentions. ✦ The heroine Namiko had contracted consumption and was forced to leave Takeo, a naval officer. Takeo's mother unilaterally arranged the divorce while he was on an exercise with the fleet. ✦ Sakae Shioya and E.F. Edgett translated this novel as *Nami=ko* (Tokyo: Yûrakusha, 1905). Tokutomi himself chose the English title, including the odd equal sign (=) before the *ko*. This suffix attaches directly to feminine names without punctuation. *Hototogisu* has been translated into at least six other languages.

LUTHER BURBANK (1849–1926)—American plant breeder and horticulturist born in Lancaster, Massachusetts. Working in California, Burbank developed new varieties of (a) fruits: apples, blackberries, nectarines, peaches, prunes, and raspberries; (b) vegetables: asparagus, corn, peas, the Burbank potato, squash, and a spineless cactus suitable for feeding livestock; and (c) flowers: various lilies and the famed Shasta daisy. ☆ Most Japanese of Mushakôji's milieu were familiar with Burbank's work, if not with the detailed contents of his eight-volume work, *How Plants are Trained to Work for Man* (1921), which appeared three years before Mushakôji published this poem.

MACHINES AND PEOPLE—Idealists like Mushakôji saw machines as dead and inauthentic items that demean existence; ☞ page 49 ff. He hoped nevertheless that they might serve as handy tools to improve human life. That would sanctify them and prevent capitalists from transforming people into mindless machines. ✦ Interestingly, Freud regarded the automobile a "prosthetic god," for it gives drivers the illusion they are Mercury.

MALIGNED—The last word in the poem—*kobito* [literally, small person • midget • pygmy]— implies being Lilliputian in character rather than in size. I thus render *kobito* "spiritual dwarf." ✦ This term has an ancient lineage and complex nuances. Current dictionary definitions refer primarily to the literal sense of smallness. In Confucian contexts, where the compound occurs as *hsiao-ren* [small person], however, the issue is invariably spiritual rather than physical qualities. That is true, too, in most of Mushakôji's contexts (☞ THUMBLING). ✦ The compound *hsiao-ren* appears frequently in the Chinese classics as a foil to the morally superior "great" man, the *ta-ren*. Note, for example, two similar selections from the *Mencius*: (a) Book VI, Part I, Chapter XIV:2: "He who nourishes the little belonging to him is a little man [*hsiao-ren*], and he who nourishes the great is a great man [*ta-ren*]." And (b) Chapter XV:1: "Those who follow that part of themselves which is great are the great men. Those who follow that part which is little are little men." That is surely the sense that Mushakôji has in mind. ★ The Chinese correlative *ta-ren* approaches Mushakôji's idea of giant [*kyojin*]; ☞ GIANT.

MAN FISHES—This image reflects an ancient conceit in Chinese poetry urged by quietists, Taoists, and the like. In East Asia, fishing in "the stream of life" has long been associated with finding or attempting to find the meaning of life. The result of that sincere quest should be spiritual calm and stability: in short, one catches food for the soul.

MAN ON THE FLUTE—Flutes universally symbolize poetry (or the spirit of poetry), the flute player the poet; ☞ PLAYING THE FLUTE.

MAN PAINTING A MOUNTAIN—For other mountain poems, ☞ pages 127 and 134 f.

MANY HARDSHIPS—Refers to the autumn of 1936 when Mushakôji was returning from his European sojourn. He had never been separated for such a long time from family and friends. By then he was physically exhausted and also extremely homesick. After visiting many spots in Europe, he sailed to New York, rode trains across America, then boarded a ship for home, thus girding the globe. ★ Other poems dealing with this trip include: ☞ "From My Three Children" and "Time Passes Fast" (page 82), and "Many Hardships" and "On a Train to San Francisco" (page 83). His journey lasted from 27 April to 10 December. ◆ Saitô Hiroshi (1886–1939) was a classmate who since 1934 had served as the Japanese Ambassador in Washington, D.C. After he died in Washington, the U.S. battle cruiser Astoria returned Saitô's remains to Japan.

MARY MAGDALENE—She has long been mistakenly identified with the unnamed repentant prostitute who washed the feet of Jesus (*Luke* 7:36–50). Christ later cast out seven demons or evil spirits from Mary of Magdala (*Mark* 16:9 and *Luke* 8:2). ◆ The New Testament further identifies Mary Magdalene as a female follower of Jesus, a woman "who ministered to him" when he was in Galilee (*Matthew* 27:56 and *Mark* 15:40). She is reported standing under the cross (*John* 19:25), mentioned as one of the women who took spices to the tomb on Easter morning (*Mark* 16:1), and as one who later told the disciples that she had spoken with Jesus (*Luke* 24:10 and *John* 20:18).

MASTER! MASTER!—Mushakôji bases this poem on an example found in the New Testament. In *Matthew* 18:21–22 Peter asks Jesus, "'Lord, how often shall my brother sin against me and I forgive him? As many as seven times?' Jesus said to him, 'I do not say to you seven times, but seventy times seven.'" In short, as long as a brother or sister asks for forgiveness, there is no limit to the number of times one should forgive.

MICHELANGELO—The Italian architect, engineer, painter, poet, and sculptor Michelangelo Buonarroti (1475–1564) was one of the masters of the Italian Renaissance. He created some of the all-time eminent works of art, including the first of several *Pietàs* (1497–1499), the marble sculpture *David* (1501–1504)—carved from a damaged marble block (he regarded himself primarily a sculptor), the profound content and sublime style of the paintings on the ceiling of the Sistine Chapel executed between 1508 and 1512, and the plans for Saint Peter's Church in Rome. Many historians point to Michelangelo as the perfect embodiment of the ideal of universal excellence.

MOMMY—Mushakôji (born 1885.05.12) divorced Takeo Fusako after 10 years of childless marriage and in 1922 married Igô (a reading of Iikawa) Yasuko (born 1900.03.09); cf.

Chronology. ☆ The statement after the last line is the poet's.

MORAL PRINCIPLE—This title somewhat freely renders the Japanese *daidô* ["the great Way," human morality]. Buttressing this concept is the deeply-held conviction that the East Asian spirit is so superior to the spirit of Westerners that it can overcome their material advantages. ☆ Taken to ludicrous extremes (as by some in China's 1900 Boxer Rebellion), this conviction gave many the entirely false assurance that their spiritual superiority could overcome Western bullets.

MORNING OF MY SEVENTY-FOURTH BIRTHDAY—This work refers to the date 12 May 1959.

MOTOMARO'S DEATH—For details, ☞ SENKE MOTOMARO. ↘ I am not sure what Mushakôji means by saying that Senke died like ☞ VAN GOGH and ☞ REMBRANDT (i) • (ii) • (iii). ↘ *Banzai* (10,000 years) might also be rendered, Long live…"X"!

MU CH'I'S PICTURE OF PERSIMMONS—For details on Mu, ☞ IN CHINA MU CH'I. ↘ It is mysterious that Mushakôji notes there are seven persimmons in this picture. I resisted the temptation to correct his text to six. This again illustrates the truth that a factual miscue does not necessarily demolish the poetry. ↘ The title is "The [6] Persimmons," blue-black ink on paper, 14.25" wide. The Daitoku Temple in Kyôto preserves this masterpiece. ↘ Commentators in Japan and the West have for many years admired this "elusive work," perhaps Mu Ch'i's most famed drawing. Arthur Waley describes this picture as "passion…congealed into a stupendous calm." ↘ One art critic writes, "Few other Ch'an [Zen] paintings are so convincingly the product of an instantaneous flash of inspiration or so perfectly illustrate the way the Ch'an painter can register his vision in ink splashes." ↘ Had it not been for Japanese Zen monks who preserved Mu Ch'i's art and assured his fame (☞ also LIANG K'AI), it is likely he would be unknown in his homeland. A Western critic laments, "Chinese art critics and scholars had little appreciation for the kind of painting which he produced." ☆ The word "ravine" in line 5 echoes the meaning of the second graph of the painter's religious name. ☞ *HOTEI—ATTRIBUTED TO MU CH'I* and *I PRAISE MU CH'I AND LIANG K'AI*.

MY DESK—Mushakôji's trip to Berlin and elsewhere lasted from 27 April to 10 December; ☞ Chronology, 1936. ↘ Older brother Kintomo (born 1882) was then Japan's Ambassador to Germany. ↘ In the traditional manner, Mushakôji counts the months he was away. Though absent from Japan only a few days in April, that month enters the count of the months he was not there. Following the "scientific" count, he was away 7.5 months. ☆ Other verse in *Long Corridor* related to this journey includes, ☞ "From My Three Children" and "Time Passes Fast" (page 82), and "Many Hardships" and "On a Train to San Francisco" (page 83). ☆ Inokashira Park lies adjacent to Kichijôji Station on the Chûô Line. The Tokyo Metropolitan Government administers this west-side recreational area, its small zoo, and botanical garden. The park also comprises a dense grove of cedars and a spring-fed lake (once Edo's source of drinking water) that contains a tiny picturesque island. ☆ Mushakôji kept this writing desk—a thank-you gift from the man who sold him the two figurines—behind the large Western chair and desk he used when he painted. This traditional black writing table (ca. 18" high with a writing surface ca. 18" x 30") sat on the *tatami* mats near the southeast corner of Mushakôji's study. The desk faced the *shôji* (☞ explanation in HEMP PALM). For a color photograph of this table and its setting, ☞ *Nihon bungaku arubamu—Mushakôji Saneatsu* [Album of Japanese Literature—Mushakôji Saneatsu] (Shinchôsha, 1984), pages 56–57.

MY PRAYER—Line 9 from the end of STANZA 2 offers, *"Hajime ni kotoba ari"*—the exact words of the Japanese translation of *John* 1:1: "In the beginning was the Word." Here "Word • *kotoba*" registers the Greek *Logos*, as untranslatable and mystic a term as Tao (which might also be translated "the Way"); some Chinese translations of *John* have used Tao to render *Logos*. ↰ Theologians agree that rendering the *Logos* in *John* 1:1 as "Word" could mislead. They find Word inadequate here because the text's referent is an eternal Person through whom all things were made. Thus *Logos* became a term traditionally associated with Jesus, the "pre-existent Christ [the Messiah • savior]," who is also the incarnation of the Divine. Some believe a better translation of *Logos* in this context might be "gospel," the good news of God's redemption of mankind, effected through Jesus Christ. Mushakôji apparently thinks this *kotoba* means simply "language • word(s)." ☆ "The Lord God" in STANZA 3—line 5, registers *kamisama*.

NATURALISM • NATURALISTS— ① Also ☞ page 29 ff. Naturalism in painting, as it developed in France over the last two decades of the 19th century, stressed the unembellished depiction of the individual's existence. Since realistic portrayal and exactitude were of utmost importance, the artist must not only reproduce subjects as precisely as possible in real-life situations but deal with contemporary scenes of work and leisure. Of course, the naturalist painter had to imitate nature precisely. In literature, the emphasis lay similarly on strictly factual or realistic representation. Naturalism called for precise descriptions of the actual circumstances of human life, whether on the farm or in the city. ↰ The significance of being up-to-date and individualistic conditioned naturalist novelists and critics like Emile Zola (1840–1902) to lend support to Impressionist painters, whose modernity appealed to them. Zola and others were not betraying their commitment to naturalism but rather stressing its penchant for dealing in a functional and modernist manner with contemporary life and the way they thought society conditioned, influenced, or degraded the individual. The realist's views on these matters usually assumed an urban milieu, though Japan was then overwhelmingly agricultural.

② Zola, the chief naturalist theorist, believed that the writing of literary works should proceed from a detailed observation and documentation of real life. He urged writers to imitate scientists and present only the facts—tell what happened and how. They were not to ask why the events occurred, for Zola thought that novels occupy a time and space that suspends moral values. Everyday human experiences alone should be the focus of the writer's non-judgmental descriptions. The goals of objective analysis, which must avoid idealism or subjectivism, centered then on the natural, social, and economic forces that drive or determine the thinking and behavior of all who live in the modern world. ↰ Naturalist writers saw society as the chief corrupting influence on citizens, who are far too weak and deluded to resist the superhuman powers of societal forces. That's why no one can hold individuals responsible. Life is violent and people are, after all, little more than glorified animals that the environment conditions. The realist accordingly believed that a genuine novelist dare not shun the ugly, the seedy, or the shady. Naturalists saw themselves representing the modern vision, at once tragic and crudely deterministic, that celebrates the downfall of the individual by the material and mechanistic forces of the world around us.

③ Out of a concern to modify the social conditions they described, many naturalist novelists concentrated on awakening readers to the sordid aspects of urban life and the people's harsh lot. Writers hoped to reveal the foibles, lack of knowledge, and frustrated hopes of humanity—all of which cried for compassion. Concerted attempts to avoid "romantic transfigurations" of life's data infused naturalist literature with nerves, flesh, and blood. There are no souls, few joys, and rarely characters with a developed sense of free will. This produces stories shadowed with gloom, hopelessness, boredom, pain, and suffering. ☆ Mushakôji and his ☞ SHIRAKABA colleagues saw these views as humanly degrading. The naturalist's assertion that individuals cannot be held responsible for their lot they regarded utterly repugnant. Much of Mushakôji's poetry attempts, indeed, to counterbalance these aspects of naturalist theory. He wanted to underline the spiritual not the animal side of humankind, the positive not the negative. In the never-ending tension between hope and actuality, Mushakôji opted always for hope. ✜ He also shared with Shirakaba colleagues the belief that it would be very hard to maintain the spirit of humanism in an art forced to serve political aims like improving society.

NATURALLY—Mushakôji's *jôbutsu* means "to become a Buddha" or enter Nirvana; ☞ I'M A PAINTER. Here I render it "enlightenment." Whether one enters Nirvana or becomes a Buddha [*hotoke*], *jôbutsu* implies waking to the truth and thus being freed of desires and attachments. Either expression may, moreover, mean to die—a state with no desires.

NEO-IMPRESSIONISTS— ① For the context of Impressionism, ☞ NATURALISM above. For the aftermath of Neo-Impressionism, ☞ CUBISM • CUBIST. ✜ Mushakôji's negative regard for painters representing this school relates to identifiable beliefs and preferences: he held intuitive spontaneity (☞ page 177 ff.) in highest regard, he believed in "natural" color balance, and he rejected scientific or formal planning as requirements in the creation of art. ★ The designation Neo-Impressionism dates from 1886 when the term described a movement that matured in France during the 1880s and continued into the early 1890s. The movement reacted to Impressionism, which required a painter to "depend on his intuition alone." He "could only rely on his sincerity." Impressionists rejected overprecise detailing as they attempted to "use shimmering spots of color" in open-air landscapes dominated by sparkling light. ✜ Despite the diverse aesthetics and styles of those associated with this "school" (Paul Cézanne, Edgar Degas, Pierre Renoir, et al.), most remained committed to the ideas of free technique, spontaneity, and fidelity to nature. Mushakôji could readily sympathize with these viewpoints.

② Two Frenchmen are most often mentioned as determining the direction and content of Neo-Impressionism. The first, the painter Georges Seurat (1859–1891), undertook to illustrate the basis of the Neo-Impressionist principle: the "scientific study of color and the systematic division of tone." Through a combination of research and experimentation, he discovered certain optical laws of color effects. Seurat then developed a "logical system of linear and spatial organization" that allowed the creative artist to utilize these "laws" in a systematic and effective manner. ✜ One of Seurat's aims was to restore to the painted line a simplicity and purity that would not be overshadowed by the "busy effect" of pigmentation. Orderliness produced calm and balance, an approach that created a more formal composition than Impressionism. ✜ Tonal contrasts resulted from "a methodical fragmentation of the brushstroke." This technique critics later called pointillism, which means applying paint to the canvas in small dots with brush strokes that some call "color lozenges."

③ The other painter, Paul Signac (1863–1935), served as the Neo-Impressionists' theoretician. He and Seurat tried to rationalize and codify the new practices. In their paintings they were interested both in achieving maximum luminosity and in reducing the spontaneity urged by the Impressionists. ✜ One problem with striving for maximum effect is that luminosity requires relative contrasts. Signac urged painters to use colors in their most intense forms. Painting by recipe oversimplified the artistic process, which critics claim produced at least two predictable results: sterility and boredom. Thanks to his careful preparation, exquisite composition, and thoughtfully worked-out thematic unities, however, Seurat's talent managed to transcend these pitfalls. Indeed, despite his faulty theories, he produced some of the century's most significant art works.

NEW LIFE—The language Mushakôji uses in this work reflects the *wu-wei* ["no act," that is, "no sweat," ☞ STRINGLESS HARP] ideal of Taoism and Zen; ☞ page 20. *Wu-wei* flows with life the way ☞ WATER finds its level. Without exerting itself in the least, water thus carves mountain gorges, gouges canyons, and creates river deltas.

NEW VILLAGE— ① **Ideals of the Institution**—Near the end of World War I, the *Ôsaka Mainichi Newspaper* asked Mushakôji to write an original article. He ended up producing the essay *"Atarashiki mura ni tsuite no taiwa"* [Dialogues (i.e., Questions and Answers) on the New Village]. He later published in ☞ SHIRAKABA two more question-and-answer articles. These outlined his dreams of the ideal polity • society he had been mulling over. Tolstoy's humanistic thought had partly stimulated his ideas. The increasing world-wide interest in anarchism and socialism, as well as personal concerns and values, also contributed. ↖ Mushakôji's ideal community—founded 14 November 1918 in Koyu County, Kijô Village, Miyazaki Prefecture (east longitude 131.25°, north latitude 31.93°)—would boast intellectuals committed to performing menial tasks and manual labor willingly and with pride-filled joy. This was unheard of in East Asian Confucian societies that strictly differentiated those who work with their heads and those who work with their hands (☞ PEOPLE). As long as the individual accepts responsibility, carries out assigned tasks, relishes being human, and exalts humanity, this cooperative would honor his or her individualism, free will, and personal liberty. ↖ For background details on the founding of the New Village, ☞ page 111 ff.

② **New Village East**—In 1938 Miyazaki Prefectural officials decided to build a dam and construct a hydroelectric plant near Takajô. As a result, the New Village lost 3 *tan* (ca. 75% of an acre) of its best land. The decision was thus made in 1939.09 to create another New Village in the Kantô area. Ideally, the site was to be close enough to the center of the capital to allow a round-trip in a day's time. Villagers purchased 4,000 *tsubo* (ca. 3.25 acres) in Moroyama, Iruma County, in the southwest sector of Saitama Prefecture (located north by northwest of Tokyo Station). This became the site of New Village East. ↖ In the early years, Moroyama may have required a day's travel to make a round trip. Though hardly convenient, the location is now easier to reach. New Village East boasts a modern "chicken coop" on a scale that will astonish the visitor.

③ **Dream and Reality**—Many Japanese regarded the New Village a utopian community. I avoid using the word utopia because it means "no place" and commonly refers to a dreamy political ideal not likely to be realized. That was never Mushakôji's conception. His dreams nevertheless do have a touch of the unrealistic and utopian. Creating in Japan the sort of community that might recognize individuality and help people fulfill their promise as human beings was a gigantic challenge ↖ The idealist's usual reason for establishing such a community requires escaping the present. He may believe that the disorganization of the social order or the disintegration of values requires recovery of past ideals. Or he may believe that traditional values bog down progress; ☞ page 52 ff. In either case, the social order requires refurbishing. ↖ To give society new life means moving ahead toward definite objectives. For Mushakôji, these included a polity that might embrace God, society, and human beings in one harmonious polity. He wanted to modify the human spirit without being ruthless. In the process, he hoped to realize without regimentation the urge to be an individual and still belong. ↖ Disordered social revolutions generally fail, for serious change requires orderliness. Systematic order, however, ironically threatens to undermine the very purposes of revolution. In this respect, the lack of a power-hungry authority figure in the village was very likely a boon. *Atarashiki Mura* may not have touched many Japanese over its 75–year existence; cf. Chronology. Yet it satisfied the thirst of some men and women to free their individual talent and learn to function harmoniously in a democratic context.

NEW VILLAGE—The Poems (i–vii)—Both "The New Village" ([v] page 146) and ☞ RATHER

THAN MAN refer to the Tower of Babel (☞ *Genesis* 11:1–9). ✺ This biblical myth purports to explain the existence of many unintelligible languages. The story describes people who had settled in Shinar, the alluvial plain of Babylon. Figuring they could make a name for themselves in history, they decided to build a tower that reached to heaven. ✺ The legend depicts their attempt as an insufferable example of human pride and arrogance. As divine punishment, Yahweh caused a confusion of tongues that made it impossible for the builders to communicate. The leaders had no choice then but to cancel the project. ✫ The clear import of this myth conflicts with Mushakôji's point. Professor Iida suggests that Mushakôji had in mind attempting the impossible. It is clear, too, that Mushakôji requires conditions that the original builders ignored: remaining obedient to God and nourishing wisdom.

NEW VILLAGE GREETS ITS FORTIETH YEAR (1958)— ☞ NEW VILLAGE. "Hurrah" registers *banzai* • 10,000 years, meaning, Long live…"X"!

NOT GOD—Rendering *kami* as God presents a problem. Although *kami* defies precise translation, it is rarely advisable to render it "God" except in Judeo-Christian usage. Mushakôji belonged to no sect, and yet he clearly uses *kami* in ways that resemble Christian contexts. ✫ *Kami* can refer to dead spirits, to a host of "spirits" in nature and mythology, as well as to the living great—including military heroes. In essence, however, *kami* describes the subjective reaction of veneration or wonder in the face of greatness, the numinous, or whatever inspires awe. The source of inspiration could be a supernatural being, a person, or even a rock or a tree. ✺ The single Japanese word *kami* thus embraces a large number of English terms for gods or spirits. These include: Ariel, dryad, fairie, faun, fay, lares, Mab, naiad, Nereid, nymph, oread, penates, pixy, satyr, and sylph. ✫ The way Mushakôji uses *kami* is another matter. I choose to capitalize God in rendering his verse because he seems to have in mind an almighty creature he elsewhere calls the Maker or Creator; ☞ page 235 ff. His *kami* likely includes Jehovah, Allah, and God the Father in the Christian sense. Mushakôji believes that this *kami* stands above Japan's national or local deities. ✫ *Tsumi* renders both the legal word for "crime" (an offense against the law) and the religious word "sin." Translating this term can be hazardous, for some uses carry undertones of "guilt."

OH, GOD (i) • (ii)—Mushakôji addresses God using the familiar *omae* [you], which in Japanese often implies a superior speaking to an inferior. The poet no doubt equates *omae* with the familiar "thee." By contrast, in his 1965 dialogues with the Maker • Creator he uses *anata*, the more formal and distancing "you"; ☞ page 235 ff. He also uses *omae* in addressing the historical Buddha; ☞ BUDDHA'S GOSPEL.

OLD MAN ON LIFE'S SUPEREXPRESS—"Pure tears" in the last line serves consistently as Mushakôji's symbol for—actually, as physical proof of—sincerity and truth.

ON A TRAIN TO SAN FRANCISCO—Mushakôji was enroute home after more than a half-year absence visiting his diplomat brother Kintomo, then the Japanese Ambassador to Germany. Mushakôji attended the 1936 Berlin Olympics and visited every famous European museum and art gallery he could; ☞ Chronology, 1936. He had boarded the train in Chicago. For related poems, ☞ "From My Three Children" and "Time Passes Fast" (page 82), and "Many Hardships" and "On a Train to San Francisco" (page 83).

ON MY DESK—This full-sized desk used mainly for painting sat adjacent to the small, black writing table described in ☞ MY DESK, page 126. Mushakôji did much of his painting from a chair but wrote his manuscripts and did his calligraphy kneeling on the floor in the traditional Japanese manner. ☆ On grappling with a mountain, ☞ pages 187 ff.

ON THIS DAY JESUS WAS BORN—From the outset, members of the New Village celebrated December 25, the traditional date of Christ's birth, as one of their major festivals. For the other holidays, ☞ NEW VILLAGE and page 113, first full paragraph.

ONE REED LEAF—Tall grasses with hollow stems and broad leaves, reeds or rushes [*ashi*] thrive in wet soil. Their leaves, which faintly resemble swords, have blade-like edges.

ONE WHO SAW GOD—God's words to the persona (lines 10–11 from the bottom: *"Waga aisuru ko yo. / Waga tame ni hatarake"*) echo statements reported at the baptism of Christ, just before he began his ministry: "Thou art my beloved son [*watashi no aisuru ko*]" (R.S.V. *Mark* 1:11; ☞ also *Matthew* 3:17 and *Luke* 3:22). ☆ Throughout time, those involved in a sacred mission customarily sought for their endeavors a ritualistic blessing from the ancestors, the gods, heaven, etc. It is impossible to determine whether Mushakôji consciously meant to create this echo. Because he regarded himself "a son of God," however, not even a purposeful appropriation of this biblical event qualifies as blasphemy. This desire for a blessing, in fact, provides a deft touch entirely consistent with Mushakôji's beliefs and values—not to mention echoes of the trials experienced at the New Village by the spring of 1920 when this poem was published.

OUR WARRIORS ADVANCE ON ATTU— ① This poem, published at the end of 1943, celebrates the earlier sacrifice of the small Japanese garrison on Attu, which lies in the westernmost group of the volcanic Aleutian Islands (extending west from the tip of the Alaska Peninsula). ☆ In early June 1942, Japanese bombed the American base on Attu, invaded, and occupied it. They also took Kiska and Agattu. American troops stormed Attu on 12 May 1943 and regained control on the 29th. Japanese forces withdrew from Kiska two months later. The Battle of Minatogawa (the name of a river flowing through the city of Kôbe in Hyôgo Prefecture) took place in 1336. It was one of the most decisive battles in Japanese history—perhaps comparable to the firing on Fort Sumter in the American Civil War or possibly as pivotal in importance as Gettysburg.

② Professor Iida points out that Mushakôji connects the attitudes of the heroic Japanese garrison with those of the samurai at Minatogawa, particularly warriors on the losing side under Kusunoki Masashige (?–1336). These warriors realized that defeat was inevitable and yet willingly went into battle and fought their best. Mushakôji praises the heroes on Attu who gave their lives as freely and as bravely as the samurai at Minatogawa. ☆ Incidentally, the Battle of Minatogawa ushered in a 56-year period of dual emperors (the Northern and Southern Courts) and propelled the general Ashikaga Takauji (1305–1358) into power as the first Ashikaga Shôgun. ☆ The Yamazaki Unit [*butai*] identifies the Hokkaidô-based regiment of 2,576 men headed by Colonel Yamazaki Yasuyo. His wireless reports provide grist for the legends surrounding the garrison's "honorable death in battle" [*gyokusai*: a sacrificial act often reported in American news articles covering the war as a "banzai charge"]. ☆ Mushakôji notes at the end of this work that he originally wrote this poem for a radio broadcast and states that this version has been "slightly [*sukoshi*] rewritten." It is exceedingly rare for him ever to rewrite a poem. He prefers to re-write a piece till he gets it "right."

PANGLOSS—The simple-minded Dr. Pangloss appears in *Candide* (1759). In this work, Voltaire—pen name of François Marie Arouet; 1694–1778—satirically takes to task human follies and vices that affect people in every field of endeavor, including (especially?) science and philosophy. Pangloss (meaning "All Tongues"), is Candide's pedantic and absurd tutor, a man who bubbles with incomprehensible optimism. He loves to aver that "All is for the best." He is an unabashed disciple of Baron Gottfried Wilhelm von Leibnitz (1646–1716), the German philosopher and mathematician who wrote that present society is not simply good but "the best of all possible worlds." The tedious pedant Pangloss foists this beguiling logic on his pupil Candide, adding speciously that "since everything is made for an end, everything is necessarily for the best end." No such monumental nonsense exists in Mushakôji's corpus.

PEOPLE—For more than two millennia, Confucianists have taught that those who labor with their bodies should serve those who labor with their heads. Scholars and writers in East Asia consequently had, and still have, extremely strong prejudices against manual labor. They will avoid any task that causes profuse perspiration or calluses, gets one's hands dirty, or involves intensive use of muscles and "back power." Most regarded such work as taboo activity for a legitimate member of the intelligentsia. What Mushakôji proposes thus remains a revolutionary concept. ✶ It is not difficult to find intellectuals who worked when they were students. Their part-time tasks [*arubaito*], however, rarely qualify as manual labor. I have met only one who has worked in a factory of any kind, and he was born and reared in the slums. I have yet to discover a single one who ever done *arubaito* as a manual laborer—on a garbage truck, on a road gang or a freeway construction crew, as a carpenter's helper, as a farm hand or grounds keeper, etc.

PEOPLE OF THE FUTURE—Each of my three parts appears in MSZS as a separate poem.

PLAYING THE FLUTE—This instrument, metaphor for artist or poet, stands universally for poetry or the spirit of poetry. The flute player stands for the poet. Euterpe, the Muse of lyric poetry, carries a flute, but Erato, the Muse of erotic poetry, usually carries a lyre. ✶ Flutes traditionally associate not only with funerals because of their melancholy airs but their tunes were said to "stir the loins." Thus they connect with joy and the anguish of the lover. Additionally, because people regarded the phallic shape as masculine and the sound as feminine, it is no surprise that flutes were once associated also with courtship, weddings, and desire. Flutes furthermore symbolize the explosive imagination that, in direct opposition to science, attempts to allow free association and ambiguity. ✶ The modern French poet Guillaume Apollinaire (1880–1918) treats the instrument in his poem *"Les Collines"* [The Hills, from *Calligrammes* (1918)] as follows: "… it is myself / Who am the flute I play upon. / A whip to punish other men."

POTATO (i) • (ii)—Three drawings of potatoes exist in *Mushakôji Saneatsu no jigazô— suketchichô yori* [Mushakôji Saneatsu Self-Portraits—From the Sketchbooks], ed. by Watanabe Kanji (Moroyama: Atarashiki Mura, 1995), pages 56–57.

PREFACE POEM—Refers to the 1947 collection *Kanki* [Joy]; cf. page 372.

PURE PEOPLE—For *wu-wei* (ca. line 75), ☞ STRINGLESS HARP and page 20 ff.

PURSE— ① The title of this poem is *"Kanabukuro"* [literally "moneybag"]. Because moneybag can refer to a rich or extravagant person, I think it prudent here to use another term, thus purse. ✶ Knowledge of underlying social caste attitudes in this poem may enhance appreciation. The educated in Mushakôji's day were familiar with the Confucian caste system that regulated society during the Tokugawa Era (1615–1868). His peers were equally acquainted with society's negative attitude toward merchants and money. Some fastidious samurai (whose stipends were measured in bushels of rice) were so eager to distance themselves from any hint of the merchant mentality that they refused to allow their children to learn how to count or even to master basic math skills. ✦ For more than 2,000 years, the Confucian ideologue relegated merchants to the bottom of the caste structure. Society must check merchants' influence because their income enables them to compensate themselves. This inevitably removes them from normal patterns of reward and punishment for virtuous behavior. Since merchants have no incentive to seek public rewards, they constitute a menace to society. It is true, too, that merchants make a living without "earnest labor." Not only do they charge interest on loans, they create profits by underpaying producers, over-charging buyers, and extracting high fees for their services. Confucianists consequently thought that merchants drain off valuable resources accumulated by "honest" workers.

② The Confucian caste system adopted by the state and adhered to throughout the Tokugawa era (1615–1868) consisted of four classes, the *shi-nô-kô-shô*: warriors [*shi*] (i.e., samurai, the new bureaucrats), peasants [*nô*], artisans or craftsmen [*kô*], and merchants [*shô*]. Aristocrats and those with "imperial" connections stood above society and beyond these regulations ✦ Caste rules were easiest to observe in castle towns, of which Edo, i.e., Tokyo, was the most important because the Tokugawa Shôguns resided there. Living areas in all such towns were parceled out by social caste. Among the four classes, samurai from various levels lived in the choicest areas contiguous to the castle. Farmers lived outside town. Then came the artisans and, finally, at the very bottom, the merchants. They lacked official "political clout," social status, and military power. Sumptuary rules tried to inhibit them from flaunting their wealth, which enabled many to exert enormous social and cultural influence in Japan's cities.

RATHER THAN MAN—The eclectic values expressed here reflect sentiments urged by Taoists and Mencius, as well as Jesus (cf. the Sermon on the Mount where Christ proclaims the new values of the kingdom of God; ☞ *Matthew*, chapters 5–7). ✦ The Tower of Babel myth, reported in *Genesis* 11:1–9, explains why people speak different languages and can no longer communicate with one another; ☞ NEW VILLAGE (v). The place was called Babel because Yahweh punished the people's ambitions by making communication impractical. That forced them to abandon their arrogant project.

REAL PERSON—Throughout the corpus, Mushakôji consciously employs the term *ningen* [human • humanity • humankind • person • mortal] in a normative manner. That is, he has in mind the **ideal** way(s) human beings were meant to (or should) be or behave. He does not embellish *ningen* with modifiers, whether "real" or "authentic"; ☞ page 49 ff. I believe, however, that adding these modifiers is a justifiable reading of his intentions.

READING HODLER'S BIOGRAPHY—For details on this Swiss artist, ☞ HODLER.

REMBRANDT (i) • (ii) • (iii)—The Dutch painter Harmensz Ryn • Rijn Rembrandt (1606–1669) produced works unmatched in their portrayal of subtle human emotions. ✦ His masterpieces include historical and religious scenes, group portraits such as *The Anatomy Lesson of Dr. Tulp* (1632) and *The Night Watch* (1642), as well as self-portraits that span his career. ✦ The one Mushakôji describes in (i) is doubtless the 1652 oil (ca. 44" x 31"), preserved in the Vienna Art History Museum. This depicts Rembrandt when he faced financial ruin. Thumbs in belt, elbows out, he looks sober but determined—perhaps even defiant. ✦ A lover of life, he frequently depicted old age, spiritual depths, and people who convey the impression of looking inward. ✦ In 1634 he married Saskia van Uylenburgh, daughter of a prosperous art dealer. She died of TB in 1642. A woman from a highly-placed family, Saskia provided Rembrandt an entrée to people he may not otherwise have been able to meet or paint. She also modeled for him. Their first three children died in infancy. Only Titus (1641–1668) survived; ☞ HENDRICKJE!

REMBRANDT'S ETCHING OF FAUST—For biographical details, ☞ REMBRANDT (i) • (ii) • (iii) above. ★ The amorphous Japanese word *e* becomes picture • painting • etching • sketch, and the like, depending on my knowledge of the item to which Mushakôji refers. ★ The powerful dramatic poem *Faust* (1808 and 1832) by Goethe (☞ JAPAN BRIMS WITH HOPE ①) immortalized the tale of Dr. Faustus. German legend depicts Faust as an avidly grasping magician and alchemist who, according to myth, sold his soul to Satan in exchange for knowledge and power over others. ★ Mushakôji doubtless refers to Rembrandt's 8" x 6" etching titled, "Faust in His Study Watching a Magic Disc." The title of this etching alone suggests what appeals to Mushakôji.

RETURN OF TOBIAS—Tobit names a pious old man who during the Babylonian captivity remained fiercely loyal to Jehovah. Tobit, the apocryphal book of the Bible that relates this man's story, dates from around the late third century B.C. ➤ Against the protestations of his wife Anna, who feared her son might not return, the blind Tobit dispatches his only son Tobias to collect a debt. Accompanied by the angel Raphael, Tobias also catches a gigantic fish in the Tigris and later uses its gall to cure his father's blindness. ★ Between 1610 and 1630, several painters illustrated this well-known incident. Other Rembrandt paintings with these names include *Tobias and His Family* (1626) and *Tobit and Anna* (1626). Rembrandt's mother was the model for Anna.

RHAPSODIZING ON MY BIRTHDAY— ① Mushakôji turned 26 on 12 May 1911. ★ French painter Paul Cézanne (1839–1906) is regarded as "the most outstanding innovator of the 19th century." As a young artist attracted to the sensual and the romantic, he most adored ☞ COURBET and ☞ DELACROIX. Cézanne later leaned for a time toward the Impressionists (☞ NEO-IMPRESSIONISTS) but later became more and more lyrical. At the height of his powers, he produced a sense of space by shifting the angles of vision, bisecting horizontal and vertical lines, and the like. He avoided shadows and invented a new kind of light created by pure color. This led him to fresh ways to fashion form and line. Some call him the first ☞ CUBIST. ★ For details on the Swiss painter, ☞ HODLER. For details on the Dutch painter, ☞ VAN GOGH. ★ "Ask, and it will be given you" (R.S.V.) is from Christ's Sermon on the Mount, ☞ *Matthew* 7:9 and *Luke* 11:9.

② Otaru, the Hokkaidô port city on the Sea of Japan (☞ Chronology, 1911), refers to a side trip Mushakôji made from Sapporo to visit his first love, Otei; ☞ AUTUMN HAS COME, FEELING LONELY and the Chronology, 1900, 1903, and 1911. She was at the time living in Otaru with her husband. Otei is, of course, the referent of "my first love" in the last line of the poem. In the original, Mushakôji wrote "second mother," which I alter to accord with his later decision to make a similar change in story titles. ➤ In 1914 he published in *Shirakaba* the story *"Dai ni no haha"* [My Second Mother], dealing with his three-year infatuation with Otei. In 1946 he renamed this story *"Hatsukoi"* [First Love]. ➤ One scholar explains this odd reference to his first love by quoting a statement Mushakôji made concerning Otei: "Unless I study and become a truly noteworthy [*erai*] person, I won't be qualified to love Otei." His birth mother raised him, but this second mother—the ideal or archetypal woman—provided him with ideals for which to strive. This is the function of a wife. With such backing, he could become a man who fervently works to achieve his goals. ★ This dynamic has been worked out in Mushakôji's 1919 novel *Yûjô* [Friendship], ☞ Chapter 5. Here Mushakôji portrays identical thoughts through his hero, Nojima, who thinks about being worthy of Sugiko, the heroine. ★ In 1930 Mushakôji listed this as one of his favorite poems; ☞ page 365.

RODIN— ① Mushakôji refers to his Rodin sculpture ☞ "In My Tiny Room," page 191. ↘ François Auguste René Rodin (1840–1917), the prolific French sculptor and draftsman of the late Romantic period, was one of the giants of 19th century art. After working in Belgium, he studied in Italy where the influence of ☞ MICHELANGELO emancipated him from academicism. Submitting to academic rules that stifle creativity (by stressing externals to the exclusion of the spirit) enslaves an artist to stereotypes. That will surely guarantee mediocrity. ↘ Rodin, who preferred always to identify himself as a man of the people, recalled with some pride, "Until the age of 50, I had all the worries of poverty." Poets, statesmen, and artists celebrated his work and honored both his creativity and personal magnetism. ↘ By 1880 Rodin was well enough established that the French government commissioned him to do the bronze door of a Parisian art museum. This led to his mighty *Gates of Hell* (1880–1917), an exceedingly ambitious but unfinished project that occupied him on and off till his death.

② Rodin's dedication to work and art never flagged. It mattered little whether he was working in conditions of poverty or, particularly after 1900, in the backwash of renown. Fame burdened him, however, with many a surprising call on his time. For example, George Bernard Shaw paid the equivalent of $18,000 for a marble bust of himself, and Oxford University conferred on Rodin an honorary doctorate. ✩ Like the best Impressionists, Rodin could capture life's fleeting moments in stone and nevertheless unfailingly preserve a sense of transience. He did not regard a work "finished" until it adequately expressed his idea, whether it called for a polished marble figure or for one barely gouged out of a virgin block. ↘ While he was also a supreme realist, Rodin's works have the quality of communicating a "passionate immediacy" that appealed to Mushakôji. Most educated people the world over have been exposed to one or more of Rodin's masterpieces, including especially *The Thinker* (1880) and *The Kiss* (1886). ✩ Japanese also honor Rodin for his personal interest in East Asian art and for his penetrating study of the Japanese dancer-actress Hanako (bust, 1908). Rodin is furthermore mentioned in NEW VILLAGE and VIEWING A BOURDELLE PAINTING. ✩ Volume VIII of *Shirakaba*, a massive special issue devoted to Rodin, appeared in 1910.11.

SEEK THE KINGDOM OF GOD—On Mushakôji's use of God [*kami*], ☞ NOT GOD. For his views on the kingdom of God, ☞ TO LIVE IN THE KINGDOM OF GOD.

SELF-ADMONITIONS WHEN I PAINT—On sprouting wings, ☞ pages 46 and 366, No. 6.

SENKE MOTOMARO (1888–1948)— ① Poet born in Tokyo as the first son (by a mistress) of Baron Senke Takatomi. The Baron was born into a family of hereditary chief priests at the Izumo Shrine, but after the 1868 Meiji Restoration he switched to the world of bureaucracy. There the central government favored him with several appointments. He was Governor of Saitama, then of Shizuoka and Tokyo before becoming Minister of Justice on the Saionji Cabinet (1908.03–.07). Baron Senke also had some renown as a traditional poet. Motomaro's mother, who had a good deal of training and talent as a painter, unwittingly became his lover in Tokyo. She was not aware that Takatomi had a wife and three daughters living in his native village. ↘ Motomaro, resentful toward his father because of the complex family arrangements, left home during his teenage years with the romantic dream of living on an uninhabited island in the South Pacific. Back in the real world, he began around age 17 to submit manuscripts to the literary columns of Tokyo newspapers. ↘ He studied free verse, tanka, and haiku with a number of well-known teachers. Like Mushakôji, various Japanese authors as well as the works of Tolstoy (☞ TOLSTOY'S WORDS) influenced Senke. Works of Anton Pavlovich Chekhov (1860–1904) that deal with the inability of people to communicate also moved him. Through a coterie magazine he helped edit, he happened to meet Mushakôji. They soon became fast friends. Motomaro also associated with other artists vaguely connected with the Shirakaba, e.g., the poet and sculptor Takamura Kôtarô (1883–1956).

② In 1913 Motomaro married against his father's wishes and left home so he could begin life as a writer. Senke began publishing his stories in a Shirakaba satellite magazine—in no way sufficiently lucrative to put food on his table. After his son was born in 1916, he began writing free verse and published his first collection in 1918. There was no money in poetry, either. ↖ Senke's works, powerfully influenced by idealism, glow with a sense of love and goodness. Steadfastly optimistic, he never tired of glorifying the life of the common people. His second verse collection appeared in 1919. Other slight collections followed regularly. Throughout, his work indicates his adoration of nature and people. He also displays a tendency to praise talent—good reasons for Mushakôji to find him a like-minded friend. Senke was presumably influenced as well by the thought of ☞ WHITMAN and Emile Verhaeren (1855–1916), whom scholars consider the leading Belgian poet writing in French. He was especially noted for writing Symbolist poetry that dealt with Flanders but also wrote verse plays. ★ Senke's first son became a war casualty in 1944. His wife died of sickness in 1946. Despite being lonely and impoverished, he styled himself the "Poet of Paradise" [*rakuten no shijin*] and continued writing vigorously. A cold developed into bronchial pneumonia and he died at age 61 in 1948. In 1964 Yayoi Shobô published his *Zenshû* [Works] in two volumes.

SESSHÛ'S *THUNDERBOLTS*—Sesshû Tôyô (1420–1506) was a Zen-type painter who penetrated to the heart of whatever he depicted. The uncharacteristic subject matter of this picture overshadows elements of Sesshû's style common to his most famous works. ↖ For a ca. 3.25" x 3.75" reproduction of this picture ☞ MSZS:IX:175. ★ Sesshû was born in Bitchû • Bishû, now the western part of Okayama Prefecture. After becoming a Rinzai Zen priest, he studied in China (1467–1469). Later he produced in the Chinese style many folding screens and India ink-on-paper landscapes, some with faint coloring. Sesshû is especially renowned for his imagined "portrait" of Bodhidharma • Dharma (Daruma in Japan), the sixth century Indian monk who introduced Ch'an [Zen] Buddhism to China. As the first Zen patriarch, Dharma reputedly excised his eyelids to lessen the chances that he might doze off during meditation. ↖ Roly-poly Daruma dolls, some of which serve as piggy banks, are like our weighted tumbler dolls that cannot be pushed over. Daruma dolls hence associate with tenacity and good luck. ★ With respect to the four celestial gods [*tenjô no shigami*] named in this poem, note that four is a homonym for death. *Tenjô* also can mean death. The traveler symbolizes man's journey through life. ★ Mushakôji uses "she" in stanza 3 presumably because the Japanese word for lightning [*inazuma*] contains the graph for wife [*tsuma* • *-zuma*].

SHIGA AND I—Mushakôji's life-long friendship with the novelist ☞ SHIGA NAOYA dates from 1902, that is, from their middle school days at the Peers' School.

SHIGA NAOYA— ① Mushakôji was 86 when his lifelong friend, the novelist Shiga Naoya (1883–1971), died at 88 years, eight months. Shiga has often been labeled the "patron saint [actually, *shôsetsu no kamisama*, the god] of the novel." The persona depicted in many of his stories is, however, far from being a god. Indeed, terribly indulged by his paternal grandmother (for many years he was the only grandchild), Shiga was the strong-willed first son and heir of a menacing, intractable, blunt, curt, and distant father. Outsiders regarded his father, a nouveau riche businessman and banker of samurai stock, a trustworthy man. At home, however, he was as cold and as demanding as his mother—who lived with him and terrorized Naoya's birth mother. Despite having at least three or four maids in the Shiga mansion, Naoya's mother was mercilessly forced to work around the house. Nor was she allowed much of a relationship with her son. Perhaps it was a blessing that she died when Naoya was age 13.

② Shiga's father regarded him an arrogant, obstinate, lackadaisical, slothful, and parasitic crybaby. Naoya disclaimed this assessment, though he did admit he had little desire to write enough to be economically independent. He was an avid athlete but a consistently indifferent student. Because he failed several grades at the Peers' School (his father's income qualified him to enter), however, he ended up in the same class as Mushakôji. They later developed a life-long friendship. Shiga was far more interested in being free and doing what he wanted than in conforming to rules, whether set by academics or society. ✚ Throughout the first 35 years of his life, he was always more prepared to obey his private feelings than either to exercise common sense or to show conventional courtesy to others. Little irritated him more than doing anything mindlessly or "by the numbers," as Japanese social conventions require.

③ Ego and an instinctive grasp of human experience dominate Shiga's literary output, which is as meager as Mushakôji's is copious. Shiga's oeuvre, moreover, is as barren of idealism and commitment as Mushakôji's is rich in them. Although some will surely regard as despicable (or at least distasteful) the individual whom many of his stories portray, Shiga's superb style and obvious honesty easily overcome negative reactions. ✚ Many Japanese readers find his strong personality irresistibly addictive. The direct, unvarnished style and honest personal revelations of Shiga's early autobiographical works boast a reputation out of proportion with his slim output. Confessional literature of this kind may pander to the voyeuristic interests of many Japanese readers, yet critics agree that Shiga's stories have had a profound impact. They continue to appeal to readers able to identify, for example, either with the author's early struggles with sexuality (as described in the 1912 novella *Ôtsu Junkichi,* the name he adopts as his alter ego) or with the tensions experienced with his father. These he resolved in 1917 and described in *Wakai* [Reconciliation], a highly praised novelette.

④ In these novellas, as in his short stories and in his single long novel, *Anya kôro* [A Dark Night's Passing, completed only in 1937], Shiga portrays the "truth" in what he took to be a forthright manner. That included avoiding "unnatural" or "surprising" turns of plot. Like Mushakôji, Shiga refused to falsify his feelings, mask his human frailties and pettiness, or distort perceptions merely to achieve a literary objective or special reaction from his reader. This makes his work significant to partisans and critics alike. Donald Keene perspicaciously notes that Shiga's oeuvre could only be written after Japanese literature had "passed through a baptism of individualism from the West." Many Shiga stories indulge in auto-therapy that seeks to define selfhood. Others focus on warped or sickly states of mind. Examples from either genre deservedly belong to world literature. The long-lasting high literary value and wide recognition accorded Shiga's work differs radically from Mushakôji's writings.

SHIRAKABA— ① This term translates as White Birch[es]. One of the earliest to sprout green leaves in the spring, this tree can reach a height of 90' or more. ✚ Western associations have little to do with Mushakôji's use. It is interesting, nonetheless, that birch rods were used in antiquity to drive out the old year and witches, as well as to purge delinquents or lunatics of evil spirits. Mushakôji claimed in a 1964 interview (aged 79) that the name derived from a "tranquil forest of white birch trees on Mt. Akagi" in Gunma Prefecture outside Maebashi. ✚ Shirakaba names both a magazine (160 issues between 1910.04 and 1923.09) and a loosely-amalgamated group or "school" [ha] of writers and artists. These men were attracted vaguely to ☞ HUMANISM (also page 29 ff.), in the simplest sense of interest in human beings—their welfare, worth, values, and happiness. ✚ Most adherents were as opposed to ☞ NATURALISM as they were devoted to modern Western art. It is often impossible to differentiate between the "school" (which I do not italicize) and the journal (which I do). The founders consisted, for example, of poets, playwrights, essayists, a folklorist, an art historian, and many novelists. All were alumni of or dropouts from the Peers' School [Gakushûin]. They thus enjoyed relatively blessed social and economic backgrounds. From the socialist viewpoint, therefore, Shirakaba writers—regarded as spoiled scions of privileged families—were disqualified from making meaningful statements about or contributing to Japanese society. Some of the most catty and petty remarks about Shirakaba writers come from Marxists, who uncritically accept environmental determinism and other dogmas. Rendered insensitive by his theories, the Marxist refuses to believe that men "born with a silver spoon in their mouths" are capable of either compassion for the poor or interest in social reform.

② The four drivers behind both magazine and "school" were Ôgimachi Kinkazu (1881–1960; ☞ KINOSHITA), ☞ SHIGA NAOYA (1883–1971), Mushakôji (1885–1976), and ☞ KINOSHITA Toshiharu • Rigen (1886–1925). Until his love suicide, the novelist and essayist Arishima Takeo (1878–1923) published many works in the journal. He was more a cheer-leading elder than, properly speaking, a prime mover. ↖ The 15 or so second-level "founders," for the most born slightly later, included: Sonoike Kin'yuki (1886–1974), a novelist who dropped out of the Gakushûin because of illness. Kojima Kikuo (1887–1950), an art historian—famed for his research on ☞ LEONARDO da Vinci—who became a professor at Tokyo University. Nagayo Yoshirô (1888–1961), novelist and playwright. Satomi Ton (1888–1983), novelist. Yanagi Muneyoshi (1889–1961), thinker and founder of the folklore movement—he hoped that even everyday utensils might be lovely works of art. And Kôri Torahiko (1890–1924), a playwright who emigrated to England were he worked for 13 years. He died in a Swiss sanitarium.

③ From the outset, the editors of *Shirakaba* made clear an important objective. The magazine would cover a wider territory and have broader appeal than the customary literary journal, which typically specialized in publishing only the work of its associates. ↖ As early as its eighth issue, for example, *Shirakaba* (1910.11) devoted a special number to the French sculptor Auguste ☞ RODIN (1840–1917) and his work. Also, the 600-page edition celebrating the fifth anniversary of the inauguration of *Shirakaba* featured many illustrations by and information on William Blake (1757–1827), the British poet, engraver, artist, and mystic. ↖ The magazine consistently featured illustrations of the paintings of famous modern Western artists. These included several from France: the painter Paul Cézanne (1839–1906; ☞ RHAPSODIZING ON MY BIRTHDAY), the painter and woodcut artist Paul Gauguin (1848–1903), and the painter, sculptor, and lithographer Henri Matisse (1869–1954).

④ Much attention was also accorded the Dutch painter Vincent ☞ VAN GOGH (1853–1890), whom Mushakôji takes credit for introducing to Japan, and the Norwegian painter and graphic artist Edvard Munch (1863–1944), who in 1893 produced *The Shriek*—that world-famed picture that so poignantly characterizes modern angst. ↖ Of course, the founders and colleagues also used *Shirakaba* as a handy forum for their fiction, poetry, drama, essays, translations, and art. Furthermore, writers like ☞ SHIGA NAOYA first published on the pages of the *Shirakaba* many works now regarded as masterpieces of the Japanese short story. These include "Han's Crime" (1913.10), "The Kidnapping" (1914.01), and "At Kinosaki" (1917.05). The *Shirakaba* regularly presented translations of European literature, including, for example, a drama by Johan August Strindberg (1849–1912), the Swedish playwright. Koizumi Magane (1886–1954), a *Shirakaba* adherent, translated this play. In his dramas, poetry, short stories, novels, and pamphlets, Strindberg was a scourge of the authoritarian Establishment. This brand of "political action" appealed to the humanist in Mushakôji and others.

⑤ The *Shirakaba* made important contributions to art in Japan. Its articles enhanced the appreciation of modern European works. Though contributions to Western art history were seminal, writers also expanded the acknowledgment of Asian art and increased public awareness of the quality of several pre-modern painters lightly regarded in China. For example, ☞ poems describing the work of Liang K'ai, Mu Ch'i, and Wu Chun, all 13th century Ch'an [Zen] painters. ↖ The magazine served as a major conduit to Western writers, introducing, among others, Walt Whitman (1819–1892), Henrik Ibsen (1828–1906), Leo Tolstoy (1828–1910), Romain Rolland (1866–1944), and Maurice Maeterlinck (1862–1949). ☆ Shirakaba founders were, in a sense, born into humanism, ☞ page 29 ff. Only a privileged background allowed entry to their alma mater. Though several like Mushakôji came from relatively "impoverished" aristocratic families, not a one grew up in dire poverty. ☆ The idealist-humanist Shirakaba colleagues, for their part, felt antagonism toward their NATURALIST competitors' lack of attention to individual autonomy. Mushakôji's HUMANISM called always for cultivating rather than indulging the self. ☆ As Mushakôji's poems show, one aspect of the hope that many Shirakaba writers shared was belief in a Being who transcends social forces and human life. Whether one perceives the transcendent as man's will, God, or nature, this view increased tensions with the naturalists, who rejected all such ideals.

SINCERITY— ① Mushakôji may fit the critical description of the extraordinarily naive, uncomplicated, and simple-minded bard. For all that, his verse exudes concepts and concerns, and often presents insights, that are far from ordinary. One of these is sincerity. Mushakôji often uses words like *honki* [earnestness] that imply sincerity even if they do not translate directly as or perfectly correspond to it. Throughout his canon he so frequently refers to the concept that the reader can hardly ignore its importance. Nor is it possible to downplay. Sincerity ranks with spontaneity (☞ page 177 ff.), hope, authenticity (☞ page 49 ff.), beauty, love (☞ page 114 ff.), and truth as core foci for Mushakôji. ↖ Sincerity implies being or becoming as opposed to having or acquiring. It always associates with the humanist interest in the whole person. Gaps between seeming and being greatly interested Mushakôji. Does what a poet writes coincide with what he actually feels? When there is no gap—that is, when a poet's words are perfectly consonant with what he truly feels—he may be regarded authentic or sincere. That is the only kind of person Mushakôji respected. It is the only kind of poetry he aspired to produce. The primary virtues of the sincere writer include living up to his ideals, remaining true to his values, and refusing to counterfeit his feelings. All require writing spontaneously from the heart [*kokoro*], and all imply authenticity. ↖ These qualities obviously cannot promise the work greatness, critical recognition, or monetary success. That is impossible short of having talent and then fleshing it out with appropriate ideas, insights, style, and technique. Mushakôji knew that. His view, however, was that sheer talent without sincerity or authenticity produces shallowness. Judgments—whether simple-minded or brilliant, sensitive or intractable—concerned him less than stating his distinct preference for authentic poets. Their writing might boast virtue if not literary excellence.

② That's why Mushakôji insisted on starting with sincerity, even if at the outset it lends no literary merit to the work. Poets who begin there at least escape being enticed by the greatest act of insincerity: tweaking the reader's emotions in ways that do not touch—and are not native to the heart of—the writer. ↖ That marks the irresponsible bard whose insincerity shows little respect for the reader. Thus, though their rhetoric and techniques may impress, in the end such poets are unlikely to move people consistently. Heart must communicate with heart. Mushakôji never tires of calling for honesty, earnestness, true-heartedness, and openness—attributes of sincerity and authenticity. ↖ The quality of the poet's person, in short, becomes a major issue. This contrasts markedly with the confessional naturalist writer who, in fact, exalted dubious character traits. Candor about the id was his path to truth and sincerity. At almost every point, therefore, Mushakôji's views of sincerity imply a reproach of self-conscious naturalist and academic writers. Objects of his faultfinding might also include Marxists and those who toady to the critical Establishment. ☆ Mushakôji would agree that sincerity is subjective and a value judgment that makes no pretensions at objectivity. The fact that these qualities disqualify sincerity from serious scholarly discourse only verified to him how important an ideal it must be to the poet.

SOMEONE SAID—Doing one's best and leaving the rest to fate, a Confucian teaching, has been an orthodox view for at least two millennia; ☞ pages 24, 34, and 274.

SONG OF A MOUNTAINEER—For other poems on mountains, ☞ pages 127 and 187 ff.

SONG OF THE VISIONARY—By 1917, when Mushakôji published this work, Japan had theaters, art museums, hospitals, and dormitories. Professor Iida suggests that Mushakôji may have in mind building an **ideal** theater, museum, etc.—at any rate, the kind Japan did not have at that time. He may be thinking that Japan also needed an "ideal" dormitory because dorms tended to manifest all the least admirable characteristics of Japan's vertical society. ↖ One problem in translating this poem is Mushakôji's frequent use of *chikara*, a word with a wide horizon. Possibilities range across English words like strength • power • ability • effort • action • force • vigor • energy.

SORDID POEM—In both the text and the title, "sordid" renders *kitanai*, written in *katakana*. This implies italics, which I chose not to use here. ↖ White birch registers ☞ SHIRAKABA (and page 29 ff.), the anti-naturalist magazine (published in 160 issues between 1910.04 and 1923.08) that Mushakôji et al. founded and edited. ↖ Even the meanest and most trivial criticism, in short, "fertilizes" the efforts of those putting out the journal.

SPRING—For Otei, Mushakôji's teenage flame whose lack of response made him miserable, ☞ AUTUMN HAS COME, FEELING LONELY, RHAPSODIZING ON MY BIRTHDAY, and the Chronology, 1900, 1903, and 1911. ☆ Mushakôji's *bôfu* doubtless refers to *hamabôfu* [*Umbelliferae*], sometimes called glehnia. The roots of this perennial imported from China have medicinal value. It has a ca. 4" high stem and from late summer to fall blooms small white, five-petaled flowers. The persona is not picking the flowers but pulling up the plant's young edible roots ("uprooting" registers *toru*). ☆ Mushakôji writes that the *hamabôfu* is not easy to identify or find. That is why he felt a sense of satisfaction in being able to gather quite a few; ☞ MSZS:XI:662. ↖ This 1915.05 work refers to World War I, then raging in Europe. ☆ Kugenuma names an area near Fujisawa, a city lying east of Kamakura on Sagami Bay. Mushakôji lived there briefly between 1915.01 and 1915.09; ☞ Chronology. This seacoast district is a popular summer retreat from the heat and humidity of urban areas.

SQUASH AND POTATO—Mushakôji later altered the original title in two ways: he converted the graphs to *kana* and he changed the designation of potato from *bareisho* to *jagaimo*. Either word designates a potato, but the former is more old-fashioned. *Bareisho* may therefore be more appropriate in texts with literary expressions or classical verb forms.

STONE BY THE WAYSIDE—Mushakôji's title for this poem means "the stone dropped by the road." This differs noticeably from *Robô no ishi* [literally, "roadside stone"]—the famous children's story by novelist and playwright Yamamoto Yûzô (1887–1974). My version of Mushakôji's title may thus urge a resonance that does not exist.

STRINGLESS HARP—The term "non-action" in the last line renders *mui* ["no do"; *wu-wei* in Chinese], the Taoist • Zen concept; ☞ NEW LIFE and page 20 ff. Alan W. Watts (1915–1973) renders *wu-wei* "no sweat." This suggests an essential dimension of the term:

effortless and natural action—like ☞ WATER seeking its level. The innate purity of such behavior gives it magnetism or virtue in the ancient sense of affective power. *Wu-wei* also implies authentic behavior that, because it is neither aggressive nor manipulative, lends the individual the capacity to inspire and transform.

SUN AND MOON—For reasons not clear to me, only the first part of this poem appears in MSZS:XI:14. I render the full version from an anthology dated 1968.06; ☞ page 373. For other poems on the sun, ☞ WONDERS OF THE SUN. ★ East Asians see the sun as masculine (*yang* • *yô*) and the moon as feminine (*yin* • *in*). Mushakôji does not use "he" and "she," but he has the moon speak in appropriately deferential, feminine Japanese.

SUNFLOWERS IN OUR VILLAGE— ☞ NEW VILLAGE and VAN GOGH. Van Gogh made his *Sunflower* paintings in 1888. ★ Two graphs of the 3-graph term for sunflower [*himawari*] invert the two characters for Hyûga, the location of the first New Village in Kyûshû; ☞ IN HYÛGA'S HILLS. The visual echo between the two words (one literally, "sun-face-hollyhock," the other "face-the-sun") cannot be realized in English. ★ I am unable to identify Arai. Watanabe Kanji compiled an official chronology as well as a number of works dealing with Mushakôji; ☞ page 287. ★ The village journal, *Kono Michi* [This Path] (1960.04–1974.11), had been renamed from *Atarashiki Mura* [New Village] eight years earlier. ★ For other poems on the sun, ☞ WONDERS OF THE SUN.

SURRENDER OF SINGAPORE—A note at the end of this 1942 poem indicates that it initially appeared in the *Manshû Shinbun* [Manchurian Newspaper]. ★ Singapore, an island at the tip of the Malay Peninsula, commands the eastern entrance to the Strait of Malacca that separates Malay and Sumatra. Because this location is a major sea-lane, Singapore's site has long been recognized as having strategic significance. The British East India Company obtained possession of it in 1819. Five years later the island came under government control, and Britain made Singapore its major naval base in Asia. ★ All defenses were, unfortunately, oriented to attack from the sea. This allowed Japanese forces to cross with little trouble the Johore Strait, which separates the island from the Malay mainland. They then readily subdued the garrison. The British surrendered on 15 February 1942 and Japanese occupied the island until after their 1945.09 unconditional surrender. ★ Singapore became an independent republic in August 1965.

TEARDROP—In stanzas 6–7, I render *seiyoku* [sexual desire • carnal passion] variously because Mushakôji often refers to Eros as the life force; ☞ BEAUTIFUL WOMAN. ★ The expression "God is love," some eight lines from the end, derives from I *John* 4:16. For the meaning of this expression, ☞ discussion of *agapé*, page 114 ff.

TESSAI—Tomioka Tessai (1836–1924) was a modern Japanese painter who all his life obstinately adhered to the ideals of the Southern School of Chinese ink painting (Nanga). Tessai, who was widely read in Confucianist and Buddhist thought, created a world for himself that walled out the flood of Western ideas and realistic painting. ★ His immense output alone is astonishing, but his work displays such originality and power that Japanese and Western critics alike cannot help but recognize his genius. Despite rejecting modernist European methods, themes, and concerns, the thoroughgoing individuality of Tessai's production makes some critics perceive its affinity with 20th century Western painting. ★ Few artists will impress Mushakôji more than those who can fully express their true individuality, despite using the most ancient of methods, and simultaneously give the impression that they are "modern."

THAN THE MALCONTENT— ☞ LIVING IN THE KINGDOM OF GOD These two poems form a unity.

THAN THIS PATH—In 1953 Mushakôji wrote this 1920 work on a stele at Moroyama to commemorate the 35th anniversary of the New Village.

THIS BOOK—Refers to *Watashi no kaigara* [My Shell], a collection of paintings, prose, and poetry that Ikeda Shoten issued in 1962. For details, ☞ page 372.

THIS SMALL POETRY COLLECTION—This 1925 poem refers to *Shi hyakuhen* [One Hundred Poems], which Mushakôji himself selected. For data on this book, ☞ page 371.

THOSE ABLE TO ENTER HEAVEN— ☞ TO LIVE IN THE KINGDOM OF GOD. Mushakôji does not use the term "heaven" in any strict Christian sense. His interest is rather in qualifying by proper behavior and hard work to make a paradise on Earth; also ☞ page 28.

THOSE I CAN'T DESPISE—In this poem, and in most statements voicing parallel sentiments, Mushakôji assumes that feelings of love and hate rise unbidden from his heart or innermost self. Because raw feelings never result from conscious decisions but are unconscious, they can't be explained or prescribed. It is a psychological verity that though human beings ought to love and respect each other, some people are easier to love or hate than others. Like almost all feelings, this is inexplicable.

THREE MEN AND A GIRL—Dante Alighieri (1265–1321) is the Florentine poet best known for his classic, *The Divine Comedy*. This masterpiece of world literature, completed in 1321, describes how the Roman poet Virgil • Vergil (70–19 B.C.), author of the epic *Aeneid*, guides Dante through hell and purgatory. The one who escorts Dante through heaven is his lifelong idealized love (possibly Beatrice Portinari [1266–1290], whom he first saw when he was nine). Beatrice may be the girl to whom Mushakôji refers.

THUMBLING—This registers *Issun bôshi* [literally, "the 1"–high monk"], often rendered Tom Thumb, who was however a historical personage. *Issun bôshi* most often refers to a character in a Japanese fairy tale analogous to the Grimm brothers' "Thumbling." ★ *Issun bôshi* also can imply a mean or small-minded person, the sense in which Mushakôji uses it here. He contrasts a spiritual dwarf with no sense of individuality (☞ *hsiao-ren* in GIANT and MALIGNED) with the focused, mature individual.

TITLING REMBRANDT'S PAINTING OF A BEGGAR—For data on the painter, ☞ REMBRANDT (i) • (ii) • (iii). ★ Several small etchings of cripples and beggars date from the late 1620s. In a 1968 study, one critic comments that Rembrandt's outcasts "arouse a feeling of wrath at the plight of man, and it is plain that he identified himself with them...."

TITIAN'S *GIRL IN A FUR*—This painting is from the artist's middle period. For data on the Venetian painter Titian, ☞ VIEWING A TITIAN PAINTING. The woman is the oft-painted model of the painting *La Bella* in a well-known 1536 picture.

TO A CHINESE BROTHER—This doubtless refers to Chou Tso-jên (born 1885; Japanese read Shô Sakujin), who is the younger brother of the celebrated writer Lu Hsün (1881–1936). Chou studied in Japan at Rikkyô University, married a Japanese girl (Hata Nobuko), and taught modern Japanese literature at Beijing University. He was a dedicated supporter of humanistic writers like Mushakôji. ☆ The city of Sochou (Japanese read Soshû), in the southeastern section of Kiangsu • Chiang-su • Jiangsu Province, is not far from Shanghai. Sochou, with a 1965 population of 63,000, serves as a market and distribution center for the surrounding area and hinterland.

TO AMERICA—This wartime work appeared in the January 1944 issue of Mushakôji's magazine, *Bareisho* [Potato]; ☞ SQUASH AND POTATO for contrast with *jagaimo*. The content would be more appropriate to the months immediately before Pearl Harbor. By early 1944—though not all citizens were aware of or would care to admit it—the tide had definitely turned against Japanese forces in the South Pacific theater.

TO LIVE IN THE KINGDOM OF GOD—Mushakôji, whose uncle Kadenokôji Sukekoto introduced him to the Bible when he was in his early teens, gradually gained a degree of familiarity with the eloquent Meiji translation of the Scriptures. He found particular interest in the *Gospel According to St. Matthew*. His later readings of Tolstoy deepened Mushakôji's grasp of the Gospels. Among several other works related to Christian themes, he wrote in 1920 a critical biography of Jesus; ☞ Chronology. ☆ Throughout the corpus we find biblical phrases, images, or references. Mushakôji found in the Scriptures ideas that echoed his personal spiritual commitments. "The kingdom of God" [*kami no kuni*], the key phrase in *Matthew* where it appears 30 times, is an example. This expression implies a concept that—because it resonates with ideal ethical concepts implicit in the Tao—would in no way alienate the mind of many an ancient Chinese philosopher. ☆ The last two lines refer to a passage in Christ's Sermon on the Mount (☞ *Matthew* Chapters 5–7). The King James Version renders them: "And why beholdest thou the mote that is in thy brother's eye, but considerest not the beam that is in thine own eye?" (*Matthew* 7:3 and *Luke* 6:41). The New English Bible renders mote "speck of sawdust" and beam "great plank." ☞ Mushakôji pairs "Than the Malcontent" (page 269) with this work. ☆ For an explanation of *kami* as God, ☞ NOT GOD.

TO MY ELDERS—This title renders *"senpai ni."* In Japan's hierarchical, age-graded society, one's *senpai* are older or have seniority on the job. Even second graders are first graders' *senpai*. We are unlikely to use the term "elders" in that situation. In such a society those who have even a day of seniority have the right to lord it over those less senior than they. ☆ This poem exploits several idiomatic uses of hoops [*taga*], the metal or bamboo rings that secure the staves of a tub or barrel, hold the vessel together, and help keep it from losing its shape. ☜ One idiom based on this image is "loosen the hoops" [*taga o yurumu*], which means to deteriorate or fall apart as a result of aging. When this expression refers to an institution, it suggests a process of growing laxness or deterioration. Another idiom is "remove the hoops" [*taga o hazusu*], which means to eliminate constraints or rules. Professor Iida supplied most of this data. ☆ Hoops metaphorically imply external rules that fence people in or attempt to shape and restrict them.

TO SENKE—For biographical details, ☞ Senke Motomaro.

TO THEIR WORK—Throughout, "Long live" renders *banzai* ["10,000 years"], which is also the original for each "Hurrah!" in line 3 from the end.

TOLSTOY'S WORDS—The Russian writer and philosopher Count Leo (or Lev) Nikolayevic (1828–1910) produced the celebrated novels *War and Peace* (1864–1869) and *Anna Karenina* (1873–1876), among others. Both offer profound psychological insights. Tolstoy's later theories of ethics and morality recommended non-participation in and passive resistance to evil. ✯ From Mushakôji's viewpoint, the salient feature of Tolstoy's thought was his idealism. He believed that ideas shape and determine reality and will help human beings overcome whatever situation they find themselves in. Tolstoy also found human beings susceptible to historical forces. Marx, by contrast, was a materialist who thought that material relationships (one's environment, class, and the like) are the sole determinants of nature, reality, and the human condition.

TWENTY-FIVE YEARS OF THE NEW VILLAGE—For the New Village, founded 1918.11, ☞ NEW VILLAGE. For other background, ☞ page 111 ff. ✯ "Long live" at the end of the poem registers *banzai* • 10,000 years, which might also be translated "Hurrah!"

TWO CALLERS— ① For the New Village and Hyûga in Kyûshû, ☞ NEW VILLAGE, IN HYÛGA'S HILLS, and page 111 ff. The colleagues purchased the land in the fall of 1918 and opened the village on 14 November. ✯ Hirakushi [means flatcomb; some read Hira-gushi] Denchû (1872.02–1979.12) was a renowned wood sculptor born Tanaka Taku-tarô in Ibara, Okayama Prefecture. His native city built and maintains the three-story Denchû Art Museum, opened in 1982. ✎ The Hirakushi family adopted him when he was ten. A year later they apprenticed him to an Ôsaka doll master. Zen Buddhism also influenced him. As his professional name he adopted Denchû, the Chinese pronuncia-tion of Tanaka (the surname of his biological father). ✎ He moved in 1897 to Tokyo, where his work later won many honors. From 1970 till his death at almost 108, he lived in the western suburb of Kodaira, not far from Mushakôji's Chôfu house. Denchû's former Kodaira house is now a museum open to the public since 1984.
   ② Hirakushi carved exquisitely detailed figurines, including classical personages, Zen priests, etc. His larger works range from the 6' high masterpiece, a Nô dancer, in the foyer of the National Theater, to splendidly alive 8.5" tall figures. These include a strik-ing ca. 4' high gilt replica of Yakushi Nyôrai, the Buddha who mitigates suffering. Hirakushi's unpainted figurines demonstrate his ability to make the most of the wood's grain and nature. Some of his painted dolls (ca. 20"–30" high) resemble lifelike minia-ture people. (Professor Nagata Masao kindly supplied much of this data.) ✯ The 102-year-old visitor, Tsue Ichisaku, stopped by on 15 May 1966. Just after World War I, Tsue helped show Mushakôji and colleagues around the Hyûga area. He also advised New Villagers on agricultural methods; ☞ Chronology. ✯ Mushakôji wrote this 1972 poem in January, four months shy of his 87th birthday.

TWO LIONS—The Japanese borrowed the expression *"Nito o ou mono wa itto o ezu"* [He that hunts two hares at once will catch neither] from an ancient Roman proverb. The lesson is "don't bite off more than you can chew" but concentrate on doing well one task at a time. ✯ The British poet, mystic, and artist William Blake (1757–1827) produced paintings and poetic works with an enigmatic, visionary quality. Notice, for example, *Songs of Innocence* (1789) and *The Marriage of Heaven and Hell* (ca. 1790). I have been unable to discover the source of Mushakôji's specific reference to the two lions.

UNOPENABLE DOOR—The first stanza relates to a celebrated passage in Chapter XXI of *Mon* [The Gate, 1914] by Natsume Sôseki (1868–1916). It is hard to imagine that any educated person of Mushakôji's generation might be unfamiliar with this passage. ✎ In this excerpt, Sôseki describes the feelings of Sôsuke, the anti-hero of *Mon*. He had just returned from a Zen temple in Kamakura after a fruitless but wrong-headed search for enlightenment [*satori*]—something one must achieve through personal discipline and effort, that is, with his own strengths [*jiriki*]. ✎ Sôsuke had, however, gone to the temple hoping to have the gate opened *for* him. Of course nobody could open the gate— achieve enlightenment—for him. He had to do it himself. Sôsuke rationalizes that he has been fated to stand forever outside the gate, unable to enter because nobody would respond to his knocking. In a word, he had learned nothing about Zen or *satori.*

VAN GOGH— ① Mystical experiences drove the Dutch post-impressionist painter Vincent Van Gogh (1853–1890) to study theology. He served briefly from 1878.11 as a lay missionary to coal miners who lived under miserable conditions in Borinage, Belgium. His behavior alienated the miners, however, and so his superiors dismissed him in 1879.07. ✦ Early works such as *The Potato Eaters* (1885) portray the dark gloom of peasant life. Van Gogh liked to depict people at work. Three years later, he abandoned somber colors and his work suddenly sparkled with reds, greens, blues, and yellows. He was also an avid admirer of Japanese wood prints. ✦ Bold, rhythmic brush strokes and vivid colors characterize later works, including numerous self-portraits, a series of wonderfully warm and bright sunflower paintings (1888), and the remarkable *Starry Night* (1889). Mushakôji generally rejects the ☞ NEO-IMPRESSIONISTS, who under the leadership of Seurat and Signac urged the use of brilliant colors. Despite his unaccountable rejection of Seurat's brilliance, Mushakôji adored Van Gogh's colorful palette.

② Vincent's long struggle with depression and delirium—he claimed that he painted only to make life bearable—ended in mid-summer of his 37th year. He went behind a manure pile in a nearby farmyard and used a pistol to shoot himself in the stomach. Entirely lucid till the end, he was able to stumble the 200 yards back to his room in an inn where he died 36 hours later. ☞ VAN GOGH'S DRAWING OF A FOUNTAIN and VAN GOGH'S PAINTING OF AN OLD MAN. ✶ Mushakôji finds an interesting difference in the suicides of Van Gogh and General Nogi Maresuke (1849–1912), who became Headmaster at the Gakushûin in 1907, the year after Mushakôji graduated. ✦ The painter's death suggested to him a profound "humanism," none of which he noted in the general's demise. While Mushakôji does not clarify the meaning of this observation, it is obvious that he admired Van Gogh's free choice and individualistic act. By contrast, General Nogi's suicide adhered to the ancient custom of following in death his lord Mutsuhito, the Meiji Emperor—a special suicide called *junshi.* Nogi's act shocked most intellectuals, for they imagined that they lived in a more enlightened age.

VAN GOGH'S DRAWING OF A FOUNTAIN—For data on Van Gogh, ☞ VAN GOGH above. ✶ This 45" x 48" India ink drawing, which dates from 1889, is titled, *In the Garden of the Hospital at Saint-Rémy.* Van Gogh was committed to that hospital between 1889.05 and 1890.05. ✦ Early in 1889 the Arles police seized him and had him incarcerated in a barred cell for dangerous lunatics. Later he was moved at his request to the asylum at Saint-Rémy where he was assigned two rooms, one of which he used for painting. This hospital was originally an Augustinian monastery dating from the 12–13 century. ✶ The shaded fountain in the center of a circular stone pool dominates the picture. The wing that contains Van Gogh's room is visible through the tree to the right rear of the fountain. ✦ A mid-20th century photograph exactly duplicating the picture's perspective reveals that none of the trees around the fountain now remain.

VAN GOGH'S PAINTING OF AN OLD MAN—For biographical details ☞ VAN GOGH. ✦ I am not certain to which painting Mushakôji refers, but it may be the 32" x 25" 1890.05 oil on canvas titled in one version, *Old Man in Sorrow* and in another, *On the Threshold of Eternity.* This painting shows a balding man seated by the hearth, elbows on his thighs, face buried in his hands. Two similar paintings executed in 1882 exist as well. ✶ Van Gogh admired the French painter of rural scenes and peasant life, Jean-François Millet (1814–1875), born into a poor farming family. Millet's moderately dark colors and gloomy atmosphere were early influences. In fact, Van Gogh copied several Millet pictures as exercises. ✦ Millet always drew from memory and never directly from nature.

To this day, he continues to be admired for the straight-forward technique, simple mood, and the ennobled ambience of his paintings—especially those that captured the spirit of 17th century French peasants, whom he often depicted at work. Millet also developed a spontaneous sketching technique that exhibited power similar to (and which some regard as far less sentimental than) what his paintings achieved. ★ One critic finds Millet's figures "emanations of the soil." A different scholar says of *Man with a Hoe* (1858+), "The fusion of man and his tool…has never before been more cogently expressed." These statements provide ample reasons why Mushakôji finds Millet's work of interest. ✦ I cannot identify Millet's painting of a weeping woman.

VIEWING A BOURDELLE PAINTING—The career of the prolific French sculptor, painter, and designer Emile Antoine Bourdelle (1861–1929) was influenced by ☞ RODIN, whose assistant he became in 1890. ✦ Bourdelle was preoccupied with the relation between architecture and sculpture. Many of his works are judged flamboyant. Bourdelle also produced ceramics, drawings, and illustrations. ✦ A romantic sculpture of Beethoven with wind-swept hair was an early success. The musician was one of his favorite subjects for busts (Bourdelle did at least 21 likenesses of him). ★ Mushakôji and his ☞ SHIRAKABA associates take credit for making Rodin's work known in Japan through the pages of the *Shirakaba*. ★ I cannot identify this painting of a woman in the wind.

VIEWING A RENOIR NUDE—The French impressionist painter Pierre Auguste Renoir (1841– 1919) took up sculpture after 1913. Aware of his gift for drawing, his father apprenticed him to a porcelain maker. Under his guidance, the boy decorated plates. Renoir's savings paid his tuition at an art school (1862), where Claude Monet (1840–1926) was a classmate. ✦ After 1874 Renoir did a series of female nudes "bathed in translucent and dissolving light." He painted far too many nudes to identify this painting. ★ A talented artist invests far less time and energy in a work than one with vastly inferior skills. Mushakôji's un-talented painting is thus "worth" more than Renoir's.

VIEWING A TITIAN PAINTING—The Italian-Venetian painter Tiziano Vecellio • Vecelli (ca. 1485–1576) ranks among the chief artists of the Renaissance. At nine he was sent to Venice as a painter's apprentice. Before long he was being commissioned by churches to paint frescoes and execute various religious works. By the next decade, his portraits become more sumptuous with fine tonal gradations. ☞ TITIAN'S *GIRL IN A FUR.*

VIEWING LIANG K'AI'S *DANCING HOTEI* (i) • (ii)— ☞ LIANG K'AI. The Chinese hermit-priest Hotei ["Cloth Sack"] lived during the T'ang Dynasty and died in 917. The Japanese designate him one of the seven Gods of Fortune and invariably portray him with a huge pot belly and a smiling face. ✦ Considered the god of contentment and happiness, Hotei carries a large cloth bag around with him (thus his name). The sack holds his few possessions as well as the fortunes for those who believe in his virtues.

WATER—Perhaps water is the favorite Taoist metaphor of the power of the un-willed and of being natural. Despite a lack of intentionality, water is capable of achieving all things simply by being itself, simply by seeking its level. ★ In the fifth century B.C. the Taoist philosopher Lao Tzu put it succinctly in this description of water's power and symbolism: "What is of all things most yielding / can overcome that which is most hard. / Being substanceless, it can enter in / even where there is no crevice. / That is how I know the value / of action which is actionless. / But that there can be a teaching without words, / value in action which is actionless, / few indeed can understand." ✦ Lao Tzu also said, "[the truth] that the yielding conquers the resistant and the soft conquers the hard is a fact known by all men, yet utilized by none...."

WHEN I'M WORKING—In line 5 I freely translate *osejiwarai* [a flattering smile] as "inviting smile." Professor Iida points out that Mushakôji's usage is somewhat peculiar. *Osejiwarai* invariably assumes a conscious or manipulative act, not possible for a baby.

WHEN I'M WRITING POETRY—Shinko, Mushakôji's oldest daughter, was born in December 1923. He published this poem exactly a year later. ★ The *engawa* is too narrow and too specifically a Japanese structural element to justify rendering it porch or verandah. This wood-floored corridor (some 3'–5' wide) runs along the sunny south side of a traditional Japanese home. Sliding glass doors separate the *engawa* from the yard or garden. These doors are usually shuttered at night with sliding wooden panels [*amado* • rain doors]. ☞ SHÔJI (sliding doors or windows covered with rice paper and hence translucent) customarily separate the *engawa* from the family's living space.

WHEN PAN PLAYS HIS PIPES—Pan is the pastoral god charged with assuring the fertility of woods, fields, and flocks. He made his pipes or flutes from the hollow stems of reeds. ⭰ Playing his pipes connects with pining for lost love. Pan wanted to ravage the nymph Syrinx. To escape the hideous Pan—who had a human face, a hairy body, and the legs, horns, and ears of a goat—Syrinx begged the gods for help. They facilitated her escape by transforming her into a bed of reeds. Pan used these reeds to make his instrument. ⭰ Pipes of different length are connected with the even ends open, uneven ends plugged. The player generates sound by blowing across the openings. Other names include mouth organ, panpipe, and syrinx (in honor of the nymph). Historians claim that this instrument is actually of Chinese origin.

WHITMAN (i) • (ii) • (iii)— ① The American poet Walt Whitman (1819–1892) published *Leaves of Grass* in 1855. This collection—a monument to unconventional non-metered and un-rhymed verse—celebrates the self, death as a process of life, universal brotherhood, love for common people and workers, the excellence of democracy, and love for America. ⭰ Whitman's father, a Long Island carpenter and builder, communicated to Walt a respect for democracy and the inner life. In his youth he was apprenticed to a printer, later taught in schools (1836–1841), then dabbled in journalism. Despite his radical and independent opinions, some found the young Whitman dandified. This foppish impression changed suddenly in 1850 at age 31 when he grew a beard. He then emerged as the Whitman we recognize: the prophetic bard of an ideal America.
② Ralph Waldo Emerson (1803–1882) and Henry David Thoreau (1817–1862) both perceived the genius and ground-breaking nature of *Leaves of Grass*. Most commentators, however, belittled the book's free-wheeling structure and diffuse language. Though Whitman's diction is full of physicality, far from genteel, and uniformly "unpoetic" in any traditional sense, one critic thought it bristled with "oceanic energies." ⭰ Whitman's confidence that whoever "touches this [book] touches a man" echoes Mushakôji's beliefs that verse constitutes a record of his inner self; ☞ page 364, No. 3. Most of Whitman's "Song of Myself" must have struck sympathetic chords in Mushakôji, who had similar hopes to recover the innocence, the self-reliance, and the unselfish love (☞ page 114 ff.) that idealists fondly imagine characterized primal man. ★ (iii)—For William Blake, ☞ TWO LIONS; ☞ REMBRANDT (i) • (ii) • (iii). ★ Could the 13,600 figure relate to the number of supporters of the New Village?

WHO IS MY FATHER?—Mushakôji was 2.5 years old when his father died in 1887. He was 43.5 when his mother died in 1928. Some statements are clearly not factual.

WITH ANOTHER'S FLUTE—The flute is a metaphor for poet or artist; ☞ PLAYING THE FLUTE.

WITHOUT GOD—For an explanation of the Japanese term *kami*, ☞ NOT GOD.

WONDERS OF THE SUN—Related works "Sun" and "Sun and Moon" follow on page 100. ★ The graphs for Hyûga, the site of the New Village in Kyûshû, also contains the character for sun; ☞ IN HYÛGA'S HILLS and SUNFLOWERS IN OUR VILLAGE.

WU CHUN'S *HOTEI*—Wu-chun Shi-fan (?1177–1249), a Rinzai Zen monk active during the Southern Sung dynasty, was invited in 1233 to lecture to the Chinese Emperor. Mushakôji confesses in a note that he does not completely understand Wu's lines in the first stanza (they appear in the painting directly above Hotei, where Wu centered the four lines). ↖ What most impresses Mushakôji, however, are the consummate skills of these ancient Zen monk painters. The depiction of Hotei worshipping the moon also suggests a commitment to the laws of the universe. For the poet, this symbolizes the unity of mind and matter. ★ A 3" x 1.75" reproduction of this miniature appears with the poem, ☞ MSZS:XI:172. ★ On Hotei, ☞ VIEWING LIANG K'AI'S *DANCING HOTEI*.

YEAR TWO OF THE GREATER EAST ASIA WAR—A note at the end of the poem indicates that this February 1943 work first appeared in the *Manshû Shinbun* [Manchurian Newspaper]. ★ By May 1942, Japan controlled a vast area from Burma through the Netherlands Indies (including the Philippines and Indo-China), to the northern shores of New Guinea, through the Solomon and Gilbert Islands in the South Pacific, and then due north to Kiska and Attu at the tip of the Aleutians. ↖ In early June 1942, the Japanese Navy suffered grievous losses of aircraft and carriers at the Battle of Midway. By the time this poem appeared, Guadalcanal in the Solomons had been wrested from Japanese control. The Japanese public was largely unaware of the crippling effect the losses at Midway had on Japan's air and sea power. From the people's view, the Empire was intact and Japan's glorious armies still invincible.

APPENDIX I

CHRONOLOGICAL LISTING OF THE POEMS

This appendix allows one to read the poems in the order they appeared. I alphabetize the titles in groupings where all poems appeared in the same month. Poems with no month appear after those that list a month. A question mark after a date (e.g., 1926?) indicates an estimate based on the known publication dates of nearby poems. I insert these items at the end of each year grouping. All dates I derive from *Mushakôji Saneatsu Zenshû* [Mushakôji Saneatsu, Works], Volume XI. Parentheses enclose the source of each poem in the *Works*, Volume XI. After the bullet or raised period stands the page number for each translation in *Long Corridor*.

✦   ✦   ✦

1908.01—Love Tragedy (XI:182) • 167
1909.09—Autumn has Come (XI:4) • 164
1909.10—Feeling Lonely (XI:4) • 164
1909.10—Like a Tortoise (XI:5) • 85
1909.10—Loneliness (i) (XI:232) • 63
1909.10—Long Corridor (XI:5) • 55
1910.04—Lean on Me (XI:184) • 166

1911.04—Genius and Artiste (XI:187) • 186
1911.04—Gossip (XI:186) • 55
1911.04—I'm Made of Steel (XI:186) • 66
1911.04—Rumors about Him (XI:188) • 56
1911.05—Critic and Painter (XI:189) • 213
1911.05—Dostoyevski's Face (XI:12) • 77
1911.05—Master! Master! (XI:11) • 107
1911.05—My Present Work (XI:9) • 155
1911.05—Rhapsodizing on My Birthday (XI:6) • 91
1911.05—Substitute Foreword (XI:188) • 220
1911.05—Three Men and a Girl (XI:11) • 163
1911.06—Critics' Disdain (XI:190) • 215
1911.06—I Feel like Laughing (XI:6) • 60
1911.07—Death (XI:10) • 85
1911.07—Eggshell (XI:13) • 77
1911.07—Fountain's Lament (XI:14) • 107
1911.07—Giant (i) (XI:13) • 78
1911.07—God's Will (XI:12) • 266
1911.07—Hodler (XI:12) • 211
1911.07—Japan Brims with Hope (XI:13) • 274
1911.07—Loneliness (ii) (XI:12) • 63
1911.07—Van Gogh (XI:11) • 210
1911.07—Whitman (i) (XI:11) • 229
1912.12—Lord of the Castle (XI:15) • 76

1913.04—For Me (XI:194) • 66
1913.08—Angler's Soliloquy (XI:194) • 130

1913.08—Giver (XI:195) • 132
1913.93—To My Wife (XI:192) • 69
1913?—What the Genius Said (XI:193) • 81
1914.03—I (i) (XI:197) • 61
1914.03—My Friend (XI:196) • 159
1914.03—To My Mind (XI:16) • 60
1914.04—They (XI:15) • 107
1914.04—To My Elders (XI:15) • 82
1914.04—To the Critic (XI:15) • 216
1915.04—Rembrandt (i) (XI:21) • 206
1915.05—Spring (XI:22) • 165
1915.08—That Lion (XI:201) • 87
1917.04—Song of the Visionary (XI:206) • 100
1917.09—Sordid Poem (XI:22) • 220
1917.10—Friend (XI:239) • 159
1917.10—Joy (XI:22) • 107
1917.10—Joy of Friendship (XI:205) • 159
1918.12—America's Wilson (XI:214) • 275
1918.12—Japan Has Been Left Behind (XI:214) • 275
1919.06—God and Humankind (i) (XI:217) • 262
1919.06—To a Chinese Brother (XI:217) • 167
1919.06—Whitman (ii) (XI:466) • 229
1919.09—Machines and People (XI:219) • 155

1920.01—God (i) (XI:221) • 261
1920.02—Six Songs of Work (XI:222) • 141
1920.03—Chinese (XI:224) • 169
1920.03—How Describe God? (XI:224) • 240
1920.04—At the Workshop (XI:224) • 137
1920.04—Be Honest (XI:223) • 105
1920.04—Beautiful Flowers (XI:24) • 73
1920.04—Big Ship (XI:230) • 104
1920.04—Big Tree (XI:25) • 213
1920.04—Buddha (XI:26) • 75
1920.04—Buddha's Gospel (XI:230) • 262
1920.04—Child (XI:27) • 58
1920.04—Death's Desolation (XI:225) • 85
1920.04—Flowers (XI:23) • 74
1920.04—Forgetting God (XI:26) • 263
1920.04—Foundation (XI:229) • 117
1920.04—From Childhood (XI:23) • 58
1920.04—However (XI:225) • 85
1920.04—In Earnest (i) (XI:24) • 246
1920.04—Loved by God (XI:24) • 253
1920.04—My Work (i) (XI:223) • 155
1920.04—My Work (ii) (XI:231) • 156
1920.04—One Called God (XI:225) • 261
1920.04—One Who Saw God (XI:28) • 241
1920.04—Rather than People (XI:223) • 262
1920.04—To a Friend (XI:231) • 172
1920.04—To Talk of Myself (XI:25) • 60
1920.04—Well, All Right (XI:24) • 59

1920.04—Well, Me Too (XI:25) • 62
1920.04—What You Write (XI:227) • 226
1920.04—Worthless Pouch (XI:25) • 231
1920.04—Write • Cultivate the Land (XI:23) • 143

1920.05—Good Brothers and Sisters (XI:235) • 170
1920.05—His Children (XI:234) • 173
1920.05—In Concert (XI:236) • 138
1920.05—In the Kingdom of God (i) (XI:295) • 246
1920.05—Sapling and Spring (XI:28) • 71
1920.05—Skylark (XI:250) • 223
1920.05—To a Chinese (XI:236) • 169
1920.06—God and Humankind (ii) (XI:243) • 263
1920.06—I (ii) (XI:30) • 62
1920.06—Song of a Gigantic Tree (XI:29) • 70
1920.07—Artists (XI:248) • 271
1920.07—Beautiful Woman (XI:249) • 69
1920.07—Endless Rain (XI:263) • 72
1920.07—Fire From a Single Match (XI:248) • 138
1920.07—I'm a Standard-Bearer (XI:264) • 139
1920.07—Lots and Lots of Poets (XI:263) • 217
1920.07—Maligned (XI:260) • 56
1920.07—My Work (iii) (XI:249) • 156
1920.07—Naturally (XI:249) • 254
1920.07—New Life (XI:246) • 67
1920.07—New Village (i) (XI:255) • 146
1920.07—New Village (ii) (XI:258) • 146
1920.07—Only to the Right (XI:261) • 216
1920.07—Reading Hodler's Biography (XI:264) • 211
1920.07—Water (XI:262) • 102
1920.07—When My Heart is Pure (XI:259) • 247
1920.07—Tasks I Cannot Do (XI:249) • 157

1920.09—Being True to God (XI:273) • 262
1920.09—Does God Exist? (i) (XI:273) • 240
1920.09—God's Love (i) (XI:276) • 253
1920.09—In the Kingdom of God (ii) (XI:274) • 173
1920.09—Leave Everything to God (XI:275) • 273
1920.09—Not God (XI:273) • 260
1920.09—Oh, God (i) (XI:271) • 266
1920.09—Oh, God (ii) (XI:271) • 266
1920.09—Seek the Kingdom of God (XI:269) • 120
1920.09—Those Able to Enter Heaven (XI:274) • 273
1920.11—Always in the Village (XI:285) • 148
1920.11—In the Village (XI:285) • 270
1920.11—My Work (iv) • (XI:279) • 156
1920.11—Playing the Flute (XI:43) • 221
1920.11—To Senke (XI:286) • 227
1920.11—Village Air (XI:285) • 148
1920.12—Rivers Flow (XI:288) • 254
1920.12—Traveler! (XI:287) • 105

1920.00—God (ii) (XI:30) • 261
1920.00—Growth (XI:33) • 62
1920.00—In Earnest (ii) (XI:39) • 154
1920.00—Love (i) (XI:42) • 174
1920.00—My Visions (XI:38) • 144
1920.00—Neither a Sage . . . (XI:39) • 63
1920.00—New World (XI:255) • 108
1920.00—No Matter What (XI:34) • 62
1920.00—One More Step (XI:33) • 254
1920.00—People (XI:267) • 246
1920.00—People Compelled to Work (XI:37) • 118
1920.00—People of the Future (XI:35) • 118
1920.00—People of the Past (XI:36) • 117
1920.00—Slaves of Toil (XI:267) • 137
1920.00—Someone Said (XI:266) • 67
1920.00—Talented (XI:238) • 138
1920.00—Than this Path (XI:40) • 254
1920.00—This Mission (XI:276) • 146
1920.00—To Someone (XI:37) • 166
1920.00—Toil (i) (XI:267) • 138
1920.00—Toil (ii) (XI:267) • 138
1920.00—We (XI:36) • 118
1920.00—We're a Grove of Cedars (XI:40) • 71
1920?—Believe Me (XI:280) • 64
1920?—Idealist Who Walks Testing a Stone Bridge (XI:280) • 100
1920?—Without God (XI:280) • 240

1921.01—Build It! (XI:288) • 151
1921.01—Village Doctor (XI:291) • 149
1921.02—God (iii) (XI:44) • 261
1921.02—On this Day Jesus Was Born (XI:44) • 268
1921.05—God's Love (ii) (XI:301) • 253
1921.05—I Respect (i) (XI:301) • 64
1921.05—New Village (iii) (XI:299) • 271
1921.05—New Village (iv) • (XI:299) • 273
1921.05—Self-Reliant (XI:298) • 270
1921.05—Sun and Moon (KK:12:36 [1st part, XI:14]) • 102
1921.07—To Live in the Kingdom of God (XI:308) • 269
1921.07—Someone Like Me (XI:308) • 171
1921.07—Sun (XI:307) • 101
1921.07—Than the Malcontent (XI:308) • 269
1921.08—I Believe (XI:314) • 64
1921.00—When I Was Ailing (XI:297) • 159
1921.00—Trees in the Rain (XI:319) • 72

1922.02—Does God Exist? (ii) (XI:323) • 240
1922.03—I'm a Worker (XI:348) • 135
1922.04—To Be Loved (XI:317) • 167
1922.04—With Love and Gratitude (XI:318) • 170
1922.05—New Village (v) • (XI:328) • 146
1922.05—Your Work (XI:330) • 140
1922.06—Apple Trees and Pear Trees (XI:334) • 91

1922.11—After a Fit of Anger (XI:334) • 173
1922.11—My Mind (XI:335) • 83
1922.11—Rembrandt's Etching of Faust (XI:334) • 208
1922.11—When I Was a Child (i) (XI:335) • 57

1923.01—Pine Trying to be a Cedar (XI:336) • 71
1923.01—Seeds I Sowed (XI:336) • 132
1923.02—Those I Can't Despise (XI:325) • 173
1923.03—Aged Rembrandt (XI:47) • 207
1923.03—New Village (vi) (XI:340) • 147
1923.03—*Return of Tobias* (XI:48) • 207
1923.03—Tolstoy's Words (XI:340) • 77
1923.04—Bookshop (XI:337) • 104
1923.04—One Hundred Eggs (XI:339) • 157
1923.05—However Fine the Instrument (XI:49) • 224
1923.05—Flies (XI:343) • 88
1923.05—Humanity (XI:343) • 107
1923.05—Two Women (XI:342) • 69
1923.05—When Pan Plays his Pipes (XI:342) • 221
1923.06—Comical Couple (XI:344) • 171
1923.06—Song of a Mountaineer (XI:346) • 134
1923.07—Chinese Painting (XI:50) • 196
1923.07—Death's Dread (XI:49) • 84
1923.07—Sexual Desire (i) (XI:346) • 163
1923.07—Things I Cannot Do (XI:352) • 142
1923.07—When He Works (XI:50) • 143

1923.08—Buddha and Jesus (XI:351) • 262
1923.08—I'm a Huge Rock (XI:353) • 62
1923.08—I'm an Egotist (XI:350) • 63
1923.08—Work with My Pen (XI:350) • 219
1923.09—Creativity (XI:356) • 226
1923.09—Fleet-footed Rumors (XI:344) • 56
1923.11—Lofty Aspirations (XI:52) • 67
1923.00—Because He Wrote a Poem (XI:330) • 226
1923.00—Closing My Eyes (XI:51) • 74
1923.00—Does God Exist? (iii) (XI:327) • 241
1923.00—In the Typhoon (XI:327) • 103

1924.01—Where is God? (XI:381) • 268
1924.03—People I Respect (XI:365) • 65
1924.03—Sleeping Lion (XI:367) • 87
1924.04—Luther Burbank (XI:373) • 139
1924.04—When You Want to do Two Things at Once (XI:361) • 121
1924.05—Eve (XI:364) • 68
1924.05—Mud (XI:364) • 211
1924.05—Volcano (XI:362) • 75
1924.05—What We Call the City (XI:361) • 108
1924.06—Florist (XI:369) • 75
1924.06—*Go* Master (XI:358) • 215
1924.06—Good Instruments (XI:371) • 224
1924.06—Musical Instrument (XI:371) • 224

1924.06—Neo-Impressionists (XI:369) • 196
1924.06—Parents (XI:370) • 58
1924.06—Infant's Joy (XI:373) 57•
1924.08—King of the Hill (XI:374) • 63
1924.08—Nouveau Riche (XI:376) • 106
1924.08—What the Fly Told the Lion (XI:374) • 87
1924.08—Why Love One Person? (XI:358) • 162
1924.10—Dürer's *St. Jerome* (XI:394) • 271
1924.10—Flowing River (XI:382) • 103
1924.10—Others' Sense of Independence (XI:395) • 120
1924.10—People With Tails (XI:394) • 231
1924.11—At the New Village (XI:396) • 148
1924.12—Doing My Work (XI:392) • 119
1924.12—Fine Work of Art (XI:390) • 192
1924.12—Government Officials (XI:390) • 76
1924.12—I Adore Fall (XI:396) • 74
1924.12—If They Don't Work (XI:394) • 119
1924.12—Lenin's Embalmed Remains (XI:390) • 77
1924.12—Ludicrous Folks (XI:392) • 214
1924.12—When I'm Working (XI:395) • 143
1924.12—When I'm Writing Poetry (XI:392) • 119

1925.01—Jesus and St. Francis (XI:385) • 273
1925.01—To Their Work (XI:398) • 270
1925.01—Within Me (XI:400) • 129
1925.02—Giant (ii) (XI:57) • 78
1925.03—Kinoshita! (XI:403) • 227
1925.03—To the Dentist (XI:401) • 275
1925.04—Revolutionary (XI:408) • 130
1925.05—To Fate (XI:411) • 274
1925.06—From the New Village (XI:414) • 147
1925.06—When I Was a Child (ii) (XI:418) • 58
1925.07—In Hyûga's Hills (XI:419) • 145
1925.07—Watching Fish Swim (XI:418) • 90
1925.08—Giant Appeared (XI:427) • 80
1925.08—Giant's Calligraphy (XI:428) • 226
1925.08—This Small Poetry Collection (XI:431) • 217
1925.10—Even in Japan (XI:432) • 276
1925.11—Arrow Shooter (XI:55) • 225
1925.00—Whenever I see a Japanese Movie (XI:414) • 103

1926.07—Hendrickje! (XI:52) • 208
1926.07—To Japan (XI:360) • 276
1926.00—Mary Magdalene (XI:424) • 68
1926.00—Purse (XI:424) • 104
1926?—Man Fishes (XI:57) • 91
1927.06—Van Gogh's Painting of an Old Man (XI:445) • 210
1927.07—Painting Pictures (XI:444) • 191
1927.09—I'm a Bell (XI:445) • 247
1927.09—On a Painting of Soy Beans (XI:445) • 184
1927.09—Titling a Sketch of an Apple (XI:56) • 186
1927.00—Giant's Footprint (XI:59) • 80

1927.00—Unopenable Door (XI:61) • 154
1928.01—Good Script (XI:456) • 130
1928.01—Growth Potential (XI:448) 151•
1928.01—I Dare (XI:456) • 232
1928.01—On My Desk (XI:456) 127
1928.01—Incoherent Picture (XI:456) • 212
1928.05—Lost Titles (XI:57) • 230
1928.05—In China Mu Ch'i (XI:450) • 203
1928.05—In My Tiny Room (XI:450) • 191
1928.09—Wild Geese and Drakes in the Zoo (XI:451) • 90
1928.11—Devoted Critic (XI:453) • 216
1928.11—Work (XI:454) • 120
1928.11—World of Cooperation (XI:455) • 145

1929.01—Artist and Critic (XI:57) • 213
1929.01—I Simply (XI:461) • 216
1929.01—One Critic (XI:461) • 215
1929.01—One Painter (XI:461) • 215
1929.01—To Critics (XI:461) • 216
1929.02—If You Break Every Oil Lamp (XI:462) • 105
1929.06—Courbet (XI:466) • 209
1929.06—Daumier (XI:467) • 209
1929.06—Delacroix (XI:467) • 209
1929.07—Sexual Desire (ii) (XI:468) • 163
1929.09—Visionary (XI:468) • 100
1930.02—Work Alone (XI:470) • 117
1930.08—Romance and Work (XI:493) • 164
1931.02—Age of Adversity for the Race Horse (XI:472) • 89
1931.02—Aged Toilers (XI:472) • 121
1931.04—Sexual Desire and Love (XI:474) • 163
1931.04—Viewing a Renoir Nude (XI:474) • 209
1931.06—Rembrandt (iii) (XI:476) • 206
1931.08—Giants Only Walk (XI:76) • 79

1933.01—Self-Admonitions When I Paint (XI:477) • 187
1933.02—Whitman (iii) (XI:479) • 229
1933.03—Horse Deprived of Liberty (XI:477) • 89
1933.03—I'm a Patriot (XI:479) • 276
1933.03—Weary Fellow (XI:477) • 185
1933.05—One Reed Leaf (XI:481) • 204
1933.06—Rembrandt (ii) (XI:68) • 206
1933.06—Things I'd Like to Write (XI:67) • 218
1934.02—Study (XI:70) • 104
1934.03—Two Horses (XI:69) • 88
1934.03—Two Lions (XI:69) • 86
1934.07—Desk and Cot (XI:483) • 126
1934.07—Angry Lion (XI:70) • 87
1934.07—Life's Work (XI:70) • 155
1934.07—Thumbling (XI:70) • 155
1935.01—Viewing a Bourdelle Painting (XI:484) • 210
1935—Man (XI:85) • 94
1935?—Giant (iii) (XI:73) • 78

1936.06—Expert Archers (XI:488) • 225
1936.08—Joy of Seeing a Fine Picture (XI:76) • 186
1936.08—Viewing a Titian Painting (XI:94) • 205
1936.11—Many Hardships (XI:489) • 83
1936.11—On a Train to San Francisco (XI:116) • 83
1936.12—Real Person (XI:116) • 60
1936.00—Time Passes Fast (XI:488) • 82
1936 • 1940—From My Three Children (XI:498) • 82
1937.04—Nature's Eye (XI:490) • 74
1937.04—Titling Rembrandt's Painting of a Beggar (XI:490) • 207
1938.00—God and Satan (XI:491) • 267
1938.00—Love that Conquers Death (XI:491) • 253
1939.03—Grim Reaper (XI:78) • 84
1939.03—Mountaineering (XI:78) • 188
1939.03—Tessai (XI:78) • 204
1939.07—Dedicated to God (XI:494) • 266
1939.12—New Village (vii) (XI:495) • 147
1939.00—Efforts (XI:555) • 153
1939.00—Man Painting a Mountain (XI:556) • 187
1939.00—Squash and Potato (XI:556) • 182
1939?—For the Mountain Climber (XI:79) • 135

1940.11—Canary that Forgot Its Song (XI:522) • 121
1940.00—Broad-Minded Man (XI:499) • 105
1940.00—Gentle Rain (XI:498) • 73
1940.00—Giant Advances (XI:496) • 79
1940.00—Path to Triumph (XI:500) • 274
1941.05—In Praise of Potatoes (XI:108) • 183
1941.10—Viewing Liang K'ai's *Dancing Hotei* (i) (XI:95) • 197
1941.11—Man on the Flute (XI:111) • 221
1941.11—We're a Mass of Steel (XI:507) • 277
1941?—Painting Vegetables (XI:83) • 181
1941?—People I Like (XI:114) • 65
1941?—Self and Others (XI:114) • 106
1941?—Stringless Harp (XI:114) • 242
1942.01—Daily Renewal (XI:114) • 143
1942.04—Moral Principle (XI:518) • 65
1942.04—Surrender of Singapore (XI:507) • 277
1942.10—Some Dozen of Us (XI:510) • 149
1942.10—Titian's *Girl in a Fur* (XI:510) • 205
1942.00—Man who Works Earnestly (XI:511) • 153
1942.00—Objects I'd Like to Paint (XI:512) • 188
1942.00—Painter (XI:106) • 184
1942.00—Still Life (XI:81) • 186
1942 • 1957—Potato (i) (XI:104) • 183

1943.02—Year Two of the Great East Asian War (XI:507) • 279
1943.12—Our Warriors Advance on Attu (XI:514) • 281
1943.12—Twenty-Five Years of the New Village (XI:515) • 150
1944.01—To America (XI:517) • 277
1944.00—Artist and a Frog (XI:100) • 190
1944.00—Day by Day (XI:101) • 154

1944.00—Two on a Mountaintop (XI:102) • 231
1945.00—Shiga and I (XI:97) • 161
1945.00—Two-Horse Cart (XI:98) • 89
1945.00—Viewing Liang K'ai's *Dancing Hotei* (ii) (XI:95) • 198
1946.00—I Praise Mu Ch'i and Liang K'ai (XI:117) • 201
1947.04—Van Gogh's Drawing of a Fountain (XI:523) • 211
1947.00—Preface Poem (XI:89) • 219
1948.04—Motomaro's Death (XI:524) • 228
1948.08—Senke Motomaro (XI:524) • 228
1948.11—Stone by the Wayside (XI:525) • 224
1948.00—Poem of an Old Painter (XI:525) • 190
1948.00—Stars in the Heavens (XI:528) • 172
1948.00—Wolf and Sheep (XI:528) • 86
1949.01—Stone, Stone (XI:528) • 106
1949.04—Poet of the Seas and the Skies (XI:526) • 223
1949.11—Joys of Painting Pictures (XI:522) • 189

1950.03—Dying to Paint a Picture (XI:536) • 182
1950.03—I'm a Painter (XI:535) • 190
1950.03—Old Hen (XI:535) • 86
1951.00—Beautiful World We Desire (XI:534) • 158
1951.00—I Can Do It, I Can Do It (XI:536) • 66
1951.00—Joy of Work (XI:91) • 122
1951.00—You and I are Beautiful (XI:95) • 65
1958.11—New Village Greets its Fortieth Year (XI:540) • 150
1959.05—Morning of My Seventy-Fourth Birthday (XI:541) • 94
1959.09—Who is My Father? (XI:541) • 59
1959.12—More I Paint (XI:543) • 124
1959.12—One of My Paintings Sold (XI:544) • 192
1960.01—I'm a Pine (XI:548) • 71
1960.01—Three Cooks (XI:548) • 133
1961.09—Whatever I Observe (XI:551) • 212
1961.10—Impaired Painter (XI:552) • 189
1961.10—My Shell (XI:551) • 66
1961.10—Silence (i) (XI:553) • 75
1961.10—This Book (XI:551) • 217

1962.06—Leonardo da Vinci's Lilies (XI:554) • 205
1962.09—Liang K'ai (XI:560) • 197
1962.09—Mu Ch'i's Picture of Persimmons (XI:561) • 204
1962.00—Potato (ii) (XI:553) • 183
1962.00—Silence (ii) (XI:554) • 186
1963.00—I Respect (ii) (XI:559) • 64
1963.00—In this World (XI:557) • 133
1963.00—New Year (XI:560) • 140
1963.00—Stroke of Luck (XI:560) • 131
1964.11—Optimist Meets the Optimistic Creator (XI:133) • 242
1964.12—Health (XI:565) • 96
1965.03—My Prayer (XI:136) • 247
1965.04—Teardrop (XI:141) • 254
1965.06—Vision? (XI:571) • 99
1965.11—Pure People (XI:166) • 263

1965?—*Hotei*, Attributed to Mu Ch'i (XI:172) • 198
1965?—Liang K'ai's *Harpist Under a Pine* (XI:170) • 200
1965?—Sesshû's *Thunderbolts* (XI:174) • 123
1965?—Wu Chun's *Hotei* (XI:171) • 199

1966.06—Genuine and Lovable People (XI:578) • 170
1966.00—Since Childhood (XI:573) • 58
1966.00—Two Men (XI:567) • 212
1966.00—With Another's Flute (XI:574) • 223
1967.01—Listening to the Piano (XI:580) • 272
1967.05—Living and Working (XI:582) • 156
1968.04—Two Human Types (XI:596) • 246
1968.07—Sunflowers in Our Village (XI:600) • 151
1968.10—Old Man on Life's Superexpress (XI:602) • 97
1969.03—Mommy (XI:607) • 69
1969.00—Son of My Father, My Mother (XI:183) • 59
1969.00—Transitional Period (XI:183) • 108
1970?—Me of Words (HS:I:7) • 8

1971.02—Fresh Painting (XI:622) • 185
1971.11—As Long as I'm Alive (XI:625) • 162
1971.11—Old Painter (XI:624) • 127
1972.01—Two Callers (XI:629) • 99
1972.05—At Eighty-Eight (XI:631) • 95
1972.06—My Eighty-Seventh Birthday (XI:631) • 95
1972.00—Lovable People (XI:627) • 170
1973.02—My Desk (XI:634) • 126
1973.07—Hemp Palm (XI:637) • 125
1974.01—When I Paint (XI:641) • 194
1975.02—Old Man's Dreams (XI:651) • 96
1975.06—Wonders of the Sun (XI:653) • 101
1975.09—Clay Figurine — *Haniwa* (XI:655) • 106
1975.12—Love (ii) (XI:655) • 174

APPENDIX II

VIEWS OF MUSHAKÔJI'S WORK

The following entries present views that an older, prewar generation of Japanese critics or literary figures offer of Mushakôji and his work. From seven to nineteen years younger than he, all are near contemporaries. I arrange the remarks by seniority, the oldest critic first. From each I select several mostly positive statements. These observations are not limited to the poetry. In several cases, moreover, I have willy-nilly culled the remarks from several different sources.

✦   ✦   ✦

(1) **The poet and novelist Satô Haruo** (1892–1964) thought Mushakôji had the ability to inspire the reader's heart. The surfaces of his work, however, look extremely jejune and empty. This, Satô claimed, urged many observers to consider much of Mushakôji's canon simple-mindedly childish. That justifies their rejecting him outright as a serious author. Probably no novelist was as laughed at in the early days of his career. Mushakôji nevertheless writes quite sensitively and has a clear grasp of the laws of nature. He is relentlessly idealistic and optimistic, yet he later won a degree of popularity.

Satô claims that no one in all Japanese literature displays as clearly as Mushakôji the unity between speech and writing. In his time there was, indeed, a huge gap between the printed word and what passed in fiction as "natural conversation." Many of his works produced snickers because he collapsed this gap and produced true-to-life dialogue. Mushakôji was a pioneer in the use of such natural, everyday conversational expressions as *ki ga suru* [I feel like..., one feels that..., I'm in the mood for...; cf. page 40].

Mushakôji believed that art derives from the heart, not the head—from man's intuitive not from his logical faculties. Although it quite taxes one's patience trying to read his collected works, Satô thinks that few will tire of individual selections. In shorter works extraneous detail and repetitive observations do not cloud Mushakôji's sincerity. He has shown with unrivaled earnestness how someone in the arts might respect individuality and still allow the subjective to dominate. No writer has been imitated on these points as often as he.

Satô believes that we can compare Mushakôji's appearance in Japanese literary circles with the emergence in the history of modern thought of the Swiss-French philosopher and moralist Jean Jacques Rousseau (1712–1778). Mushakôji, like Rousseau, held that people are essentially good until corrupted by a society that does not allow its citizens to realize their well being and achieve liberty. Rousseau's approach to education similarly stressed developing innate qualities rather than cramming students' heads with countless facts devoid of understanding.

(2) **The novelist Tanizaki Jun'ichirô** (1886–1965) thought that Mushakôji reacted to political events in a uniform manner and hoped that he would never be sidetracked from the path he chose and felt he must take. That made him reluctant always to jump on any and every bandwagon. He did, however, get involved in writing pieces to support the war effort. Possibly Mushakôji wrote more plays than he wrote novels. There are excellent pieces among them that are more than just simple-minded. Despite composing very rapidly, Mushakôji's sentences reveal a passion whether he writes as a novelist or a dramatist.

His critical views of paintings are especially interesting. They do not focus on minute details of technique but rather on the work's overall feeling or impact. Apparently he wants people to react with the feeling of *Wonderful!* or *How awesome!* He seeks, in short, emotional not intellectual reactions to what he writes. The way he praises each piece he comments on elicits in readers the sense that they stand in the presence of a masterpiece. He stresses the joy of observing and appreciating the work, which in turn makes observers feel blithe and happy.

(3) **Tokyo University Professor of Japanese literature Hisamatsu Sen'ichi** (1894–1976) notes Mushakôji's efforts to combat the naturalist's excessive objectivity. Giving each individual free rein results, he believed, in harmony among all people. This motivated him to encourage individuals to express themselves fully. His corpus boasts a sense of humor and sunny atmosphere not seen in other Japanese writers. Some works demonstrate, however, that on the other side of his sunny optimism is a man tuned to the darker aspects of society and fully sensitive to the gamut of human problems. Though his expressions are simple and direct, his works consistently grapple with problems of existence and humanity. This quality gives Mushakôji a singular importance among thinkers and writers in modern Japan.

(4) **The critic and modern Japanese literature specialist Inagaki Tatsurô** (1901–1986) thinks that Mushakôji's artistry had many facets and that his contributions cover a vast range. Inagaki finds throughout Mushakôji's poetry a splendid consistency of purity or genuineness [*junsuimi*]. He never loses his desire for life. His unique poetic is definitely his own. Many of his poems deal with ideas of truth, love, and beauty—of humanity and of nature. There is in his verse not a shred of falseness or of pose, nor a hint of the fake or the pretended—no airs whatsoever, no affectations to scholarship, wisdom, or brilliance. Reading him makes one feel cleansed and freshened. Some poems praising painters are particularly lovely.

(5) **The poet Kusano Shinpei** (1903–1988) finds Mushakôji's sentences unique and clear—whatever genre you choose to read, his language and expressions are the same. Mushakôji's works are also always affirmative. They do not, however, confront us with the real world of suffering, pain, slaving for a living, and the like. Interestingly, the poem he wrote on his 50th birthday seems more energetic than the one he wrote on his 26th birthday.

Not even contemporary high school students can possibly write such simple, straight-forward, lucid, plain, and unadorned sentences. Their compositions are all twisted and cramped, for they are perhaps trying too hard to impress adults. There is no other poet like him. He has no peers.

(6) **The literary critic Senuma Shigeki** (1904–1988) thinks the common reader, not the specialist, will most enjoy the work of Mushakôji. His literature makes no sharp breaks with the past nor does it seek to be up-to-date. Mushakôji has nonetheless produced best sellers. The novelist Satô Haruo [cf. #1 above] wrote that by 1924 Mushakôji's work had significantly affected literary circles. But Senuma comments that most other observers recognize little or no influence.

Senuma does point out, however, that even Mushakôji's off-beat heroes were popular among general readers. Note, for example, the antiquarian book dealer who stubbornly sacrificed profits to specialize in works on the great teachers of the world [one of Mushakôji's long-standing interests]. Professional critics regard him differently. Most steadfastly refuse to acknowledge Mushakôji as a thinker in the customary sense. They prefer to regard him a *seishin no hito*—a man of the spirit. This evaluation doubtless stems from Mushakôji's tendency to honor and accept the natural self. He seeks the full realization of every human being's selfhood.

His ideas are idealistic, always optimistic, and inevitably moralistic. These and the utter domination of the subjective in Mushakôji's work invites the jaunty evaluation of him as "the chief • god of fools" [*baka no kami*; after all, fools were once viewed as prophets having a touch of divinity]. For all that, Mushakôji is a thinker in his own right and a splendid artist. He speaks, moreover, to those who find solace in religion and faith. In fact, something in his thought is most appropriate to the lost sheep who seek salvation from the darkness of society.

(7) **The literary critic Kamei Katsuichirô** (1907–1966) regards Mushakôji a seriously religious person [*shûkyôteki ningen*]. Kamei—who sees an emphasis on infinite love as a primary characteristic of religiosity—interprets Mushakôji's straightforward thinking as a desire to return to "fundamental human concerns" [*gensen shisô*, literally, "original sentiment" • "ur-thought"]. Infinite love, perceived as the will of nature, drives Mushakôji to an eclectic interest in ethical heroes. He praises Christ, respects Gautama, shows interest in Confucius, and finds Socrates fascinating. No matter what he evaluates, his typically East Asian both-and temperament avoids the Western either-or view of the world.

A persistent strain of uncomplicated naiveté or "innocence" [*mushin*] allows Mushakôji to accept various approaches to life and the absolute. He furthermore recognizes a wide variety of ethical paragons. The problem for the literary critic is that [as Kamei has long asserted] religion and literature are absolutely incompatible (cf. pages 240–241). The world of creative fiction simply cannot be made congruous with religious faith because their basic natures differ so drastically. In Mushakôji's work they do not, however, seem entirely incompatible. It is true, nonetheless, than the more religious his work becomes the more difficult it is to identify as literature. At some point he produces a literature that is no more religious or philosophical than it is literary.

The fountainhead of such a religious view, not to mention faith itself, must be a sense of awe or dread. Of course, Mushakôji has a reverential sense of awe toward the Creator. More universally one can point to the apprehension of death as a motivating force to faith. Not many writers in Japan have so consistently talked about death as Mushakôji. He saw death not negatively as the erasure of life but positively as life's fulfillment. Throughout, his central concern has been to actualize the gifts that fate dealt him. He believed accordingly that he could regard himself a fulfilled and happy man regardless of when his life ended.

His positive, constantly affirmative, and always appreciative views of the real world characterize much of his work and all of his life. He could—and did—discover a use and a purpose for everything. This open, accepting attitude offers critics wide latitude to criticize his work. Because the nature of what he produces differs so radically from the norms, no writer's corpus is easier to make fun of than his. Evaluated on its own terms, however, Mushakôji's powerfully affirmative literature of self-fulfillment displays both primitive simplicity and unfathomable wisdom. It does indeed suggest a return to the most fundamental human ideas.

APPENDIX III

MUSHAKÔJI ON HIS POETRY

Below are fourteen summaries and paraphrases of comments that Mushakôji has made about his verse. I arrange them in chronological order. These comments often parallel or exemplify descriptions of his poetic principles; cf. page 177 ff. Unless otherwise noted, the texts appear in *Mushakôji Saneatsu Zenshû* [Mushakôji Saneatsu, Works], Volume XI; hereafter MSZS. In no case, however, do I render his remarks in full. Most dates indicate when Mushakôji wrote each statement. The book in which he published it usually appeared several weeks or months later. In place of the usual terms for Foreword, Preface, and the like, Mushakôji uses a number of intriguing words that I do not venture to render.

Even the briefest excerpt illustrates Mushakôji's uniformly subjective definitions of poetry. His discussions are at times general. At other times they say specifically what he takes to be the value or nature of his verse. I include only portions I deem relevant to appreciating his views. Like his verse, these statements never derive from discursive logic, close reasoning, fine analysis, or careful rewriting. Rather, they fit the spontaneous, intuitive patterns that characterize his aesthetic. This makes his observations of special interest, to be sure, even though they by no means suffice as an adequate analysis of, or a full introduction to, his work. His intuitive remarks may nonetheless cast light on the attraction his verse holds for some readers in Japan concerned with authenticity or spontaneity.

✦   ✦   ✦

(1) *"Jobun no kawari"* [Substitute Preface], from *Zatsu sanbyaku rokujûgo* [Miscellany of 365 (poems)], Kôyasha, 1920.06.03; MSZS:659.

I don't know if I'm a poet.

In any event, I wrote what I wanted to write. I let surface whatever would come to the surface.

People have likes and dislikes. I didn't compose these poems based on my likes and dislikes. I produced them as they came to life. I wrote them down just as they came to mind. I intended to write nothing false. The rest I leave to you. I'd like you to accept what you feel like accepting and reject what you feel like rejecting.

(2) *"Jibun no shi"* [My Poems], from *Seimei ni yakudatsu tame ni* [Helping People Live], Shunjûsha, 1925.08.15; MSZS:660.

We recently set up a small print shop in the New Village and plan to issue a number of bantam books at reasonable cost. Because our typesetting remains amateurish, however, we decided to begin with one of my poetry collections. Next I'd like to put out a collection of the verse of SENKE MOTOMARO. At this moment we don't yet have the entire manuscript in hand, so the book will be slightly delayed. I'd like to gather together some Senke poems that especially appeal to me. I'm interested in having this volume clarify the reasons I respect him as a modern Japanese poet.

My arena as a poet differs entirely from Senke's. I suspect the main characteristic of my poetry consists of its impulsive declarations stated in unadorned, straightforward, and tranquilly-charged language. Some few do acknowledge me as a poet, but I write many works that lie between poetry and impressions. In compiling this collection I tried to select from among them those I personally regard as poetry.

(3) *"Ushiro ni"* [Afterword], from *Shishû* [Selected Poetry], Hyûgadô, 1930.03.13; MSZS:661–662.

I suspect there are not many who truly grasp what I am doing in my verse. At least those conversant with the poetry that literary figures in this country produce apparently do not regard my verse as poetry.

I found it somewhat amusing that the poet-novelist Murô Saisei [1889–1962] wrote consolingly that I had mastered the "skeleton of poetry" but hadn't quite managed its "flesh and skin." Yet he appears to acknowledge that my verse is poetry. In most cases, anthologies of modern poetry omit my works. I don't fuss about that. I like my poems despite the fact that people don't much recognize them.

Why do I like them? Because they forthrightly say what I want to say.

Moreover I have confidence in this style of verse. Obviously I do not imagine that my poetry is the only style there is. Many other more poetic types of verse are possible. I think, however, that my poetry has its own strong points.

If you read this book, I think you'll understand not only what kind of person I am but also the sort of poet I am. I suspect some may enjoy these poems. That, at least, is my hope.

(4) *"Jibun no shi ni tsuite"* [About My Poetry], from the journal *Dokuritsujin* [The Self-Reliant], 1930.05; MSZS:662–664.

I write once again regarding my poetry. When I comment on my verse, I think it's natural to look at it the way others would like to see it. That's why I don't intend to complain about whether somebody disparages or disdains my poems.

I think, however, that it also might be a good idea at this time to write down honestly and plainly what I personally think about my poetry.

I figure I know best what my poetry is worth.

To begin, if I were to list poems of mine that I like best, I'd offer "Spring" (1915, page 165) and "Closing my Eyes" (1923, page 74). Among my poems, these two are the most poetic. I don't think either will suffer embarrassment if compared to other modern Japanese poems published through 1926.

The following two may differ slightly from my other verse, but I think they will give a clear savor [*aji*] of my work. I also like their style. Of course, since it's my own style this means it best matches me.

I like "Spring" because I find it hard to reject the way the poem reflects the variations in and candidly expresses vernal rhythms.

I like "Closing my Eyes" because I have confidence in its singular simplicity.

I like a number of my shorter works, too. Although some of these fall somewhat short of qualifying as poetry, they have a sensitivity of sorts. Take, for example, "Child" (1920, page 58).

These are typical of the poems I write. Do you think they have little worth?

Do you think my verse has less value than the many poems in modern anthologies?

There is no end to citing poems I'm fond of. Naturally, among my verse are many works that have yet to become poetry. I'm well aware of that, so I all but omitted them from my most recent collection.

I don't have the leisure to berate the work of other poets. Nor am I interested in doing so. A number of present-day poets are quite good. I do not think SENKE MOTOMARU is the only one writing excellent poetry. I like certain poems by Shimazaki Tôson [1872–1943], but a lot of his work I don't like. I could mention others, as well.

But I think neither that my verse fails as poetry nor that I am alone in imagining I have some quite creditable [*nakanaka rippana*] poems.

I regard it neither an honor nor a disgrace to be excluded from consideration as a modern Japanese poet. How others look at my work, however, obviously has no affect on my personal confidence in the worth of my verse.

Following is a partial listing of my own favorite poems: "Rhapsodizing on my [26th] Birthday" (1911, page 91), "Loneliness" ([ii] 1911, page 63), "The Fountain's Lament" (1911, page 107), "Rembrandt" ([i] 1915, page 206), "The Aged Rembrandt" (1923, page 207), *"The Return of Tobias"* (1923, page 207), "One Hundred Eggs" (1923, page 157), "Arrow Shooter" (1925, page 225), and "Hendrickje!" (1926, page 208).

It's my personal opinion that anyone who presents these works to Japan's poetry Establishment may justifiably demand considerable praise.

(5) *"Hajime ni"* [Foreword] to *Jinsei shishû* [Poems on Life], Nôsan Gyoson Bunka Kyôkai, 1945.12; MSZS:664.

More often than not I write poetry to revitalize myself. I write such poems when in life or work my self-confidence has eroded or when I think it most appropriate to write a poem to cheer myself up. Conversely, I also write poems when I'm in such very, very high spirits that I can't help expressing myself. Beyond that I may write a poem when I long for something.

Whatever the occasion, I somehow feel that I'd like to encourage those who do the same sort of work we're doing. I'll be happy, therefore, if these poems cheer and give a pinch of consolation to those who labor in agriculture.

Among these works are pieces written about working together with the brothers and sisters in our New Village fields.

(6) *"Atogaki"* [Afterword], from *Kanki* [Joy], Sôzansha, 1947, reprinted in Nagami Shichirô, *Mushakôji Saneatsu shishû* [Poems of Mushakôji Saneatsu], *Sekai no shi* #34 [Poetry of the World, Volume 34], Yayoi Shoten, 1966, page 146.

    I think there are various types of poetry. I don't know what kind of poetry mine is. It depends on who makes the evaluation, of course, but there may be some who won't even be able to agree that my verse is poetry.

    Shall I call it free verse? I haven't particularly made a study of poetry. It's only that as I am writing something, I little by little become more deeply involved in it and my words take wing. I think that then, to begin, poetry naturally "happens." In any event, I write my poems at such times.

    Prose is limited to the ground. Sometimes it crawls, sometimes it walks, sometimes it runs. It cannot, however, disengage itself from the ground. When a plane taxies down the runway, still incapable of liftoff, you don't yet have poetry. But when it lifts off you get a poem. That, at any rate, is how I look at it. When words take wing, you end up with poetry.

(7) *"Shi ni tsuite"* [On Poetry], from the magazine *Shigaku* [Poetics] (1948.04); MSZS:665–667.

    I've never made a special study of poetry. Not just poetry. I've never especially studied either fiction or drama, either. When I feel like writing a poem, I write it. There are also times when I write one because I've been asked.

    I write exactly what emerges from my inner self, so I'm not saying I write verse simply because it's this or that kind of expression.

    That's why even if I'm asked to write about poetry, I'm in a bind to say something about it in a general way. Perhaps I could do so if I wrote about the special poetry I'm familiar with. Or I think I could write about poetry if I could do it as a solitary human being, or simply as a person who likes to read poetry.

    It seems to me, therefore, that I can't say much that will be informative [*sankô*]. I'll try nevertheless to write something about how I personally view poetry.

    Because I love poetry, I'm anxious to read good poems and I want them available. There aren't even many good novels at hand, however, and apparently there are even fewer good poems.

    One problem in Japan is our love of tanka and haiku. These forms dominate verse writing. You can't say that those who compose traditional poems are incapable of writing free verse [*shi*], but if waka and haiku had less popularity (a term I detest!) I imagine many more people would now be writing modern poetry. That would raise the level.

    However earnest the writer, if he uses crudities or if his style lacks cohesion, he won't end up with good poetry. I suspect that artless expressions will require thorough revision.

    I don't mean to suggest that there are no good modern poems in Japan. But I do think it would be wonderful both if there were more excellent ones and if there were more and more collections so good that one wants always to have them handy.

    Poems that fail to elicit in me the slightest desire to read them, poems that lack allure, are like salt that has lost its savor. They have no merit.

(8) *"Jo"* [Preface], from *Fue o fuku* [Playing the Flute], Atarashiki Mura, 1951.03; MSZS:667.

The primary reason I'm publishing this collection is that I want to donate the royalties to the New Village East in Moroyama, Saitama. I was, however, also interested in issuing a collection of my favorite poems. I hope that this book will be a good memorial for and provide assistance to the village.

I will consider it a double joy if those who buy this poetry collection are people who are fond of my verse and of the New Village East.

(9) *"Jo"* [Preface], from *Mushakôji Saneatsu shishû* [The Poetry of Mushakôji Saneatsu], *Shinchô Bunko* [Shinchô Library], 1952.07; MSZS:668.

For the most, I write poetry when I feel the need to console or motivate myself. When, moreover, I become involved in writing something, I often get carried away. At such times I'm inspired to spontaneity or I write pieces that directly convey my true feelings. When I read over what I'd written, I find much of it offers clear insights into my inner life. That's why when I look back I find many poems that give me a sense of nostalgia. That is to say, my verse makes clear to me the development of and changes in my inner life.

Most works written when I was young dealt with the misery [*sabishisa*] of isolation or the misery of being unable to feel confident in my writing. Some poems also record how I gradually regained confidence in my work. Some deal with the founding of the New Village, and some tell of the excitement or resignation I experienced in those days. I suspect that anyone one reads through all my verse will understand what half my life was like.

This explains why I feel a surprising affection for my verse, though I don't know to what extent it may communicate to the reader. If, however, it is true that the sincere heart communicates with the sincere heart, I suspect there are works here that will touch some readers. I feel that these poems are most typically me.

(10) *"Atogaki"* [Afterword], from *Shishû* [Poetry Collection], Shinchôsha, *Zenshû* [Works], Volume 21, 1956.07.25; MSZS:668–669.

Most of my poetry collections I wrote on various occasions to animate my mind and give me the will to live. At times when I couldn't stand feeling isolated, I consoled myself writing poems about isolation. To encourage myself when dispirited, to compose myself when disturbed, and the like—on whatever the occasion, I wrote verse intent on revealing my inner self.

I've written in detail elsewhere about my poetry, so you'll see what I mean if you read what I wrote. But I can say this: whichever work I read reveals to me how I felt when I wrote it, so the poem becomes a reminiscence.

I've written any number of works, but this single volume of poetry reveals most profoundly, I think, what sort of person I am.

I'm wondering if my work doesn't differ completely from the poetry others write and if it's even appropriate to call it poetry. I do think, however, that these works are what true poetry should be like. It merely seems to me that, since I've intemperately used my own expressions, there may be passages that won't make sense to others.

I mean that I sang my songs like a song bird, though one cannot say my tunes are especially lovely.

I believe nevertheless that these poems will console those capable of sympathizing with what I write. It's no exaggeration that those who make no sense of my verse lack spiritual affinity with me.

This, however, hardly brings shame on the reader. It brings shame on me, the writer. Nevertheless, I have no intention of betraying my self so as to please the reader.

Nor do I intend being either an apologist or a booster of my verse. Most of all I'd like you just to read it without prejudice.

If you read this collection, I think you'll understand how my thinking and life have changed from my youth. It seems to me, however, that each poem can stand on its own, and that each does tell the truth.

(11) *"Bôtôbun"* [Foreword], from *Waga jinsei* [My Life], Shinchôsha, 1956.10; MSZS:669.

Were someone to ask me what sort of person I am and what kind of life I've lived, I'd hand him a copy of one of my poetry collections and respond, "This is me." In my time I've written quite a few different pieces, some dealing with my personal affairs. But I feel that my poetry reveals the most about my true intentions.

Naturally, because on different occasions I express myself differently, I suppose that some who read my poems may not be able to figure out why I wrote any particular one of them. After having read through them one by one, moreover, I suspect that readers may instead miss getting a clear idea of the meanings invested in each poem and so lose interest in my verse as poetry.

Furthermore, when I compose verse I do not write with the hope that the reader will look at it all that carefully. I presume that if a sharp critic interested in such things looks into why I wrote such a poem he will to some extent be able to understand the reason. But it is possible that the excessively insightful critic might totally miss the point, overstate himself, and increasingly misconstrue my meaning.

Indeed, I suspect I'm the one who best understands what I felt when I wrote the poems. If I were to make my feelings public, I suppose it would be clear that my poetry collections most honestly express my self.

Actually, whichever of my poems I read clearly brings to mind what I felt when I wrote it.

I don't know to what extent my verse has value as poetry. I know only that on each occasion the poems deeply express my actual feelings. That's a fact. It does, to be sure, depend on the poem. At times the intensity of the emotion makes it impossible not to express myself that way.

Because I am reminded in each case of what I was like when I wrote the poem, however, I discover that my present self has changed considerably.

(12) *"Hashigaki"* [Preface], from *Jinsei sanka* [In Praise of Life], Ie no Hikari Kyôkai, 1963.08.21; MSZS:670.

If you read my verse it will be clear to you that my primary concern as an individual is how best to exist in our society. When I was young I wrote many poems thinking that despite my cheerless mood [*sabishisa*] I wanted somehow to carry on cheerfully.

Nor did I want to let unrequited love and the dread of death get the better of me. I truly desired to make the most of myself, and I longed to perceive my mission in life. Many poems emerged from these yearnings. When after marriage I began work at the New Village, the central issue for me became how to exist. And I adored work.

It's been my habit to write poetry to encourage myself to discharge my mission in life. That is to say, more often than not my verse makes me reflect on how to live as a person, or it equips me with fortitude, gives me the resolve to live, and allows me the satisfactions of life. Furthermore, I write if I can when I want to write—and then I write the truth straight from the shoulder.

From time to time I write didactic poems. These are more to teach myself than others.

In any event, writing these poems has given me the courage to live. Not to mention the joy of living. And so, since they have encouraged me, I think my poems will encourage my readers, as well, for we are equally human.

This applies, however, only to those who in some sense inwardly feel that they want to make the most of themselves. I suspect this book will have no utility for those thinking only about how to make money or how best to get ahead in the world. I imagine that people with a strong drive toward the inner life will get the most enjoyment from reading this book.

I hope, too, that such people might appreciate my work.

(13) *"Maegaki"* [Foreword], *Mushakôji Saneatsu shishû* [Poems of Mushakôji Saneatsu], Chôbunsha, 1966.07.29; MSZS:670–671.

I rejoice that these days I get the impression people have more or less come to understand my poems. When I first began writing verse, I recall being told to refrain from dabbling in poetry.

Because I wanted to write poems, however, I wrote them—in short, as long as I have felt driven to express myself in that medium, I've been writing verse.

Most of what I wrote in my youth consoled me in my solitude. I also wrote poems to inspire myself. Later on, moreover, I wrote verse because I wanted to speak the truth, to express my longings, or at times to cheer myself up.

There are, furthermore, poems written forthrightly in response to the feelings of the moment. Or there are times when you could say "aspirations are the mother of verse." My expressions reflect in my own style [*chôshi*] what I most wanted to write. Prior to concerning myself with what might appeal to the reader, I want to feel satisfied if I can express myself in a way that best suits me.

I've never made an issue of whether what I write is or isn't poetry. I've wanted only to say exactly what I felt to be the truth.

During the fifty some years I've been writing verse, however, I'm glad to see that public opinion has changed. People now regard my poems as poetry. They have also met my expectations and come to read my verse with an open mind [*sunao ni*].

Although I regard my poems as poetry, I wish I had written more truly poetic and beautiful works—if only I could do so! Perhaps I am by now too old for that.

I'm glad, however, that there are all kinds of people in the world, so I'm happy being the way I am.

(14) *"Jo"* [Preface], from *Jinsei no tokkyûsha no ue de hitori no rôjin* [An Old Man on Life's Superexpress], Keibisha, 1969; MSZS:671–672.

It's been my intention to write honestly whatever I wanted to write. I have most confidence in what I have created. I do not choose to deal with problems in terms of acquired knowledge [*chishiki*]. I want to discuss problems as honestly as possible in consonance with my heartfelt feelings [*honshin*].

I'd like to write honestly, as much as possible lining up the words as they come into my head. And I'd like to write up whatever I feel I really want to write about.

Perhaps not everything has conformed to these ideals, but as far as possible I wanted to avoid writing about undesirable [*fujun*] topics. I want to write down what I feel like writing once my true feelings become fervent [*honki*].

I trust the feelings of the human heart. I trust that which created these feelings. I have trust in that whereby humans can become sincere about their thoughts.

That is, I trust the One who created the human heart. We live as we have been made. I think that whatever I feel sincere about and wish to write up is worth writing up sincerely. It seems to me it is impossible for human beings to become sincere about issues that lack value to them.

A human being cannot in his own self-centered way become fervent or earnest about trivia. That's because he can only become earnestly sincere about what can have value for him. That's an interesting point about people. One cannot do genuine [*junsui*] work by writing out of ambition, by catering to the reader, or by aiming to make money. I want to do genuine work.

As long as I exist as a human being, I figure I'd like to say honestly whatever I feel like saying as a human being.

APPENDIX IV

POETRY COLLECTIONS

The following inventory includes collections listed in Volume XI of *Mushakôji Saneatsu Zenshû* [Mushakôji Saneatsu: Works], pages 679–684 and 686–691. I follow the *Works* in adding a number of entries that are not, strictly speaking, verse collections. Each does, however, contain a number of new poems, as indicated.

✦　　　✦　　　✦

『雑三百六十五』 *Zatsu sanbyaku rokujûgo* [Miscellany of 365 (Poems)], 曠野社 • Kôyasha, 1920.07, 297 pages.

『新しき村詩集』 *Atarashiki mura shishû* [New Village Poetry Collection], 新しき村出版部—曠野社 • Atarashiki Mura Shuppanbu [New Village Publications—Kôyasha], 1924.01, 350 pages.

『詩集』武者小路実篤全集第九巻 *Shishû • Mushakôji Saneatsu zenshû daikyûkan* [Mushakôji Saneatsu: Works • Poetry Collection, Volume IX], 芸術社 • Geijutsusha, 1924.03, 579 pages.

『新しき村詩集、其二』 *Atarashiki mura shishû, Sono ni* [New Village Poetry Collection, Number 2], 新しき村出版部 • Atarashiki Mura Shuppanbu [New Village Publications], 1924.04, 349 pages.

『詩百篇・自選』 *Shi hyakuhen • Jisen* [One Hundred Poems • Self-selected], 新しき村印刷部 (日向新しき村) • Atarashiki Mura Insatsubu—Hyûga Atarashiki Mura [New Village Printers—Hyûga], 1925.09, 126 pages.

『詩集』 *Shishû* [Poetry Collection], 日向堂 • Hyûgadô, 1930.04, 370 pages.

『無車詩集』 *Musha shishû* [Musha (a pun; literally, Wheel-less) Poetry Collection], 甲鳥書林 • Kôchô Shorin, 1941.04, 336 pages.

『武者小路実篤画集と画論』 *Mushakôji Saneatsu gashû to garon* [Mushakôji Saneatsu: Paintings and Views of Painting], 座右宝 • Zayûhô, 1942.03. This book contains 22 poems.

『新しき村詩集』 *Atarashiki mura shishû* [New Village Collection], 馬鈴薯叢書 • *Bareisho Sôsho* [Potato Series], 扶桑閣 • Fusôkaku, 1943.12, ? pages.

『野菜讃』 *Yasaisan* [In Praise of Greens], 愛宕書房・Atago Shobô, 1944.05. This book contains 21 poems.

『詩と劇』 *Shi to geki* [Poetry and Drama], 筑摩書房・Chikuma Shobô, 1945.10. This book contains nine poems.

『人生詩集』 *Jinsei shishû* [Poems on Life], 農山漁村文化協会・Nôsan Gyoson Bunka Kyôkai, 1946.03, 63 pages.

『歓喜』 *Kanki* [Joy], 双山社・Sôzansha, 1947.08, 193 pages.

『笛を吹く』 *Fue o fuku* [Playing the Flute], 新しき村・Atarashiki Mura Printers, 1951.04, 67 pages.

『武者小路実篤詩集』 *Mushakôji Saneatsu shishû* [Poetry of Mushakôji Saneatsu], 詩人全書の一冊, from *Shijin zensho* [Poets' Works], 醋燈社・Kantôsha, 1951.10, 245 pages.

『武者小路実篤詩集』 *Mushakôji Saneatsu shishû* [Poetry of Mushakôji Saneatsu], 新潮文庫, *Shinchô bunko* [Shinchô Library], 新潮社・Shinchôsha, 1953.01, 195 pages.

『武者小路実篤詩集』 *Mushakôji Saneatsu shishû* [Poetry of Mushakôji Saneatsu], 市民文庫, *Shimin Bunko* [Citizens' Library], 河出書房・Kawade Shobô, 1953.07, 101 pages.

『武者小路実篤詩集』 *Mushakôji Saneatsu shishû* [Poetry of Mushakôji Saneatsu], 角川文庫, *Kadokawa bunko* [Kadokawa Library], 角川書店・Kadokawa Shoten, 1953.07, 182 pages.

『わが人生・詩を通して見た我が内面生活』 *Waga jinsei・shi o tôshite mita waga naimen seikatsu* [My Life・My Inner Life Viewed through Verse], 新潮社・Shinchôsha, 1956.07, 226 pages.

『武者小路実篤全集第二十一巻』 *Mushakôji Saneatsu zenshû dainijûikkan* [Works of Mushakôji Saneatsu, Volume 21], 新潮社・Shinchôsha, 1956.08, 430 pages.

『私の貝殻』 *Watashi no kaigara* [My Shell], 池田書店・Ikeda Shoten, 1962.03. This book contains 25 poems, including eight new works about his painting.

『詩集人生讃歌』 *Shishû jinsei sanka* [Poems in Praise of Life], レインボウ・ブックス 7, *Reinbô bukkusu* #7 [Rainbow Books #7], 家の光協会・Ie no Hikari Kyôkai, 1963.10, 198 pages.

『武者小路実篤詩集』 *Mushakôji Saneatsu shishû* [Poetry of Mushakôji Saneatsu], 銀河選書 6, *Ginga sensho* #6 [Milky Way Choice Books #6], 大和書房・Yamato Shobô, 1964.04, 260 pages.

『のんきな男とのんきな造物者』 *Nonki na otoko to nonki na zôbutsusha* [Optimist and the Optimistic Creator], 私家版— 非売品・*Shikaban — hibaihin* [Private Edition — Not for Sale], 1965.12, 102 pages.

『或る男と創物者』 *Aru otoko to sôbutsusha* [A Man and the Maker], 角川書店・Kadokawa Shoten, 1966.02, 201 pages.

『武者小路実篤詩集』 *Mushakôji Saneatsu shishû* [Poetry of Mushakôji Saneatsu], 世界の詩 34, *Sekai no shi* #34 [Poetry of the World #34], 弥生書房・Yayoi Shobô, 1966.06, 154 pages.

『詩集と人生語録』 *Shishû to jinsei goroku* [Poetry Collection and Aphorisms on Life], 講談社・Kôdansha, 1966.12, ? pages.

『武者小路実篤詩集』 *Mushakôji Saneatsu shishû* [The Poetry of Mushakôji], カラー版・日本の詩集 12, *Karâ ban・Nihon no shishû* 12 [Color・Japanese Poetry Collections, #12], 角川書店・Kadokawa Shoten, 1968.06, 270 pages.

『人生の特急車の上で一人の老人』 *Jinsei no tokkyûsha no ue de hitori no rôjin* [An Old Man on Life's Superexpress], 皆美社・Kaibisha, 1969.03, 225 pages.

『実篤人生詩集』 上・下 *Saneatsu jinsei shishû* [Saneatsu: Poems on Life] *jô・ge*, Volumes I and II, 芳賀書店・Haga Shoten, 1970.06, 220 and 219 pages. These volumes contain many small cuts of Mushakôji's paintings.

NB: The *Zenshû* notes that the two volumes of 『実篤人生詩集』 were first published in 1965; my personal copies give 1970 as the date of the first edition.

『自選詩画集』 *Jisen shigashû* [A Collection of Verse and Paintings—Selected by the Author], 欅書房・Keyaki Shobô, 1970.09, 116 pages.

『武者小路実篤全集』 第十一巻・詩 *Mushakôji Saneatsu zenshû, daijûikkan・shi* [Mushakôji Saneatsu: Works, Volume XI・Poetry], 小学館・Shôgakukan, 1989, 716 pages.

ENGLISH INDEX

With two exceptions, the complete originals of every poem in *Long Corridor* appear in Volume XI of *Mushakôji Saneatsu Zenshû* [Mushakôji Saneatsu Works], Shôgakukan, 1989, hereafter MSZS. One exception, "The Me of Words" (cf. page 8), I take from *Saneatsu jinsei shishû • jô* [Saneatsu's Poems of Life, Volume 1], Haga Shoten, 1970, which I designate HS:I. The other, "Sun and Moon," comes from *Mushakôji Saneatsu shishû* [Poetry of Mushakôji Saneatsu], Volume 12 of *Nihon no shishû* [Japanese Poetry], Kadokawa Shoten, 1968, which I designate KK:12. Only the first ten lines of this poem exist in MSZS:XI:14; cf. page 102. The full twenty-three-line version has, however, been anthologized several times since its 1921 publication. For details on and Chinese graphs of the poetry books, cf. Appendix IV: Poetry Collections, page 371 ff. In all other cases where differences exist, I follow the version contained in MSZS. NB: regard an apostrophe as a space.

The date after each title usually indicates when the poem was first published. In some instances, however this is the date Mushakôji wrote the work. Dates listed in the Table of Contents of MSZS:XI adhere to the Western calendar. But in the text, where he sometimes dates his poems, Mushakôji is inconsistent. At times he follows the Western calendar, at times the indigenous reign era. Where dates seem not to agree, I follow the Table of Contents. If an undated poem lies between poems of the same year, I use that year. Poems that the editors of MSZS do not date and that appear between poems with quite different publication dates have a question mark ? after the assumed year of publication.

After the colon is the page number in the designated volume. The page number in *Long Corridor* follows the bullet • or raised period. To fit the space, I sometimes abbreviate longer titles; ☞ the translated text for the full version. Most titles, incidentally, Mushakôji takes from his first line, for he consciously avoids influencing the way a reader might interpret the work. In translation it is at times impossible to duplicate this convention. Small Roman numerals in parentheses—(i), (ii), or (iii)—differentiate identical English titles. These designations, which rarely appear in Mushakôji's originals, I add for convenience. The Roman numerals XI refer uniformly to Volume XI of MSZS. All initial articles I omit.

✦   ✦   ✦

After a Fit of Anger (1922.11; XI:334) • 173
Age of Adversity for the Race Horse (1931.02; XI:472) • 89
Aged Rembrandt (1923.03; XI:47) • 207
Aged Toilers (1931.02; XI:472) • 121
Always in the Village (1920.11; XI:285) • 148
America's Wilson (1918.12; XI:214) • 275
Angler's Soliloquy (1913.08; XI:194) • 130
Angry Lion (1934.07; XI:70) • 87
Apple Trees and Pear Trees (1922.06; XI:334) • 91
Arrow Shooter (1925.11; XI:55) • 225
Artist and a Frog (1944; XI:100) • 190
Artist and Critic (1929.01; XI:57) • 213
Artists (1920.07; XI:248) • 271
As Long as I'm Alive (1971.11; XI:625) • 162
At Eighty-Eight (1972.06; XI:631) • 95

At the New Village (1924.11; XI:396) • 148
At the Workshop (1920.04; XI:224) • 137
Autumn has Come (1909.09; XI:4) • 164

Be Honest (1920.04; XI:223) • 105
Beautiful Flowers (1920.04; XI:24) • 73
Beautiful Woman (1920.07; XI:249) • 69
Beautiful World We Desire (1951; XI:534) • 158
Because He Wrote a Poem (1923; XI:330) • 226
Being True to God (1920.09; XI:273) • 262
Believe Me (1920?; XI:280) • 64
Big Ship (1920.04; XI:230) • 104
Big Tree (1920.04; XI:25) • 213
Bookshop (1923.04; XI:337) • 104
Broad-Minded Man (1940; XI:499) • 105
Buddha (1920.04; XI:26) • 75
Buddha and Jesus (1923.08; XI:351) • 262
Buddha's Gospel (1920.04; XI:230) • 262
Build It! (1921.01; XI:288) • 151

Canary that Forgot Its Song (1940.11; XI:522) • 121
Child (1920.04; XI:27) • 58
Chinese (1920.03; XI:224) • 169
Chinese Painting (1923.07; XI:50) • 196
Clay Figurine — Haniwa (1975.09; XI:655) • 106
Closing My Eyes (1923; XI:51) • 74
Comical Couple (1923.06; XI:344) • 171
Courbet (1929.06; XI:466) • 209
Creativity (1923.09; XI:356) • 226
Critic and Painter (1911.05; XI:189) • 213
Critics' Disdain (1911.06; XI:190) • 215

Daily Renewal (1942.01; XI:114) • 143
Daumier (1929.06; XI:467) • 209
Day by Day (1944; XI:101) • 154
Death (1911.07; XI:10) • 85
Death's Desolation (1920.04; XI:225) • 85
Death's Dread (1923.07; XI:49) • 84
Dedicated to God (1939.07; XI:494) • 266
Delacroix (1929.06; XI:467) • 209
Desk and Cot (1934.07; XI:483) • 126
Devoted Critic (1928.11; XI:453) • 216
Does God Exist? (i) (1920.09; XI:273) • 240
Does God Exist? (ii) (1922.02; XI:323) • 240
Does God Exist? (iii) (1923; XI:327) • 241
Doing My Work (1924.12; XI:392) • 119
Dostoyevski's Face (1911.05; XI:12) • 77
Dürer's St. Jerome (1924.10; XI:394) • 271
Dying to Paint a Picture (1950.03; XI:536) • 182

Efforts (1939; XI:555) • 153
Eggshell (1911.07; XI:13) • 77
Endless Rain (1920.07; XI:263) • 72
Eve (1924.05; XI:364) • 68

Even in Japan (1925.10; XI:432) • 276
Expert Archers (1936.06; XI:488) • 225

Feeling Lonely (1909.10; XI:4) • 164
Fine Work of Art (1924.12; XI:390) • 192
Fire From a Single Match (1920.07; XI:248) • 138
Fleet-footed Rumors (1923.09; XI:344) • 56
Flies (1923.05; XI:343) • 88
Florist (1924.06; XI:369) • 75
Flowers (1920.04; XI:23) • 74
Flowing River (1924.10; XI:382) • 103
For Me (1913.04; XI:194) • 66
For the Mountain Climber (1939?; XI:79) • 135
Forgetting God (1920.04; XI:26) • 263
Foundation (1920.04; XI:229) • 117
Fountain's Lament (1911.07; XI:14) • 107
Fresh Painting (1971.02; XI:622) • 185
Friend (1917.10; XI:239) • 159
From Childhood (1920.04; XI:23) • 58
From My Three Children (1936 • 1940; XI:498) • 82
From the New Village (1925.06; XI:414) • 147

Genius and Artiste (1911.04; XI:187) • 186
Gentle Rain (1940; XI:498) • 73
Genuine and Lovable People (1966.06; XI:578) • 170
Giant (i) (1911.07; XI:13) • 78
Giant (ii) (1925.02; XI:57) • 78
Giant (iii) (1935?; XI:73) • 78
Giant Advances (1940; XI:496) • 79
Giant Appeared (1925.08; XI:427) • 80
Giant's Calligraphy (1925.08; XI:428) • 226
Giant's Footprint (1927; XI:59) • 80
Giants Only Walk (1931.08; XI:76) • 79
Giver (1913.08; XI:195) • 132
Go Master (1924.06; XI:358) • 215
God (i) (1920.01; XI:221) • 261
God (ii) (1920; XI:30) • 261
God (iii) (1921.02; XI:44) • 261
God and Humankind (i) (1919.06; XI:217) • 262
God and Humankind (ii) (1920.06; XI:243) • 263
God and Satan (1938; XI:491) • 267
God's Love (i) (1920.09; XI:276) • 253
God's Love (ii) (1921.05; XI:301) • 253
God's Will (1911.07; XI:12) • 266
Good Brothers and Sisters (1920.05; XI:235) • 170
Good Instruments (1924.06; XI:371) • 224
Good Script (1928.01; XI:456) • 130
Gossip (1911.04; XI:186) • 55
Government Officials (1924.12; XI:390) • 76
Grim Reaper (1939.03; XI:78) • 84
Growth (1920; XI:33) • 62
Growth Potential (1928.01; XI:448) • 151

Health (1964.12; XI:565) • 96
Hemp Palm (1973.07; XI:637) • 125
Hendrickje! (1926.07; XI:52) • 208
His Children (1920.05; XI:234) • 173
Hodler (1911.07; XI:12) • 211
Horse Deprived of Liberty (1933.03; XI:477) • 89
Hotei, Attributed to Mu Ch'i (1965?; XI:172) • 198
How Describe God? (1920.03; XI:224) • 240
However (1920.04; XI:225) • 85
However Fine the Instrument (1923.05; XI:49) • 224
Humanity (1923.05; XI:343) • 107

I (i) • (1914.03; XI:197) • 61
I (ii) • (1920.06; XI:30) • 62
I Adore Fall (1924.12; XI:396) • 74
I Believe (1921:08; XI:314) • 64
I Can Do It, I Can Do It (1951; XI:536) • 66
I Dare (1928.01; XI:456) • 232
I Feel like Laughing (1911.06; XI:6) • 60
I Praise Mu Ch'i and Liang K'ai (1946; XI:117) • 201
I Respect (i) (1921.05; XI:301) • 64
I Respect (ii) (1963; XI:559) • 64
I Simply (1929.01; XI:461) • 216
I'm a Bell (1927.09; XI:445) • 247
I'm a Huge Rock (1923.08; XI:353) • 62
I'm a Painter (1950.03; XI:535) • 190
I'm a Patriot (1933.03; XI:479) • 276
I'm a Pine (1960.01; XI:548) • 71
I'm a Standard-Bearer (1920.07; XI:264) • 139
I'm a Worker (1922.03; XI:348) • 135
I'm an Egotist (1923.08; XI:350) • 63
I'm Made of Steel (1911.04; XI:186) • 66
Idealist Who Walks Testing a Stone Bridge (1920?; XI:280) • 100

If They Don't Work (1924.12; XI:394) • 119
If You Break Every Oil Lamp (1929.02; XI:462) • 105
Impaired Painter (1961.10; XI:552) • 189
In China Mu Ch'i (1928.05; XI:450) • 203
In Concert (1920.05; XI:236) • 138
In Earnest (i) (1920.04; XI:24) • 246
In Earnest (ii) (1920; XI:39) • 154
In Hyûga's Hills (1925.07; XI:419) • 145
In My Tiny Room (1928.05; XI:450) • 191
In Praise of Potatoes (1941.05; XI:108) • 183
In the Kingdom of God (i) (1920.05; XI:295) • 246
In the Kingdom of God (ii) (1920.09; XI:274) • 173
In the Typhoon (1923; XI:327) • 103
In the Village (1920.11; XI:285) • 270
In this World (1963; XI:557) • 133
Incoherent Picture (1928.01; XI:456) • 212
Infant's Joy (1924.06; XI:373) • 57

Japan Brims with Hope (1911.07; XI:13) • 274

Japan Has Been Left Behind (1918.12; XI:214) • 275
Jesus and St. Francis (1925.01; XI:385) • 273
Joy (1917.10; XI:22) • 107
Joy of Friendship (1917.10; XI:205) • 159
Joy of Seeing a Fine Picture (1936.08; XI:76) • 186
Joy of Work (1951; XI:91) • 122
Joys of Painting Pictures (1949.11; XI:522) • 189

King of the Hill (1924.08; XI:374) • 63
Kinoshita! (1925.03; XI:403) • 227

Lean on Me (1910.04; XI:184) • 166
Leave Everything to God (1920.09; XI:275) • 273
Lenin's Embalmed Remains (1924.12; XI:390) • 77
Leonardo da Vinci's Lilies (1962.06; XI:554) • 205
Liang K'ai (1962.09; XI:560) • 197
Liang K'ai's *Harpist Under a Pine* (1965?; XI:170) • 200
Life's Work (1934.07; XI:70) • 155
Like a Tortoise (1909.10; XI:5) • 85
Listening to the Piano (1967.01; XI:580) • 272
Living and Working (1967.05; XI:582) • 156
Lofty Aspirations (1923.11; XI:52) • 67
Loneliness (i) (1909.10; XI:232) • 63
Loneliness (ii) (1911.07; XI:12) • 63
Long Corridor (1909.10; XI:5) • 55
Lord of the Castle (1912.12; XI:15) • 76
Lost Titles (1928.05; XI:57) • 230
Lots and Lots of Poets (1920.07; XI:263) • 217
Lovable People (1972; XI:627) • 170
Love (i) (1920; XI:42) • 174
Love (ii) (1975.12; XI:655) • 174
Love that Conquers Death (1938; XI:491) • 253
Love Tragedy (1908.01; XI:182) • 167
Loved by God (1920.04; XI:24) • 253
Ludicrous Folks (1924.12; XI:392) • 214
Luther Burbank (1924.04; XI:373) • 139

Machines and People (1919.09; XI:219) • 155
Maligned (1920.07; XI:260) • 56
Man (1935; XI:85) • 94
Man Fishes (1926?; XI:57) • 91
Man on the Flute • (1941.11; XI:111) • 221
Man Painting a Mountain (1939; XI:556) • 187
Man who Works Earnestly (1942; XI:511) • 153
Many Hardships (1936.11; XI:489) • 83
Mary Magdalene (1926; XI:424) • 68
Master! Master! (1911.05; XI:11) • 107
Me of Words (1970?; HS:I:7) • 8

Mommy (1969.03; XI:607) • 69
Moral Principle (1942.04; XI:518) • 65
More I Paint (1959.12; XI:543) • 124
Morning of My Seventy-Fourth Birthday (1959.05; XI:541) • 94
Motomaro's Death (1948.04; XI:524) • 228

Mountaineering (1939.03; XI:78) • 188
Mu Ch'i's Picture of Persimmons (1962.09; XI:561) • 204
Mud (1924.05; XI:364) • 211
Musical Instrument (1924.06; XI:371) • 224
My Desk (1973.02; XI:634) • 126
My Eighty-Seventh Birthday (1972.05; XI:631) • 95
My Friend (1914.03; XI:196) • 159
My Mind (1922.11; XI:335) • 83
My Prayer (1965.03; XI:136) • 247
My Present Work (1911.05; XI:9) • 155
My Shell (1961.10; XI:551) • 66
My Visions (1920; XI:38) • 144
My Work (i) (1920.04; XI:223) • 155
My Work (ii) (1920.04; XI:231) • 156
My Work (iii) (1920.07; XI:249) • 156
My Work (iv) (1920.11; XI:279) • 156

Naturally (1920.07; XI:249) • 254
Nature's Eye (1937.04; XI:490) • 74
Neither a Sage . . . (1920; XI:39) • 63
Neo-Impressionists (1924.06; XI:369) • 196
New Life (1920.07; XI:246) • 67
New Village (i) (1920.07; XI:255) • 146
New Village (ii) (1920.07; XI:258) • 146
New Village (iii) (1921.05; XI:299) • 271
New Village (iv) (1921.05; XI:299) • 273
New Village (v) (1922.05; XI:328) • 146
New Village (vi) (1923.03; XI:340) • 147
New Village (vii) (1939.12; XI:495) • 147
New Village Greets its Fortieth Year (1958.11; XI:540) • 150
New World (1920; XI:255) • 108
New Year (1963; XI:560) • 140
No Matter What (1920; XI:34) • 62
Not God (1920.09; XI:273) • 260
Nouveau Riche (1924.08; XI:376) • 106

Objects I'd Like to Paint (1942; XI:512) • 188
Oh, God (i) (1920.09; XI:271) • 266
Oh, God (ii) (1920.09; XI:271) • 266
Old Hen (1950.03; XI:535) • 86
Old Man on Life's Superexpress (1968.10; XI:602) • 97
Old Man's Dreams (1975.02; XI:651) • 96
Old Painter (1971.11; XI:624) • 127
On a Painting of Soy Beans (1927.09; XI:445) • 184
On a Train to San Francisco (1936.11; XI:116) • 83
On My Desk (1928.01; XI:456) • 127
On this Day Jesus Was Born (1921.02; XI:44) • 268
One Called God (1920.04; XI:225) • 261
One Critic (1929.01; XI:461) • 215
One Hundred Eggs (1923.04; XI:339) • 157
One More Step (1920; XI:33) • 254
One of My Paintings Sold (1959.12; XI:544) • 192
One Painter (1929.01; XI:461) • 215

One Reed Leaf (1933.05; XI:481) • 204
One Who Saw God (1920.04; XI:28) • 241
Only to the Right (1920.07; XI:261) • 216
Optimist Meets the Optimistic Creator (1964.11; XI:133) • 242
Others' Sense of Independence (1924.10; XI:395) • 120
Our Warriors Advance on Attu (1943.12; XI:514) • 281

Painter (1942; XI:106) • 184
Painting Pictures (1927.07; XI:444) • 191
Painting Vegetables (1941?; XI:83) • 181
Parents (1924.06; XI:370) • 58
Path to Triumph (1940; XI:500) • 274
People (1920; XI:267) • 246
People Compelled to Work (1920; XI:37) • 118
People I Like (1941?; XI:114) • 65
People I Respect (1924.03; XI:365) • 65
People of the Future (1920; XI:35) • 118
People of the Past (1920; XI:36) • 117
People With Tails (1924.10; XI:394) • 231
Pine Trying to be a Cedar (1923.01; XI:336) • 71
Playing the Flute • (1920.11; XI:43) • 221
Poem of an Old Painter (1948; XI:525) • 190
Poet of the Seas and the Skies (1949.04; XI:526) • 223
Potato (i) (1942 • 1957; XI:104) • 183
Potato (ii) (1962; XI:553) • 183
Preface Poem (1947; XI:89) • 219
Pure People (1965.11; XI:166) • 263
Purse (1926; XI:424) • 104

Rather than People (1920.04; XI:223) • 262
Reading Hodler's Biography (1920.07; XI:264) • 211
Real Person (1936.12; XI:116) • 60
Rembrandt (i) (1915.04; XI:21) • 206
Rembrandt (ii) (1933.06; XI:68) • 206
Rembrandt (iii) (1931.06; XI:476) • 206
Rembrandt's Etching of Faust (1922.11; XI:334) • 208
Return of Tobias (1923.03; XI:48) • 207
Revolutionary (1925.04; XI:408) • 130
Rhapsodizing on My Birthday (1911.05; XI:6) • 91
Rivers Flow (1920.12; XI:288) • 254
Romance and Work (1930.08; XI:493) • 164
Rumors about Him (1911.04; XI:188) • 56

Sapling and Spring (1920.05; XI:28) • 71
Seeds I Sowed (1923.01; XI:336) • 132
Seek the Kingdom of God (1920.09; XI:269) • 120
Self and Others (1941?; XI:114) • 106
Self-Admonitions When I Paint (1933.01; XI:477) • 187
Self-Reliant (1921.05; XI:298) • 270
Senke Motomaro (1948.08; XI:524) • 228
Sesshū's *Thunderbolts* (1965?; XI:174) • 123
Sexual Desire (i) (1923.07; XI:346) • 163
Sexual Desire (ii) (1929.07; XI:468) • 163

Sexual Desire and Love (1931.04; XI:474) • 163
Shiga and I (1945; XI:97) • 161
Silence (i) (1961.10; XI:553) • 75
Silence (ii) (1962; XI:554) • 186
Since Childhood (1966; XI:573) • 58
Six Songs of Work (1920.02; XI:222) • 141
Skylark (1920.05; XI:250) • 223
Slaves of Toil (1920; XI:267) • 137
Sleeping Lion (1924.03; XI:367) • 87

Some Dozen of Us (1942.10; XI:510) • 149
Someone Like Me (1921.07; XI:308) • 171
Someone Said (1920; XI:266) • 67
Son of My Father, My Mother (1969; XI:183) • 59
Song of a Gigantic Tree (1920.06; XI:29) • 70
Song of a Mountaineer (1923.06; XI:346) • 134
Song of the Visionary (1917.04; XI:206) • 100
Sordid Poem (1917.09; XI:22) • 220
Spring (1915.05; XI:22) • 165
Squash and Potato (1939; XI:556) • 182
Stars in the Heavens (1948; XI:528) • 172
Still Life (1942; XI:81) • 186
Stone by the Wayside (1948.11; XI:525) • 224
Stone, Stone (1949.01; XI:528) • 106
Stringless Harp (1941?; XI:114) • 242
Stroke of Luck (1963; XI:560) • 131
Study (1934.02; XI:70) • 104
Substitute Foreword (1911.05; XI:188) • 220
Sun (1921.07; XI:307) • 101
Sun and Moon (1921.05; KK:12:36 [1st part, XI:14]) • 102
Sunflowers in Our Village (1968.07; XI:600) • 151
Surrender of Singapore (1942.04; XI:507) • 277

Talented (1920; XI:238) • 138
Tasks I Cannot Do (1920.07; XI:249) • 157
Teardrop (1965.04; XI:141) • 254
Tessai (1939.03; XI:78) • 204
Than the Malcontent (1921.07; XI:308) • 269
Than this Path (1920; XI:40) • 254
That Lion (1915.08; XI:201) • 87
They (1914.04; XI:15) • 107
Things I Cannot Do (1923.07; XI:352) • 142
Things I'd Like to Write (1933.06; XI:67) • 218
This Book (1961.10; XI:551) • 217
This Mission (1920; XI:276) • 146
This Small Poetry Collection (1925.08; XI:431) • 217
Those Able to Enter Heaven (1920.09; XI:274) • 273
Those I Can't Despise (1923.02; XI:325) • 173
Three Cooks (1960.01; XI:548) • 133
Three Men and a Girl (1911.05; XI:11) • 163
Thumbling (1934.07; XI:70) • 155
Time Passes Fast (Fall 1936; XI:488) • 82
Titian's *Girl in a Fur* (1942.10; XI:510) • 205

Titling a Sketch of an Apple (1927.09; XI:56) • 186
Titling Rembrandt's Painting of a Beggar (1937.04; XI:490) • 207

To a Chinese (1920.05; XI:236) • 169
To a Chinese Brother (1919.06; XI:217) • 167
To a Friend (1920.04; XI:231) • 172
To America (1944.01; XI:517) • 277
To Be Loved (1922.04; XI:317) • 167
To Critics (1929.01; XI:461) • 216
To Fate (1925.05; XI:411) • 274
To Japan (1926.07; XI:360) • 276
To Live in the Kingdom of God (1921.07; XI:308) • 269
To My Elders (1914.04; XI:15) • 82
To My Mind (1914.03; XI:16) • 60
To My Wife (1913.93; XI:192) • 69
To Senke (1920.11; XI:286) • 227
To Someone (1920; XI:37) • 166
To Talk of Myself (1920.04; XI:25) • 60
To the Critic (1914.04; XI:15) • 216
To the Dentist (1925.03; XI:401) • 275
To Their Work (1925.01; XI:398) • 270
Toil (i) (1920; XI:267) • 138
Toil (ii) (1920; XI:267) • 138
Tolstoy's Words (1923.03; XI:340) • 77
Transitional Period (1969; XI:183) • 108
Traveler! (1920.12; XI:287) • 105
Trees in the Rain (1921; XI:319) • 72
Twenty-Five Years of the New Village (1943.12; XI:515) • 150
Two Callers (1972.01; XI:629) • 99
Two-Horse Cart (1945; XI:98) • 89
Two Horses (1934.03; XI:69) • 88
Two Human Types (1968.04; XI:596) • 246
Two Lions (1934.03; XI:69) • 86
Two Men (1966; XI:567) • 212
Two on a Mountaintop (1944; XI:102) • 231
Two Women (1923.05; XI:342) • 69

Unopenable Door (1927; XI:61) • 154

Van Gogh (1911.07; XI:11) • 210
Van Gogh's Drawing of a Fountain (1947.04; XI:523) • 211
Van Gogh's Painting of an Old Man (1927.06; XI:445) • 210
Viewing a Bourdelle Painting (1935.01; XI:484) • 210
Viewing a Renoir Nude (1931.04; XI:474) • 209
Viewing a Titian Painting (1936.08; XI:94) • 205
Viewing Liang K'ai's *Dancing Hotei* (i) (1941.10; XI:95) • 197
Viewing Liang K'ai's *Dancing Hotei* (ii) (1945; XI:95) • 198
Village Air (1920.11; XI:285) • 148
Village Doctor (1921.01; XI:291) • 149
Vision? (1965.06; XI:571) • 99
Visionary (1929.09; XI:468) • 100
Volcano (1924.05; XI:362) • 75

Watching Fish Swim (1925.07; XI:418) • 90

Water (1920.07; XI:262) • 102
We (1920; XI:36) • 118
We're a Grove of Cedars (1920; XI:40) • 71
We're a Mass of Steel (1941.11; XI:507) • 277
Weary Fellow (1933.03; XI:477) • 185
Well, All Right (1920.04; XI:24) • 59
Well, Me Too (1920.04; XI:25) • 62
What the Fly Told the Lion (1924.08; XI:374) • 87
What the Genius Said (1913?; XI:193) • 81
What We Call the City (1924.05; XI:361) • 108
What You Write (1920.04; XI:227) • 226
Whatever I Observe (XI:551) • 212
When He Works (1923.07; XI:50) • 143
When I Paint (1974.01; XI:641) • 194
When I Was a Child (i) (1922.11; XI:335) • 57
When I Was a Child (ii) (1925.06; XI:418) • 58
When I Was Ailing (1921; XI:297) • 159
When I'm Working (1924.12; XI:395) • 143
When I'm Writing Poetry (1924.12; XI:392) • 119
When My Heart is Pure (1920.07; XI:259) • 247
When Pan Plays his Pipes (1923.05; XI:342) • 221
When You Want to do Two Things at Once (1924.04; XI:361) • 121
Whenever I see a Japanese Movie (1925; XI:414) • 103

Where is God? (1924.01; XI:381) • 268
Whitman (i) (1911.07; XI:11) • 229
Whitman (ii) (1919.06; XI:466) • 229
Whitman (iii) (1933.02; XI:479) • 229
Who is My Father? (1959.09; XI:541) • 59
Why Love One Person? (1924.08; XI:358) • 162
Wild Geese and Drakes in the Zoo (1928.09; XI:451) • 90
With Another's Flute (1966; XI:574) • 223
With Love and Gratitude (1922.04; XI:318) • 170
Within Me (1925.01; XI:400) • 129
Without God (1920?; XI:280) • 240
Wolf and Sheep (1948; XI:528) • 86
Wonders of the Sun (1975.06; XI:653) • 101
Work (1928.11; XI:454) • 120
Work Alone (1930.02; XI:470) • 117
Work with My Pen (1923.08; XI:350) • 219
World of Cooperation (1928.11; XI:455) • 145
Worthless Pouch (1920.04; XI:25) • 231
Write • Cultivate the Land (1920.04; XI:23) • 143
Wu Chun's *Hotei* (1965?; XI:171) • 199

Year Two of the Great East Asian War (1943.02; XI:507) • 279
You and I are Beautiful (1951; XI:95) • 65
Your Work (1922.05; XI:330) • 140

JAPANESE INDEX

After each Japanese title I insert its English translation—sometimes abbreviated to fit the space; see text for the full version—as it appears in *Long Corridor*. Small Roman numerals in parenthesis, for example, (i), (ii), or (iii), differentiate identical English titles. These numerals do not often appear in Mushakôji's originals.

End parentheses enclose the Japanese source of each work in Mushakôji's *Works*, Volume XI. The year of first publication in a collection (with page number after the colon) appears for poems not in these anthologies; cf. page 375 for details.

The page number in *Long Corridor* follows the bullet • or raised period. Slightly more information appears in the English Index. For full data on the poetry books, see Appendix IV: Poetry Collections, page 371.

Mushakôji registers Van Gogh using at least three different *katakana* phonetic registrations. I make no attempt to reconcile his "spellings."

✦   ✦   ✦

Ai, Love (i) (XI:42) • 174
Ai, Love (ii) (XI:655) • 174
Ai to kansha de, With Love and Gratitude (XI:318) • 170
Aisareru tame, To Be Loved (XI:317) • 167
Aisubeki hito, Lovable People (XI:627) • 170
Akanbô no yorokobi, Infant's Joy (XI:373) • 57
Aki ga kita, Autumn has Come (XI:4) • 164
Akuguchi iwarete, Maligned (XI:260) • 56
Ame ga furitsuzuku, Endless Rain (XI:263) • 72
Ame wa shitoshito to, Gentle Rain (XI:498) • 73
Ame no naka no kigi, Trees in the Rain (XI:319) • 72
Amerika ni atau, To America (XI:517) • 277
Amerika no Uiruson, America's Wilson (XI:214) • 275
Ano shishi, That Lion (XI:201) • 87

Arashi ni, In the Typhoon (XI:327) • 103
Aratana toshi, New Year (XI:560) • 140
Aru gaka to aru kaeru, Artist and a Frog (XI:100) • 190
Aru gaka, One Painter (XI:461) • 215
Aru hihyôka, One Critic (XI:461) • 215
Aru hihyôka to aru gakka, Critic and Painter (XI:189) • 213
Aru hito wa itta, Someone Said (XI:266) • 67
Aru kokkei na jinshu, Ludicrous Folks (XI:392) • 214
Aru ôkina ki no uta, Song of a Gigantic Tree (XI:29) • 70
Aru otoko, Man (XI:85) • 94
Aru Shina no kyôdai, To a Chinese Brother (XI:217) • 167
Aru Shinajin, To a Chinese (XI:236) • 169
Aru tomodachi, Friend (XI:239) • 159
Aru tozansha no uta, Song of a Mountaineer (XI:346) • 134

Ashi no ha ichimai, One Reed Leaf (XI:481) • 204
Ataeru mono, The Giver (XI:195) • 132
Atarashii seikatsu, New Life (XI:246) • 67
Atarashii sekai, New World (XI:255) • 108
Atarashiki mura, New Village (i) (XI:255) • 146
Atarashiki mura, New Village (ii) (XI:258) • 146
Atarashiki mura, New Village (iii) (XI:299) • 271
Atarashiki mura, New Village (iv) (XI:299) • 273
Atarashiki mura, New Village (v) (XI:328) • 146
Atarashiki mura, New Village (vi) (XI:340) • 147
Atarashiki mura, New Village (vii) (XI:495) • 147
Atarashiki mura man nijûgonen, Twenty-Five Years of the New (XI:515) • 150
Atarashiki mura ni te, At the New Village (XI:396) • 148
Atarashiki mura yonjûnen o mukaete, New Village Greets (XI:540) • 150
Atarashiki mura yori, From the New Village (XI:414) • 147
Attsutô yûsaitachi no shingun, Our Warriors Advance (XI:514) • 281

Ban•goho, Van Gogh (XI:11) • 210
Bareisho, Potato (i) (XI:104) • 183
Bareishosan, In Praise of Potatoes (XI:108) • 183
Benkyô, Study (XI:70) • 104
Boku kara miru to, To My Mind (XI:16) • 60
Boku wa aikokusha da, I'm a Patriot (XI:479) • 276
Boku wa kantan ni, I Simply (XI:461) • 216
Budda no fukuin, Buddha's Gospel (XI:230) • 262
Budda to iu, Buddha (XI:26) • 75
Buruderu no e o mite, Viewing a Bourdelle Painting (XI:484) • 210

Chichian no aru e o mite, Viewing a Titian Painting (XI:94) • 205
Chichian no kegawa kiru onna, Titian's *Girl in a Fur* (XI:510) • 205
Chinmoku, Silence (i) (XI:553) • 75
Chinmoku, Silence (ii) (XI:554) • 186
Chûjitsu na hihyôka, Devoted Critic (XI:453) • 216

Da ga, However (XI:225) • 85
Daitôa sensô daininen no haru, Year Two of the Great East Asian War (XI:507) • 279
Daidô, Moral Principle (XI:518) • 65
Daizu no e ni, On a Painting of Soy Beans (XI:445) • 184
Dare ga nan to ittemo, No Matter What (XI:34) • 62
Dekiru, dekiru, I Can Do It, I Can Do It (XI:536) • 66
Den Mokkei Hotei, *Hotei*, Attributed to Mu Ch'i (XI:172) • 198
Detarame na e, An Incoherent Picture (XI:456) • 212
Deyurâ no sei Zerômu, Dürer's *St. Jerome* (XI:394) • 271
Dôbutsuen no gan ya kamo yo, Wild Geese and Drakes (XI:451) • 90
Dokuritsu suru mono, The Self-Reliant (XI:298) • 270
Dokyô o suete, I Dare (XI:456) • 232
Dorakuroa, Delacroix (XI:467) • 209
Doro, Mud (XI:364) • 211
Doryoku, Efforts (XI:555) • 153
Dosutoefusukî no kao, Dostoyevski's Face (XI:12) • 77
Doumie, Daumier (XI:467) • 209

E ga kakitakute, Dying to Paint a Picture (XI:536) • 182
E o kakeba, The More I Paint (XI:543) • 124
E o kaku toki no jikai, Self-Admonitions When I Paint (XI:477) • 187
E o kaku wa, Painting Pictures (XI:444) • 191
E o kaku yorokobi, The Joys of Painting Pictures (XI:522) • 189

Fude no shigoto, Work with My Pen (XI:350) • 219
Fuefuku otoko, Playing the Flute • (XI:43) • 221
Fuefuku otoko, Man on the Flute • (XI:111) • 221
Fuheika yori, Than the Malcontent (XI:308) • 269
Fujiyû na gaka, Impaired Painter (XI:552) • 189
Fukuro wa kusatta, Worthless Pouch (XI:25) • 231
Funkazan, Volcano (XI:362) • 75
Futari no kyaku, Two Callers (XI:629) • 99
Futari no onna, Two Women (XI:342) • 69
Futari no otoko, Two Men (XI:567) • 212

Gakki, Musical Instrument (XI:371) • 224
Geijutsuka, Artists (XI:248) • 271
Gohho no funsui no e, Van Gogh's Drawing of a Fountain (XI:523) • 211
Go no meijin, Go Master (XI:358) • 215
Gooho no e no rôjin, Van Gogh's Painting of an Old Man (XI:445) • 210

Hachijûhassai no jibun, At Eighty-Eight (XI:631) • 95
Hae, Flies (XI:343) • 88
Hae wa shishi ni itta, What the Fly Told the Lion (XI:374) • 87
Haisha ni, To the Dentist (XI:401) • 275
Hana mo, Flowers (XI:23) • 74
Hanazukuri, Florist (XI:369) • 75
Haniwa, Clay Figurine (XI:655) • 106
Haru, Spring (XI:22) • 165
Hatarakanaide irarenai ningen, People Compelled to Work (XI:37) • 118
Hatarakanakereba, If They Don't Work (XI:394) • 119
Hataraki no uta—roku, Six Songs of Work (XI:222) • 141
Hataraku toki ni wa, When He Works (XI:50) • 143
Hendorikke yo, Hendrickje! (XI:52) • 208
Hibari, Skylark (XI:250) • 223
Hibi shin, Daily Renewal (XI:114) • 143
Hitori no gakka, Painter (XI:106) • 184
Hitori no hito ni, To Someone (XI:37) • 166
Hitori no onna to sannin no otoko, Three Men and a Girl (XI:11) • 163
Hitotsu no shinsen na e, Fresh Painting (XI:622) • 185
Hihyôka ni, To the Critic (XI:15) • 216
Hihyôka ni, To Critics (XI:461) • 216
Hihyôka no keibetsu, Critics' Disdain (XI:190) • 215
Hirakarenai to, Unopenable Door (XI:61) • 154

Hodorâ, Hodler (XI:12) • 211
Hodorâ no denki o yonde iru, Reading Hodler's Biography (XI:264) • 211
Hoittoman, Whitman (i) (XI:11) • 229
Hoittoman, Whitman (ii) (XI:466) • 229
Hoittoman, Whitman (iii) (XI:479) • 229

Honki ni, In Earnest (ii) (XI:39) • 154
Honya, Bookshop (XI:337) • 104
Hyaku no tamago, One Hundred Eggs (XI:339) • 157
Hyûga no yama no naka ni, In Hyûga's Hills (XI:419) • 145

Ibu, Eve (XI:364) • 68
Ichinichi ichinichi, Day by Day (XI:101) • 154
Ichiji ni futatsu no koto o . . . , When You Want to . . . (XI:361) • 121
Idai na kokorozashi, Lofty Aspirations (XI:52) • 67
Ii gakki, Good Instruments (XI:371) • 224
Ii geijutsuhin, Fine Work of Art (XI:390) • 192
Ii kyakuhon no, Good Script (XI:456) • 130
Ikitari hataraitari, Living and Working (XI:582) • 156
Ikite iru aida, As Long as I'm Alive (XI:625) • 162
Ikko no ningen, Real Person (XI:116) • 60
Ikura gakki, However Fine the Instrument (XI:49) • 224
Ima no jibun no shigoto, My Present Work (XI:9) • 155
Ippon no matchi no hi, Fire from a Single Match (XI:248) • 138
Ippon no shuro, Hemp Palm (XI:637) • 125
Ishi, ishi, Stone, Stone (XI:528) • 106
Ishibashi o tataite aruku risôka, Idealist Who Walks Testing (XI:280) • 100
Isshô no shigoto, Life's Work (XI:70) • 155
Issunbôshi, Thumbling (XI:70) • 155
Itteki no namida, A Teardrop (XI:141) • 254
Izumi no nageki, The Fountain's Lament (XI:14) • 107

Jagaimo, Potato (ii) (XI:553) • 183
Jibun ni dekinai shigoto, Tasks I Cannot Do (XI:249) • 157
Jibun no kodomo, His Children (XI:234) • 173
Jibun no shigoto, My Work (iii) (XI:249) • 156
Jibun no shigoto ni, To Their Work (XI:398) • 270
Jibun no suki na hito, People I Like (XI:114) • 65
Jibun to tanin, Self and Others (XI:114) • 106
Jibun wa aki ga suki da, I Adore Fall (XI:396) • 74
Jibun wa byôki shite, When I Was Ailing (XI:297) • 159
Jibun wa chichi to haha no ko da, Son of My Father, My Mother (XI:183) • 59
Jibun wa jibun ni dekinai, Things I Cannot Do (XI:352) • 142
Jibun wa jibun ni totte, For Me (XI:194) • 66
Jibun wa kakumeika, Revolutionary (XI:408) • 130
Jibun wa shinjite, I Believe (XI:314) • 64
Jibun wa wagamama mono de, I'm an Egotist (XI:350) • 63
Jibun, I (i) (XI:197) • 61
Jinrui, Humanity (XI:343) • 107
Jinsei no tokkyûsha no ue de hitori no rôjin, Old Man on Life's Superexpress (XI:602) • 97
Jitsu ni ôku no shijin, Lots and Lots of Poets (XI:263) • 217
Jiyû o ushinatta uma, Horse Deprived of Liberty (XI:477) • 89
Jo no kawari, Substitute Foreword (XI:188) • 220
Joshi, Preface Poem (XI:89) • 219
Junsui na aisubeki hitobito, Genuine and Lovable People (XI:578) • 170
Junsui no ningen, Pure People (XI:166) • 263

Kabocha to jagaimo, Squash and Potato (XI:556) • 182

Kaigara, My Shell (XI:551) • 66
Kakitai mono, Things I'd Like to Write (XI:67) • 218
Kakitai mono, Objects I'd Like to Paint (XI:512) • 188
Kako no ningen, People of the Past (XI:36) • 117
Kaku • Tagayasu, Write • Cultivate the Land (XI:23) • 143
Kame no gotoshi, Like a Tortoise (XI:5) • 85
Kami, God (i) (XI:30) • 261
Kami, God (ii) (XI:44) • 261
Kami, God (iii) (XI:221) • 261
Kami de nai mono, Not God (XI:273) • 260
Kami nashi ni wa, Without God (XI:280) • 240
Kami ni aisare, Loved by God (XI:24) • 253
Kami ni chûjitsu de aru koto, Being True to God (XI:273) • 262
Kami ni sasagerareta, Dedicated to God (XI:494) • 266
Kami no ai, God's Love (i) (XI:276) • 253
Kami no ai, God's Love (ii) (XI:301) • 253
Kami no ishi, God's Will (XI:12) • 266
Kami no kuni de wa, In the Kingdom of God (ii) (XI:274) • 173
Kami no kuni ni, In the Kingdom of God (i) (XI:295) • 246
Kami no kuni ni sumu no ni, To Live in the Kingdom of God (XI:308) • 269
Kami no kuni o motomete yo, Seek the Kingdom of God (XI:269) • 120
Kami o mita mono, One Who Saw God (XI:28) • 241
Kami o wasurete, Forgetting God (XI:26) • 263
Kami to akuma, God and Satan (XI:491) • 267
Kami to iu mono, One Called God (XI:225) • 261
Kami to jinrui, God and Humankind (i) (XI:217) • 262
Kami to ningen, God and Humankind (ii) (XI:243) • 263
Kami to wa nani zo ya, How Describe God? (XI:224) • 240

Kami wa aru ka nai ka, Does God Exist? (i) (XI:273) • 240
Kami wa aru ka nai ka, Does God Exist? (ii) (XI:323) • 240
Kami wa aru ka nai ka, Does God Exist? (iii) (XI:327) • 241
Kami wa doko ni iru, Where is God? (XI:381) • 268
Kami yo, Oh, God (i) (XI:271) • 266
Kami yo, Oh, God (ii) (XI:271) • 266
Kanabukuro, Purse (XI:424) • 104
Kanemochi ni wa natta, Nouveau Riche (XI:376) • 106
Kanshaku o okoshita ato, After a Fit of Anger (XI:334) • 173
Kare no fûhyô, Rumors about Him (XI:188) • 56
Karera, They (XI:15) • 107
Katoki, Transitional Period (XI:183) • 108
Kawa no nagare, Rivers Flow (XI:288) • 254
Kenkô, Health (XI:565) • 96
Kensetsu se yo, Build It! (XI:288) • 151
Kibô ni michite'ru Nihon, Japan Brims with Hope (XI:13) • 274
Kikai to ningen, Machines and People (XI:219) • 155
Kimi mo boku mo utsukushii, You and I are Beautiful (XI:95) • 65
Kinoshita yo, Kinoshita! (XI:403) • 227
Kiso, Foundation (XI:229) • 117
Kitanai shi, Sordid Poem (XI:22) • 220

Kôba de, At the Workshop (XI:224) • 137

Kodomo no toki, When I was a Child (ii) (XI:418) • 58
Kodomo, Child (XI:27) • 58
Kodomo no toki kara, Since Childhood (XI:573) • 58
Kokoro no kioi toki, When My Heart is Pure (XI:259) • 247
Koi no higeki, Love Tragedy (XI:182) • 167
Koi to shigoto, Romance and Work (XI:493) • 164
Kokkei fûfu, Comical Couple (XI:344) • 171
Kono chiisaki shishû, This Small Poetry Collection (XI:431) • 217
Kono hon, This Book (XI:551) • 217
Kono michi yori, Than this Path (XI:40) • 254
Kono yo ni wa, In this World (XI:557) • 133
Kotoba no watashi to chinmoku, The Me of Words (HS:I:7) • 8
Kôun, Stroke of Luck (XI:560) • 131

Kurô ôkushite, Many Hardships (XI:489) • 83
Kurubê, Courbet (XI:466) • 209
Kûsô ka, Vision? (XI:571) • 99
Kûsôka, Visionary (XI:468) • 100
Kûsôka no uta, Song of the Visionary (XI:206) • 100
Kyojin, Giant (i) (XI:13) • 78
Kyojin, Giant (ii) (XI:57) • 78
Kyojin, Giant (iii) (XI:73) • 78
Kyojin no ashiato, Giant's Footprint (XI:59) • 80
Kyojin no kaita ji, A Giant's Calligraphy (XI:428) • 226
Kyojin wa dete kita, Giant Appeared (XI:427) • 80
Kyojin wa susumu, Giant Advances (XI:496) • 79
Kyojin wa tada aruku, Giants Only Walk (XI:76) • 79
Kyôryoku no sekai, World of Cooperation (XI:455) • 145
Kyôryoku shite, In Concert (XI:236) • 138

Mâ ii, Well, All Right (XI:24) • 59
Maria magudarena, Mary Magdalene (XI:424) • 68
Matsu ga sugi ni narô, Pine Trying to be a Cedar (XI:336) • 71
Me o tsumutte, Closing My Eyes (XI:51) • 74
Michibata no ochita ishi, Stone by the Wayside (XI:525) • 224
Migi ni bakari, Only to the Right (XI:261) • 216
Mirai no ningen, People of the Future (XI:35) • 118
Mite iru to, Whatever I Observe (XI:551) • 212
Mizu, Water (XI:262) • 102
Mô ippo, One More Step (XI:33) • 254
Mokkei no kaki no e, Mu Ch'i's Picture of Persimmons (XI:561) • 204
Mokkei to Ryôkai o sanbisu, I Praise Mu Ch'i and Liang K'ai (XI:117) • 201
Mokkei wa Shina de wa, In China Mu Ch'i (XI:450) • 203
Moshi kono shigoto, This Mission (XI:276) • 146
Motomaro no shi, Motomaro's Death (XI:524) • 228
Mu Jun, Hotei, Wu Chun's *Hotei* (XI:171) • 199
Mugenkin, Stringless Harp (XI:114) • 242
Mura ni wa itsumo, Always in the Village (XI:285) • 148
Mura no himawari, Sunflowers in Our Village (XI:600) • 151
Mura no isha, Village Doctor (XI:291) • 149
Mura no kûki, Village Air (XI:285) • 148
Mura no naka, In the Village (XI:285) • 270

Nagai rôka, Long Corridor (XI:5) • 55
Nagareru kawa, Flowing River (XI:382) • 103
Nanajûyonkai tanjôbi no asa, Morning of My Seventy-Fourth Birthday (XI:541) • 94
Nanji no shigoto, Your Work (XI:330) • 140
Naze aru hito o ai shi, Why Love One Person? (XI:358) • 162
Nemureru shishi, Sleeping Lion (XI:367) • 87
Nihiki no uma, Two Horses (XI:69) • 88
Nihon ni, To Japan (XI:360) • 276
Nihon ni mo, Even in Japan (XI:432) • 276
Nihon no katsudô o miru to, Whenever I see a Japanese Movie (XI:414) • 103
Nihon wa torinokosareta, Japan Has Been Left Behind (XI:214) • 275
Nijû no ningen, Two Human Types (XI:596) • 246
Nikumenai mono, Those I Can't Despise (XI:325) • 173
Ningen, People (XI:267) • 246
Ningen yori mo, Rather than People (XI:223) • 262
Nitôdate no basha, Two-Horse Cart (XI:98) • 89
Nitô no shishi, Two Lions (XI:69) • 86
Nonkimono, nonki na zôbutsusha ni au, Optimist Meets the (XI:133) • 242

Oitaru mendori, Old Hen (XI:535) • 86
Oitaru Renburanto, The Aged Rembrandt (XI:47) • 207
Oitaru rôdôsha, Aged Toilers (XI:472) • 121
Okâchan, Mommy (XI:607) • 69
Ôkami to hitsuji, Wolf and Sheep (XI:528) • 86
Ôkina atama no otoko, Broad-Minded Man (XI:499) • 105
Ôkina fune, Big Ship (XI:230) • 104
Ôkina ki, Big Tree (XI:25) • 213
Omae no kaku mono, What You Write (XI:227) • 226
Ore no kodomo no toki kara, From Childhood (XI:23) • 58
Ore no kûsô, My Visions (XI:38) • 144
Ore no shigoto, My Work (ii) (XI:231) • 156
Ore no shigoto, My Work (iv) (XI:279) • 156
Ore no shinken, In Earnest (i) (XI:24) • 246
Ore no tomo ni, To a Friend (XI:231) • 172
Ore o shinze yo, Believe Me (XI:280) • 64
Ore wa kishu, I'm a Standard-Bearer (XI:264) • 139
Ore wa kodomo no toki ni, When I Was a Child (i) (XI:335) • 57
Ore wa seijin demo, Neither a Sage . . . (XI:39) • 63
Ore wa sonkei suru, I Respect (i) (XI:301) • 64
Ore wa, ore wa, To Talk of Myself (XI:25) • 60
Oretachi wa sugi no ki, We're a Grove of Cedars (XI:40) • 71
Oshiro no tonosama, Lord of the Castle (XI:15) • 76
Osoreru shishi, Angry Lion (XI:70) • 87
Ôumi to ôzora no shijin, Poet of the Seas and the Skies (XI:526) • 223
Oya, Parents (XI:370) • 58
Oyama no taishô, King of the Hill (XI:374) • 63

Pan ga fue o hiku toki, When Pan Plays his Pipes (XI:342) • 221
Piano o kiite, Listening to the Piano (XI:580) • 272

Ranpu o kowaseba, If you Break Every Oil Lamp (XI:462) • 105
Renburanto, Rembrandt (i) (XI:21) • 206

Renburanto, Rembrandt (ii) (XI:68) • 206
Renburanto, Rembrandt (iii) (XI:476) • 206
Renburanto no Fuasuto no e, Rembrandt's Etching of Faust (XI:334) • 208
Renburanto no kojiki no e ni dai suru, Titling Rembrandt's (XI:490) • 207
Renin no mîra, Lenin's Embalmed Remains (XI:390) • 77
Reonarudo•da•uinchi•yuri, Leonardo da Vinci's Lilies (XI:554) • 205
Ringo no e ni daisu, Titling a Sketch of an Apple (XI:56) • 186
Ringo ya nashi no ki, Apple Trees and Pear Trees (XI:334) • 91
Rôdô, Toil (i) (XI:267) • 138
Rôdô, Toil (ii) (XI:267) • 138
Rôdô no dorei, Slaves of Toil (XI:267) • 137
Rôgaka no shi, The Poem of an Old Painter (XI:525) • 190
Rôjin gaka, Old Painter (XI:624) • 127
Rôjin no yume, Old Man's Dreams (XI:651) • 96
Runoâru no aru rafu o mite, Viewing a Renoir Nude (XI:474) • 209
Rûsâ bâbanku, Luther Burbank (XI:373) • 139
Ryôkai, matsushita kinkyaku, Liang K'ai's *Harpist Under a Pine* (XI:170) • 200
Ryôkai no odori Hotei o mite, Viewing Liang K'ai's (i) (XI:95) • 197
Ryôkai no odori Hotei o mite, Viewing Liang K'ai's (ii) (XI:95) • 198
Ryôkai yo, Liang K'ai (XI:560) • 197

Sâ ore mo, Well, Me Too (XI:25) • 62
Sabishii, Feeling Lonely (XI:4) • 164
Sabishisa, Loneliness (i) (XI:12) • 63
Sabishisa, Loneliness (ii) (XI:232) • 63
Sakana no oyogi no, Watching Fish Swim (XI:418) • 90
Sakka to hihyôka, Artist and Critic (XI:57) • 213
Sanfuranshisuko ni yuku kishachû nite, On a Train to (XI:116) • 83
Sanjô ni futari, Two on a Mountaintop (XI:102) • 231
Sannin no kodomo kara, From My Three Children (XI:498) • 82
Sannin no ryôrinin, Three Cooks (XI:548) • 133
Seibutsu, Still Life (XI:81) • 186
Seichô, Growth (XI:33) • 62
Seichôryoku, Growth Potential (XI:448) • 151
Seiji no yakunin, Government Officials (XI:390) • 76
Seiyoku, Sexual Desire (i) (XI:346) • 163
Seiyoku ni, Sexual Desire (ii) (XI:468) • 163
Seiyoku to ren'ai, Sexual Desire and Love (XI:474) • 163
Seken, Gossip (XI:186) • 55

Senke ni, To Senke (XI:286) • 227
Senke Motomaro, Senke Motomaro (XI:524) • 228
Senpai ni, To My Elders (XI:15) • 82
Sesshû, Kaminari, Sesshû's *Thunderbolts* (XI:174) • 123
Shaka to Yaso, Buddha and Jesus (XI:351) • 262
Shi, Death (XI:10) • 85
Shi ni katsu ai, Love that Conquers Death (XI:491) • 253
Shi no kyôfu, Death's Dread (XI:49) • 84
Shi o kaite iru to, When I'm Writing Poetry (XI:392) • 119
Shi o kaita kara, Because He Wrote a Poem (XI:330) • 226
Shi yo shi yo, Master! Master! (XI:11) • 107
Shiga to boku, Shiga and I (XI:97) • 161

Shigoto, Work (XI:454) • 120
Shigoto koso, Work Alone (XI:470) • 117
Shigoto no yorokobi, Joy of Work (XI:91) • 122
Shigoto o shite iru to, When I'm Working (XI:395) • 143
Shigoto o suru no wa, Doing My Work (XI:392) • 119
Shina no e, Chinese Painting (XI:50) • 196
Shinajin, Chinese (XI:224) • 169
Shinapôru kanraku, Surrender of Singapore (XI:507) • 277
Shinigami, Grim Reaper (XI:78) • 84
Shin-inshôha, Neo-Impressionists (XI:369) • 196
Shinken ni shigoto o suru otoko, The Man who Works (XI:511) • 153
Shinu sabishisa, Death's Desolation (XI:225) • 85
Shippo no aru ningen, People With Tails (XI:394) • 231
Shitsudai, Lost Titles (XI:57) • 230
Shizen no mama ni, Naturally (XI:249) • 254
Shizen no me, Nature's Eye (XI:490) • 74
Shôjiki de are, Be Honest (XI:223) • 105
Shôri no michi, Path to Triumph (XI:500) • 274
Shunme fugû jidai, Age of Adversity for the Race Horse (XI:472) • 89
Sonkei suru ningen, People I Respect (XI:365) • 65
Sôsaku suru mono, Creativity (XI:356) • 226
Subete o kami ni makasete, Leave Everything to God (XI:275) • 273

Tabibito yo, Traveler! (XI:287) • 105
Taiyô, Sun (XI:307) • 101
Taiyô no fushigisa, Wonders of the Sun (XI:653) • 101
Taiyô to tsuki, Sun and Moon (KK:12:36) • 102
Tamago no gara, Eggshell (XI:13) • 77
Tanin no dokuritsusei, Others' Sense of Independence (XI:395) • 120
Tanin no fue de, With Another's Flute (XI:574) • 223
Tanjôbi ni saishite no bôsô, Rhapsodizing on My Birthday (XI:6) • 91
Ten ni hoshi, Stars in the Heavens (XI:528) • 172
Tengoku ni hairiuru mono, Those Able to Enter Heaven (XI:274) • 273
Tensai, The Talented (XI:238) • 138
Tensai to geinin, Genius and Artiste (XI:187) • 186
Tensai wa itta, What the Genius Said (XI:193) • 81
Tessai, Tessai (XI:78) • 204
Tobiasu no kaeri, *The Return of Tobias* (XI:48) • 207
Tokai to iu mono, What We Call the City (XI:361) • 108
Toki no sugiru no wa hayai, Time Passes Fast (XI:488) • 82
Tomodachi no yorokobi, Joy of Friendship (XI:205) • 159
Torusutoi no kotoba, Tolstoy's Words (XI:340) • 77
Tozan, Mountaineering (XI:78) • 188
Tsukareta otoko, Weary Fellow (XI:477) • 185
Tsukue no ue no, On My Desk (XI:456) • 127
Tsukue to nedoko, Desk and Cot (XI:483) • 126
Tsuri shite iru otoko, A Man Fishes (XI:57) • 91

Unmei ni, To Fate (XI:411) • 274
Urashima Tarô no dokuhaku, Angler's Soliloquy (XI:194) • 130
Uta o wasureta kanariya, Canary that Forgot Its Song (XI:522) • 121
Utsukushii hana, Beautiful Flowers (XI:24) • 73

Utsukushii onna, Beautiful Woman (XI:249) • 69
Uwasa no ashi no hayasa, Fleet-footed Rumors (XI:344) • 56

Waga shigoto, My Work (i) (XI:223) • 155
Waga tomo, My Friend (XI:196) • 159
Waga tsukue, My Desk (XI:634) • 126
Waga tsuma ni, To My Wife (XI:192) • 69
Waga uchi ni, Within Me (XI:400) • 129
Wakaki ki to haru, Sapling and Spring (XI:28) • 71
Waratte yaritai, I Feel like Laughing (XI:6) • 60
Ware ni tayore, Lean on Me (XI:184) • 166
Warera, We (XI:36) • 118
Warera jûsûnin, Some Dozen of Us (XI:510) • 149
Warera wa nozomu utsukushii sekai, Beautiful World We (XI:534) • 158
Warera wa tetsu no katamari da, We're a Mass of Steel (XI:507) • 277
Watashi, I (ii) • (XI:30) • 62
Watashi no atama, My Mind (XI:335) • 83
Watashi no chichi wa dare, Who is My Father? (XI:541) • 59
Watashi no chiisai shitsu, In My Tiny Room (XI:450) • 191
Watashi no e ga ureta, One of My Paintings Sold (XI:544) • 192
Watashi no hachijûnanakai no tanjôbi, My Eighty-Seventh (XI:631) • 95
Watashi no maita tane, Seeds I Sowed (XI:336) • 132
Watashi no negai, My Prayer (XI:136) • 247
Watashi no yô na ningen, Someone Like Me (XI:308) • 171
Watashi wa e o kaku toki, When I Paint (XI:641) • 194
Watashi wa gaka, I'm a Painter • (XI:535) • 190
Watashi wa hataraku mono de aru, I'm a Worker (XI:348) • 135
Watashi wa kane da, I'm a Bell (XI:445) • 247
Watashi wa matsu de aru, I'm a Pine (XI:548) • 71
Watashi wa ôkina iwa da, I'm a Huge Rock (XI:353) • 62
Watashi wa sonkei suru, I Respect (ii) (XI:559) • 64
Watashi wa tetsu nari, I'm Made of Steel (XI:186) • 66

Ya o iru mono, The Arrow Shooter (XI:55) • 225
Yama o kaku otoko, Man Painting a Mountain (XI:556) • 187
Yama o noboru otoko ni, For the Mountain Climber (XI:79) • 135
Yasai no e ni, Painting Vegetables (XI:83) • 181
Yaso to Sei Furanshisu, Jesus and St. Francis (XI:385) • 273
Yaso wa umareta konnichi, On this Day Jesus Was Born (XI:44) • 268
Yoki e o miru yorokobi, The Joy of Seeing a Fine Picture (XI:76) • 186
Yoki kyôdai shimai, Good Brothers and Sisters (XI:235) • 170
Yorokobi, Joy (XI:22) • 107
Yumi no meijin, Expert Archers (XI:488) • 225

The highest achievement possible to man is
the full consciousness of his own feelings
and thoughts, for this gives him the
means of knowing intimately
the heart of others.

—— Johann Wolfgang von Goethe ——

Yakusha

Box #666, Stanwood, WA 98292–0666
U. S. A.

Cinderellas (198 works) • 335 pages
Selected poetry of Sekine Hiroshi
$30 Postpaid, Boards—ISBN 1-880276-55-0

Egg in My Palm (290 works) • 279 pages
Selected poetry of Tsuboi Shigeji
$30 Postpaid, Boards—ISBN 1-880276-61-5

Long Corridor (465 works) • 398 pages
Selected poetry of Mushakôji Saneatsu
$30 Postpaid, Boards—ISBN 1-880276-70-4

Rainbows (565 works) • 359 pages
Selected poetry of Horiguchi Daigaku
$30 Postpaid, Boards—ISBN 1-880276-50-X

Rats' Nests (365 works) • 251 pages
Collected poetry of Hagiwara Sakutarô
$30 Postpaid, Boards—ISBN 1-880276-40-2

That Far-Off Self (460 works) • 2nd edition • 367 pages
Collected poetry of Maruyama Kaoru
$35 Postpaid, Boards—ISBN 1-880276-49-6

Twisted Memories (360 works) • 279 pages
Collected poetry of Kinoshita Yûji
$30 Postpaid, Boards—ISBN 1-880276-25-9

★   ★   ★

Threading the Maze • 1997
Anthology of the Above Seven Modern Poets
$25 Postpaid, Boards—ISBN 1-880276-87-9

Through a Prism • 1998?
Anthology of Modern Japanese Verse for Youth
$25 Postpaid, Boards—ISBN 1-880276-93-3

Order direct from **Yakusha** and subtract $10 from each title.

—— *Translations from the Japanese by Robert Epp* ——